John Roland Phillips

Memoirs of the Civil War in Wales and the Marches.

1642 - 1649. Vol. 2

John Roland Phillips

Memoirs of the Civil War in Wales and the Marches.
1642 - 1649. Vol. 2

ISBN/EAN: 9783337015206

Printed in Europe, USA, Canada, Australia, Japan

Cover: Foto ©ninafisch / pixelio.de

More available books at **www.hansebooks.com**

MEMOIRS

OF

THE CIVIL WAR IN WALES

AND THE MARCHES.

1642—1649.

BY

JOHN ROLAND PHILLIPS

OF LINCOLN'S INN, BARRISTER-AT-LAW.

IN TWO VOLUMES.

VOL. II.

LONDON:

LONGMANS, GREEN, & Co.

1874.

CONTENTS.

DOCUMENT		PAGE
I.	A Petition from Flintshire to the King at York. August, 1642	1
II.	Parliament Order to call out Militia in Pembrokeshire ...	4
III.	Chester declares against the Array. August	8
IV.	The King at Shrewsbury and Chester, various letters. Sept. ...	10
V.	Marquis of Hertford takes Cardiff for the King. Aug. ...	23
VI.	Visit of Prince of Wales to Raglan Castle. Oct.	26
VII.	Mint at Shrewsbury—the King departs thence. Oct. ...	30
VIII.	Nantwich in trouble for opposing the King	33
IX.	After the battle of Edghill—old Rhyme.	36
X.	Welsh under Marquis of Hertford defeated at Tewkesbury. Dec.	38
XI.	Shropshire Royalists' resolution for the King. Dec. ...	42
XII.	Agreement of Neutrality in Cheshire. Dec.	44
XIII.	The History of the Cheshire Neutrality	46
XIV.	Fight at Middlewich—Sir W. Brereton defeats Royalists. Jan. 1643	49
XV.	Battle of Torperley. Feb. 21.	52
XVI.	Brereton's Account of Battle of Middlewich	54
XVII.	Sir Thomas Aston's Account ditto	56
XVIII.	List of Prisoners ditto	62
XIX.	Defeat of Lord Herbert at Gloucester. March 25	63
XX.	Monmouth and Chepstow taken by Waller	66
XXI.	Surrender of Hereford. April 25	69
XXII.	Sir Thomas Myddelton's Commission as Major-General of North Wales	71
XXIII.	Naval Fight at Milford Haven. Aug. 7	76
XXIV.	Proceedings in Pembrokeshire. Aug.—Oct.	82
XXV.	Parliament Victory near Chester.	86
XXVI.	Marquis of Ormond to Archbishop of York as to Defence of Anglesey, and Transportation of Soldiers from Ireland to Chester. Oct. 26	89
XXVII.	Ormond to Orlando Bridgman. Nov. 11	91
XXVIII.	Sir Thomas Myddelton and Brereton advance into N. Wales —Archbishop of York to Ormond	93
XXIX.	Myddelton summons Denbigh Castle	95
XXX.	Ormond to Mayor of Chester—Transportation of Soldiers. Nov. 15	98
XXXI.	Archbishop of York to Ormond. Nov. 18	99

DOCUMENT		PAGE
XXXII.	Attempt to win over to Parliament the Irish Soldiers landed in N. Wales...	101
XXXIII.	Orlando Bridgman to Ormond	103
XXXIV.	Siege of Hawarden Castle. Nov. and Dec.	106
XXXV.	Ormond to Mayor of Chester—More forces from Ireland ...	109
XXXVI.	Landing of Irish forces in North Wales, and repulse of Brereton and Myddelton	111
XXXVII.	Encounter at Middlewich. Jan., 1644	116
XXXVIII.	Protestation of Royalists in Carmarthenshire, Pembrokeshire, and Cardiganshire. Jan. 11.	118
XXXIX.	Defeat by Mytton of Cavaliers at Ellesmere. Jan. 12 ...	121
XL.	Ormond to Lord Byron—More Soldiers from Ireland ...	124
XLI.	Fairfax raises Siege of Nantwich. Jan. 25	125
XLII.	Prince Rupert appointed to the command of North Wales, Cheshire, and Shropshire	134
XLIII.	State of Shrewsbury in February	136
XLIV.	Intercepted letter of Sir Thomas Fairfax	138
XLV.	Lukewarmness of Royalists in Monmouthshire	139
XLVI.	Success of Parliament forces in Pembrokeshire—Defeat of Earl of Carbery—Haverfordwest, Tenby, &c., taken. March and April	140
XLVII.	Three Letters from Mr. John Vaughan of Trawscoed, relating to affairs in Pembrokeshire, &c.	154
XLVIII.	Swansea summoned for the Parliament	158
XLIX.	Charge of inhumanity against Admiral Swanley at Milford...	161
L.	Ordinance for Associating the Counties of Pembroke, Carmarthen, and Cardigan	163
LI.	Earl of Denbigh, &c., to Committee of both Kingdoms as to State of Shropshire and Cheshire	166
LII.	Archbishop of York on Appointment of Sir John Mennes to be Governor of Beaumaris	168
LIII.	Oswestry taken from the Royalists by Earl Denbigh and Col. Mytton. June 23.	171
LIV.	Rumours of design to betray Oswestry—Denbigh's letter ...	177
LV.	Siege of Oswestry raised by Myddelton and Denbigh ...	179
LVI.	Gerard in South Wales—Successes of Royalists	189
LVII.	Capture of Royalist Horse at Welshpool. Aug. 5. ...	194
LVIII.	Fight at Tarvin, near Chester. Aug. 21, 1644	196
LIX.	Defeat of Royalists at Malpas, Cheshire. Aug. 26 ...	198
LX.	Siege of Montgomery raised by Brereton and Myddelton, and Lord Byron defeated. Sept. 18	201
LXI.	Col. Massey takes Monmouth for the Parliament. Sept. 26...	210
LXII.	Powis Castle taken by Sir Thomas Myddelton. Oct. 2 ...	212
LXIII.	State of North Wales—York to Ormond. Oct. 30 ...	214
LXIV.	Monmouth retaken by Royalists. Nov.	217
LXV.	Myddelton takes Abbey Cwmhir. Dec.	219
LXVI.	General Laugharne takes Cardigan Castle. Dec. ...	222
LXVII.	Myddelton besieges Chirk Castle	224
LXVIII.	Lord Byron defeated at Beeston Castle. Jan. 18, 1645 ...	225
LXIX.	Of the taking of Cardigan Castle and Town, and of an attempt to regain it	226

DOCUMENT		PAGE
LXX.	Shrewsbury taken by Parliament. Feb. 22	235
LXXI.	An intercession on behalf of Prisoners of War	239
LXXII.	Of ravages committed by Rupert's soldiers	240
LXXIII.	Siege of Hawarden Castle. April	242
LXXIV.	Complaint of Archbishop of York against Sir John Owen being appointed Governor of Conway	243
LXXV.	Lord Byron's Account of defenceless state of Chester. April 26	245
LXXVI.	Laugharne defeated at Newcastle-Emlyn by Gerard, and driven back to Pembroke and Tenby. April	248
LXXVII.	Symonds' Diary of King's sojourn in South Wales. June 18—Aug. 8	255
LXXVIII.	Digby to Rupert as to King's intention to stay in Wales ...	264
LXXIX.	Defeat of Royalists at Colby Moor, co. Pemb.—Haverfordwest retaken by Laugharne. July 28	266
LXXX.	Symonds' Diary of King's second visit to South Wales. Sept. 6—Oct. 1	268
LXXXI.	Defeat of Royalists on Rowton Heath. Sept. 24 ...	272
LXXXII.	Carmarthen surrendered to Laugharne. Oct. 12... ...	273
LXXXIII.	Col. Morgan and Sir Trevor Williams take Monmouth. Oct. 24. Defeat of an attempt to regain it	279
LXXXIV.	Sir William Vaughan defeated by Mytton near Denbigh. Nov. 1	282
LXXXV.	Declaration of Gentlemen of Brecknockshire for Parliament. Nov. 23	284
LXXXVI.	Prisoners taken at Surprisal of Hereford. Dec. 18 ...	286
LXXXVII.	Efforts to relieve Chester. Jan., 1646	288
LXXXVIII.	Surrender of Chester to Parliament. Feb. 1	292
LXXXIX.	Revolt of Royalists in Glamorganshire. Feb.	298
XC.	Surrender of Ruthin to Mytton. April 8	301
XCI.	Aberystwith Castle yielded to Parliament. April 14 ...	305
XCII.	Mytton's proceedings in North Wales. April—June ...	306
XCIII.	Carnarvon taken by Mytton. June 4	309
XCIV.	Anglesey and Beaumaris submit to the Parliament. June 14	312
XCV.	Siege of Raglan. June—August	314
XCVI.	Conway Town taken by storm, and Castle summoned. Aug. 18	325
XCVII.	Salesbury yields Denbigh Castle. Oct. 26	328
XCVIII.	Surrender of Harlech—the last Royalist garrison in Wales. March 15, 1647	332
XCIX.	Fresh revolt of Royalists in Glamorganshire	335
C.	Outbreak of second Civil War in 1648—Poyer's refusal to disband—Discountenanced by other officers	344
CI.	Col. Poyer defeats Col. Fleming and takes Pembroke ...	347
CII.	Further revolt of troops—Arrival of forces from Bristol before Pembroke	349
CIII.	Some troops disband—chiefly Cardiganshire	351
CIV.	Advance of General Horton into Glamorganshire ...	352
CV.	State of South Wales—Royalist tactics	353
CVI.	Brecknock taken by Horton—Fight in Carmarthenshire. April 29	355
CVII.	Of the same—Emlyn Castle fortified—State of the country	358

DOCUMENT		PAGE
CVIII.	Suppression of insurrectionists in Brecknockshire—Horton advances to Glamorganshire—Laugharne joins Poyer ...	360
CIX.	Battle of St. Fagans. May 8. Defeat of Royalists and list of prisoners	365
CX.	Flintshire and Denbighshire faithful to Parliament ...	370
CXI.	Montgomeryshire declares to assist Parliament. May 20 ...	373
CXII.	Chepstow after a siege is taken. May 25	375
CXIII.	Surrender of Tenby to Cromwell. May 31	377
CXIV.	War breaks out also in North Wales—Defeat of Sir John Owen	380
CXV.	An attack on Denbigh Castle. July...	385
CXVI.	Cromwell before Pembroke. May—July. Passages during the siege—Letters of Cromwell, &c.	387
CXVII.	Suppression of revolt in Anglesey. July—Oct.... ...	399

DOCUMENTS

ILLUSTRATING TRANSACTIONS

IN THE YEAR 1642.

I.

A Petition from Flintshire to the King at York.

To the King's Most Excellent Majesty,—The humble petition of the Gentry, Ministers, and Freeholders of the County of Flint. Presented to his Majesty at York, the fourth of August, 1642.

DOCUMENT I. A.D. 1642.

Sheweth,—That your petitioners do, with all due submission, thankfulness, and joy of heart, acknowledge the happiness they have enjoyed of a long peace under your gracious government, and your goodness in yielding to a ready redress of such grievances as have grown in that time of ease and security, and in enacting such laws in this Parliament as your petitioners hope will prevent the like for the future.

They are further tenderly apprehensive of your Majesty's transcendent goodness, in your free condescending to give your people so full and clear an account of your actions and intentions, and rest thoroughly persuaded of the sincerity and constancy of your Majesty's resolution to maintain the true Protestant religion in

DOCUMENT

A.D. 1642.

its primitive purity, the laws of the land in their genuine sense, the just privileges, freedom, and frequency of Parliaments, with the property and liberty of the subject thereupon depending, and your Majesty's willingness to join with your great council in granting or enacting any other good laws that may be for the public weal of your people, who, as they have ever flourished, and been most happy and secure in all acts and ordinances passed by the three estates, and most peaceably governed under the known laws of the land.

So it is the humble prayer of us, your Majesty's most loyal subjects (prostrating at your Majesty's feet our persons and estates) for protection (according to your oath) from those dangers we should be driven into, by being bound by any rule, order, or ordinance whereunto your Majesty, together with both Houses of Parliament, shall not assent.

We also further supplicate your Majesty so to maintain us in that ancient and necessary privilege, as not to suffer us to be governed but by the known and established laws of the land.

And your petitioners, as in duty, and by the oaths of allegiance and supremacy, they conceive themselves bound, shall not only pray for the preservation of your Majesty's sacred person, honour, estate, and lawful prerogative, but shall always be ready to hazard their lives and fortunes for the maintenance and defence of the same against all powers and persons whatsoever.

His Majesty's Answer to the Petition.

His Majesty hath commanded me to return this answer to this petition:—That his Majesty is much pleased with the duty and affection expressed by the petitioners, and with so evident a testimony that the grievances he hath redressed, the laws he hath passed, and the declarations he hath made, have produced the effect for which they were intended, viz., the satisfaction, gratitude, and confidence of his subjects, which he doubts not but the whole course of his government will daily increase. That his Majesty is no less pleased to see them so sensible of what hath and ever will best preserve their happiness and security, and that

DOCUMENT I. A.D. 1642.

therefore they only desire to be governed by that rule, which he is resolved only to govern by, the known and established laws of the land, assuring them, that according to his oath, he will always protect them from the invasion of any other assumed arbitrary power whatsoever, as long as he shall be able to protect himself, being resolved of nothing more than to stand and fall together with the law. And that he will not expect they should any longer express their duties to him by the hazard of themselves and fortunes for the preservation of his person, honour, estate, and lawful prerogative, against all powers and persons whatsoever, than his Majesty shall ever be mutually ready to discharge his duty towards them by the hazard of himself and fortune for the preservation and defence of the religion and laws established, of the just privileges and freedom of Parliament, and of the liberty and property of his subjects, against whomsoever they shall endeavour either to destroy or oppose them.

(Signed) FALKLAND.

At the Court at York, Aug. the fourth, 1642.[1]

[1] From a pamphlet entitled "A Petition of the Gentry, Ministers, and Freeholders of the County of Flint, presented to his Majesty at York, August the fourth, 1642, with his Majesty's most gracious answer thereunto. London: Printed by A. Norton, 1642, August 12."

II.

Order to call out the Militia in Pembrokeshire on behalf of the Parliament, and to prevent the execution of the Commission of Array.

DOCUMENT II. A.D. 1642.

Instructions for Sir Hugh Owen,[1] Sir John Stepney,[2] Baronets, and John Wogan the elder,[3] members of the House of Commons and Committee, to be sent into Pembrokeshire and the town of Haverfordwest, and for Sir Richard Phillipps,[4] Baronet, John Laugharne,[5] Alban Owen,[6] Thomas ap Price,[7] Hugh Bowen,[8] Arthur Owen,[9] Roger Loit,[10] Griffith White,[11] John Phillips,[12] Lewis Barlow,[13] John Ellyott,[14] John Edwardes,[15] and Thomas Warren,[16] Esquires, for the preservation of the said county and town.

Whereas it doth appear to the Lords and Commons in Parliament now assembled, that the King, seduced by wicked counsel, doth make war against the Parliament, and for that it is not improbable that under colour of raising a guard for his Majesty's

[1] Of Orielton, member for Pembroke.

[2] Of Prendergast, member for Haverfordwest
[3] Of Wiston, member for the County.
} These two, though here placed in the Parliamentary Committee for the Militia, soon after declared for the King.

[4] Of Picton Castle.

[5] Of St. Brides, father of (the afterwards celebrated) Major General Laugharne.

[6] Of Henllys.

[7] Of the Ricketson family. There was a Thomas ap Rice, of Scotborough, H.S. for 1610.

[8] Of Llwyngwair or Pentre Evan.

[9] Son of Sir Hugh.

[10] Of Stackpole Court.

[11] Of Henllan, Castlemartin.

[12] Of Ffynongain.

[13] Of Criswell.

[14] A lawyer who will hereafter figure.

[15] Of Trefgarn or Sealyham.

[16] Of Trewern.

DOCUMENT II. A.D. 1642.

person, or some other pretence, the knights, gentlemen, freeholders, and inhabitants of the county of Pembroke and town of Haverford the West may be drawn together. Therefore you and every of you shall take special care that the ordinance concerning the militia be forthwith put in execution through the county; and the Sheriff, and all other officers, are hereby enjoined to assist you and every of you therein. And if any person whatsoever shall levy, or endeavour to levy, any soldiers, or draw or keep together the trained bands or other armed forces of the said county, or any other forces, by colour or pretence of any commission or warrant from his Majesty, under the great seal or otherwise, without the order or consent of both Houses of Parliament, you are to make known to the trained bands and other inhabitants of the said county, that those who shall appear upon any such warrants, or obey any such commission, shall be held disturbers of the public peace, and those who shall not appear upon any such warrant or commission, nor do anything in execution thereof, shall be protected by both Houses of Parliament.

And you and every of you are hereby required to draw together such of the trained bands and other forces of the said county as shall be expedient for the suppressing of all such assemblies, and for apprehending of all, or any person or persons as shall, after admonition and command by you or any of you, made unto them, to forbear the execution of any such commission or warrant, or the calling, or gathering, or keeping together of any such forces or assemblies, still persist in doing the same; and likewise such as bear arms by colour of any warrant or commission from his Majesty, under the great seal, or otherwise without order or consent of both Houses of Parliament; and also all such disaffected persons as shall be found raising any parties or factions against the Parliament, to be sent up hither to answer such their offences as to law and justice shall appertain.

And you and every of you, the above said members of the House of Commons, shall, in the name of the Lords and Commons, require and command the Sheriff of the County of Pembroke and town of Haverford to publish throughout the said county and town, the declarations formerly printed by both Houses of Parliament.

You and every of you shall further take care that such

DOCUMENT II. A.D. 1642.

resolutions and orders of both Houses (as have been or shall be delivered or sent down unto you or any of you) be put in execution, and shall require the Sheriff and Justices of the Peace, and all other his Majesty's officers and subjects, to be aiding and assisting to you and every of you for that purpose.

You shall declare unto all men that it hath been and still shall be the care and endeavour of both Houses of Parliament to provide for his Majesty's safety; that they do not, nor ever did, know of any evil intended to his Majesty's person which might move him to require any extraordinary armed guard; that his greatest safety is in the affection and fidelity of his subjects, and in the advice and counsel of his Parliament, and his greatest danger in withdrawing himself from them, so that under colour of doing him service, disaffected and malignant persons, obnoxious to justice for their great crimes, have raised forces, which they labour to increase, to the disturbance and hazard of the Kingdom. You, the said members of the House of Commons, and every of you, shall endeavour to clear the proceedings of the Parliament from all imputations and aspersions, and shall from time to time certify us of all things which you conceive necessary for the present service; and that we may have a speedy account of it, and that our directions to you, as well as your advertisements to us, may have a clear and ready passage, you and every of you shall lay a strict charge upon all postmasters that they do not suffer any letters or other dispatches to or from the Parliament to be intercepted or stayed. And if any shall presume to make stay of those dispatches, you and every of you shall direct the postmasters to repair to the Justices of the Peace, constables, and all other officers, for their aid and assistance, who are hereby required to take a special care that there may be no such interruption.

You and every of you shall take care that none of the recusants' arms or ammunition of the said county be carried, or taken out of the county, upon any pretence or command whatsoever, without warrant of both Houses of Parliament. And you and every of you shall give order and direction to the Sheriffs, Justices of the Peace, and other officers, to require and command all the Popish recusants in that county to confine themselves to their dwellings, according to the statute in that case provided; and if any such recusant shall be found to transgress therein, you and every of you shall cause the Justices of the Peace forthwith to bind them to their good behaviour, and upon refusal or neglect to give security accordingly, to commit them to prison, and further to proceed against them according to the law.

DOCUMENT II. A.D. 1642.

You shall also, in the name of both Houses of Parliament, require all such persons who have in their custody any part of the public magazine of your county, to deliver the same unto you, or some of you, to be employed for the service of the said county.

And you and every of you are likewise to give charge from both Houses of Parliament to all captains and lieutenants, and other officers of the militia, that they be obedient to such directions as they shall from time to time receive from the lieutenant of the county, or his deputies, or any of them, for the due performance of any commands of the said Houses.

And you and every of you shall resist and repel, and are hereby authorized to resist and repel by the power of the said county, and by all other ways and means, all such force and violence as shall be raised or brought by any person or persons to the hindrance or disturbance of their present service, or for the arresting or seizing the persons of you or any of you, or of any others that shall be employed in the performance of the ordinances, instructions, and commands of both Houses of Parliament, for anything done in execution thereof; and the Sheriff and the Justices of the Peace of the same county and town, and all other officers and subjects, are hereby enjoyned to be aiding and assisting to you, and every of you, for the better and more speedy execution of the premises.

And the Lords and Commons do hereby declare that they will protect, defend, and assist all manner of persons for such actions as they shall perform in pursuance of these instructions and other orders and commands of the said Houses of Parliament. [1]

JOHN BROWNE, Cleri.-Parliament.

[1] Journals of the House of Lords, vol. 5, p. 364, under date Thursday, the 18th August, 1642. A similar order, directed to Sir Wm. Brereton for Cheshire, was printed in a pamphlet which is preserved in the British Museum, K. P. No. 68—37.

III.

Chester declares against the Array, August, 1642.

DOCUMENT III. A.D. 1642.

The citizens and inhabitants of the City of Chester, being summoned to appear before his Majesty's Commissioners at the Roodee, within the liberties of the said city, upon Friday, being the 1st of July, 1642, for the clear manifestation of their allegiance to his Majesty and duty to the Parliament, do declare,

That as it is a sacred truth that a Kingdom divided cannot stand, so it is a legal principle that his Royal Majesty is the head, and the Parliament the representative body of this Kingdom, and that in the cordial union of his Majesty and the Parliament consists the safety, glory, and hope thereof.

And they for their parts heartily wish they may be accursed as Corah and his accomplices, that do or shall purposely occasion or foment any difference betwixt his Majesty and his Parliament. And therefore they do further declare their readiness, with their lives and fortunes, to obey his Majesty as their most dear and dread Sovereign, according to their due allegiance and their resolution to defend the privileges of Parliament, according to their free and just protestation; and that as God and the fundamental laws of this Kingdom have joined his Majesty and the Parliament together, so they cannot agree unto a disjointed obedience, but do declare themselves enemies to all such as shall go about to put his Majesty and the Parliament asunder.

And for this resolution they have received encouragements from his Majesty's own declarations, attested with forty of the nobility and prime councillors, whereby he had most graciously assured them, and all other his people, that he hath no more thoughts of making war against his Parliament than against his own children; and that he will defend the just privileges of Parliament and maintain and observe the Acts assented unto by his gracious Majesty this present Parliament, without violation, for which, as for other his Majesty's several gracious protestations for the defence of the Protestant religion, and the laws of the land, they return most humble thanks to his Majesty.

DOCUMENT III. A.D. 1642.

Petition intended to be presented against the Array.

To the Right Honorable and Worshipful the Lords and Gentlemen now in the Commission of Array to be executed in this City of Chester.

The humble petition of divers his Majesty's loyal subjects within the City of Chester,

Humbly Sheweth,—That your petitioners, hearing of the said Commission, and conceiving it to be in the judgment of both Houses illegal and contrary to the express ordinance of Parliament, and also of dangerous consequence, do humbly pray that the execution thereof be stayed, themselves excused from obeying the same, and that you would be pleased rather to mediate betwixt his gracious Majesty and the honorable Houses of Parliament for a reconciliation than to put your petitioners to such desperate consequences, being as they humbly conceive against their protestation so to deceive their obedience, oppose the privileges of Parliament, and withstand their own rights and privileges.[1]

[1] From a pamphlet entitled "The Petition and Resolution of the Citizens of the City of Chester, as it was intended to be presented to the Commissioners of Array, but for special reason was afterwards waived, and the following Declaration (*i.e.*, the first here given) presented by Citizens that were summoned to appear before his Majesty's Commissioners at the Rood, in the Liberties of the said City, for the clear manifestation of their allegiance to his Majesty and duty to the Parliament. Printed at London for Thos. Banks and William Ley, 1642 (Aug. 20)."

IV.

The King at Shrewsbury and Chester—Copies of various Letters, Anonymous and otherwise.[1]

A.

DOCUMENT IV. A.D. 1642.

His Majesty came to Salop on Tuesday last with great strength, both of men and arms, where he stayed till Friday, and then came to Whitchurch and went to Chester. I was one that was appointed to attend him thither, which I did with divers more gentlemen and freeholders. His Majesty and the Prince dined in Whitchurch and so went for Chester. When we came to Milton Green, there was Mr. Richard Edgerton, of Ridley, with some 600 musketeers; and then when we came to Hatton Heath, there was the Lord Rivers with all his forces, and my Lord Cholmley with horse and foot, very complete, beyond the other. So they, having displayed their colours, gave his Majesty a volley of shot; which being done, his Majesty, having ridden once or twice about the army, taken notice of the Sheriff and his company, with divers other gentlemen who were there, then came to Rowton Heath, where was Sir Thomas Aston with what company he had, who did show themselves as the others had done.

Then his Majesty set forwards for Chester. At Boughton, where the liberty of the city beginneth, the two Sheriffs of Chester, with all their company, attended. Then coming to the Bars, there attended the Mayor and Aldermen, where the Mayor delivered both Mace and Sword into his Majesty's hand, who received them and gave them to him again, and so he marched before the King,

[1] The copies of letters, marked A, B, and C, are extracted from a pamphlet entitled "A true Relation of his Majesties coming to the Town of Shrewsbury, on the 20th of this inst. September, and his passage thence, the 23rd day, to the City of Chester, &c., collected out of several letters from men of good credit to their friends in London. London: Printed for R. R., September 29, 1642." K. P. 75—3.

with all the Aldermen and Sheriffs, with all the companies in the town with their gowns, and all the trained bands of the city, who discharged just as his Majesty passed by. Thus was his Majesty attended to the Court, with all the bells ringing, and drums and trumpets sounding.

B.

September 24, 1642.

Yesternight, about four or five o'clock, the King came into the city attended with two troops of horse that came with him, and after his Majesty, came Sir Thomas Aston with his troop. The Mayor and Aldermen standing on a scaffold in Eastgate-street, before Thomas Parnell's door. Sergeant Brierwood made a speech; but there was such great shouting for joy that I think his Majesty scarce heard him. And all the companies standing with their arms in Eastgate-street, to entertain his Majesty and the Sheriffs and Sheriff-peers, and such as have been leave-lookers, rid out of the town in scarlet (as they use to ride out at Midsummer) to meet his Majesty with all our trained bands. The Mayor rid before his Majesty, carrying the sword from the scaffold to the Bishop's Palace, as I am told for truth by them that saw them. The Lord Dillon and another Irish Lord, a great rebel, came with his Majesty into the city. Sir Richard Wilbraham met his Majesty and fell down on his knees to him, but his Majesty would not take notice of him. He and Sir Thomas Delves are committed to the Sheriff. Both these knights declared themselves for the Ordinance of the Militia. It is thought there are warrants out for the apprehending of many other gentlemen.

Yesterday, about two hours before his Majesty came there, came a troop of the Lord Strange his horse, and 80 horse-loads of muskets and bandaliers, and such like provisions which were laid in our common hall, and there are 200 more at the Lord Strange his house that came from Newcastle. The Lord Strange hath delivered those arms that were taken from Papists in Lancashire to them again, and threatened the Mayor of Liverpool to batter down the town if he would not deliver them. It is said there are 5,000 coming through

DOCUMENT IV. A.D. 1642.

Lancashire, which came out of the north for his Majesty. Yesternight, at 9 o'clock, the Lord Strange came into this city with one or two troops of horse. This day all betwixt the age of 16 and 60 years of the trained bands of the county are summoned to appear before his Majesty at Hoo Heath, two miles from Chester.

Upon Wednesday last the town of Nantwich were in some fear lest they should be disarmed, and stood upon their guard, and some aid came to help them; but that night following, about 1,000 horse came thither. The Lord Cholmley came with them, with the Commission for the Array. They were to have a parley, and the town would have been delivered, so that they might have their arms and liberties. This while, the other side got in at back gardens, and disarmed all, plundering some houses. The day following they went to Sir Richard Wilbraham's and Sir Thomas Delves', and disarmed them, took their horses and three cart-loads of armour from them, and do further proceed, doing much harm at many other places and houses. It is thought our Mayor and Aldermen do intend to give the King a sum of money.

C.

September 23rd, 1642.

Good Sir,

The latter end of your letter is somewhat comforting, in that you write there are some dragoons coming into Cheshire for our relief, but surely they are not come, and now will come too late, for we are all plundered and undone.

Nantwich is taken by my Lord Grandison's army, and the town disarmed, and many houses plundered who stood for the Parliament and the militia, the owners of them driven to run away for safety of their lives, for they have threatened them much; and after they had disarmed the town they came into the country and disarmed all the great houses. First, Sir Thomas Delves', then my Lord Crewes's, then Sir Richard Wilbrahams's, and so all the other gentlemen round about us. They plundered their houses—they being forced not only to leave their own houses but also the Town of Nantwich and their poor tenants and countrymen to the mercy

DOCUMENT IV. A.D. 1642.

of these merciless villains, who will have what they list; nay, they will have what we have not for them, or else they will set a pistol to our throats and swear God damn them, they will make us swallow a bullet! Some of them are not content to take what arms they can find, but also money, plate, linen, clothes, writings, meat, drink, and not these with content, but steal our horses, and drive our women and children into such fear that they over-run (? leave) their houses and lie in the fields, ditches, and woods. I do not hear of the like cruelty that hath been used anywhere, but in that miserable and bleeding Kingdom of Ireland. We are like to be worse yet, for this day the King is at Chester, and all the whole country from 16 years to 60 is to meet and attend his Majesty and the Commissioners of the Array, not far from Chester, with all their arms which are left. None dare refuse to go. The malignant party will inform against them, and then they are threatened to be all carried away with my Lord Grandison's army. The best of it is, if we stay at home, we are now their slaves. Being naked they will have of us what they list, and do with us what they list; I believe we shall be made the seat of war, and so be utterly ruined and undone for want of help in time and true hearts among ourselves * * * * * * * *
To hear the pitiful shrieking, weeping, and howling of women and children, did more trouble me than anything else. God grant I never hear the like.[1]

[1] Another correspondent gives a somewhat different version of the affair. Writing from Nantwich on the 24th September, he says—"The day following [Grandison's entry] they took arms from Crew Hall for 20 men, but did no other violence. Sir Thomas Delves left his house empty and much arms on the hall table for them. They dealt more harshly at Mr. Vernon's, taking many other things besides arms. No violence that I could hear of was offered to any man's person in Nantwich on Wednesday, but to one Radcliff, an honest man about Westaston, who was shot in the hands and shoulder because he was slow in delivering his musket. They have also been in divers other houses in Barthomly parish, the parson's for one, and what they have done on the other side of the town I know not. The gentlemen and trained bands are to attend his Majesty this day on Hatton Heath."

D.

A True and Exact Relation of the King's Entertainment in the City of Chester.

DOCUMENT IV. A.D. 1642.

The King came to Chester from Salop upon Friday, about five of the clock, but he brought with him no great company. The Lord Rivers, Lord Cholmley, and Sir Thomas Aston, came each of them with a troop of horse to wait on his Majesty into the city besides those that came with him. There went out of the city to Boughton about forty that had been sheriffs, and some others on horseback and foot clothes, and rode before him into the city; and at the Hong Stairs there was a scaffold made for the Aldermen to stand and receive him (as they had done his father before time), and they kneeled down, and the Recorder made a speech or oration to the King, not such a one as is conceived much to his credit. Your father promised to send you a copy that you may print it to his shame, for I take it he is full of malice and pride, and but an ignorant man in his own profession.[1] After the oration our Mayor[2] gave the King the sword, the mace, and the staff, and the King gave them again to him, and the Mayor got on his horse and carried the sword before the King unto the Bishop's palace,[3] where he stayed till Tuesday and departed towards Salop, taking Wrexham in his way, and there dined with Master Lloyd,[4] a lawyer, and the King's attorney for Flintshire, and thence to Salop, where he is.[5]

Our Mayor and his brethren presented him with £200 in gold and to the Prince £100. It was well taken, but by the report

[1] This speech of Mr. Recorder Brierwood was by no means as bad as the above writer would wish us to believe. It will bear favourable comparison with modern addresses to Sovereigns, and contains no more than the usual platitudes. Believing in his Majesty's "indeered love for his subjects, and to the Protestant Religion," he freely promised the King the "adventure of their lives and fortunes for his defence."

[2] Thomas Cowper, Ironmonger. [3] Bishop Bridgman.

[4] Sir Richard Lloyd. He was knighted by the King on the second visit which he soon afterwards made to Wrexham. See Randle Holme's Notes, Harl. MSS. 2125—fol. 313.

[5] While at Wrexham he delivered a speech, which see post. H.

DOCUMENT IV. A.D. 1642.

of some a greater sum was expected, but those know not our having, for I persuade myself before it be collected amongst the citizens, it will be thought a very great sum. His stay amongst us was very peaceable, and his departure very cheerful. The Mayor and Aldermen brought him out of the liberty on horseback. It is reported he left a garrison amongst us, but he left none, he only commanded that 100 of the country soldiers should be put into the castle. What we shall have put upon us I know not, but all those not of the Array[1] are observed. Some of our country gentlemen, as Sir Richard Wilbraham, Sir Thomas Delves, Mr. Mainwaring of Badely, Mr. Wilbraham of Darfold, Mr. Birkenhead, the Pronotary and his son,[2] are all commanded to wait upon the King, and went with him to Salop where they are all yet.

I am informed that some have a commission to search our houses in Chester, what for, as yet, I know not, but I hear my house is set down for one to be searched. If they plunder not, I do not fear them. We have great store of soldiers billeted round about our city. What for, I know not, but they are very unruly, and come into many honest men's houses, especially into ministers' houses, and take away, some all, and what they please of their goods.

Since the Sabbath day last, Manchester hath been besieged by my Lord Strange, now Lord of Derby, for his father lieth dead at his little house under St. John's, but we do not know nor hear that he hath taken the town as yet, neither they yielded. This is all the passages that we have at present, so I end with my prayer to God to bring all these troubles to an end. So committing you to to God and rest.[3]

Chester, October 1, 1642.

[1] That is who did not join with the Commissioners of Array appointed by the King.

[2] Mr. Hen. Birkenhead, junior, was one of those who assisted Sir W. Brereton to oppose the Array on the 8th of August, on the occasion of the tumult. They had to seek refuge in the house of Mr Alderman Edwards (Mayor for 1636.)

[3] From "A True Relation of the King's Entertainment in the City of Chester. Sent from a citizen of note in Chester. London: Printed for C. M. October 4, 1642." (K. P. 75—25.)

E.

Bridgenorth, October 1, 1642.

DOCUMENT IV. A.D. 1642.

Our country is in a most miserable condition; there is nothing can be expected but a total ruin thereof, except God do miraculously help us with assistance from the Parliament. The King's soldiers are altogether bent on mischief, taking, wasting, and spoiling those things we should live by. They take our corn unthreshed to litter their horses, spoiling that which many a poor creature wants. If any one speak, be it a man or woman, either a pistol or a sword is straight set at the party with many grievous oaths. They know what they do, they are the King's servants, and will not be limited of their will. You may judge by this what a case we are in, and for anything we can perceive like to be worse, for as long as these outrages are permitted no question but the King's army will increase. What with Papists, Atheists, and all desperate ruffians, they have made Shrewsbury strong, as it is reported to us, many pieces of ordnance, 300 carts laden with ammunition, and our County of Shropshire is very much awed, and many well-affected persons withdraw themselves. The Sheriff here hath lately seized certain thousands of pounds at our town of Bridgenorth, intended to be sent down Severn lately to Bristol, by Mr. Charlton of Apley, Mr. Baker of Hammond, and others. We have many brags here of the Cavaliers, what victories they have had at Worcester, though we know for certain they are notorious lies, yet we dare not contradict them. It grieves the soul of every good Christian to see how his Majesty is misled. We are glad to hear of your constancy to the King and Parliament. Our affections are the same, though we dare not show it. For all the reports you have heard, you may perhaps understand by the next that Shropshire is not altogether so malignant as it is reported. Fear makes us yield to many things. I am in haste,

Yours, T. C.[1]

[1] From "A True and Exact Relation of the Proceedings of His Majesty's Army in Cheshire, Shropshire, &c." London: Printed for M. Bath. October 5, 1642. K. P. 77—3.

F.

Chester, October 1, 1642. DOCUMENT IV. A.D. 1642.

We are hear in great fears. 260 horse-loads of arms are come hither out of the North, and they tell us of 5,000 men that will come out of Lancashire, and the parts adjacent, besides what Cheshire and these parts of Wales will afford. The Lord Cholmley sets out 200 foot and 20 horse. The Lord Grandison, with 200 horse, hath possessed himself of Nantwich for the King, and hath billeted his troops in the town, who have since their entrance plundered divers houses of well-affected men in the town and country, which hath put the people round about in such a fear that many fly from the country into the city and take houses, and carry their best goods hither. I myself am come this last week to live in Chester, and have left my servants to look to the business in the country. Since my coming hither there were 200 soldiers billeted in our little village, and 13 of them appointed to my house, who, I thank God, departed without doing any more hurt than what victuals they ate, which they took in an orderly manner. His Majesty departed Chester on Tuesday, and went hence by Wrexham to Shrewsbury, whence he came. At his departure from us he put 100 men for a garrison with the castle, and commanded Sir Thomas Delves, Sir Richard Wilbraham, Mr. Philip Mainwaring, of Badely, and Mr. Birkenhead, the Pronotary, and his son, to wait upon his Majesty, and to be confined to the Court. The same day the King went Captain Salisbury and his men did burn Sir William Brereton's decoy; and the King's soldiers in all places where they come grow very insolent, and do much spoil and mischief. The Commissioners of Array by the King's coming hither are much strengthened in these parts, for the aforesaid men whom the King hath taken away with him were the chief of those that attempted to put the militia in execution. The report is here that the King likes the city so well that he intends shortly to return and winter with us. My Lord Strange, now Earl of Derby (for on Monday last his father died here in Chester), is gone with great forces against Manchester, who have fortified themselves, and resolve to keep him out with all the might they can. They have three pieces of

DOCUMENT IV. A.D. 1642. ordnance. My Lord Strange hath six pieces. Bullets have been exchanged on both sides, and two of my lord's men slain, and some commanders, which hath so far incensed him that he is resolved to have the town or to die before it. The times are like to be miserable. God grant a happy reconcilement.

G.

September the last.

On Tuesday last, at night, his Majesty came safe to Shrewsbury from Chester. And upon warrant, granted out the Friday before, most part of the gentry, clergy, freeholders, and substantial inhabitants of the county, appeared before him last Wednesday at Shrewsbury, in a meadow called the Gay, where his Majesty and the Prince came in person, and made a short speech, which, the crowd being great, I could hear little of, but the substance of that he intended to speak was put in writing and read to the people, which was to this effect: That such was the insolences of a rebellious and malignant party against him, who had robbed and spoiled him of his goods, and kept his revenues from him, and had now set forth an army marching against him, that now he was enforced to desire the aid and relief of his good subjects to supply him in this necessity for the defence and safety of his person, the preservation of the true religion and maintenance of our laws and liberties, hoping they would be as liberal to their abilities in supplying him as others that were grown wanton with plenty had been bountiful to maintain the war against him; but yet rather than he would put too heavy a pressure upon his good subjects he would melt down his own plate and sell and mortgage his land to maintain his just rights and ours. There was no money or plate parted with that I did see, for his Majesty referred it to his High Sheriff and other Commissioners to use the time and method they thought fit, and so we should be called again to express our affections to them. The Lord grant us faith and constancy to undergo all troubles that lie upon us, and send a happy and speedy reconciliation betwixt Prince and people to God's glory and our comfort.

DOCUMENT IV. A.D. 1642.

Our country is now in a woful condition by reason of the multitude of soldiers daily billeted upon us, both of Horse and Foot. I have had of those guests all this week, and expect little better next week. We had in town on Thursday night last some 12 or 14 captains besides other officers, and near upon 2,000 soldiers belonging to them. All the country around, within 12 or 14 miles of Shrewsbury, are full of soldiers. Your father had some four for his part, being some of those that came from Nantwich, which after they had made what spoil they could there are now billeted a good part of them in Prince parish. They are of my Lord Grandison's regiment, and such for condition that I think the earth affords not worse. They have plundered divers men's houses in a most woful manner. Your friend and mine hath had in money and goods taken from him to the value of £50. A gentleman of quality was forced to shift for himself and leave his house, and they have taken possession of it and live upon the spoil of his household provision, corn, and cattle, near 20 men, and at least 40 horses, since Monday last, and show no sign of parting as yet; but endeavour the ruin of his house and goods; and if any fault be found threaten to burn it to the ground. We have escaped reasonably well in the town as yet with some little loss. I praise God for it, I have none as yet; but how long I and many others shall be free the Lord above doth know, for we have one outrage or other committed daily. They ride armed, up and down, with swords and pistols, muskets, and dragoons, to the great terror of the people, that we scarce know how in safety to go out of doors. They take men's horses, break and pillage men's houses, both night and day, in an unheard-of manner. They pretend quarrel with the Roundheads, as they call them, but for aught I see they will spare none if they may hope to have good booty. Prince Robert (Rupert) came to Shrewsbury last Monday night. I saw him myself on Wednesday. The Marquis of Hertford is reported to be there likewise. So with my best respects unto you, I remain,

Yours, whose hand you know.

October 1, an. 1642.[1]

[1] From "Some late Occurrences in Shropshire, &c. London: Printed for H. Blunden. October 5, 1642." (K. P. 77—4.)

II.

DOCUMENT IV.

A.D. 1642.

The King's Speech to the Inhabitants of Denbigh and Flintshire, delivered at Wrexham on the 27th of September.

I am willing to take all occasions to visit all my good subjects, in which number I have cause to reckon you of these two counties, and having lately had a good expression of your loyalty and affections to me by those levies, which at your charge have been sent me from your part (which forwardness of yours I shall always remember to your advantage), and to let you know how I have been dealt with by a powerful malignant party in this Kingdom, whose designs are no less than to destroy my person and crown, the laws of the land, and the present government both of Church and State. The leaders of these men by subtilty and cunning practices have so prevailed upon the meaner sort of people about London that they have called them up into frequent and dangerous tumults, and thereby have chased from thence myself and the greatest part of the members of both Houses of Parliament. Their power and secret plot have had such influence upon the small remaining part of both Houses, that under colour of orders and ordinances made without the Royal Assent (a thing never heard of before this Parliament), I am robbed and spoiled of my towns, forts, castles, and goods; my navy forcibly taken from me and employed against me; all my revenue stopped and seized upon; and at this time a powerful army is marching against me. I wish this were all. They have yet further laboured to alienate the affections of my good people; they have most injuriously vented many false reproaches against my person and government; they have dispersed in print many notorious false scandals upon my actions and intentions; and in particular have laboured to cast upon me some aspersions concerning the horrid, bloody, and impious rebellion in Ireland. They tell the people that I have recalled two ships appointed to guard these seas. 'Tis true. But they conceal that at the same time I sent my warrant to the Downs, commanding four as good ships to attend that service instead of those recalled, which warrant by their means could not find obedience. They forget that they then employed forty ships (many of them my own, and all of them set forth at the public charge of this and that Kingdom) to rob and pillage me of my goods, to chase my good subjects, and maintain my own town of Hull against me, and that by the absence of those ships from the Irish Sea, the rebels have had opportunity to bring store of arms, ammunition, and supplies, to their succours (to which we may justly impute the calamities which have overwhelmed my poor Protestant subjects there). They cry out upon a few suit of clothes appointed (as they say) for Ireland, which some of my forces took; but conceal that they were taken as entering into Coventry (then in open rebellion against me), where I had reason to believe they would have been disposed of amongst their soldiers who then bore arms against me. They talk of a few horses which I have made use of, for my carriages (concealing that they were certified to be useless for service in Ireland), when they themselves have seized £100,000, particularly appointed by an Act of Parliament for the relief of Ireland (where my army is ready to perish for want of it), and employed it, together with such part of the £400,000 subsidy as they have received, to maintain an unnatural Civil War at home.

Neither have they used their fellow subjects better than their King. By their power the law of the land (your birthright) is trampled upon, and instead thereof, they govern my people by votes and arbitrary orders. Such as will not submit to their unjust, unlimited power, are imprisoned, plundered and destroyed. Such as will not pay such executions as they require towards this rebellion are threatened to be put out of protection (as they call it) of the Parliament. Such as conscientiously remember their duty and loyalty to their Sovereign, are reviled, persecuted, and declared traitors; such as do desire to maintain the true Protestant religion, as it is established by the laws of the land, are traduced and called Popish and superstitious. And on the contrary, such as are known Brownists, Ana-baptists, and public depravers of the Book of Common Prayer, are countenanced and encouraged.

They exact and receive tonnage and poundage, and other great duties upon merchandise, not only without law, but in the face of an Act of Parliament to the contrary passed this present Parlia-

DOCUMENT IV. A.D. 1642.

ment, which puts all men into the condition of *præmunire* that shall presume so to oppress the people. If you desire to know who are the contrivers of these wicked designs you shall find some of their names in particular, and their actions at large, in my declaration of the 12th of August (to which I refer you). I wish their craft and power was not so much, that few of those copies can come to the view of my good people since that time that these men so thirst after the destruction of this Kingdom, that they have prevailed to make all my offers of treaty (which might bring peace to this Kingdom and beget a good understanding between me and my Parliament) fruitless in this distress into which these men have brought me and this Kingdom. My confidence is in the protection of Almighty God and the affections of my good people. And that you may clearly see what my resolutions are I shall cause my voluntary protestation lately taken, to be read to you. And I desire that the Sheriffs of these two counties will dispose copies of that, and what I now deliver unto you, having no other way to make it public, these men having restrained the use of my presses in London and the Universities.[1]

[1] Rushworth's Collection. Pt. 3, vol. II., p. 21.

V.

The Marquis of Hertford at Cardiff.

"True and Happy News-from Wales, declaring the Proceedings of the Marquis of Hertford in Glamorganshire."

DOCUMENT V. A.D. 1642.

The Earl of Bedford, since his last and happy victory over the Marquis of Hertford, the Lord Paulet, and the rest of their confederates, except Sir Ralph Hopton, one of the greatest incendiaries in that opposition and rebellion, who is departed from them and is escaped privately (as it is surmised), and returned back again into Somersetshire, but there his welcome will be very mean and slender, were chased and pursued to Minchead by the Earl of Bedford, where the Marquis, according to his expectation, but contrary to his desert, was found and entertained and received by some coal ships.

Yet the Earl of Bedford had formerly used all possible means for the prevention and stoppage of his passage over Severn.

Notwithstanding all which means formerly used by the Earl for the prevention of the Marquis his flight, having gotten the opportunity and conduct of these small coal ships, which then lay in the harbour, he got over the river and escaped into Wales, and by that means escaped the justice of the pursuing enemy. Yet, notwithstanding this unhappy escape, and the Earl's hopes to compass his ends, the cause of all his labours and vexations being frustrated by the escape of the Marquis, he did not desist from his purpose, but did pursue them with all the violence he possibly could, and at the last came in view of them, and being seconded with a happy success, he was made in part master of his desires, for although he could not catch the Marquis, who, by the help of those Welsh ships, had escaped into Wales, yet he took the Lord Paulet, Sir Henry Berkly, and two of his brothers,

DOCUMENT V. A.D. 1642.

whom he hath now in custody, and as soon as with conveniency he can, he will send them up to the Parliament, that by them they may receive condign punishment.

By letters from the well-affected party in Wales it was signified that the Marquis of Hertford had possessed himself of Cardiff Castle in Glamorganshire, and was resolved to seize upon all cattle that belonged to the Earl of Pembroke; but so soon as the inhabitants of that county had information of it, they gathered ahead and gave battle against the Marquis at Cardiff, killing some 53, with the loss of nine men.[1]

Extract from "Speciall Passages, No. 7. From Tuesday, the 20 September, to Tuesday, the 27." Sub tit. "Hereford, Sep. 21."

It is reported that the Marquis of Hertford is coming from Sherborne Castle hither. There is much tampering with the Welshmen, to charm them to go and aid the Marquis and his company; and as we are informed some of the rascal mountaineers are in the service, because they hear the common soldiers in England wear shoes and stockings in summer, and they go barefoot in the depth of winter.

From a "A Continuation of True and Speciall Passages, &c. From the 22 of September to the 29, 1642." Sub voc. "Hereford."

His Majesty is daily expected here. Some Welshmen, to the number of two thousand, have entered the town, pretending they have warrant from his Majesty to possess the same for his

[1] From "A True and Joyful Relation of a famous and remarkable Victory obtained by the inhabitants of Glamorganshire, in Wales, against the Marquesse of Hartford and the Cavaliers, who had took the Castle of Cardiffe, in the said county. October 3, 1642, &c. London: Printed for H. Fowler. Oct. 5." (K. P. 75—31.)

use. But after a day's abode there, they used themselves so inhumanly towards the townsmen and attempted to disarm them; but they (the townsmen) perceiving their intention, stood upon their guard, and have expelled many of them out of the town, and sent into the country adjacent for the assistance of the trained bands, hoping in short time to expel them quite out of that country.

DOCUMENT V. A.D. 1642.

From No. 12 of "A Continuation of Certain Speciall Passages" (K. P. 77—9), under date Monday, 3rd of October.

There was also certain information given to the House by letters that the Marquis of Hertford and his cavaliers that lately fled from Sherborne Castle, are come into South Wales, and that they have possessed themselves of Cardiff Castle, it being the Earl of Pembroke's house in Glamorganshire, which castle was very treacherously yielded up to them by one Master Herbert, the keeper thereof, an ungrateful kinsman to the Earl of Pembroke and a member of the House of Commons, but now voted against for ever sitting in the House during this Parliament. It was also informed the Marquis intends to pillage the Earl of Pembroke's lands thereabouts, and to strengthen his forces, and then march back to his Majesty.

In another newspaper of the time, entitled "Certain Special and Remarkable Passages" (K. P. 77—14), it is stated that the Earl of Bedford had followed the Marquis of Hertford to Cardiff, and had effected an entry, and was fortifying the town for the Parliament.

VI.

Charles Prince of Wales's Visit to Ragland in October.

DOCUMENT VI. A.D. 1642.

A loving and loyal Speech, spoken to our noble Prince Charles by Sir Hugh Vaughan, the 2nd of October, at Raglan Castle, in Monmouthshire, in Wales.

This country of Wales is so filled with joy by the gracious presence of you, their hopeful Prince Charles, so that they know not how to show it outwardly, or to speak unto you in such language as may declare their unfeigned and hearty gladness by your approach and residence here in Ragland Castle. The genius of that ancient building doth seem to rejoice, and the walls are now become a cabinet to keep and preserve the eldest jewel of the Royal progeny, and our dearly-beloved Prince Charles. It is the glory of the Britons that we are the true remaining and only one people of this land, and we have always been true in our affections to our King and country. The eldest son of our gracious Sovereign having so near relation unto us as to be our Prince. The Prince we now behold with tears of joy, with hearts over-flowing with an inundation of love, with wishes, with desires, and fervent prayers, that Heaven would be always auspicious to our King and Prince Charles. We know no sun that can with the influence of Royal beams cherish and warm our true British hearts, but the sun of our gracious Sovereign, who now doth shine in the horizon of Wales. We have no happiness nor hope but what we derive from your gracious aspect, and we reckon it amongst the greatest favours that Divine Providence could do us to send you, our hopeful Prince amongst us. In what the true and ancient Britons may serve you, you may command us to our uttermost strength, our lives and fortunes to be ready to assist you, the King and the Parliament, in all just actions, that none may suffer by the malignity of some ill-affected persons. Our lives, dear sir, are so true and firm to your Princely person, so that all we can promise cannot declare how ready we will be to actuate and express our love in real

DOCUMENT VI. A.D. 1642.

performances. The common people with hands and hearts are ready to help you in all honourable attempts, and our gentry will show their ancient virtue and valour in your service; and because we will not trouble you with further protestations of our real intentions we will conclude this brief narration with prayers to God to bless and preserve you. And the general voice of this country doth by this speech bid you thrice welcome to Wales.

The manner of Prince Charles his Entertainment in Ragland Castle in Wales.

As the Welshmen did in many verbal congratulations manifest the true love and affections of the British heart unto Prince Charles, now keeping Court at Raglan Castle; so to make their words, true expressions of their love and ambition to serve the Prince, they did with cheerful forwardness make divers substantial demonstrations of their professed affection.

Love is always active, and desires to be known and understood by signs, by evidences; and by many officious actions, it will appear and be visible. And this was manifest by Prince Charles his late entertainment at Ragland Castle, in Wales, which was performed with much solemnity. The Castle was prepared and made ready for his coming before his approach thither. Some of the chief rooms were richly hung with cloth of Arras, full of lively figures and ancient British stories. All the other furniture was rich and costly.

At the first entering into the Castle the aforesaid speech was by a person of good rank and quality spoken before the Prince, who in thankfulness gave them a brief answer in testimony of his accepting their love and tendered service; and besides, honoured the Knight that delivered the aforesaid speech by reaching forth his hand to kiss, whereon the Knight imprinted a kiss as the seal of his affection.

Then there was a great feast of divers varieties, especially of fowl, whereof there [is] abundance in those counties. And all this preparation did conclude in a curious banquet, while Metheglin and other British drinks were plentifully afforded unto all the

DOCUMENT VI. A.D. 1642.

courtiers. For the Welshmen are of a true generous disposition, and when they are to give entertainment to common strangers they will perform it with much civil courtesy. But especially now, having the happiness to see their young hopeful Prince in the heart of their country, they could not endeavour enough (as they thought) to make it appear that with all cordial and hearty affection the Prince was most nobly welcome into Wales. They showed a glimpse of their true British love to the King and Prince in the aforesaid speech, congratulating his coming into the country, promising him to be his true and faithful servants, and after they had feasted him and all his Court in a liberal, free, and magnificent manner, they remembered that it was an ancient custom to offer presents unto Princes to gratulate their access and coming into a country; whereupon, to declare that their love was not barren like the sea sands which yield nothing, but that as their country was plentiful, abounding with all sorts of provisions, so their hearts were large and liberal, as became them who are acknowledged to be the ancient true Britons; and to make their native liberality apparent, they as soon as the Prince was come to Radnor Castle brought unto him divers rich presents, and with many expressions of love presented them to the Prince. Some brought him pieces of plate of great antiquity, as might appear by the fashion thereof. The common people brought in provision for the maintenance of his Court [such] as young kids, sheep, calves, fish, and fowl of all sorts, and some sent in fat oxen. Everyone striving for the credit and glory of his country to exceed in several expressions of generous liberality. One Master Lewis ap Morgan, a private gentleman, sent the Prince a piece of plate with his arms engraved thereon, being very massy and of great value. Other gentlemen and squires of the county of Radnorshire being descended of ancient families, came bravely mounted to the Prince's Court at Radnor Castle, and there presented him with divers testimonies of their good will and affection—everyone in the delivery of his present desiring [and] wishing all accumulations of happiness unto their noble and gracious Prince Charles, offering, together with their presents, their services unto him, and promising to assist him and his royal father King Charles, upon any lawful design, to the maintenance [of] justice, piety, and religion, and to defend their persons from all malignants and enemies. DOCUMENT VI. A.D. 1642.

The Prince being thus entertained and nobly used by the Welshmen, he showed himself very gracious and loving unto them, and because he could not give particular thanks unto every person that presented gifts unto him, therefore in a great assembly of lords, knights, squires, gentlemen, and many common people, the Prince made a very loving speech unto them, and to gratify their liberality and remunerate their bounty, he, in this brief speech following,[1] rendered them hearty thanks for their presents, and for the tender of their service upon all good occasions.[2]

[1] The speech which this boy-prince piped with his childish voice ran as follows—bad grammar notwithstanding—"Gentlemen, I have heard formerly of the great minds, the true affections and meanings of the ancient Britanies, but my kind entertainment hath made me confide in your love, which I shall always remember. I give you commendations, praise, and thanks, for your love, your bounty, and liberal entertainment. I know you desire nothing but thanks. You shall be sure of that my favour as long as I am Prince of Wales."

[2] "A Loving and Loyal Speech, spoken unto the Excellency of our Noble Prince Charles, by Sir Hugh Vaughan, the 2 of October, at Raglan Castle, in Monmouthshire, &c., sent from a gentleman of that county, one Mr. Francis Meredith, unto Mr. Henry Roberts, belonging to the Custom House, London. Printed for John Johnson, 1642."

VII.

The King quits Shrewsbury.

A.

DOCUMENT VII A. A.D. 1642.

Sir,

My respects to you. I give you many thanks for your good remembrance of me. I could not write to you an answer by the same carrier, because they did not come of the latest unto me, and I was mightily employed about the King's business, I being an officer of the Mayor's. The King did go from hence on Wednesday last to Bridgnorth, and some of his foot soldiers did march yesterday to Stourbridge, in Worcestershire.

The King is about 16,000 strong of foot, besides horse, and every day; more and more come to him, by reason (as we are informed about us) the Parliament forces do so plunder as they go. And the King hath commanded that no plundering shall be at all, for he did cause Sir Robert Heath, who is now made Lord Chief Justice of England, to sit with a Commission of Oyer and Terminer, in our town, where six of the King's soldiers were cast for plundering and stealing.

The Mint is come to our town, and one Master Bushell doth coin every day; for abundance of plate is sent in to the King from the several counties about us, and a great deal of plate comes daily out of Wales and Cornwall to be coined here. Also the press for printing is come to this town, and this day they are setting of it up in some vacant rooms in my house.

Sir Richard Newport is made a Lord; he hath given the King 10,000 pounds. The King would have knighted the Mayor, but he refused it.

The last Sunday the King took a protestation, and the Sacrament upon it, in St. Mary's Church, in our town, to defend the true Protestant religion, established by Queen Elizabeth and his Royal father.

We hear his Majesty on Tuesday last, with his army, were at Birmingham. Prince Robert demanding 2,000 pounds, or he would plunder the town; but most of the inhabitants were (before) fled to Coventry. Upon Thursday he marched to Meriden, three miles off Coventry, and intends (as we are informed by divers reports) to march towards Banbury, and so to Oxford; for his resolution, it is thought, is to March to London or to Windsor, or thereabouts. God of his mercy turn all to good and peace of this Kingdom, and deliver us from the misery of Civil War. Thus with love to all our friends I rest, DOCUMENT VII A. A.D. 1642.

Yours to his power,

BASIL WARING.

Shrewsbury, Oct. 18, 1642.[1]

[1] From a pamphlet, entitled "The True Copy of a Letter, &c., written by one Master Tempest, &c., which was intercepted at Manchester, and sent to a Member of the House of Commons, &c., with divers Remarkable Passages from Shrewsbury and Coventry, concerning the King, &c." London: Printed for H. Thompson, 1642. (K.P. 80—15)

B.

The King to Thomas Bushell, Master Worker of the Mines Royal, acknowledging his services. DOCUMENT VII. B. A.D. 1642.

CHARLES R.,

Trusty and well-beloved we greet you well. Calling to mind your vigilant eye of care upon all occasions, and the many true services you have actually done us in these times of trying a subject's loyalty, as in raising us the Derbyshire miners for our life guard at our first entrance to this war, for our own defence, when the Lord Lieutenant of the county refused to appear in the services: supplying us at Shrewsbury and Oxford with your Mint for the payment of our army, when all the officers in the mint of our Tower of London forsook their attendance, except Sir William Parkhurst: your changing the dollars, with which are paid our soldiers, at six shillings apiece, when the malignant party cried them down at five: your stopping the Mutiny in

DOCUMENT VII. B. A.D. 1642.

Shropshire when the soldiers had left their arrears upon the country, and brought the association of the gentry to perfection: your providing us one hundred tons of lead shot for our army, without money, when we paid before twenty pounds per ton: and your helping us to twenty-six pieces of ordnance when we were at a straight for supplying of Chester, Shrewsbury, and other places: your clothing of our life guard and three regiments more with suits, stockings, shoes, and mounterees, when we were ready to march in the field: your invention for our better knowing and rewarding the Forlorn Hope with badges of silver at your own charge, when the soldiers were ready to run away through the instigation of some disaffected persons: your contracting with merchants beyond the seas for providing good quantities of powder, pistol, carabine, musket, and bullen, in exchange for your own commodities, when we were wanting of such ammunition, with divers other several services, which we hope our royal successors will never forget; and to assure you that we shall bear them in our princely remembrance, we hereby promise you on the word of a Prince to make those traitorous subjects Smyth, Wild, and Stephenson, for to restore those lands of Chawford Dene, Hampstead, and Euston, which you sold them, and to free you and your three sureties, Edmond Goodier, Charles Mordent, and the Lady Anne Wade, of the debts you owe to such rebellious persons as shall be proved [to] have assisted the Parliament (either by their purse or power) against us, to the end, that you may enjoy your desires at Euston Rock and the Rocks in Wales, which your own industry and God's providence hath helped you unto. Given under our sign manual, at our Court at Oxford, the twelfth day of June, 1642.

To our trusty and well-beloved Thomas Bushell, Esq.,
Warden of our Mint, and M[aste]r Worker, of our Mines Royal.[1]

[1] From Cart. Harl. Antiq. iii., b. 61. orig. Given also in Ellis's original letters, 2nd series, vol. iii., p. 309.

VIII.

Nantwich in trouble for its opposition to the King.

DOCUMENT VIII. A.D. 1642.

Nantwich.

Good Cousin,

Many troubles fall upo. o[r] countrey and upo. o friends but especially upon this unfortunate towne for the folly of some few w[ch] are fled, for besides y[e] losse and terrour it hath already sustaine'd by these late devouring troopes, the King hath imposed a fine upo. it of two thousand pounds, without making any distinction between the innocent and y[e] guilty. It is thought also that now at the assizes o[r] towne will be indicted and severely proceeded against. In all w[ch] perplexities how I must behave myself I must entreat yo[r] advice. Being absent at the Bathe all the while theis actions of rebellion were in agitation whereof I have y[e] testimony of divers of best credit in o[r] towne, w[ch] I have hereinclosed sent you for my iustification (if there be cause, and can have more hands anon to it if it were requisite. Also here-inclosed is a note of some p'ticulers which I heare will be charged upo. the towne. I am not well able to travel myself in regard of my old pain w[ch] I cannot yet be cured of. I have sent my man of purpose to you with theis things, y[t] in case I be named, you will make my excuse, and moove y[t] those y[t] were innocent and ignorant of theis proceedings, no way allowing or approving them may not be involved with y[e] delinquents nor beare any p[t] of their blame or burden. It may be for my name's sake[1] I may find some adversaries, otherwise, I think, I should find none, for in

[1] Referring doubtless to the conduct of his kinsmen who were strenuous supporters of the Parliament, and suffered for it.

DOCUMENT VIII.

A.D. 1642.

regard I am sworne his Maties servant I was very cautious. It was tould me y^{t} this last week Mr. Sheriff, in ye hearing of my Ld Chomley and others, did averre y^{t} I sent 2 armed men to rescue Steele, our constable, when he was under arrest, wch is most false. I myself was then at Bathe and left but only one man at Nantwich, wch was this messenger, & he will depose y^{t} at that tyme he was forth of the towne. What I write to yo^{u} I will make good by the testimony of all my neighbours. I have appointed my man to stay till Tuesday, to bring me word how things are carried, wch ye Lord grant may be for the good of us and our friends, wch I am much afraid of, for I received a letter upo. Saturday fro. Sr Ric. Wilb., intimating y^{t} something will be done this assizes agst o^{r} towne or our friends or both. I pray [you if] there shall be occasion doe what good you can for them all, for those that cannot be there to make their owne defence.

I shall entreat you to draw me a petition to his Matie for my own iustification, wch I will either deliver myself or procure some to do it for me. I think it were not amisse if I made mention of my readines at all tymes to do his Matie ye best service y^{t} lay in my power. That in the year 1639, when he went in person to make warre against ye Scots, whom he then took to be his enemyes, without eyther letter or summons fro. his Matie, I furnished myself with a curasiers armes and three horses at my owne charge, and went to his Matie to York, where I tendered my service to him, for wch he gave me his hand to kisse and gave command to my Ld Chamberlain, y^{t} I should be sworne of his Privy Chamber. I wayted upo. his Matie all y^{t} iourney in wch employment I spent betwixt 3 and 4 hundred pounds. His Maties father was pleased to make use of my house to lye at, and at my owne charge I entertayned & lodged the Earle of Strafford and his company when he came last forth of Ireland upo. his Maties service. That I was farre fro. home when theis fortifications and tumults were in Nantwich, &c., and therefore being his Maties sworne servant and loyall subject to desyre I may be severed fro. ye delinquents and not pay or contribute any thing for their falt, &c.

You may put in or take out what yo^{u} please, but certainly before I will pay any money for other men's errors, I will preferre some petition or other as you shall advise. If you please to do this any tyme this week I hope will serve turne. I am almost asleep, as you may see by my scribling, and therefore fro. this sheet I will go to another, and bid you and all my cousins good night, who am

DOCUMENT VIII. A.D. 1642.

Yo^r assured lov. cousin,

THO. WILBRAHAM.

9 Oct. 1642.

I had forgott to tell you y^t I heare Mr. Sheriff hath foisted in my name, among ye rest, into his catalogue. I [pray] you keep theis inclosed papers.[1]

[1] Harl. MSS., 2135, fol. 22.

IX.

After the Battle of Edghill.

DOCUMENT IX. A.D. 1642.

The Welshman's doleful ditty to the Tune of *O'hone, O'hone*

In Kinton Green[1]
Poor Taffy was seen,
O Taffy, O Taffy;
Taffy her stood
To her knees in blood,
O do not laugh, ye;
But her was led on
With false Commission,
To her unknown;
That poor Taffy herself
Might live in health,
But her got blows for her wealth;
O Taffy, poor Taffy!

The guns did so f—t,
Made poor Taffy start,
O Taffy, O Taffy;
Her go bare foot,
Then so go trot,
O do not laugh, ye;
For her was bang'd,
Because her had gang'd,
Under the Command
Of Array.
Who had for her pay
Many a sound great knock that day,
O Taffy, O Taffy.

Their grievous fight,
Did make day night,
O Taffy, Taffy;
Her would be flying,
Liked not dying,
'Twas bad Epitaphe;
Her sword and spear
Did smell for fear,
And her heart were
In a cold plight;
Made Taffy outright,
His poore britches besh—te,
O Taffy, O Taffy.

Her go in frieze,
Eat bread and cheese,
O Taffy, O Taffy;
Feed with goats,
Without old groats,
O do not laugh, ye;
Had you been there,
Where her did appear,
With cold cheer
In Knapsack,
You would then alack,
For fear have turn'd back,
O Taffy, O Taffy.

[1] Keynton is the name of the village at the base of Edgehill.

DOCUMENT IX.
A.D. 1642.

Her will now invent
How to repent,
O Taffy, O Taffy;
And for want
Of words to recant,
O do not laugh, ye;
For her will be swore,
Her will do no more,
Though her be poor;
And too true
Valour her will shew,
No more in such great crew,
O Taffy, poor Taffy.

Her do conclude
In doleful mood,
O Taffy, O Taffy;
Her will weep
To goats and sheep,
O do not laugh, ye;
For her be anger,
And then hang her,
If in danger;
Her come,
Pox upon a gun,
Has spoiled her going home,[1]
O Taffy, poor Taffy.

[1] From a pamphlet entitled "The Welshman's Public Recantation, or her hearty sorrow for taking up arms against her Parliement, &c. Printed at London for Fr. Coule, 1642." (K. P. 85—20.)

X.

An Account of the Defeat at Tewkesbury, in November, of the Welsh Forces raised by the Marquis of Hertford.

DOCUMENT X. A.D. 1642.

It is not unknown to this whole Kingdom how perverse a malignant William L. Marquis of Hertford hath declared himself in all these late distractions betwixt the King and the High Court of Parliament. . . . Being expulsed from Sherborne Castle by the valour and industry of the Earl of Bedford and his forces, and pursued to Minehead, with some 500 of his cavaliers, getting shipping in some coal boats he escaped into South Wales, and surprised Cardiff Castle, the ancient seat of the Right Honourable the Earl of Pembroke, and hath ever since made his abode thereabouts. By his persuasions partly, and partly through fear of his power, drawing the poor ignorant Welshmen to side with him in his unjust quarrel; keeping correspondence with another principal and powerful malignant in those parts, the Lord Herbert of Ragland, son and heir to the Earl of Worcester, a notorious Papist, till between them they had raised some seven thousand men, and conjoined them into a body about the fourth of this present month, near Cardiff Castle, whence, with colours flying and drums beating, they marched down from the mountains along the pleasant banks of the Severn which they passed, into Herefordshire, intending to take Hereford in their way, and, if possible, to surprise and plunder that city, and so, as it is conjectured, meant to take their way towards these parts to unite themselves with the rest of the malignants hereabouts. Their daily passes being notified to the Earl of Stamford, Lord Lieutenant in these parts of the Parliamentary Forces, he used all means convenient for the augmenting his forces by calling in the trained bands of that and the adjoining counties to his aid, and resolving if he had an opportunity to stop their passage in their journey. They being ferried over the Severn on Tuesday, the 15th of this present month, harassing and pillaging the country, they left Hereford, it being strongly fortified, and made towards Tewkesbury, in Gloucestershire, of which their proceedings, the Earl having notice, with some 4,000 men, he made after them, and on Wednesday morning found them quartered on that plain, near Tewkesbury, where the great battle was long ago fought between Edward the 4th and the followers of Henry the 5th. Being in view one of another, with glad and courageous hearts they prepared themselves for battle.

DOCUMENT X.

A.D. 1642.

The Marquis, the Lord Herbert, with their wild Welshmen, assuring themselves of an absolute victory, and so, furiously with the horse, which were some 500 of the Marquis's old cavaliers, they charged into the front of the Earl's forces, who, nothing amazed with their violent encounter, allayed the heat of their courage by heating them with good store of lead about their hearts, out of their carabines, pistols, and muskets. Yet the force of those demi-devils was so courageous that nothing could withstand their fury, but that they fell pell-mell into the body of our foot, so that some men were slain on our side though more on theirs. My Lord of Stamford's own regiment, at push of pike, keeping off the horses, while his musketeers, through their buffs and corslets, sent death into their bosoms.

My Lord Seymour, brother to the Marquis, by this time came up with some of his foot companies, their horse wheeling about as it were to take breath, left our infantry engaged against theirs. Then might easily be perceived the difference between the Earl's regiment of old soldiers and those ragged and inexperienced Welshmen, giving fire twice to once upon them, that they fell by ranks, till the Marquis himself rallying up his horsemen came into his brother's rescue. Those cavaliers, hoping to regain their loss, came up very resolutely, and were as valiantly entertained by some three troops of our horse, who were as a reserve to our foot [until] the malignants [were] beginning to make a stand, and the Welsh footmen being to be scarcely beaten on by their commanders (one Sir Rice ap Hugh Cranock, a colonel, being slain to the great discouragement of his countrymen). The Earl of Stamford, in the meantime, having got the hill and the wind, added new terror to them that were already half discomfited, pouring incessantly upon

DOCUMENT X. A.D. 1642.

them fresh volleys of shot. Having also two field-pieces, they having their opportunity to play, were discharged, killing whole squadrons of the poor half-armed Welshmen.

My Lord Seymour's horse was shot under him, and in much danger of his life, and those forces ready to be put to rout, when my Lord Herbert, with some Welsh gentlemen of quality, as Master Jenkin Vaughan, and Captain Owen ap Griffith, with the residue of their forces, charged unto their succours, and made some though not much slaughter of our men (the Welsh musketeers very bad firemen and their muskets not very serviceable), when the rear of our foot, being trained bands, stept upon the theatre of death and danger, and like good actors performed their parts very resolutely, giving in a broad front fire they galled their rear insufferably. So that the Welshmen, in spite of the Lord Herbert's persuasions, betook themselves to a shameful flight, leaving all the weight of the battle on the Marquis and his cavaliers, who stood to it still very stoutly, reviling the cowardice of the Welshmen, and resolving to sell their lives at dear rates, or purchase their liberty, if not victory. So that fighting, as it were, in a ring, they made the success of the day something doubtful, till one of their chiefs by a musket shot fell from his horse (who it was is not certainly known, but it was imagined to be my Lord Paulet), they then getting up his body, and with the Marquis, the Lord Herbert, and others, fled upon the spur over the plain, our horsemen not following them, but doing execution on the Welsh footmen, who, poor misled creatures, came as so many asses to the slaughter. Many of them flung away their arms and cried for mercy, which the Earl of Stamford very nobly granted, there yielding themselves to the number of 1,200 of those Britons prisoners, whom the Earl, after a modest reproof for their boldness in taking up arms against the Parliament, making them them sensible and sorry for their error, sent in peace to their houses, only detaining their captains, who appeared perverse and incorrigible malignants.

The Marquis, in the meantime, with his cavaliers, as fast as their fear would carry them, made towards the Severn, over which getting passage they are said to be retreated or rather fled back into South Wales. There were slain of the Marquis his army

DOCUMENT X. A.D. 1642.

some five and twenty hundreds, as their bodies did testify on the place, besides good store of wounded, most of the slaughter happening on the Welsh footmen of my Lord Herbert his regiment. The Earl commanded pits to be made, and their bodies, with those of our men, which were not above an hundred and sixty, most of the trained bands, to be buried together on the place. There were taken some eight colours. The Earl gave due thanks to the most High, the giver of all victories, acknowledging to Him alone the glory of the day, and so with his victorious forces he marched back to Hereford, keeping that city and adjacent parts in very good order and peaceable condition from the fury of the cavaliers and malignants, from whose mischievous malice pray Heaven deliver ours.[1]

[1] From a pamphlet, entitled "True News out of Herefordshire, &c. London: Printed for Fr. Wright, November 19, 1642." (K. P. 83—28.)

XI.

An Engagement of divers Shropshire Royalists to raise a Regiment of Dragoons.

DOCUMENT XI. A.D. 1642.

The Engagement and Resolution of the Principal Gentlemen of the County of Salop, for raising and maintaining of forces at their own charge for the defence of his Majesty, their country, and more particularly the Fortunes, Persons, and Estates of the Subscribers undernamed.

We, whose names are hereunder written, do hereby engage ourselves, each to the other, and promise upon the faith and word of a gentleman, that we will do our utmost endeavours, both by ourselves and friends, to raise as well for the defence of our King and country, as our own particular safeties, one entire regiment of dragooners, and with our lives to defend those mens' fortunes and families, who shall be contributors herein to their abilities. And for the more speedy expedition of the said service, we have thought fit to entreat Sir Vincent Corbet, formerly Captain of the Horse for this County, to be our chief commander over the aforesaid regiment. And likewise we have appointed the day of our appearance for bringing in of every man's proportion of his horse and money, according to the subscription of his undertaking, to be the twentieth day of December, all in the battle field.

HENRY BROMLEY, Sheriff.

Sir Richard Lee, Baronet
Paul Harris, Knight and Baronet
Vincent Corbet, Knight and Baronet
Sir William Owen
Sir Robert Eyton
Sir John Wilde
Sir Francis Oteley
Sir Thomas Scriven
Sir Thomas Eyton
Sir Thomas Lyster
Edward Kynaston, Esquire

DOCUMENT XI.
A.D. 1642.

Robert Corbet de Homfrest, Esquire
Pelham Corbet, Esquire
Roger Kynaston, Esquire
Edward Acton, Esquire
William Fowler, Esquire
Edward Crescet, Esquire
Walter Pigott, Esquire
Francis Thrones, Esquire
Arthur Sandford, Esquire
Thomas Corbet, Esquire
Edward Bawdwin, Esquire
Thomas Edwards, Esquire
Charles Bawdwin, Esquire
Walter Waring, Esquire
Richard Okely, Esquire
Henry Billingly, Esquire
Richard Church, Esquire
Thomas Phillips, Esquire
Edward Stanly, Esquire
Lawrence Bentall, Esquire
George Ludlow, Esquire [1]

[1] From a pamphlet, entitled "Wiltshire's Resolution, &c. Oxford: Printed by L. Lichfield, Printer to the University, 1642. [December 14.]" (K. P. 86—22.)

XII.

An Agreement of Neutrality in Cheshire.

Tricesimo[1] *Decembris*, 1642.

DOCUMENT XII. A.D. 1642.

An Agreement made the day above at Bunbury, in the County of Chester, for a pacification and settling of the peace of that county by us whose names are subscribed, authorised hereunto by the Lords and Gentlemen nominated Commissioners of Array and Deputy Lieutenants of the said county.

1. It is agreed that there be an absolute cessation of arms from henceforth within this county, and no arms taken up to offend one another but by the consent of the King and both Houses of Parliament, unless it be to resist forces brought into the county.

2. That all but 200 of either side shall be disbanded tomorrow, being Saturday, and on Monday all the rest on both sides, both horse and foot, shall be disbanded.

3. That all prisoners, on both sides, shall be enlarged. As for Mr. Norton, who is now prisoner at Manchester, the gentlemen appointed deputy-lieutenants do declare that he was taken without their priority or encouragement by some Manchester troops, upon a private quarrel, for taking powder and other goods belonging to one of Manchester; yet they will use their utmost endeavours to procure his enlargement, and do desire the like endeavours be used by lords and others, Commissioners of Array, for enlarging Mr. Daniel, of Dasbury.

4. That the fortifications of Chester, Nantwich, Slopford, Knutsford, or any town in Cheshire, lately made by either party, be presently demolished.

5. That all goods and arms taken on both sides now remaining in the county in specie be forthwith restored, and for all others

[1] In a copy of this Agreement in the Harleian MSS. (2135, fol. 87), the date is given as the 23rd, which seems to be correct.

that are taken out of the county, it is promised on both parts that since the benefit of this Pacification redounds to the whole county, they will use their utmost endeavours for a joint contribution of the county towards satisfaction of the owners.

DOCUMENT XII. A.D. 1642.

6. That the lords and gentlemen, Commissioners of Array, before the 8th day of January next, procure from his Majesty a letter thereby declaring, That in regard a peace is made in the county he will send no forces into the county, and if any other person shall, contrary to such declaration, bring forces into the county (passage for forces without doing any hostile act only excepted) the said lords and gentlemen will join to resist them. And if any forces without the consent of the King and both Houses of Parliament shall come into this county (the passages for forces without doing any hostile act only excepted), the said gentlemen nominated deputy-lieutenants will join to resist them and use their utmost endeavours therein.

7. In regard by the blessing of God there is like to be a peace within this county, if this agreement be, it is agreed that the Commissioners of Array shall not any further put the Commission of Array in execution, nor the gentlemen nominated deputy-lieutenants, the ordinance of the militia, or execute their commission.

8. Lastly, all the said parties do agree and promise each to other, on the word of a gentleman, as they do desire to prosper, that as well themselves as also their friends, tenant servants, and all others in whom they have any interest, shall as much as in them lies perform the agreement. And it is further desired that all the parties join in a petition to his Majesty and both Houses of Parliament, for putting an end to the great distractions and miseries fallen upon this Kingdom, by making a speedy peace. And it is agreed that Sir George Booth,[1] and all others within this county who have appeared as Commissioners of Array or as Deputy Lieutenants, by reason of the ordinance of Parliament, shall with all convenient speed subscribe this agreement.

ROBERT KILMURRY. WILLIAM MARBURY.
ORLANDO BRIDGMAN. HENRY MAINWARING.[2]

[1] Sir George Booth was an active Deputy-Lieutenant.
[2] Rushworth, Pt. 3, Vol. 2, 100.

XIII.

The History of the Neutrality in Cheshire.

DOCUMENT XIII. A.D. 1642.

After alluding to the oppression of the County of Chester by the Array, which had driven many persons out of the county and others to hide themselves, the pamphlet from which the following account is taken proceeds:—

But at last some gentlemen of generous spirits, hating this servile condition, began to raise up the country into a body for their just defence. This course proved successful every way, for then many thousands discovered themselves which way their hearts inclined who formerly durst not appear for the militia. The Commissioners of Array were forsaken of their own tenants . . . and the body of the county in a short time grew so vast that they possessed themselves of divers towns for the securing of themselves and the whole county. Nantwich was the chief; and there was their rendezvous.

This struck such terror into the hearts of the Array that they fled to the City of Chester for sanctuary, after Master Bridgman, the vice-chamberlain, had surprised it, by subtilty to speak the best of it. Thither then they brought their goods and arms, and about 4 or 500 soldiers to guard them, most of which they furnished with horses and arms out of the pillage taken from the county. This invited many malignants thither out of many other counties, who brought with them their treasure and some arms.

Master Bridgman took upon him the government of the city, which the soft spirited aldermen durst not contradict, but seemed thankfully to accept of his varnished motions. That which emboldened him thereunto was the malignant party that brought him in, which was the Recorder, the two Gamuls, and Master Throp. He sent forth his warrants, ordered the watch, imprisoned and enlarged at his pleasure; in a word, he was as imperious as the Bishop, his father, amongst the Ministers. . . . .

The Council for the managing of the new government was holden at the Palace, where the Bishop, his son, and the Lord Kilmurry, were chief, but the Lady Cholmondeley was to hold up all, without whom nothing could pass. These were the devisers, and Sir Edward Savage, and other Papistical and malignant persons, were expeditious to execute.

DOCUMENT XIII. A.D. 1642.

But things stuck not here long, for when they perceived the citizens offended at the usurpations of their new governors, the hearts of their soldiers turned against them, who were forced thither and wanted pay; also, considering that all their treasures, together with their persons, cooped up in a place slenderly secured, did invite the adversary to look after so great a prize, and knowing the country was preparing to assault the city, besides that vast body of chased men (of whom near 2,000 were well armed) they were in daily expectation of aid from the Parliament and having Manchester men (who are the terror of malignants, in Lancashire and Cheshire) ready at a call, and knowing that the best that could come of it on their part was to lose their cattle, corn, and hay, at their own houses, which lay open to the will of the oppressed country, they were very solicitous for a pacification between them and the Deputy-Lieutenants, hoping that accommodation might extend to the whole county.

Sir Richard Wilbraham and Master Roger Wilbraham, being the solicitors of the motion for peace, as heretofore they were when otherwise, the militia had been bravely executed at Beameheath. Many gentlemen for the Militia and all the soldiers at Nantwich, were exceedingly offended, thinking it a hard thing to make peace with them whom the Parliament had voted for high delinquents. But Mr. Marbury and Mr. Mainwaring, deputy-lieutenants, who took upon them this matter, hearkened to the motion, and were desirous of an accommodation.

. . . .

Both parties agreed to meet. Torperley was the place, being midway between Chester and Nantwich. Monday, December 19, was the time. The Lord Viscount Kilmurry and Master Cholmondeley were for the Array, though afterwards they changed Master Cholmondeley for Mr. Bridgman. Mr. Marbury and Mr. Henry Mainwaring were for the other part. The Array came

DOCUMENT XIII. A.D. 1642.

better provided than the others, being authorized by the rest of their Commission for confirmation of what they agreed to. The other neither then could, nor ever can, procure a confirmation from the rest of the Deputy Lieutenants, but promised their endeavour.[1] Little was done that day save the propositions drawn, and a cessation of all hostile acts concluded on both sides, and mutual intercourse for the gentlemen betwixt Chester and Nantwich till the treaty was ended, and the business [was] adjourned till Wednesday.

The two gentlemen for the county, not fully prepared for the meeting on Wednesday, because they could not procure the consent of the Deputy Lieutenants to confirm their acts, sent word the night before to prevent that meeting and to adjourn it till Thursday. The Array were glad to gain time in expectation of their forces from Shropshire, treacherously brought in to compel an agreement. They imprisoned the messenger sent to Chester, took the letters which they would not be known of, denied to Mr. George Booth entrance into Chester contrary to the agreement, hastened to Torperley, knowing that we could not meet them, that they might have matter of exception against our gentlemen. But the business was so agitated that they met at Bunbury, two miles from Torperley, because Torperley was taken up with Col. Hastings' troops upon Thursday. At Bunbury a peace was concluded. The heads of the articles are [as in the preceeding paper].[2]

[1] The Parliament soon repudiated this Neutrality, denouncing the agreement as prejudicial and dangerous.

[2] From a pamphlet, entitled "The Unfaithfulness of the Cavaliers and Commissioners of Array in Keeping their Covenants, &c. London: Printed for Thomas Underhill, Jany. 11, 1643." (K. P. 89—37.)

DOCUMENTS

ILLUSTRATING TRANSACTIONS

IN THE YEAR 1643.

XIV.

Battle at Nantwich January 28th.

DOCUMENT XIV. A.D. 1643.

The well-affected [*i.e.* those for the Parliament] in the County of Chester, having a long time expected Sir William Brereton, Baronet, for their relief (who were miserably infected by the Commission of Array), on Saturday, Jan. 28, he advanced from Congleton, in the same county, to Nantwich. Hearing Sir Thomas Aston, with his forces, intended to take that town before him, he sent a party before to secure the town for himself. [These] but few in number came seasonably. Sir William advanced after with his carriages, which he durst not leave without himself, to guard them. Sir Thomas, understanding that a party of ours had possessed themselves of the town, came against it about three o'clock; was five times valiantly repelled. In which assaults we lost but one man (slain by a poisoned bullet), though the town lay open on all sides without any trench or bank. When he saw his hopes for that town frustrated, he retreated and fell upon Sir William, who

DOCUMENT XIV. A.D. 1643.

was not above 150 strong, but Sir Thomas had near 400. Besides that, he had all other advantages, for he had first surveyed and chosen his ground in a lane near the town; had made his van strong, flanked them on either side, and there stood in battalia till Sir William came, who had no notice of his enemies but by a boy who told him of their approach, which caused them to order themselves for an assault in chance that news were true. But they were gotten into the jaws of death before they were aware; for it being dark, near six o clock, they discerned the enemy, more by their whispering than by the eye. . But God, to whom the night is all one as the day was a pillar of fire unto them, and gave them so much light as served to the obtaining of a glorious victory. Sir Thomas let fly, but without success, and Sir William discharged his drakes which wrought more terror than execution, for the ground was very rough. The enemy cried, "Let us fly, for they have great ordnance." Captain Goldgay dismounted his dragooners, and turned his horses upon them, which brought them into confusion, and charged upon them very sore. All the rest fell to it with their pistols and carbines. But that service was very short, for there was neither time nor place to wheel about or renew the charge. Then they fell to it by dint of sword and the weight of their battle-axes, with which they belaboured the enemy that the prisoners confess they never felt the like blows in any other service. In a short time so many were unhorsed and beaten down, that all the work that remained was the taking of prisoners, horses, and arms. Sir William, who first had carried it with brave resolution, was the first that took prisoners, seconded by many more, who apprehended more than they could secure.

Sir Thomas, seeing how things went, fled (as we hear) on foot three miles, and then got a horse on which he fled to Whitchurch. Sir Vincent Corbet crawled away on all fours, lest he should be discerned, and then ran on foot bare-headed to Over, six miles. Many were dispersed abroad in the fields, and divers found there next day. One man, with a stick in his hand, disarmed three men, and took them prisoners, &c. What number of men we slew is uncertain, but some were seen dead in the lane, some afterwards were found dead in the fields, and some graves were discovered. We took 110 of their horse, and near 120 prisoners. Amongst

DOCUMENT XIV. A.D. 1643.

those Captain Bridgman and Captain Cholmley,[1] with other commanders and officers. Three of ours (as I take it) were slain, and two or three were prisoners, whom they took into Chester with triumph, having made them six in number by men they had taken up on the highway. Sir Thomas, after some days, returned to Chester with about fifty or sixty horse, but for his honour they sent many of their horses privately out to meet him, and so he returned as a man well reinforced. It is very probable they lost more horses than we got, by which stroke they were sorely shaken and their friends discomfited. We, for our part, had a solemn day of thanksgiving, and fell to the managing of the weighty affairs of the county.[2]

[1] Capt. Bridgman was a son of the Bishop of Chester, and Capt. Cholmley "base son to the Lord Cholmondeley."—Harl. MSS., 2125, fol. 315.

[2] From a pamphlet, entitled "Cheshire's Successe since their pious and truly valiant Colonel, Sir William Brereton, Baronet, came to their rescue, &c. London: March 25. Printed for Thomas Underhill, and are to be sold in Wood Street." (K. P. 99—6.)

XV.

The Battle of Torperley, February 21.

DOCUMENT XV.
A.D. 1643.

On Tuesday, Feb. 21, we had a pitched battle at Torperley, midway betwixt Chester and Nantwich, which was thus occasioned: We sent forth our warrants to require all betwixt 60 and 16 years old, to meet us at Torperley, to find out the strength of the county, and who were for us in case we had need of them. The enemy had notice of it, and gave it out they would meet us there. We were not sure of it, because we are not sure of anything they say or swear, yet we went out about 1,500 strong, as I take it, to guard the country. They came also from Chester, and were on the ground before us. When we surveyed their posture, we thought they lay in ambuscado a little from the town, where four ways meet. We, judging that place impassable, advanced no further, but wheeled to the right hand, to plant on good ground, near a place called the Swan's Nest. But whilst we were on our march, they got the ground before us, where they stood in battalion. They had all the advantages that could be, the wind clear and strong, a firm even soil, well mounted, a hole towards us where they planted divers musketeers, laid an ambuscado in a hedge, and planted their ordnance amongst their horse. We marshalled ours on a field over against them, towards Tilston Hill, a valley with a straight passage being betwixt us. We had no ordnance, nor could we reach them with our muskets. They had as fair a mark as they could desire, for our infantry were at the bottom of the hill in command of their muskets, and our cavalry were on the high ground butt for their cannon. We saluted one another with fire and lead, they played on us for the space of an hour with cannon and musket, yet we lost not a man, only three were shot [who were] scarcely wounded, and a horse's hoof hit with a (musket) ball out of a cannon, which was a miraculous providence of God in the judgment of all men. Besides our forces there, we had 200 in Beeston Castle, which we sent for to join with us, reserving 30 to keep the Castle, which they finding out by their scouts sent two troops to intercept them. Having by treachery gotten their word, they saluted them as friends, gave them the word, shook hands, and the more deluded them by Captain Green, who was very like a lieutenant of ours, and whom they dressed in a habit most like him. But being within them, they bid them throw down their arms and [saying], "Let the Roundheads cry for quarter." Whereupon ours retreated a little and then gave fire, which so amazed them that both troops fled. Sir Thomas pistolled one, who for that day bare the colours, and our party report they saw divers of theirs fall upon their firing.

DOCUMENT XV.
A.D. 1643.

The issue of that day's work was thus:—We retreated to the Heath to find out a better ground, considering we might suffer much; but could make no execution upon them. Where we rallied new ground was not to be found there, it being a "cone grew" (*sic*). Part of the army making a retreat, the rest followed. Not out of fear, for our enemy durst not meet us on even terms, but to get home before we were nighted. The enemy by their scouts discovered about 700 of our club-men coming near them from the forest, in a good posture, and suspected that we had wheeled to the left, while the others were ready to charge on the other hand, which struck them with such fear, that they fled to Chester. The Commission of Array stayed at the Cross in Torperley, not daring to come to the battle, whereby they had the precedency in the fight. Thereby Torperley escaped plundering, and the parsonage the ruin threatened [it.] For they stayed not to drink a draught of beer, but bad them solemnize another day of thanksgiving, scoffing at the Ordinance.[1] They triumphed in Chester [that] they had got Sir William's hat and feather, a great trophy, though upon examination it was found to be one of their own soldiers's.[2]

[1] Ordinance of the Militia.

[2] From "Cheshire's Successe," ante.—With reference to this attack at Torperley, *Mercurius Aulicus* (9th week) states that the King's forces were conducted by Sir Nicholas Byron. "The rebels held out not above an hour. There were killed of them between threescore and fourscore, one whole company taken, who cried for quarter and gave up their matches; but three of the King's party being wounded and not one slain." (K. P. 91—41.)

XVI.

Battle of Middlewich, March 13, 1643—*Sir William Brereton's Account.*

DOCUMENT XVI. A.D. 1643.

This day is deservedly set apart to be a day of thanksgiving for that complete and great victory which the Lord hath given us on Monday last, even when the enemy came out armed with power (of flesh) and resolution to destroy and over-run all the rest of the country. In which design they were so hopeful and confident that they took the boldness to encamp themselves in Middlewich, a town between Nantwich and Northwich, where I was, and where we had begun to fortify and place a garrison. We conceived this attempt of most dangerous consequence, and therefore thought fit to allow them no rest nor to give them time to fortify. To this end there was a strong party of horse sent from Northwich upon Saturday night last, upon their first coming there, who gave them an alarm.

The next day, being the Sabbath, could not be observed, it being the work of the whole day to prepare for our defence, and how to annoy our enemy,—towards whom I went out upon Sunday in the afternoon, with betwixt two and three companies of dragooners, who went near to Middlewich, and gave them an alarm there, but without any intention to assault them in their quarters,—they being very strong on foot and well-armed, and we had no foot at all then there, our greatest care being to preserve the country from plundering, and to let the enemy know we durst look them in the face and come even to their very door. This evening, March 12, being Sunday, we resolved and concluded to meet the Nantwich forces the next morning, who were appointed to come unto us by six o'clock in the morning. But we were in fight more than four hours before they came in to our assistance; during which time [the enemy] played full upon us with their cannon, but without any success at all, there being only one or two men hurt, but not mortally. During which time our musketeers (we had not above 200, our greatest force of foot being at Nantwich) behaved themselves very gallantly, and made good three passages, and kept the enemy in play till the Nantwich forces came in to our assistance, who came on so resolutely and with such undauntedness of spirit, even to the amazement and admiration of the enemy whom they beat from their works and from their cannon. And as they entered one end of the town our soldiers entered the other, and with no less courage and resolution. Colonel Ellis, Sergeant-Major Gilner [Gilmore], Sir Edward Moseley, and ten captains more, besides other officers (a list of whose names you will find here inclosed), who betook themselves into the church and steeple, from whence they did much annoy us for some short time. But within an hour after the Lord was pleased to make us possessors of the church and steeple, and of the commanders and soldiers who were therein, and of their ordnance, magazine, and great store of arms. So, as I believe, since the beginning of this unnatural war, God hath not given many more completer (*sic*) victories, nor hath there been many more prisoners taken, there being not many fewer than 500 prisoners, and very many of them commanders and considerable persons.

DOCUMENT XVI. A.D. 1643.

I desire the whole praise and glory may be attributed to Almighty God, who infused courage into them that stood for His cause, and struck the enemy with terror and amazement. For further particulars I must refer you to a fuller relation.

We hear nothing from London how things go there, but our confidence is in the Lord of Heaven to the protection of whose Providence I desire to commend you, and so conclude, and rest

Your ———

WILLIAM BRERETON.

Nantwich, 15th March, 1643.[1]

[1] From "Cheshire's Successe." (K. P. 99—6.)

XVII.

Sir Thomas Aston's Account to the Commissioners of Array for the County of Chester.

DOCUMENT XVII. A.D. 1643.

MY LORDS,

Though I know not what it is to apprehend feare of any man's threates, nor know any cause given them against mee in p^r^ticler, yet I must thanke yor care of my person, and shall have more cause to acknowledge yor sence of my hono^r^ that you will receive and divulge a true accompt of this unfortunate business wherin I desire noe favor, but that the truth may be known, and let that quit or condemn mee.

Yo^r^ Lo'pps know how our progress was retarded att our setting forth, the soldiers mutineing for pay on Friday night, and Mr. Bavand's haveing not issued it on Saturday morning, nor the pr'visions, till it was soe late that I was forced to leave two troopes of horses in the forest to guarde it to,—though they lay in danger that night. Att our arrival att Middlewich, a letter overtook us from the Governor, recommending to us certaine propositions from the Lo. Brereton, wch were that he might have a convoy for his lady, and children, and goods, to Chester, and then he would bring in his men. Upon consultation had with the Sherif, Sir Edw. Ffitton and Colonel Ellis, it was helde soe considerable an addition, that it was worth our stay; and thereupon sent him a letter under all our hands, desireing that thoughe it were Sunday, he would p'vide carriage for his goods and come away, for that further delay would not be safe for him, nor could our designs admit it. Yet his lordship did not accordingly, but came on Sunday himself to Middlewich to confer further with us, of wch notice was speedily given to Northwich, and (by intelligence since from them) that occasioned this sudden attempt upon us to prevent him from joining with us, whose intentions were indeed by this appearance. The accomodating this, together with the sherife's desire to sumon the countrey with theire contribucon and assistance, necessitated a ioynt consent to stay there on Monday, the rather hopeing the diversion of the danger from Namptwich, by praying the Governo^r that they might receive an alarm from Whitchurch forces. But instead of a support or countenance from thence, the forces there were disbanded. And to whatever accident wee studie to impute the miscarriage of this design, that was the ruin of this (and I pray God it prove not soe of both counties). Their whole force and power being thereby let loose upon us to assail us on three sides in an open town where it was impossible for horse to doe service, yet the imputacon of the misfortune must not be laid upon the horse. Theire duty was not neglected. On our passage to the enimy, a party of dragooners and horse, under Capt. Spotswood's command, was ordered to give them an alarme at Northwich (though with more caution than it was executed), the Lieutenant imprudently engaging himself, wch he was expressly forbidden. Soe that way was secured. Capt. Prestwich was lodged on the other passage, and his scouts discovered them, thoughe they followed close. They fell upon some of his men ere they could clear their scattered quarters; but he chased them back to their foot, rescued some prisoners, and at the bridge he wheeled about and kept them at a stande, till the foote came downe. Att their approach before the bridge from Northwich the Welsh forces advanced, so we unwillingly (thought it were but to line hedges) that 2 troops of horse, the Mayor's and Captain Bridgeman's, were sent downe to face the enemy in a narrow passage within half a musket shot, wherein several of them were shot, otherwise the foot could not have advanced or stayed by it.

Testat.
Tho. Prestwich
Tho. Roston

Testat.
Tho. Holme
Maior
R. Wiltshire
Jo. Wiltshire
Fr. Aston

Bridgman's troope being called off to face the enimy from Namptwich, the Maior's troope and the gent. still made good that place, till such time all our foote (being of the Welsh) by Maior Gilmore's commands, quit the passage, and the enimies musqueteers advanced on both sides the lane beyond the hedges (where they could not possibly charge), and beat them backe that street, and being guarded by musqueteers in a breast worke, after once discharging att randome they quit the work and ranne away.

Testat.
Tho. Prestwich
Tho. Roston

Another part of the enimy approaching another passage called

DOCUMENT XVII. A.D. 1643.

Waring Bridge, Capt. Prestwich his troope was commanded thither to stay by the foote, which were of Capt. Massie's companie, wch hee did, till all those foote likewise were comanded off and made good theire retreat.

Upon the approach of the third partie from Namptwich, I appointed the two trained bands of 200 men to make good that corner being onely a street and well advantaged by ditches and bankes on both sides, wch. with the addition of some small trenches they presently made, were conveniently defensible by those that would have stayed in them.

And to check their approach, I drew out a partie of sixtie comanded horse, the other troopes being to backe them in the lane, (there being noe other ground for horse), and to make way for them to charge, I drew off some comanded musqueteers sixscore before them to line the hedges, that the enimy might not take the advantage of the ditches on both sides, to fall the horse in the fflank upon theire charge. But the enimy, advanceing with a great body of musqueteers on either side the lane, at a great distance before theire horse, the Lieutenant that commanded them, and all our musqueteers, after the first fire given on them, fell downe and crept away leaving their armes, soe that the enimies foot receiving noe check, our horse could not charge, but to be flanked and cut off by the musqueteers on both sides the lane. And Colonel Ellis having drawne a piece of ordnance in the reare of ou^{r} horse they were forced to wheel off to let his ordnance play. Finding the greatest of their strength to advance that way I cauled a partie of Capt. Sporswood's dragooners to make good the churchyard, placed a guard in the breastworks at the other end of the towne, drew the other piece of canon to the churchyard, planted it there with advantage to secure the street; they attempted to approach in and brought up a companie of musqueteers of Colonel Ellis's, comanded by a Captain I know not, to assist their two trained bands to make good their passage, who, as soone as they came up to the canon, laid themselves all downe in a valley and their armes by them, that I was forced to ride amongst them, and with my sword I beate them up, and myself on horseback brought them up

Testat.
Wm. Ratcliffe
Th. Raper
Fr. Aston
Nath. Naper
Jo. Wiltshire

DOCUMENT XVII. A.D. 1643.

to the hedge where the other musquetcers lay, and neither of both did or durst put up theire heads, but shot their peeces up into the ayr, noe one foot officer by them to ranke or order them. During all which time my owne troope, Napper's, Capt. Ratcliff's, and the Lord Cholmeley's troops, stood directly in the reare of them, and not a man moved though diverse of theire horse were shot under them. Till our canon made one shot wch grazed a great way short and mounted over theire heads, and a second shot into a banke not fortie yards from the canoneer, att wch they (shouting) advanced fast upon our foot, who all instantly forsooke theire stand and ran away, leaving the horse within pistol shot of the enemy and a great ditch betwixt them, att which the horse wheeled backe; but all men there must witnesse I stayed them perforce standing expected to shot (*sic.*) till the canon was brought off, and noe one foot man being left by it but Colonel Ellis, who drew it off with his owne hands, some of the horsemen helping to bring it off to the church. Before wch. upon the first falling off of those Bropton hundred and the Welsh from the first hedge, all the whole stand of pikes in the rear of the horse clearly ran away, and all the musqueteers placed for the defence of the street ende quit their trenches, having never discharged a shot or never seen the enimy or cause of feare, but their fellows flying. The horse then made, though a speedie yet an orderly, retreat into the high street, and I repaired to the churchyard expecting to have found it made good by the parties left there to that purpose. But I found all the foot wedged up in the church like billetts in a woodpile, noe one man at his armes. Trusting then only to the canon to scoure the two cheife streets which lay with as much advantage as was possible for pieces to be planted, and that the enimy approached in three streets upon the horse, who were that condition as sheep in a pen exposed to slaughter, and hindered the use of our ordnance upon the enimy, I commanded them to draw up into a field att the end of the towne, but the end being barricaded by Capt. Spaswood (*sic.*) occasioned a separation of them, that they dispersed several ways, and by reason of ditches could not meet off three fields breadth till they came past Kinderton House.

I then repaired to the canon I had placed to scoure the streets, and found no canoneer with the one, the other drawing the canon

DOCUMENT XVII. A.D. 1643.

off, att which being offended, hee said hee could not gett one foot man to assist him, nor could I draw out ten musqueteers out of church would it have saved the worlde. Among these Colonel Ellis himselfe was entered, the canon deserted, the reason as I understand it—I shall not censure it. The enimy falling directly in three streets upon me, and discharging upon mee in the church-yard, the horse marched out of sight. I alone, all I could possibly hope to doe was to rally the horse again if possible, to wheel about, and to fall in the rear of them; but by reason of several cross lanes I had lost the whole body of the horse, save a few stragglers, with wch I had small hope to repell the enimy that had expulsed us. Perceiving the enimy had possessed the towne, and hearing they were turned towards Warrington, I sent a messenger after them to rally at Rudheath, intending to goe by Brereton, and with that convoy to redeeme the Lo. Brereton's force, but they were advanced (by whose conduct I know not) past recall, yet I went to him myselfe, both to give him account of the action and to know his resolution. Finding him fixed, and that the Sherife and Sir Edw. Ffitton were gone toward Whitchurch, I repaired thither to see if the gent. of that countie were in condition to lend any considerable assistance whereby I might joine with them; but I found the trained bands disbanded, those few dragooners in feare of daily surprize. Soe, hopeless of any present relief, I returned to rally my men, desiring (if I can bee conceived to bee noe further usefull according to his Majesties command) I may repose in a quiet quarter to rebreak (?) my men, and repaire to the armye. Where the occasion of this disaster can fix on me, I shall gladly be informed. The design was approved, desired by all.

The stay at Middlewich was not occasioned by mee, was necessary, was assented to by all. The principal business, the Lo. Brereton's men, the magazine lay there. The intelligence failed not, but was seasonable, though raw men with unreadie officers were long in answering the alarme, and drew out without either powder or shot. The horse could do noe more, unless there had beene place for it, nor could any horse suffer with more unmoved courage till they were clearly deserted by the foot. And I think no man there will denie but I was to my best assisting in every part of the action. I came in the rare of the horse from the field, and was the last horseman in the towne.

It is the plain truth, the enemy haveing no diversion, but att liberty with theire full power to fall on us from all parts, were much too hard for us in a place not defensible. And without some more experienced foot officers, I must freely say noe number will bee found sufficient to withstand readie men.

DOCUMENT XVII. A.D. 1643.

If the event must condemne the man, the service of this countrey will be but an uncomfortable undertaking. But I cannot believe clamour or malice can take any impression in your Lo'pps., till you are satisfied in some p'ticular, wherein I have failed of my dutie more than it hath been my unhappiness, or improvidence, or both, to expose myself to play an after game soe oft for the redemption of my countrey; to w[ch] extremity most of yo[r] Lo'pps can witness, it was not brought by the good will or default of

Your humble servant,

THOMAS ASTON.[1]

March 17, 1643.

[1] Harl. MSS., 2135, fol. 93. Original Letter.

XVIII.

Prisoners taken at Middlewich, March 13, 1643.

DOCUMENT XVIII. A.D. 1643.

Colonel Ellis
Major Gilmore
Sir Edw. Moseley, Bart.

CAPTAINS.

Capt. Corbet
Capt. Starkin of Darlin
Capt. Hurleton
Capt. Massy of Coddington
Capt. Morris
Capt. Davenport of Woodford
Capt. Eyton
Capt. Horton
Capt. Lloyd
Capt. Jones
Capt. Mason

TWO CLERKS.

Mr. Corbett
Mr. Edw. Charleton

LIEUTENANTS.

Tho. Dodd, Lieutenant to Capt. Hurleton
Charley
Marvey
Hossar
Jernnings

ENSIGNS.

Weane
Proudlove
Morris
Davenport

CANONEERS.

Harding
Gorton

Two Corporals
Two Quartermasters
448 common soldiers
100 Horse
Two Field Pieces
Two barrels of powder, besides that which was taken and divided among the soldiers
Two barrels of Match
400 Arms

Testat.

T. C.[1]

[1] Harl. MSS., 2135, fol. 92.

XIX.

The Welsh, under Lord Herbert, defeated at Highnam, near Gloucester, by Sir William Waller.

Bristol, 1st April, 1643. DOCUMENT XIX. A.D. 1643.

SIR,

I presume the report of Sir William Waller, his good success against the Welsh is very common with you. Yet, lest you may not have full information of the truth, I have made bold to insert it upon assured knowledge. Sir William pretending, when he went from Malmesbury, to fall upon Cirencester, sent thither all his prisoners, whereof one hundred have taken oath to fight for the King and Parliament, and are entertained into pay; but Sir William made for the Forest of Dean, and to get passage over the river made use of 30 boats that were intended for service at Worcester, and with them made a bridge over the Salvin [Severn]; and so marched, forcing his passage through the forest to Highnam, a place where the Welsh forces were entrenched, and fell upon the rear of them, while other forces out of Gloucester fell upon the front, and so encompassed them, slew many, took 1,326 prisoners, 500 horses, besides commanders, a list whereof I herewith send you, as also a publication made by the Council of War at Bristol, with the names of the Council to which I refer you. Since which overthrow of the Welsh, some other of the King's forces took a troop of Sir William Waller's horse, but he soon recovered it again and about 51 horse more of theirs, nine hundred pounds in money, and store of victual sent in by the country. A judicious gentleman, your friend, told me that the house of Raglan and all Wales cannot raise another such army for horse, arms, and commanders. He [of Raglan] hath

DOCUMENT XIX. A.D. 1643.

spent at the least three score thousand pounds in the expedition. [The rest of the letter is of no interest.]

Your humble servant,

T. W.

A Catalogue of the names of the most eminent officers of the Lord Herbert's army, taken prisoners at Highnam, upon the 25th of March, 1643:—

Serjeant-Major General Bret

Serjeant-Major Fox

Serjeant-Major Griffith, a Recusant

Serjeant-Major Throgmorton

Colonel Trevor Williams, Bart., a Commissioner of Array in Monmouthshire

Lieut.-Col. Wigmore, a Captain of a Train Band in Herefordshire

Lieut.-Col. Dukes, a Yorkshireman

Captain Kemes, whose father is Steward to the Lord Herbert, and Commissioner of Array

Captain Henry Lingurne [Lingen], a Commissioner of Array of Herefordshire, a gentleman of £3,000 per annum, and a Recusant

Captain Lochard, late High-Sheriff of Radnorshire, a Recusant[1]

Captain Berrington, a gentleman of £2,000 per annum

Captain Elton, son of Mr. Ambrose Elton, a Justice of the Peace of Herefordshire

Captain Adams, Muster-Master General and Prevancer, a Recusant

Captain John Abraall, heir to Rich. Abraall, of Juxten

Captain Gainsford, a Commissioner of Array for Monmouthshire

Captain Arnold Bursill, brother to Col. Bursill, a man of £2,000 per annum

Captain Brooke, a Somersetshire man

Captain Lews *(sic.)*

Captain Hooke

Captain Philip Morgan

Captain Roger Williams

Captain Lewis Thomas

[1] Latchard of Bettws, H. S. in 1642.

DOCUMENT XIX. A.D. 1643.

Captain Thomas Hunt
Captain Sympson
Lieut. Thomas Lingurne, brother to Capt. Henry Lingurne, a Recusant
Lieut. Lochard, a Recusant
Lieut. Weare
Lieut. Butler
Lieut. Charles Somerset
Lieut. James Wigmore, brother to Lieut.-Col. Wigmore
Lieut. Thomas Morris
Lieut. Pawlet
Lieut. Knowles
Cornet Roger Vaughan, of Ruerden
Cornet Carny [Carne]
Cornet Lee
Cornet Bradford
Ensign Charles Madock
Ensign John Thomas
Two sons of Capt. Charles Booth—Ensigns
Ensign Pilkington [1]

[1] From a pamphlet, entitled "The Copy of a Letter sent from Bristol, wherein is set down the Relation of the Great Victory obtained by Sir William Waller against the Welsh forces under Lord Herbert, &c. April 4, printed for R. D., 1643." (K. P. 99—30.)

XX.

Monmouth and Chepstow taken by Sir W. Waller.

DOCUMENT XX. A.D. 1643.

My Lords and Gent.,

We hear it is not well taken that you heard not of the taking of the Welsh at Highnam, nor of the loss of Malmesbury. Upon our coming to Gloucester we immediately sent [an account]. It seems many of our letters miscarry.

For Malmesbury we committed it to Sir Edward Hungerford. We left him not without commanders. He had two Sergeant-Majors, able men, and the companies of his own regiment, and a company of dragoons, with ammunition and two hundred muskets to put into the countrymen's hands, who offered themselves very freely. We conceived that Sir Edward Hungerford's power in the country, with that strength, would easily have defended that place. But for reasons best known to himself he quitted it. It was not for us to have stood long there, nor for the advancement of your service for us to garrison towns, unless it is intended we shall leave the field.

From Malmesbury, marching day and night, we came to Framelet Ferry,[1] and having our boats from Gloucester ready we passed our army over the Severn, and forthwith to Huntley, and so to Highnam, where, before the enemy had any notice, we fell upon their back, and in a short time, without the loss of above two, they rendered up the place upon quarter, where we had one thousand four hundred and forty-four common prisoners, well armed, commanders and gentlemen about one hundred and fifty, many of the chief of Wales and Herefordshire.

We then marched for Wales. The Welsh left their garrisons, they quitted Newnham, Rossbridge, Monmouth, and Chepstow. We entered those towns very weary of the Welsh ways over the

[1] Frampton Passage. Somer's Tra ts V., 310.

DOCUMENT XX. A.D. 1643.

mountains, and sensible of their wants. And hearing Prince Maurice was near us on the one side, and the Lord Herbert with his contracted garrisons on the other, and not being able to overtake the Lord Herbert's forces, we resolved for Gloucester, through Prince Maurice's army. And upon Monday, at night, being the 10th of this instant, having sent away our ordnance and baggage, with our foot to guard it, over Wye to Aust, and so on the far side of the river for Gloucester, we marched from Chepstow all night for Prince Maurice's quarters, with our horses and dragoons. He quartered at Little Dean, and his forces at Newnham, Michael Dean, and Ross. The right time for beating up a quarter was past before we gained Newnham. Upon the first alarm at Newnham, away they hasted to Little Dean, and there we found their force in a body, and their horse on a hill upon the other side of the town. Their foot came towards us, and having given one volley of shot they retired, and our dragoons, following in order, entered the town, so we had full possession of the Prince's quarters. We stood about three hours expecting their charge, the report being they had vowed we should never return.

Our design at this time was only to make our way through their army, so, leaving a forlorn hope of horse and dragoons to keep the passage in the town, we marched in their sight towards Gloucester. When they saw us gone they came down from the hill and fell hotly on our forlorn hope, and some few they killed and some they took. We conceive their loss was as great, that they lost as many men, and two of very good quality. Last night we came to Gloucester, and sent forth Lieut.-Colonel Massey to take Tewkesbury, which this morning he did. There were eight commanders, but we missed Col. Slater, he being gone last night to give information at Oxford that all Sir William Waller's forces were routed. We doubt not you will hear strange reports. Believe this, God hath been good unto us beyond our thoughts. The taking and keeping Tewkesbury is of great consequence to these parts. Prince Maurice's design of taking us in the Forest is now spoiled. And so have we the bridge he passed over. But he makes haste, we fear he will find another before we can give a stop; if not, we hope he may taste a little of Wales as well

DOCUMENT XX. A.D. 1643.

as we have done. We writ you a letter for some arms and ammunition. We earnestly beg they may be sent, and two hundred swords of Kennet's making at Hounslow. We desire your praises of God, and your prayers for,

My Lords and Gentlemen,

Your faithful servants,

WILLIAM WALLER.

ARTHUR HASLERIG.[1]

Gloucester, this 12th of April, 1643.

We are now marching towards Tewkesbury.[2]

[1] Sir Arthur Haslerig was one of the "five members" whom the King attempted to seize by force in Parliament.

[2] From a pamphlet, entitled "The Victorious and Fortunate Proceedings of Sir William Waller and his Forces in Wales, &c. London, April 17: Printed for John Wright in the Old Bailey, 1643." (K. P. 102—2.)

XXI.

The Surrender of Hereford to the Parliament.

Mercurius Bellicus, April 30.

DOCUMENT XXI. A.D. 1643.

Upon Sunday last[1] Sir William Waller marched from Gloucester towards Hereford with his forces to quiet that country. He shot three pieces at the city on Monday morning, and then summoned it by a trumpet, to which Coningsby, the governor, returned this answer:—"That if he could show a commission from the King they would surrender it to him, otherwise they would keep it for him." Thereupon he assaulted the town in three several places, and some sallies and contestations there were. But before three o'clock their sally was turned to a parley, and two were sent out of the town to Sir William Waller, who sent likewise two to them offering them quarter and no more. Herbert Price, a commander there, then came out, and brought other articles with some high language; but Sir William stuck strictly to his first proposition, which, after some injurious detention of his hostages, they yielded to, only their courtship would have some complimental forms added to his rough demand—That gentlemen should have quarter and civil usage, ladies be treated honourably, the citizens, bishops, dean and chapter, preserved from plunder and not imprisoned for anything past: that all the arms,[2] ensigns, ammunition, and the government of the town, should be surrendered to him, which was done on Tuesday morning. He took some persons of quality, as Coningsby, Price, Sir William Crofts, Sir Richard Cave, and others, and the Lord Scudamore, who was not sent to Gloucester with the rest,

[1] Rushworth dates it the 25th April. Vol. ii., pt. iii., 263.

[2] Between 2,000 and 3,000 arms were delivered. "Speciall Passages," No. 38. (K. P. 105—17). *Aulicus* states that not above 60 arms were taken.

DOCUMENT XXI. A.D. 1643.

but his honourable word taken to appear at the Close Committee upon summons; and all this (through mercy) with the loss of one man and the hurt of three or four soldiers.[1]

The names of the Commanders and Officers, Cavaliers (besides the common soldiers) taken at Hereford by Sir William Waller, April 25, 1643.

The Lord Scudamore
The Lord Scudamore's son
Colonel Herbert Price[2]
Sir Richard Cave
L. Colonel Coningsby[3]
Master Coningsby
} Sometimes Members of the House of Commons, this Parliament.
Sir Walter Pye
Sir William Crofts
L. Colonel Thomas Price
Serjeant-Major Mintridge, who is dangerously wounded
Sir Samuel Aubrey
Serjeant-Major Dalton
Captain Somerset
Captain Sclater
Doctor Rogers
Doctor Godwyn
Doctor Evans[4]

[1] From "*Mercurius Bellicus*, April 30. London: Printed for Samuel Gellibrand, May 1, 1643."

[2] Herbert Price, of the Priory, Brecon, M.P. for that borough.

[3] This was Sir William Coningsby, governor of Hereford.

[4] From a pamphlet, entitled "A most True Relation of divers notable Passages of Divine Providence, &c. London: Printed for Lawrence Blaikelocke, 1643." (K. P. 105—12.)

XXII.

Parliamentary Commission to Sir Thomas Myddelton, to be Serjeant-Major-General of the Forces in North Wales.

An Ordinance of the Lords and Commons assembled in Parliament, concerning divers ill-affected Persons and Papists within the Counties of Denbigh, Montgomery, Flint, Merioneth, Carnarvon, and Anglesey, &c. DOCUMENT XXII. A.D. 1643.

Die Lunæ, 12 *Junii*, 1643 } Whereas the Lords and Commons, now assembled in Parliament, have received credible information, that very many Papists, notorious delinquents, and other ill-affected persons, inhabiting within the several Counties of Denbigh, Montgomery, and Flint, in the dominion of Wales, have, in mere opposition to, and contempt of, the power and authority of this present Parliament, entered into an hostile and dangerous association amongst themselves, and with many other persons of like condition with them, inhabiting in other adjacent counties, for the raising and promoting of an intestine and Civil War within this Kingdom; and in pursuance thereof have (contrary to their allegiance) levied, and do daily levy, great forces, both of horse and foot, within their said several counties, compelling the common people by impress, imprisonment, and other violent courses, to enter into acts of hostility and rebellion with them, and enforcing the inhabitants of the said counties, by illegal, unjust, and unsupportable taxations, to support and maintain them in their said rebellion and force, contrary not only to the ancient known laws of this Kingdom, but also to several Acts made and consented unto by his Majesty this present Parliament; and multitudes of his Majesty's good Protestant subjects have been, and daily are, robbed of all their estates, imprisoned, ruined, and destroyed by them; which proceedings of the said persons do tend not only to the disturb-

DOCUMENT XXII. A.D. 1643.

ance of the peace and tranquillity of this Kingdom, but also to the subversion of the fundamental government thereof, and of the Protestant Religion therein professed; in case they should receive to their aid any considerable number of the Irish rebels, which is not improbable, it being the aim (as it is probable) of all the Papists now in arms in this Kingdom, and in the Kingdom of Ireland, to free themselves from the laws established against them; and the cruel and bloody outrages committed by them upon the Protestants of both Kingdoms (in ruining whole families, consuming by fire whole towns, and using his Majesty's name for their authority to countenance their treasonable practices), making it evident to all men that the said Rebellion and Civil War in both Kingdoms have sprung from the same root, and must needs live and die together:—The said Lords and Commons taking the same into their serious consideration, do hold it necessary (for the more speedy suppressing of the said rebellion and reducing of the said Papists, delinquents and ill-affected persons to their due obedience), that the said Counties of Denbigh, Montgomery, Flint, Merioneth, Carnarvon, and Anglesey, and the adjacent counties, be with all speed secured as well from insurrection as foreign invasion, being seated on the Irish coasts.

Be it therefore ordained by the Lords and Commons in Parliament assembled—That the Lord-Lieutenants for the said several counties, and all Colonels, Lieutenant-Colonels, Serjeant-Majors, Captains, and other officers, and all persons well-affected to the Protestant Religion and the peace of the Kingdom, inhabiting within the said several counties, shall and lawfully may associate themselves together, and likewise enter into mutual association to and with the said several Lord-Lieutenants, Committee or Committees of Parliament, Colonels, Lieutenant-Colonels, Serjeant-Majors, Captains, and other officers, and all other persons inhabiting within the several Counties of Chester, the County of the City of Chester, and the Counties of Salop and Lancaster, and any other adjacent county or counties; and actually aid, succour, and assist one another in the mutual preservation and defence of themselves, and of the peace of all the said counties from all rapine, plundering, and spoiling, by the said delinquents, Papists, and others, the said ill-affected persons. And that the said Lord-Lieutenants, and other officers, shall have power to raise forces of horse and foot, and to lead them into any place or places which shall be fitting and convenient, either within or out of all or any of the said several counties; and to give battle to and to fight with all such forces as are or shall be raised against the Parliament, and against all other forces raised, or to be raised, without the authority and consent of both Houses of Parliament; and likewise against all such persons as do or shall make any insurrection, or otherwise plunder or destroy any of his Majesty's good subjects, and them to invade, resist, suppress, subdue, pursue, kill, slay, and put to execution of death, and by all means to destroy, as enemies of this Kingdom. And also to perform all other things needful for the preservation of the safety and peace of all the said several counties and parts adjacent; observing from time to time such other directions as they shall receive from both Houses of Parliament, or from his Excellency the Earl of Essex, Lord General. And that all the said persons, and others, the inhabitants of the aforesaid counties, that shall enter into any such association by virtue of this ordinance, or do any other act or acts in obedience to and pursuance of this, or any other ordinance of the two Houses of Parliament, shall for his and their so doing, be saved, defended, and kept harmless, by the power and authority of Parliament.

And the said Lords and Commons, taking likewise into their serious consideration as well, the danger this whole Kingdom is likely to fall into, if any of the Irish rebels or other foreign forces should land in any of the aforesaid several counties, being maritime, and bordering on the Irish seas, and should join with the said delinquents, Papists, and others, the said ill-affected persons, now already in arms against the Parliament, as also the necessity of appointing a commander of the forces which shall be raised within the said Counties of Denbigh, Montgomery, Flint, Merioneth, Carnarvon, and Anglesey, or in any of them, for the aforesaid service:—That the said Earl of Essex, the Lord General, shall be desired to grant a commission unto Sir Thomas Myddelton, Knight, being one of the Members of Parliament, to command in chief, as Serjeant-Major-General of all the forces, both of horse and foot, raised or to be raised in all or any of the said several counties [of North Wales], or in any of them, for the service aforesaid;

DOCUMENT XXII. A.D. 1643.

and to have power to lead, command, and carry the same to such place and places, within the said several counties or without, as he shall think fit and necessary for the defence and preservation of the peace of them, or any of them; and likewise to give the same order and instructions, in his said Excellency's absence, for regulating the soldiers which are or shall be under his command, as his Excellency hath given to his army; and to use martial law to compel obedience thereunto as occasion shall require; and also to make, nominate, and appoint all other commanders under him, for the levying, conducting, and leading of the said forces, as he shall, from time to time, think fit; and to raise soldiers in all or any of the said several counties, for the aforesaid service.

And whereas the inhabitants of the said several Counties of Denbigh, Montgomery, Flint, Merioneth, Carnarvon, and Anglesey, are now wholly subject to the power and tyranny of the Commissioners of Array, and others of the said delinquents, by reason whereof no Commissioners have been named for the putting in execution of any of the Ordinances of Parliament, in any of the said counties—the well-affected in these parts being over-awed.

Be it therefore ordained that the said Sir Thomas Myddelton shall have full power and authority to name and appoint commissioners, solicitors, and agents, for the putting in execution of the ordinance for the seizing and sequestering of the estates, as well real as personal, of certain notorious dilinquents in the said several counties; and to require and take account or accounts, from time to time, of such commissioners, solicitors, or agents, of their doings and proceedings therein; and to receive into his charge and custody all such sums of monies, horses, cattle, plate, goods, and other things whatsoever, which shall be seized and sequestered in all or any of the said last-mentioned several counties, by virtue of the said ordinance of sequestration, and the same to keep for the public service and employment of the Parliament and Kingdom, rendering an account thereof to the two Houses of Parliament only, or to such persons as they shall appoint; and to receive the submission of such persons inhabiting within the said several counties, as shall, upon due summons, come in and yield obedience to the power and authority of the two Houses of Parliament, and willingly aid and assist the said Sir Thomas Myddelton in the

DOCUMENT XXII. A.D. 1643.

said service; and to forbear to put the said ordinance of sequestration in execution against the said persons, until the further pleasure of the two Houses be signified therein.

And be it further ordained that the said Sir Thomas Myddelton shall have full power and authority, and hereby is authorised, to impose and lay such assessments and taxes upon the said several counties for the maintenance of the forces, according to the several ordinances for the levying of money, which shall be raised for the preservation of the peace of the said counties, and reducing of the said Papists and delinquents to their due obedience to the power and authority of Parliament; and to cause the same, by distress or otherwise, to be levied upon the inhabitants of the said counties accordingly, rendering an account thereof to the two Houses of Parliament. And if any person or persons so assessed, or taxed, shall refuse to pay his or their assessment, or convey away his or their goods, or other personal estate, so as the sums of money so assessed or taxed cannot be levied according to this ordinance, then the Sir Thomas Myddelton shall have power, and is hereby authorised, by himself, or such other persons as he shall appoint, to seize and sequester the estates, both real and personal, of all and every such person and persons as shall so refuse to pay his or their assessment, or shall convey away or obscure his or their personal estates, or any part thereof, as aforesaid, so that the same cannot be found or met with whereon to make distress, as being persons ill-affected to the Commonwealth, and refractory and disobedient to the power and authority of Parliament; and to detain and keep the same for the public service of the Parliament and the Kingdom, rendering an account thereof to the two Houses of Parliament.

Ordered by the Commons assembled in Parliament—
That this Ordinance be forthwith printed and published.

H. Elsynge, Cler. Parl. D. Com.[1]

[1] From a pamphlet entitled as above. "Printed for Edw. Husbands, July 11, 1643."

XXIII.

A Naval Fight at Milford Haven, wherein Capt. William Smith, in the "Swallow," took two of the King's Men-of-War. August 7, 1643.

DOCUMENT XXIII. A.D. 1643.

Sir,

According to my last unto you I set sail on the 3rd of August, 1643, out of Kinsale, to play to the eastward, and between the Saul-tiers and the Smalls I made a sail some two leagues to the eastward, on the fifth of the same month, in the morning, and at even, fetching her up, she proved to be a vessel belonging to North Yarmouth, and come from Strangford, in Ireland, laden with wood, and bound for Milford, in Wales, to deliver there. And inquiring what news, the master told me that he met with Capt. Jordan, in the *Expedition*, who had taken a Hamburger, burthen about 300 tons, of force sixteen guns, being laden with salt and other provisions. She came from Rochelle, in France, and was bound for the relief of the rebels, and was taken before St. David's Head, on the coast of Wales. The master further informed me that he believed Capt. Jordan was gone for Milford, and I having a great desire to meet with Capt. Jordan, I bore in for that harbour, not knowing how he may be engaged, and in case I found him not there, then to desire the gentlemen of that county to send Hue and Cry to apprehend the passengers whom Capt. Jordan had forced on shore before he got possession of the prize. When I came before the harbour's mouth a fisherman came on board, who told me that in Milford there were two ships, men-of-war, one of which was the *Fellowship* of Bristol, burthen of about 400 tons, of force 24 guns, having in her four captains, viz., Capt. Barnaby Burley, Capt. Brooks, Capt. William Hayle, and Capt. Richard Nelson. The said captains had summoned aboard the *Fellowship* all the gentry in those parts, and certified that the King had taken Bristol, and that all the Kingdom did now repair unto his Majesty to seek his gracious pardon, and that the Parliament's forces were all overthrown: that his Majesty would soon march for London—

DOCUMENT XXIII.

A.D. 1643.

all Kent being now in arms to assist the King, and Chatham and Rochelle taken; therefore they would advise that county presently to present a petition to his Majesty in tender of their services unto him, and also to raise such a considerable sum of money as they in their wisdom should conceive meet to comply with his Majesty's occasions, and so come aboard them, and they would present them to his Majesty; but in case they should not do this, then they and their posterity were ruined for ever, for Prince Rupert would immediately come down and plunder their country. And [that] his Majesty had sent them out to command all his Majesty's ships, and other ships that were on that or the Irish coast, that on their allegiance they should repair to Bristol, where the commanders and mariners should have his Majesty's pardon, and the commanders should receive from his Majesty both employment, honour, and great reward, and the mariners should have a large gratuity.

Upon this intelligence I called to me all the officers of the *Swallow*, and then the ship's company, informed them what I had heard, and that the ship was rich, having aboard her divers goods belonging to the merchants of Bristol, to preserve from plunder, all which the owners of the ship had traitorously delivered, with their ship, into the hands of the cavaliers, and that if they would fight for it, their love and zeal to God's cause would be made visible to all men, and it would very much daunt the enemy, and be a good example to others to trace them in the steps of valour and virtue. Also, it would manifest their thankfulness to the Parliament who had conferred such favours, as first a gratuity, then the increase of wages, all which must needs bring a blessing on them, and that I did not doubt but that it should please God to deliver the ships into our hands; and then, demanding their resolutions, they cried all as one man, "God bless the King and Parliament," and that they would stand by me to the last man. And then I bore in for the harbour, it being Monday, the 7th of August, 1643, where I found the said ship at anchor; but the Commanders had made us from the top of a hill before we came in, and had fitted their ships and put aboard their waistclothes; and when I came within shot there came off a boat from the *Fellowship* towards the *Swallow*, and in it one Capt. John Brooks, holding forth a white flag, who desired a parley upon condition that I would

DOCUMENT XXIII. A.D. 1643.

let him return aboard the *Fellowship* if we could not accord, to which I consented. Then he came aboard, and leaping down into the waist, he cried "God bless King Charles," to which we all said "Amen." The which being done, the said Captain desired to have private conference with me, but I refused it, saying, I desire to hear nothing from him but what the whole ship's company might hear; but he pressed it the second time, and being denied, the said Captain turned to the ship's company, relating nnto them the words formerly specified, in demonstrating the King's grace and mercy extended towards us in case we should comply and carry the ship to Bristol. But then I commanded him to silence, saying it did seem strange to me that he should dare to take the King's name in his mouth, in regard that both he and his confederates appeared to me to be pirates and sea rovers, in that they had taken and rifled a double shallop that belonged to his Majesty's fleet; but the said Captain replied, "That they had a commission for what they had done under the hand of Sir John Pennington, and that Captain Hayle had another under the hand of Prince Rupert, and that Sir John Pennington was High Admiral by Patent under the Great Seal of England." I told him I had no intelligence of any such Patent, either from the Parliament or from the Honourable the Earl of Warwick, or any order to obey it, and for that of Prince Rupert, he being a stranger, I could not perceive by what virtue or power his Highness could give commission to any to rob or take his Majesty's ships, or other ships belonging to any of his Majesty's loyal subjects. And, therefore, until I could be better satisfied, I would use my best endeavour to seize on their persons and ships as pirates, or sink by their side.

And in the interim of this discourse the *Swallow* was come to anchor on her broad side, and then Capt. Brooks desired me to certify so much in writing to Capt. Burley; and while I went into the cabin to write, the *Fellowship* had cut her cable and was under sail, intending to run ashore, and being informed thereof by the master, we came out, and I commanded the gunner to give fire to a piece of ordnance, the which was done, but within a cable length the *Fellowship* came aground; and in pursuit of her we cut, and also came aground a little ahead of her, and then I gave her two pieces of ordnance. Whereupon Capt. Burley appeared on the poop, and cried, "Captain, hold, hold." Then I commanded him aboard, who, when he came, told me he would deliver up the ship if I would promise, on the faith of a gentleman, to set the commanders and ship's company on shore, or give them a double shallop to carry them to Bristol, the which, if I refused to do, he had left those on board who would set the ship on fire. Then I replied unto him, that burn she should, for I was resolved not to part with any one man of them, for I valued them more than I did the ship. But in the mean time I had sent a letter to the master and ship's company, that if they would deliver up the other two captains with their ship, I promised them all a free entertainment, and that they should have their wages paid and all such goods as they could make appear justly to belong to any of them. Upon receipt of which letter the master and mariners did deliver up the ship without the loss or hurt of one man (God be praised), only when the *Hart Frigate* parted from us to run ashore, we gave her an unhappy shot, killed two men, and hurt one. But Capt. Nesson, who commanded in her, carried her eight miles up the river, and ran her ashore in a creek; but she was pursued by Capt. Row. Williams, and then was exchanged divers shots between them. But Nesson ran away, with most of his men, and left her, and the next day Capt. Williams brought her off, in which service that gentleman doth crave his Lordship's protection.

Having perfected this service, the next day I set sail in pursuit of my Admiral, to acquaint him with our proceedings, and also that Bristol was lost, and the fleet is now repairing there to command our fleet, wherein Sir John Pennington is to come out admiral, that so we might use our best endeavours to nip these proceedings in the bud, and having acquainted my Admiral therewith, it is agreed on that forthwith we repair to Milford to endeavour to get our ship's want of victuals supplied, etc.

Your most loving brother, to serve you,

William Smith.

From aboard his Majesty's ship, the
Swallow, making sail for Milford,
Aug. 17, 1643.

[Capt. Smith, having heard the "character which fame sounds in the ears of all men that come into these parts, of his worth and

DOCUMENT XXIII. A.D. 1643.

good affection, which he and the rest of the gentlemen of the county bear to the public cause," writes to Griffith White on the 7th of August, from aboard the *Swallow*, desiring him and the rest of the gentlemen of the county to send Hue and Cry, to attach the "wandering rebellious persons," thought to be Jesuits and Priests, who had been driven ashore by the expedition, reported to be possessed of much jewels and money, for the relief of the rebels in Ireland, and to have come from Rochelle in France, to which Griffith White sends

Answer.

ALLWORTHY SIR,

I much rejoice at your constant preservation and good success, which I hope the Lord in his mercy will continue, and my prayers and means shall not be wanting. I have imparted your desire of supplying your wants of victuals unto the gentlemen, whose willingness I presume will not be wanting, and this night I am sure to hear their answer, which I hope will give you real content. What lies in my power to assist you I shall not be wanting, being ready to corroborate my protestation with my life and means, not any way daunted with the poor flaws of ill-fortune that hath lately befallen us. God will not suffer his chosen to suffer in the superlative degree, but to greatly chastise them lest they attribute too much to the arm of flesh. God, I hope (and make no doubt), will make a period to these unnatural wars, and our religion, laws, and liberties preserved in their desired purity. I desire to wait on you, but reserve myself till I receive your commands. In the interim I am your servant, and present my service unto you, and will remain,

Your friend to serve,

GRIFFITH WHITE.[1]

August 9, 1643.

Another Letter on the same day.

NOBLE SIR,

Since the last letter I sent you this post-noon I understand, by an honest gentleman, who is as I am, that Hayle, your

[1] This must have been him of Henllan, Castlemartin, who was High Sheriff of Pembrokeshire in 1626.

DOCUMENT XXIII. A.D. 1643.

now prisoner, hath divulged, in the presence of some gentlemen of quality of this county, that the inhabitants of this county should not reap their corn—in case they did, they should not enjoy it. My desire is that you would please vouchsafe this courteous favour to examine and fish out the cause and ground of this report, and withal, if you find this to be true, which cannot but prove prejudicial to the public good, that you would write a letter and direct it in general to the gentry of this county (omitting particulars), which I verily believe will turn the hearts of those who are now in the way of collapsing, since the taking of unconstant Bristol, and unite their hearts with ours who are constant to the cause. I desire, if your resolution comply with me (which I doubt not of), to hasten your letter with all speed, which I know will be very thankfully received, and for my own particular I shall and will remain your very loving [friend] to serve you,

GRIFFITH WHITE.

[To which Capt. Smith replies, for the satisfaction of the writer and the gentlemen of the county, that "the menacing speeches thundered out by Hayle and his confederates" were "only the bravadoes of a proud insulting enemy, grounded neither on judgment or religion." Moreover, he tenders them the only comfort he can, viz., "That in your Maker's cause you would behave yourselves as becometh good Christians and valiant soldiers of Christ Jesus: that you would gird on your swords, muster your forces, put yourselves in battle array, and quit yourselves like men, putting yourselves under God's protection, doubt[ing] not but his Divine Majesty is both able and also will deliver all those that put their confidence in Him." He believes that the "gentry of this county very well understand the condition of this war, and that it is no other than between Christ and anti-Christ," and declares that the Parliament had been forced to take up arms for the defence of the Protestant religion, the King's honour and dignities, the privileges of Parliament, and the liberties of the subject.[1]

[1] From a pamphlet, entitled "Several Letters of great importance and good successe, lately obtained against the *Fellowship*, of Bristow, by Capt. William Smith, &c. London: Printed for Lawrence Blaiklock, at the signe of the Sugar Loafe, near Temple Barre, 1643." [August 23] (K. P. 89—37.)

XXIV.

Notes relating to Proceedings in Pembrokeshire, from August to October, 1643.

A.

As to Tenby.

DOCUMENT XXIV. A.

A.D. 1643.

We told you, even now,[1] how cheerfully Tenby, in Pembrokeshire, received the noble Earl of Carbery (his Majesty's Lieutenant-General for the Counties of Pembroke, Carmarthen, and Cardigan), for which their loyalty eight ships presently rode before the town and made at least a hundred shots against the inhabitants; but one of the Haven cannon shot one of the best ships of the eight through and through, and so set the rest a-packing, whereby the good people of Tenby received no prejudice. The design was likewise to have besieged Tenby by land, with forces from Pembroke town; but the beacons being fired (the good honest old way in time of rebellion), Carmarthenshire, and many in Pembrokeshire, arose heartily to join with the noble Earl, whereby (as the letter says) Tenby was settled with thunder and lightning, in despite of all the Pembrokeshire rebels. And afterwards the gentry freely subscribed £2,000, to be delivered within ten days to their Lord-Lieutenant to tender to his Majesty as a testimony of the loyalty and obedience of the County of Pembroke and the Town and County of Haverfordwest.[2]

[1] If any account of the entry of the Earl of Carbery into Tenby ever appeared in the pages of *Aulicus*, it must have appeared in the issue for the 34th week—a copy of which I have not been able to see. The volume of the King's pamphlets containing it is not in the British Museum, and is supposed never to have been delivered with the others, though its contents were catalogued by the original collector.

[2] *Merc. Aulicus* 37th week, p. 512. (K. P. 125—4.)

B.

As to Haverfordwest and several Hundreds in the County of Pembroke.

But the Welshmen are of another make, whose language hath no word for a Close Committee. For after the Earl of Carbery had reduced Tenby, in Pembrokeshire (the only county in Wales that had been seduced, though now most loyal to his Majesty), his lordship went to Haverfordwest, whither all the gentry of the county, and all the trained bands came unto him to manifest their loyalty to his sacred Majesty. The six hundreds of train bands are Roose, Daungleddy, Dewesland, Castlemartin, Narberth, Kemes and Kilgerran—hard names—but the inhabitants are honest gentlemen, which gentry and train bands testified their hearty obedience by their subscriptions under their hands and seals, and by a tender of two thousand pounds to be given to his Majesty, all which was most happily affected by God's blessing on the valour and prudence of the noble Earl of Carbery, whom Haverfordwest received with such cheerful expressions as I have not yet met with, which (because they are excellent words) I have here transcribed from the original:— DOCUMENT XXIV. B. A.D. 1643.

"We, the Mayor, Aldermen, and inhabitants of the Town and County of Haverfordwest, do hereby humbly declare that we will be always obedient to the King's Majesty's royal commands, and will serve him with our lives and fortunes, and will submit to his Majesty's authority, now placed in the right honourable Richard, Earl of Carbery, Lord-Lieutenant-General of the Counties of Pembroke, Carmarthen, and Cardigan; and will heartily contribute to his sacred Majesty's service to the best of our abilities. And we do further engage ourselves, upon the faith of loyal subjects, that we will not receive into our town and county any garrison force or person whatsoever, sent or to be sent from any who now are, or hereafter shall be, in rebellion against his Majesty, under the name

DOCUMENT XXIV. B. A.D. 1643. of King and Parliament, or any other name, but will dutifully receive and assist all such forces as our said Lord-Lieutenant-General shall send for the use and service of his sacred Majesty. For assurance whereof we have hereunto fixed our Common Seal, and subscribed our names the 18th day of September, and call our God to witness that we are resolved to live and die in and for the defence of his Majesty and his Government, against all the said rebels. God save the King."[1]

C.

Of the Reduction of Pembrokeshire by the Royalists, with a Protestation alleged to have been subscribed by the Gentry of the County.

DOCUMENT XXIV. C. A.D. 1643. His Majesty's good subjects go a better way to work, especially those of the County of Pembroke. For the famous haven of Milford, Tenby, Haverfordwest, and all other places in Pembrokeshire, being reduced to his Majesty by that noble and prudent Earl of Carbery, his Majesty's Lieut. General of the Counties of Pembroke, Carmarthen, and Cardigan, there now remained only Pembroke Town and castle out of his Majesty's possession, for the gaining whereof the noble gentry of this county made a protestation in these very words:—

"We, whose names are subscribed, do, upon our faith and reputations, declare and promise to the Right Honourable the Earl of Carbery, our Lieut. General, that we will oppose what in us lieth, the victualling of the ships which are or shall be manned with persons who give out that they are for the King and Parliament. That we will not contribute directly, or indirectly, to maintain the forces now in Pembroke Town and Castle, and will oppose any levy of money, or other aid, in this county, to that purpose, and will, to the utmost of our power, endeavour speedily to reduce the same to his Majesty's obedience, and to

[1] *Merc. Aulicus* for 39th week (Sept. 26), p. 539. (K. P. 127—8.)

DOCUMENT XXIV. C.
A.D. 1643.

the utmost of our power will preserve this county from incursions of shipping, and the rapine of the soldiers of that Town and Castle. All which, if we do not, as aforesaid, we do acknowledge ourselves to be most unfaithful to his Majesty, and liable to his Majesty's most heavy displeasure."

Rich. Phillips, Baronet	Thomas Price, Esq.
John Stepney, Baronet	John Boteler, Esq.
Hugh Owen, Baronet	Sampson Lort, Esq.
John Barlow, Esquire	Thomas Warren, Esq.
Alban Owen, Esq.	Will. Langhorne, Gent.
Griffith White, Esq.	James Lewes, Esq.
Roger Lort, Esq.	Lewis Barlow, Esq.
George Bowen, Esq.	John Elliott, Esq.
Hugh Bowen, Esq.	John Edwards, Esq.
Morris Canon, Esq.	Thomas Bowen, Esq.
Thomas Boteler, Esq.	John Phillips, Esq.
Thomas Perrott, Esq.	Herbert Perot, Gent., &c.[1]

These, with all the rest of the gentry of that county, having made this protestation, had so kindly and speedy an operation on the Town and Castle of Pembroke, that the inhabitants sent an instrument, under their Common Seal, to their Lieut. General the Earl of Carbery, desiring his Lordship to present it to his Majesty, wherein they do protest, upon the faith of loyal subjects, that they will maintain no forces under the name of King and Parliament, but will preserve the Town and Castle for his Majesty's use and none other. So that Pembroke Castle (famous for the birth of that valiant, wise King Henry the Seventh), being the last piece of the good work unfinished, the Principality of Wales is the first of his Majesty's dominions (as it was ever most likely) wholly reduced to his Majesty's obedience.[2]

[1] This document appearing in *Mercurius Aulicus*, a paper, above all others, given to exaggerating, and even coining news, must not be accepted altogether as true. Most undoubtedly it is not a forgery, but I think, at the same time, that some of the names appended were either written at Oxford, or put to the paper in Pembrokeshire without the consent of their bearers. Sir Hugh Owen, Mr. Griffith White, Mr. John Elliot are questionable signatures. The whole of their after-conduct is out of keeping with such a protestation. Besides the surrender of Pembroke is untrue.

[2] *Mercurius Aulicus*, 43rd week (ending Oct. 28), 1643. (K. P. 132—13.)

XXV.

A True relation of a Great Victory obtained by the Parliament's Forces against the Cavaliers near Chester.

DOCUMENT XXV.

A.D. 1643.

LOVING MASTER,

My cordial love unto you. . . . .

I praise God we are now in reasonable good quietness in this County of Chester, and the last stirring that we had was upon the 17th and 18th of October, the certainty of which you shall hear, viz. :—

Upon the 17th of October, the Lord Capel set out of Shrewsbury with all the forces he could possibly raise, both in Shropshire and all Wales, forcing them to come upon pain of death; and, besides, he had gotten Colonel Hastings, and a great party of his company, and Colonel Bagot, and the most of his forces, from Lichfield to assist him, and they marched to Priest [Prees] Heath, and Sir William Brereton and Sir Thomas Myddelton at that time, with their forces, were in Wem, a town some seven miles off Shrewsbury, which they have made a garrison town for Colonel Mytton, and had just fortified it about with mudwalls, but had not had time to make any sconces. And Sir William Brereton and Sir Tho. M., with their forces, marched after him, and came to Prees Heath likewise, and there made their rendezvous, and their trumpets sounded a challenge; but the Lord Capel would not meet them, for he had laid an ambuscade for them, which Sir W. B's. scouts perceived, and then Sir W. B. changed his ground, and the Lord Capel and his forces marched all with great speed towards Nantwich, and never stayed until they came upon Ranmore, and there two pieces of his ordnance stayed, and part of his forces and the rest came straight forwards to Acton, and were there before our men were aware. And then most of the horse and foot we had at Nantwich went out to face them, and set upon them, and drove them into the church-yard, and into Acton Church, killed four of them, and shot more, and got some few of their horses. And then when they had got the churchyard, they shot very briefly, and our men could do no good with them. Two of our men were shot. And so they came into Nantwich again (for the most of our forces were with Sir W. B.), and then we made good our town, and would have died in the defence of it. And they sallied out of the Church, and we discharged two of our pieces of ordnance at them, and that scattered them all away again, that they would never come within musket shot of our town. Then some party of them fetched a compass, thinking to have come over Beame bridge, and a party of ours went out to meet them, and our men drove them back three fields' breadth, and took seven of them prisoners, poor bare rogues. And then their horse came and fetched them away, and they fled all to Acton again as fast as they could, and there they stayed until twelve o'clock at night and plundered many thereabouts— Richard Pollit, Mr. Huits' factor, both of money and his own cheese, to the value of forty pounds; plundered at Darford Hall, and Rowland Salmon (one that stood all for them), and some others. And then, they hearing that Sir W. B., was coming, fled away again. And it fell out so that Sir W. B. had false intelligence, that he came by Drayton and so by Whoone [Woore], and missed coming in the rear of them, partly mistrusting they had lain in ambuscade for him, and then the enemy all went back to Wem, making no question but to have taken it, and swore a bloody oath it was their own. And the cavaliers made thousands of kids, some of broom *(sic)* oulder and straw, and such as they could get, and came holding them before them to get to the wall's side. In Wem there was only Colonel Mytton and his soldiers, 300 at the most, and they behaved themselves valiantly, dashed their brains upon the kids, and kept their town, and many a bloody kid there lay, and men gasping on the ground, of cavaliers, and drove them off despite their being 4,000 at the least. Indeed, our men had good walls, and the town is watered, that they came but on one side of it to hurt them in the town. One of Colonel Mytton's case of drakes killed sixty of the King's party at one shot; and they being driven off, hearing that Sir W. B. and Sir T. M. were retreated, near towards Shrewsbury, our men followed and drove their horse two miles. And then the enemy had great advantage—a hill, a stone wall, buildings, and

DOCUMENT XXV. A.D. 1643.

a wood, that night. (Next morning our men took 42 cavaliers into Nantwich.) There they stayed, and our men in a plain valley, none knowing the ground; they discharged very fast one at another, till at length our men went on the other side of the hill, and then the cavaliers would not stay. The enclosed note shows you what execution was done. So I rest, yours,

W. B.

[ENCLOSURE.]

A catalogue of those that were killed, wounded, and taken prisoners of the King's party, in this fight, being on October the 17 and 18, 1643.

Colonel Wynn,[1] slain, and then the Welshmen fled.
Colonel Scriven, wounded.
Colonel Willis. wounded, and his lieutenant taken prisoner.
Major Broughton, wounded.
Captain Chapman, taken prisoner.
Captain Manlye, wounded, and his lieutenant also.
Six carriages of dead corpse taken away, and 30 more men left on the ground.
Captain Lieutenant *(sic)* Chapman, taken prisoner.
Captain Ellis, slain.
Captain Davies, wounded and taken prisoner.
A barrel of powder blown up, and burnt eight or nine of their men
A great carriage burst and their mortar piece broken.

On the next day, three of Sir W. B.'s troops took seventeen of their men in a town in Wales [viz.]:—Captain Damport, two cornets, one ensign, one serjeant, one surgeon, and eleven common prisoners, and they are brought to Nantwich.

Major Marrow slain in Wem, on our side, and one soldier more. Six killed, at Lee Bridge, of Sir W. B.'s, and 15 shot. This is the most certain news.[2]

[1] Of Melai, Denbighshire. He was H. S. of that county in 1637. He was buried at St. Chad's Church, Shrewsbury.

[2] From a pamphlet, entitled as above, "as it was sent in a letter from one that was in the fight to Mr. James Waters, in Newgate Market, and received the 24th of November, 1643." November 27. Printed by E. P., 1643. (K. P. 134—4.)

XXVI.

A Letter from the Marquis of Ormond to Dr. John Williams, Archbishop of York, concerning the Consignment of Arms, &c., for the Defence of Anglesey, and as to the probable Transportation of the Soldiers in Ireland to North Wales or Chester. Oct. 26.

DOCUMENT XXVI. A.D. 1643.

May it please your Grace,

I received your letter of the 15th of this month, and in it so noble expressions of your favour to me, that I dare only own them, as they proceed from an excess of civility in your Grace; and as a direction unto me to become more serviceable to our Gracious Master, whereunto my power holds no proportion with my will. . . . . And now, beseeching your Grace to receive my humble acknowledgments in earnest of the real services, I resolve to pray you give me leave to let you know what is done in those things you were pleased to command me.

Captain Thomas Bartlett hath aboard him fourteen barrels of powder, and some small proportion of match, for the use of the ordnance he carries with him, which are four demi-culverins, mounted with all appurtenances, and 400 shot for them. Two whole culverins would have been sent, but that the mast of his ship would not bear them. When your Grace shall send means to convey them they shall be readily sent.

The pieces are consigned to Mr. Bulkeley, at Beaumaris, and so is the powder, except one barrel which is for Capt. Bartlett's own provision. The Lord Archbishop of Dublin hath paid £10 a barrel for ten barrels, and I as much for four. This is, except money, the scantiest commodity with us; but lest this proportion should not answer his Majesty's occasion in those parts, I have a week since sent blank warrants for such Irish or outlandish merchants, or captains of ships, as are at Wexford, or in any other part in the power of the Irish, whereby they are promised,

DOCUMENT XXVI. A.D. 1643.

if they go to Beaumaris or Chester, with powder, arms, or any other necessaries for war, that they shall receive ready money for such wares, and free liberty to depart when they have sold them, and divers letters to the same effect have I written to your Grace and the Sheriff of Anglesey.

. . . .

About the 26th of last month there arrived here letters to the Lords Justices and me, from his Majesty, directing that in case a cessation of arms were here concluded on, such part of his army as might be spared from garrisoning the most important places of this province should be, with all convenient speed, transported to his service in England. To this I find ready inclination in the best and most considerable part of the army, though there have been, and is still, great industry used to corrupt the officers and debauch the soldiers. But the greatest difficulty I meet with, is the want of shipping for their transportation, and the greatest danger, I fear, when they are landed on the other side is, that if provision of shoes, stockings, clothes, and money, be not instantly made for them, it will be easy to seduce them with likely promises of having these wants supplied. And I make little doubt but the rebels there will promise all this, and perform as much as they can of it; which, if not prevented by timely provision to be made for officers and soldiers by his Majesty's servants, this part of the army will not only be useless to his Majesty, but perhaps be drawn in a great part to fight against him.

Thus much I have written to Mr. Orlando Bridgman to Chester, by this bearer, because I find he is trusted by his Majesty there; and I hold it fit to say as much to your Grace, since I know none more able or willing to serve the King in all those counties, where it may fall out we may be forced to land; and this I have more than once informed the King of.

I beseech your Grace to pardon the disorder of this letter, occasioned something by my haste. I desire to be hereafter known to you as,

Your Grace's most humble and faithful servant,

ORMONDE.[1]

Dublin, 26th Oct., 1643.

[1] "Carte's Life of Ormond. Oxford, ed. 1851." Vol. v., p. 479.

XXVII.

The Marquis of Ormond to Mr. Orlando Bridgman—as to preparations to be made for the reception of the forces from Ireland. Nov. 11.

DOCUMENT XXVII.
A.D. 1643.

SIR,

I have been since the 7th of this month . . in continual thought how to transport part of this army (according to his Majesty's command) to the port of Chester; and I am now in that forwardness that I hope a few days, with a good wind, will bring them thither to the number of about 3,000 foot, as the lists are given me by the officers, and that is the only way of muster that will be now endured. The horse artillery and some more men, I intend to follow, according as means of transportation and other important things shall admit of my own departing hence.

In the meantime I hold it necessary for me, by these, to second my former letter sent to you by Capt. Bartlett, dated the 25th of October, and to desire you that all possible provision be made for the good entertainment of the officers and soldiers, who are in the greatest want that can be imagined, and in such distemper by reason thereof, that I much fear great inconvencies will unavoidably fall upon the King's service, if they find not their condition much mended upon the instant of their landing. And if the case be such that plentiful provision cannot be instantly ready, it is absolutely needful that a competent strength of horse and foot, of whose affections you are confident, should be in readiness by force to keep the common soldiers in awe. And whatever provision is made for them this will not be amiss, for they have gotten such a head, and punishment hath been so moderately inflicted upon them by reason of their extreme sufferings, that they will be apt to fall into disorders, and will think themselves delivered from prison when they come on English ground, and that they may make use of their liberty to go whither they will.

DOCUMENT XXVII.

A.D. 1643.

There cannot go much ammunition with them this time, ten or twelve barrels will be the most; and, therefore, if they be suddenly put upon service, which I could wish they might be, preparation must be made accordingly; nor is there much more to be expected when I go, so empty our stores are.

I am, &c.,

ORMONDE.[1]

Dublin, Nov. 11, 1643.

[1] Carte's "Life of Ormond." Vol. v., p. 505.

XXVIII.

The advance of the Parliament forces into Wales under Sir Thomas Myddelton and Sir W. Brereton, detailed in a letter from the Archbishop of York to the Marquis of Ormond, Nov. 12.

DOCUMENT XXVIII. A.D. 1643.

With my humble service to your Excellency, most noble lord, you have much obliged all this country with those pieces and ammunition you were pleased to send to Beaumaris, which I have signified unto his Majesty to take notice thereof, as a service done to this country by your Excellency to secure them unto his Majesty. . . . . Capt. Bartlett being returned again to those parts (though without calling for my letter according to his promise), I humbly beseech your Excellency that he may return with some provision of powder for my use (Mr. Bulkeley having taken up all the former for the use of that island). I shall be ready with all thankfulness to return the money.

The best use I (a private man) can make of your Excellency's wise and judicious letter, was to send it up for his Majesty's perusal, with my humble advice that his Majesty would not draw over a person of that consideration in the head of an army so weak and unprovided for, without a certain and positive provision of clothes, shoes, stockings, and money, competently to engage them in his own, and to secure them from running unto the enemy, now victorious and triumphing in those parts where these forces were to land, and full of allurements to draw men to them. Thus things stood as then, now altered in many circumstances.

. . . . . .

For now (most excellent lord) the enemies are possessed of Worrall,[1] where your Excellency intended to land, are entered into Denbighshire, have taken Wrexham and Ruthin (as some say), plunder up and down the whole country, without resistance; and whether with a resolution to fortify here, or to return again and besiege Chester upon the Welsh as well as the English side,

[1] That hundred of Cheshire which will be best known to general readers as the locality in which Birkenhead is situate.

DOCUMENT XXVIII. A.D. 1643.

I am not able to conjecture. So that if the English-Irish army shall now come over, unless it be so well provided (by sea and land) as to force their entertainment in Lancashire, Liverpool (which they now seem to neglect as I am informed), or Worrall, where it is feared they will fortify, they will be necessitated to land somewhere in these parts, or at Holyhead, and so much discommodated by the poverty of the country through which they are to pass, and those two ferries at Beaumaris and Conway, which of necessity they are to waft over very incommodiously, and (as far as I can conceive) without carrying their cannon with them, but sending it by sea to meet them at Orme's Head, Abergele, Rhyddlan, or as near Conway as the enemies' advancing will permit and give them leave. And how I shall be able to keep this town of Conway (without any power of command, but that weak one of kindred and good-will), without any assistance of soldiers or Commissions of Array, is unto myself very doubtful. Because this impression upon the neighbouring counties is sudden and unexpected unto me, the Lord Capell hiding himself in Shrewsbury, and not daring to take the field, lest he be shut out from that town, the citizens whereof, with the inhabitants of that shire, having not only a mean, but a malignant estimation of his lordship.

Thus I have declared unto your Excellency what state I (a private and unemployable man) do conceive these counties to stand in at this time: that if you resolve upon any sudden transportation of those men into these parts, your Excellency may give the Sheriff, Commissioners of Array, and Justices of the Peace, timous *(sic)* notice thereof; wherein likewise I shall further any service your Excellency shall direct, as far as that foresaid estate of a private man will permit me. And remain in all things,

Most excellent lord,

Your Excellency's most humble servant,

Jo. Archbishop of York.

Conway, this 12th of November, 1643.

If your Excellency shall send over with Capt. Bartlett one company of Yorkshiremen or Welshmen, I will find them meat, drink, and shoes and stockings, until their rendezvous, provided they come armed and with some ammunition, which I will pay for.[1]

[1] Carte's "Life of Ormond." Vol. v., p. 506.

XXIX.

A Friendly Summons from Sir Thomas Myddelton to William Salesbury to deliver up the Castle of Denbigh, with the Answer.

DOCUMENT XXIX. A.D. 1613.

The former friendship and familiarity which hath passed betwixt us doth not only invite, but also engage me to use all possible means, not only to continue but to increase the same, which on my part being done and offered, however things fall out hereafter, I am excusable before God and the world.

It hath pleased God, by reason of all the distractions of the times, for the present, to put us in a way of opposition one to another—the causes being well understood, I doubt not, but the issue would be a firmer union betwixt us than ever. Sir, through all opposition God hath brought me with a considerable force to Wrexham, able both to defend myself and offend my foes; wherein I am by unquestionable power as well authorized to preserve the peace of this country from the violence of oppression used and exercised by the Commissioners of Array, and others, against the Parliament, as also to protect and receive into grace and favour such as shall willingly come in and submit to the obedience of King and Parliament. This power, by God's grace, I will labour to put in execution, and this is the intent of my coming into these parts. Sir, I understand that for the present you are in arms in Denbigh Castle, and governor thereof—and being formerly satisfied of your ingenuous disposition, I cannot doubt but that your intentions and mine will agree, and on your part produce such actions as may conduce to your honour and safety, and the prosperity of these oppressed countries. And therefore I do hereby invite you, and desire God that you may for your own good embrace it, that you would please to submit yourself to the power and obedience of the King and Parliament, lay down your arms, and deliver up that castle to me, or those that I shall appoint, to be disposed of for their service, and for the peace and safety of these parts; which, if

DOCUMENT XXIX. A.D. 1643.

you shall do, you shall not only be protected in person and estate by me and my power, but also you shall approve yourself, as formerly you have been, a patriot and preserver of your country, a lover of religion, and an instrument of the public good; and will be by the State taken notice of as an acceptable service. Sir, now I have discharged my conscience, desiring your speedy consideration and speedy resolution, and so desire God to direct you, and remain

Your old and true friend and kinsman,

THO. MYDDELTON.

Answer.

In nomine Iesu.

SIR,

I desire not to live longer than I approve myself true to my King and country, a true lover of the Protestant religion, and yield cheerful and hearty obedience to my King and Parliament; and if the want of our obedience be your quarrel, or any part of the cause of your coming into these parts, it is an offence taken, but not given. I am not so jealous as to think you point at me as one that did exercise violence or oppression in this country. I pray God that we do not see those things now begun to be exercised, instead of being preserved from those. But to be plain—to betray so great a trust as the keeping of Denbigh Castle, though upon ever so fair pretences, may be acceptable to them that desire it, but in my opinion, in itself abominable; and must needs render him that shall do it odious to God and all good men, and I will never account him my friend that should move me to do it. But I cannot say you do so, for I shall, with all pleasure and willingness, yield it up as you desire (that is), when I am commanded by my King and Parliament. And for the discharge of that trust in the meantime, and for no other cause, I have armed myself, as well as God did enable me; and those arms (with God's leave) I shall bear and use for the service of my King and country, and not to exercise violence or oppression.

This is my answer to you, and, with God's help, the firm and constant resolution of him who is your kinsman, and would be your true friend, as far as truth and loyalty will give him leave.

DOCUMENT XXIX. A.D. 1643.

WILLIAM SALESBURY.[1]

Denbigh Castle, the 15th 9bris. 1643.

[1] From Salusbury MSS., quoted in Parry's Royal Progresses, large paper edition, p. 350. These letters were also published at the time in the pages of *Mercurius Aulicus* of January 6th, 1644, where Sir Thomas's letter is dated Wrexham, 14th November. (K.P. 139—9.)

XXX.

The Marquis of Ormond to the Mayor of Chester, respecting the Transportation of Forces from Ireland to Chester and Wales. Nov. 15, 1643.

DOCUMENT XXX.

A.D. 1643.

SIR,

His Majesty haveing commanded me by his letters beareinge date at Sudely Castle, the 7th day of September, in the Nineteenth yeare of his reigne, to take order for the transportation of part of his army in this Kingdom into his Matye's Kingdome of England, and particularly if it might be to the Port of his Citty of Chester. By wich letters his Matye did likewise declare that both officers and souldiers should upon their landinge there receave theire pay in the same proportion and manner wth the rest of his Matye's army there. And that all care should be taken that clothes, shoos, and other necessaries, should be forthw^th^ provided for them after their landinge. I am, therefore, to desire you, in his Matye's name, by virtue of the sayd letters, that as you tender his Matye's service you take care that the souldiers, under the command of Sr Fulke Hunckes, Sr Michell Ernle, Collonell Gibson, and Collonell Byron, whoe shall land there, be conveniently quartered by you, and accomodated wth such necessaries and provisions as are fitt accordinge to his Matye's Royall intentions, whereby they may be the better inabled and encouraged to doe his Matye services. And soe, not doubtinge of your diligence and care in the performance hereof, I rest,

Yo assured loving friend,

ORMONDE.

Dated at Dublin, the 15th Novem^ber^, 1643.
For the Right Woorshipfull the Mayor of Chester.
(Indorsed) rec. this 19 Nov.[1]

[1] Harl. MSS., 2135, fol. 14.

XXXI.

The Archbishop of York to the Marquis of Ormond.

DOCUMENT XXXI. A.D. 1643.

MOST EXCELLENT AND MOST NOBLE LORD,

Since I wrote to your Excellency, in acknowledgment of your most noble favours to our poor country, things in the borders of North Wales are grown rather worse than better. The people of Denbighshire and Flintshire (which border upon Cheshire and Shropshire), being disunited among themselves, and ill-united under an unfortunate commander, who never led them on to any action, but when they were entered upon the same he retired and commanded them back again, so discouraging and disheartening all those of his obedience; and now that the enemy is entered [into] those parts, dares not show his head. They, I say, thus abandoned by the Prince's Lieutenant[1] in those parts, are quite driven before a handful of rebels, like sheep, and do not know how to get, nor consequently to make, a head.

Young Booth is at Wrexham, with very near 900 men out of Manchester and Lancashire. Brereton, the general, and Myddelton, his sub-general (as they term them), are at Hawarden (which castle was betrayed by one Ravenscroft[2] to the rebels), with five or six hundred men, horse and foot, and the trained bands of Cheshire are at Mold and Holt (the castle whereof, defended by young Robinson, who hath lived much at Dublin, holds still out for the King) and by these contemptible numbers these great and populous counties, for want of a head, and arms, and ammunition, are quite routed, and scattered up and down these mountainous countrys.

Now the rebels, thus scattered up and down (the cause I trouble your Excellency with this punctual narration) in the borders of

[1] The Lord Capel.

[2] Ravenscroft of Bretton.

DOCUMENT XXXI. A.D. 1643.

Wales, all Lancashire and Worrall is conceived clear enough, and of easy landing at this conjuncture of time. So are all the ports of North Wales from Holyhead to Beaumaris, Orme's Head, Abergele, Ruthlan, or Rhyda Vorwed (?), there being no enemies yet advanced to any of these places in Denbighshire and Flintshire, and Lancashire and Cheshire, much emptied of forces, drawn out as aforesaid. This is the condition of these countries at this instant, when I have said that Chester (much aimed at by the rebels) prepares for a stout defence, and Denbigh Castle, in the way, is fortified for the King.[1]

But alas! we grow daily in more uncertainty of the landing of the forces from your parts than we were—some giving out that they are not for these parts but for Bristol, which, if it be true, these parts are quite lost, and will think themselves deserted by his Majesty. But if those forces shall land here, or in any of the ports described above, they shall be waited on by two or three thousand foot at the least, and some two or three hundred horse, to the skirts of England, all which people shall submit to their commanders, and do them good service if they come hither speedily, and have any arms and ammunition to spare their auxiliaries.

However, most noble lord, I continue my suit unto your Excellency to spare 100 able soldiers, well commanded for officers, for the guard of this strong town and castle, where they shall have good quarters, and be ready at six days' warning to return again to Dublin. I do not care of what country they are, so as they come with arms and competency of ammunition, which shall be paid for or returned. Capt. Bartlett will help [to] convey them.

If the Irish forces come not this way (I mean through some parts of Wales, or to go for Cheshire and Lancashire), the rebels will gain this country, beginning already to levy forces of our nation, whereof they never had any before. I cease to trouble your Excellency any further, being,

Most noble Lord,
Your Excellency's most humble servant,
Jo. Bishop of Yorke.[2]

Conway, 18$^{mo.}$ die. Novembris, 1643.

[1] By William Salisbury. See ante p. 96.
[2] Carte's "Life of Ormond," vol. v. p. 514.

XXXII.

The Irish Forces are attempted to be won over to the Parliament.

DOCUMENT XXXII. A.D. 1643.

SIRS,

Being assured that amongst the forces now arrived in Wales your regiments have likewise entered these parts, we have thought good, before there be any further proceeding tending towards hostility, to apply ourselves to you in this way, that so, if it be possible, you may rightly understand us, and we may not mistake you; and so happily you and we, having formerly ventured our own persons in one and the same quarrel in England and Ireland, may not, through mistakes or misinformation, be divided, and we under the brand of rebellion be made enemies. Now, Sirs, give us leave to tell you that we apprehend and are assured your voyage into Ireland was to fight against Popish rebels and for the Protestant Religion, wherein you have expressed great fidelity. We imagine you are not yet thoroughly informed of the cause of taking up of arms, or if you were, you could not be engaged against us. For this reason we have tendered our respects unto you, and if you show yourselves the gentlemen we formerly knew you at your last departure out of this Kingdom, we doubt not but to procure satisfaction from the Parliament for the service you have done in Ireland, with the like preferment here, and show yourselves as real here for the Protestant Religion as you did there, which will engage us all to remain,

Sirs,

Your affectionate and faithful friends to serve you,

WILL. BRERETON. JO. BOOTHE.
THO. MYDDELTON. PETER EGERTON.
G. BOOTHE. JO. HOLCROFT.[1]

Wrexham, Nov. 18, 1643.

[1] The last three were the most active members of the Manchester Committee.

The Answer.

DOCUMENT XXXII. A.D. 1643.

GENTLEMEN,

We were not engaged in the service in Ireland otherwise than by the King's commission. The service we have done there envy itself dares not extenuate; and although we are sensible how unworthily we have been deserted by your pretended Parliament, yet we are not returned hither without his Majesty's special commission and authority. If you have the like commission from the King for the arms you carry we shall willingly treat with you, otherwise you must give us leave to carry ourselves like soldiers and loyal subjects.

MICH. ERNLE. FRAN. BUTLER.
RICH. GIBSON. ED. HAMOND.
GEO. WYNNE.

Hawarden, Nov. 20, 1643.

Postscript.—That officer of your army which came into our quarter without safe-conduct we detain till his Majesty's pleasure be further known.[1]

[1] From *Mercurius Aulicus*, 48th week, ending December 2nd, p. 684. (K. P. 135—16.)

XXXIII.

Mr. Orlando Bridgman to the Marquis of Ormond.

May it Please your Excellency, DOCUMENT XXXIII. A.D. 1643.

Your Excellency's letters by Mr. Brent found me at Oxford, and immediately upon the receipt of them I acquainted his Majesty with the contents. Both your letters, and the experience we had from Bristol, quickened their care at Court for the accommodation of the soldiers upon their landing, so that his Majesty sent down letters to the several counties of North Wales, as also a gentleman (one Col. Tildesley) to those of Lancashire residing in these parts, for a present supply of clothes, victuals, and some proportion of money, to which there was a fair return of promises; but the enemy having fatally (whether through abominable cowardice or treachery, or both, I cannot tell) forced a passage into Wales over Holt-bridge, a place of great import, within five miles of Chester, and dividing that shire from Denbighshire, when there were as many (and those backed with a strong castle at Holt) to guard it, as [there was] to assault it. By this means [they are] for the present forced to lay aside their preparations for the public service, and provide for their own particulars. And by this means, Chester itself being in a manner blocked up, they were forced to burn all that part of their suburbs which were on the Welsh side of the city.

Their condition being represented to his Majesty, he commanded me down this fortnight, and I came happily to the landing of the forces which you sent with Sir Michael Ernley and Colonel Gibson. I presume they have related to your Excellency with what number they landed, and in what condition they now are. The enemy have wholly deserted Wales (for Holt Castle they had never taken), except Hawarden Castle, which was betrayed to them, and is now

DOCUMENT XXXIII. A.D. 1643.

blocked up by 1,000 men, most of them of the country,[1] and we are in hopes to starve them out. So that now your forces are at Chester, where we endeavour all that is possible for their accommodation, hitherto retarded by this unhappy irruption of the rebels into Wales. I have provided shoes and stockings for 1,000 or 1,200 of them, already delivered, and the rest were in making, which I hope they have by this time. I have gotten cloth and frieze sufficient for them all, not yet made into apparel, but hastened it to Chester, where I hope to have it fitted up this week and the next.[2] And I am now purposely in these parts to raise some proportion of moneys for the officers and soldiers, and have gotten about 1,000*l.* which I shall distribute with their advice to the best advantage of his Majesty's service.

I am bold to give your Excellency a more particular account of this business, both for my excuse in the unreadiness of those accommodations, which might justly have been expected, and to give your lordship an assurance that I shall be so provided for those that are now to come over, that I shall have all the shoes and stockings, and I hope, most, if not all the apparel, if they be not above 2,000 men.

And in truth, all that can be done is little enough, for the rebels do so much tamper, and underhand[edly] infuse such dangerous notions into some of them, that were it not the discretion, loyalty, and moderation of the officers, which kept them in, many of them would turn to the enemy through hopes of their arrears (which he hath cunningly promised them), though they would soon find themselves deceived, God be thanked, that treasury being now as empty as ours.[3]

The sad condition of these parts, as they were before these

[1] In one of Captain Sandford's extraordinary letters to the besieged they are asked to surrender to Col. Davies or Col. Mostyn, who were in chief command before the leaguer. These, of course, had Welsh soldiers. Furthermore, Harry Byrch, in a letter to the Secretary of the Marquis of Ormond, alluding to a breach of the conditions of surrender, throws the blame on Lord Cholmley's Cheshire regiments. Post p. 113.

[2] In the Harl. MSS., 2125, fol. 135, it is stated that when the English-Irish soldiers came to Chester, they were "faint, weary, and out of clothing. The Mayor sent through all the wards to get apparel of citizens, who gave freely, some whole sutes, some two, some doubletts, others breeches, others shirts, shoes, stockings, and hatts, to the apparelling of about 300."

[3] See Document xxxii. ante, p. 101.

forces landed, hath hastened down my Lord Byron with some 1,200 horse and foot, most from Lancashire.[1] He is advanced to Shrewsbury, and comes in the quality of Field Marshal of Cheshire, Shropshire, and North Wales, and so under my Lord Capel in those parts, who is Lieut.-General under the Prince.[2]

DOCUMENT XXXIII. A.D. 1643.

. . . .

I shall stay about Chester about a month or six weeks, during which time I shall apply myself to provide all the accommodation which I can for these soldiers, sent and happily arrived for the relief of these parts, which have reason to bless God for you as the happy instrument of their deliverance from oppression.

I humbly remain,

Your Excellency's most humbly devoted servant,

ORL. BRIDGMAN.[3]

Beaumaris, Nov. 29.

[1] "My Lord Byron marched this very day with 1,000 horse and 300 foot to join with my Lord Capel in opening the passage [for the Irish], and making one body with your Lordship's aids." See letter from Arthur Trevor to Ormond. Dated Oxon., Nov. 21. Carte's "Life of Ormond," v. 521.

[2] This shows who the Prince's Lieutenant, mentioned in Archbishop of York's letter, was. Ante p. 99.

[3] Carte's "Life of Ormond," v. 525.

XXXIV.

The Siege of Hawarden Castle by the Forces landed from Ireland and its Surrender, November and December, 1643.

DOCUMENT XXXIV. A.D. 1643.

In reply to a verbal summons to surrender, the besieged returned the accompanying letter:—

To the Gentlemen lately come from the service in Ireland.

GENTLEMEN,

We are heartily sorry that you have made such an unhappy exchange of enemies, to leave Irish to fall upon English, and Papists to fall upon Protestants. We had hoped the blood of that noble gentleman, Sir John Harcourt, and the many thousands of Protestants who have fallen by the fury of those bloody monsters of Ireland, could not so soon have been forgotten. What course the Court of England runs, how destructive to the Protestants and favourable to the Papists, you cannot but know (with us) by sad experience. And, therefore, we desire (before you pass further) your thoughts may make a pause, lest you find that God of the Protestants against you whom you have hitherto found miraculously for you. We fear the loss of our religion more than the loss of our dearest blood. Do not, therefore, we beseech you, desire us to betray it, and ourselves. We hope your second thoughts may take off the edge of your former resolutions. However, we are resolved to make good our trust, and put our lives into the hand of that God who can, and we hope will secure them more than our walls or weapons.

JOHN WARREN.
ALEXANDER ELLIOT.

Nov. 21, 1643.

The reply of Lieutenant-Colonel Marrow (who commanded the party at that time before the Castle, the rest not being yet come up):— DOCUMENT XXXIV. A.D. 1643.

Gentlemen,

It is not for to hear you preach that I am sent here, but, in his Majesty's name, to demand the Castle for his Majesty's use. As your allegiance binds you to be true to him, and not to inveigle those innocent souls that are within with you, so I desire your resolution, If you will deliver the Castle, or No?

The Rejoinder from the Castle.

Sir,

We have cause to suspect your disaffection to preaching, in regard we find you thus employed. If there be innocent souls here God will require their blood of them that shed it. We can keep our allegiance and the castle, too, and therefore you may take your answer as it is in English plain before you. We can say no more but God's will be done.

[Note.—The body of the forces from Ireland coming up on the 22nd, Sir Michael Ernley and Major General Gibson sent another summons, to which like answers were sent. Two days after that the Lord Capel came to the assistance of the besiegers.]

Captain Sandford's "Big Letter" to the Officer commanding-in-chief at Hawarden Castle, and his Consorts there.

Gentlemen,

I presume you very well know, or have heard of my condition and disposition, and that I neither give nor take quarter. I am now with my firelocks (who never yet neglected opportunity to correct rebels) ready to use you as I have done the Irish, but

DOCUMENT XXXIV. A.D. 1643.

loth I am to spill my countrymen's blood. Wherefore, by these I advise you, to your fealty and obedience towards his Majesty, and to show yourselves faithful subjects, by delivering the Castle into my hands for his Majesty's use. In so doing you shall be received into mercy; otherwise, if you put me to the least trouble or loss of blood to force you, expect no quarter for *Man*, *Woman*, *or Child.* I hear you have some of our late Irish army in your company—they very well know *me*, and that *my firelocks* use not to parley.[1] Be not unadvised, but think of your liberty, for I vow all hopes of relief are taken from you, and our intents are not to starve you, but to batter and storm you, and *then hang you all*, and follow the rest of that rebel crew. I am now no bread-and-cheese rogue, but as ever, a loyalist, and will ever be whilst I can write or name

THO. SANDFORD.

I expect your speedy answer this Tuesday night
at Broadlane Hall, where I am now your
near neighbour.

Nov. 28.[2]

[1] Which evidently shows that the tampering of the rebels, as Orlando Bridgman calls it, had been to a certain extent successful.

[2] Rushworth, part iii, vol. ii., p. 298.

XXXV.

More Forces from Ireland. Ormond to Mayor of Chester.

A

DOCUMENT XXXV. A. A.D. 1643.

SIR,

There is now shipped from hence another prte of his Matie army, under the command of Collonell Robert Byron and Collonell Henry Warren. With orders to land, if they can, at the port of Chester. I shall at this tyme onely recommende them to your care for there good accomodation, as I did those that were formerly transported from hence. In performeinge whereof you will doe his Matie acceptable service. Soe not doubting of your care herein, I rest,

Y assured loving friend,

ORMONDE.

Dublin, the 1 of december, 1643.

Mayor of Chester.[1]

B

DOCUMENT XXXV. B. A.D. 1643.

SIR,

His Maties fleet returning hither very opertunely for the transportation of the rest of the men designed from hence to his service in England, I have now sent them, and directed their landing to be as neere Chester as may be, to avoid the inconvenience that must unavoydably fall uppon them, to the very great preiudice of his Maties service, if they should be landed at Beaumoris, or at any place where provision is not made for them, as I doubt not

Harl. MSS., 2135, fol. 15.

DOCUMENT XXXV. B. A.D. 1643.

there is at Chester. On the other side, I am informed by the Commander of the Fleet, his victuall is soe neare an end that unless he be supplied there it will not be in his power to pursue what he is further directed, but must stay there to the losse of his tyme and great detriment to his Maties. service. Wherefore I shall desire you to affoard him all the assistance and furtherance you can towards his victualling. And soe I rest,

Yr assured loving friend,

ORMONDE.[1]

Dublin, 2do Decem., 1643.

[1] Harl. MSS., 2135, fol. 60.

XXXVI.

Interesting Particulars of the Landing of the Irish Forces, of the Retreat of Brereton and Myddelton, of the Siege and Surrender of Hawarden, and of the State of Wales. Letter from Capt. Byrch to G. Carr, Secretary to the Marquis of Ormond. December 12, 1643.

DOCUMENT XXXVI. A.D. 1643.

SIR,

I had forgotten more than I should if I had not remembered you. I had intended to have written to more friends, but you and they must remember how great a perindinator *(sic)* I am. This morning we are to march against as contemptible an enemy as ever we had in Ireland. Some experience we have had of it already, and I hope before to-morrow night we shall see more what valour rebels possess.

At our first landing we met with several disrespective (*sic*) warrants from Sir William Brereton, requiring all from 16 to 60 to be in arms to defend themselves from the invasion of 4,000 bloody Irish rebels. He could not have done us a greater courtesy than telling so loud a lie. (The honest Welsh received us very courteously, who were then ready to yield the bucklers, not for love, but fear of the faction.) This was required to be published through Wales that we were such; that is, as far as Sir Thomas Myddelton's faction prevailed. This caused several of the religious ministers that loved conscience and the King to withdraw themselves, and not few of the laity; though we found enough besides to bid us heartily welcome.

At Holywell, the first place we came to, though the town were mostly Papists, we were told they pillaged none but the churches (in want of linen) and the poor curate. At Northop (thither we came next) they took away the surplice again, and did no other

DOCUMENT XXXVI.

A.D. 1643.

harm.[1] It was then time of probationership amongst disarmed people; and you must understand the minister staid, and was a Scotchman. Thence to Hawarden we came, where our men besieged the Castle there (but lately and falsely betrayed by its owner a week before we came, a man entrusted much by the King and his officers, the more is his sin, one Ravenscroft), where we stayed three days; in which time we had very happily (!) six men killed, for at no less cost would our men believe that Englishmen would fight with any Englishmen, but Papists. And I cannot honestly conceal from you that three of these were killed more basely than ever you heard of any killed by the rebels in Ireland; for while some called them unto them from the top of the wall, upon pretence of old acquaintanceship, and promised them sacredly they should receive no harm by their approaching, others shot at them, and missed not.[2] The practices of their ringleader, Brereton, were not more honest nor honourable, who, the very same day that he sent his warrants as far as they could reach in Wales, writ a letter to our commanders (then on ship board), almost in form of an humble petition, extolling to the skies their brave adventures in Ireland in defence of the Protestant Religion (which God knows he is sick of), confessing the unworthy reward the Parliament gave them for that service, desiring to have them excused, promising them, if they would adhere unto them, they should have their arrears undoubtedly, and humbly entreating that it would please them to accept of a parley. It was answered as nobly as men could answer rebels.[3] I will not trouble myself to repeat it, because I believe copies are sent over by this. Well! Sir William receiving a short and flat answer what he was to trust to, and our men denying parley with rebels, he being at Wrexham, and having an army that might have done something with our men, they being newly landed (after six days being at sea many of them), many arms unfixed, many of them disaffected to ourselves, and very many

[1] In one of the old Royalist papers (most probably *Merc. Aulicus*) I have seen the statement that the surplice of Hanmer Church was found in the pocket of one of the Parliamentary soldiers taken prisoner, but I cannot give the reference, having lost or mislaid the note of it.

[2] This unmanly ruse cannot be charged to Brereton or Myddelton's men. It must have been practised by some of the Irish soldiers who had gone over to the other side.

[3] See Document xxxii. ante, pp. 101, 102.

DOCUMENT XXXVI.

A.D. 1643.

straggled among their friends[1] (though now we miss scarce any that came over with us), yet it pleased God to add such fear to him, that, we being many miles from him, for fear the Devil should take the hindmost, he made proclamation through his camp, that no man should stir, on pain of death, till further directions. As soon as that was done, lest he should be jostled at the bridge of Holt, the utmost term of the Welsh border, he most valiantly went over first, and then suffered the rest, routed only by conscience, to follow him. Flushed thus with his miraculous escape, the spirit enlightened him to look back again into Wales (which I believe he will see no more but in a map, or out of Beeston Castle); he commanded that the drawbridge should be broken down, which had been enough to make our men seek another way if they were minded for Cheshire. Which done, our much respected forces ten miles off not yet appearing, he most desperately adventured to see an arch of the great bridge broken down, for the country's good and the liberty of the subject. Good man! he says there is no fighting against us: we are Devils.

I return to Hawarden Castle (though now going a contrary way). The besieged there expected daily succours. Our men knowing the contrary fed them in that expectation to starve them. There were therein about 120 men, being all that was left of Sir Thomas Myddelton's regiment, seditious chaplain and all, except himself. Their necessity was of nothing more than water. It was taken for a miracle that it rained in winter, and they had leads to preserve it; and (which is strange) they were persuaded the water came from heaven. Our men, most part, withdrew to Chester, leaving only two companies of our own, and as I take it, 500 Welshmen to watch them. After eleven, or twelve days at most, they delivered the castle, on condition they should march away with half their arms, one colour, and £25 worth of goods. Which articles were not so well performed as I could have wished; but our men profess they could not help it, but it was the fault of some of the Lord Cholmley's men, who bid them remember Reading. For which fact, they say, Capt. Sandford hewed some of our own side sufficiently, and (which was more than the articles

[1] Allusion to this fact is made by Capt. Sandford in his letter. See Document xxxiv. ante, p. 108.

DOCUMENT XXXVI. A.D. 1643.

required) guarded them out of Wales, where they will have no cause to fear the King's enemies again, we having now garrisons in all the Marches.

Now, if you desire to know what I find by my little experience in Britain of the behaviour of our zealots, I can do no less (if no more) than confirm what you have often heard. All the honest and religious clergy of Wales were fled to Conway and other safe places, till our landing set them at liberty, which was every whit as welcome and seasonable, and even more needful in this than the weakest part of the Kingdom. All the orthodox clergy of Cheshire and Lancashire are either here, or in Yorkshire, or in prison. They say that they have lately seized upon some men that would not publish in their churches that we were Irish rebels. I myself coming into the church of Hawarden the morning after they were there, found the Common Prayer-Book scattered up and down the chancel, and some well read man, without doubt, conceiving that the Common Prayers had been in the beginning of a poor innocent old church bible, tore out almost all Genesis for failing. It stood so dangerously it was suspected to be malignant. In windows where there was oriental glass they broke in pieces only the faces; to be as frugal as they could, they left sometimes the whole bodies of painted bishops, though in their rochets. But if there was anything in the language of the beast, though it was but an *hoc fecit*, or at worst, *orate* &c. (and I but guess, for I could not read it when it was gone), which had stood many years, and might many more, without idolatry, that was dashed out. They had pulled the rails down about the table, and very honestly reared them to the wall (it was well they were in a coal country, where fuel was plentiful), and brought down the table to the midst of the church. Some of our soldiers came and swore it was not right (alas! that we have no better information), and set it close to the east wall again. At Wrexham they say (I was not there) they did the like villany almost in all points, and broke in pieces one of the best pair of organs in the King's dominions, which Sir Thomas Myddelton took for his proper pillage, to make bullets of.[1] I am weary of these truths.

[1] "About 9 Nov., 1643, Sir W. Brereton and his forces came to Faringdon and Holt, and entered through the same, and went to Wrexham

DOCUMENT XXXVI. A.D. 1643.

This day we march out, 4,000 foot at least, and 1,000 horse. We may go where we will for our enemies, if we have God's blessing, which I hope we shall not want, if not for our own for our enemies' sake. One thing I had almost forgot. On Saturday last we received a most gracious letter from his Majesty (which, if I had so much time, I would have sent you, and I hope some good man will), expressing his joy for our landing: his thankfulness for our so honest refusal of the rebels' propositions: his hopes that the time would be he might be more able to reward us for our service in Ireland: his sense of the unworthy desertion of him by the Parliament, from whom he expected better when he trusted them: his fear lest the report that they were Irish rebels might do some harm: his desire that therefore they should express in all places the detestation they have of the odiousness of that rebellion, and that by their constant prayers and sermons they would make men understand what religion they fight for. . . . .

I am, &c.,

HARRY BYRCH.[1]

Chester, at the Red Lyon, Without Eastgate,
December 12, 1643.

Flint and Holywell, and did pull down the organs, defaced the windows in all the churches, and the monuments of divers, and pulled down the arms and hatchments."—Harl. MSS., 2125, fol. 135. All this, however, it should be borne in mind, was done by the authority of an Ordinance of Parliament, by men who conscientiously believed such appendages in a house of worship idolatrous and improper.

[1] Captain Byrch to G. Carr, the Marquis of Ormond's Secretary, in Carte's Collection of Letters concerning the Affairs of England. Lond., 1739. Vol i., p. 29.

DOCUMENTS

ILLUSTRATING TRANSACTIONS

IN THE YEAR 1644.

XXXVII.

An Encounter at Middlewich, resulting in the Victory of the Irish Forces, detailed in a Letter from Sir Robert Byron to the Marquis of Ormond.

DOCUMENT XXXVII.

A.D. 1644.

MAY IT PLEASE YOUR EXCELLENCY,

I doubt not but before this comes to your Excellency's hands you will have heard of the carriage of our business with Sir William Brereton, at Middlewich, on St. Stephen's day; but lest it should suffer any mistake (as it may well do) by such as take it but by report, I think it my duty to give your Excellency this following relation:—

Having made our quarter at Beckley, at a convenient distance from Nantwich, the first business we took was the taking of a church, which after summons, they refusing to surrender, we took, and put all the men to the sword,[1] which hath made the rest love

[1] The church where this cruelty was perpetrated was Barthomley Church, "wherein were divers of the Parliamentary party, which were *most barbarously used and murdered in cold blood.*" This last statement is that of a Royalist, evidently shocked at the atrocities which began now to be perpetrated under the Byrons and the Irish, "so that they prospered not." See Harl. MSS., 2125, fol. 135.

churches the worse ever since. On Christmas-day we rose with the army, upon intelligence that Sir William was drawing to a head at Sandbach, a place famous for strong ale. When we came within a mile and a half of the place, we discovered about 200 horse of theirs, seeming to make a pass good against us. We drew up in order, and as soon as we were ready, advanced towards them, they, instead of making the pass good, drew themselves off and away, and left us their quarter, but not a drop of ale. This night we lodged at Sandbach, and having sent parties of horse abroad to know what was become of the zealous crew, in the morning, notice was brought to us they were all at Middlewich, whither we marched directly. We were but three regiments there, Warren not being yet come up, and Sir Fulke Hunckes's, with a regiment of horse, remained behind for the safety of our quarters and baggage. So Col. Gibson had the van, I the battle, and Sir Michael Ernely the rear. When we came near the town, the enemy were drawn out two musket shots from the town, and had placed themselves in hedges and ditches to as much advantage as could be. Col. Gibson drew upon my left hand, whither I know not. I fell on right before me, where I saw the enemy most busy. I disputed with them an hour and something more, and could not make them budge. All this while I had never a second. At last I discovered a few of Gibson's men coming; at the same instant I was shot. The enemy (it seems) seeing relief coming, quitted and began to run, but gave fire as they went, till they came to the town. There almost 300 of them took sanctuary in the church, the rest ran through the town, where our horse overtook them, and did pretty good execution upon them. And because we would not be hindered in our pursuit of them, we were glad to give quarter to them in the church. There were slain of them about 300 and upwards, prisoners 274. We got good store of exellent good arms, and good store of amunition. There was hurt of my regiment, myself, three captains and a lieutenant, and 41 soldiers, whereof 15 killed outright. Capt. Farrell and his lieutenant died the next day. The whole service of that day fell upon my regiment. I pray God they never do worse than they did then.

For other news, I know your Excellency receives daily advertisements from better pens, and the anguish of my hurt made

DOCUMENT XXXVII. A.D. 1644.

me heedless of [every] thing: this being the first day, I have been able to sit up, which I a little forced myself unto, that I might not seem unthinking in my respects to your Excellency, which I shall ever endeavour to preserve, being by so many obligations due from

Your Excellency's, &c.,

ROBERT BYRON.[1]

Chester, Jan. 9, 1643.

[1] Carte's Collection of Letters, &c. Vol. i, p. 34.

XXXVIII.

A further Protestation by the Royalists of the Counties of Carmarthen, Pembroke, and Cardigan, for the Reduction of the Town and Castle of Pembroke. 11*th January*, 1644.

You have heretofore heard how the whole Principality of Wales was reduced to his Majesty, all except Pembroke Castle, which made a tender to deliver up itself,[1] as we told you in the 43rd week of the last year's *Mercurius*, which being not performed according to promise, the loyal gentry and other inhabitants of the Counties of Carmarthen, Pembroke, and Cardigan, the eleventh day of this month, assembled themselves at Carmarthen, and made this ensuing Protestation:— DOCUMENT XXXVIII. A.D. 1644.

Whereas we, whose names are under-written, having met at the place aforesaid, by the direction of the Right Honourable Richard, Earl of Carbery, Lieutenant-General to his Majesty of the several Counties of Carmarthen, Pembroke, and Cardigan, &c., being sensible of the present danger the said counties now stand in (his Lordship communicating with us the intelligence sent him by letter from one of his Majesty's Secretaries of State, of great forces designed to land and in readiness to enter and invade the said counties in a hostile manner, in no way commissioned by his Majesty, such forces being thereunto more especially encouraged by the present withstanding of his Majesty's authority, now exercised by sundry persons, who, having possessed themselves of the Town and Castle of Pembroke, do in a hostile manner keep the

[1] Which is simply untrue, and existed only in Aulicus's imagination.

DOCUMENT XXXVIII. A.D. 1644.

same, refusing to submit themselves and the said town and castle to his Majesty's government and authority, contrary to the constant and known laws of the land), have solemnly protested, and hereby do, to the best of our power and ability, as well with our estates and persons, and by all other means whatsoever within our power, to withstand, resist, and repulse all such forces, as aforesaid, attempting or acting any such entry and invasion or hostility.

And whereas we are likewise sensible that the condition of the Town and Castle of Pembroke, opposing his Majesty's just authority and the laws of this Kingdom, is not only an encouragement to invite foreign or rebellious forces to enter the said counties and ruin the same; but will, in a great measure, add to and further the pernicious designs of such forces as shall enter or invade these counties, by landing at the Haven at Milford: we conceive it fit that his Lordship, when he shall think it opportune to prevent or redress the said mischiefs, should employ out of the respective counties such number of the trained bands thereof, or such able persons as shall be produced by them, or any of them, to supply their persons in the said service as he shall think requisite for reducing the said Town or Castle of Pembroke to due obedience, and securing the peace of the said counties; and that such forces be quartered and provided for, during the time of such service, by every of the said counties respectively, whereunto such forces, or any part thereof, shall happen to be commanded by his Lordship, to any the purposes aforesaid, during their residence within any of the said counties.

And whereas a greater strength of horse will be requisite for the ends and service aforesaid than usually the said counties were rated unto, we conceive it fit, and accordingly submit, that his Lordship should assess for the purposes aforesaid upon such persons as he shall think fit, of the said respective counties, such proportion of horse, as in his Lordship's judgment shall be answerable to the estate and abilities of the persons assessed, over and above the number of a hundred horse agreed to be already maintained by the said counties. That such horses, to be assessed as aforesaid, and the number of the trained bands before mentioned, be in nowise (excepting in case of present invasion) longer employed in manner aforesaid than until the said Town and Castle of Pembroke shall submit to his Majesty's authority and join in common defence with the said respective counties. DOCUMENT XXXVIII. A.D. 1644.

Fra. Lloyd[1]	W. Lloyd[6]	Lew. Barlow[13]
John Vaughan[2]	Edw. Vaughan[7]	Tho. Warren[14]
William Russell	Lodwick Lewis	Joh. Phillips[15]
David Gwynne[3]	John Vaughan[2]	Thomas Vaughan
John Vaughan[2]	Rich. Vaughan[8]	Ric. Phillipps[16]
Rowland Gwynne[4]	John Stedman[9]	Rich. Pryse[17]
John Harries	Henry Myddelton[10]	James Lewes
Nicholas Williams	John Stepney[11]	Joh. Elliot.[18]
Rice Rudd[5]	Hugh Owen[12]	

1 Probably of Danyrallt, Carm.

2 There are three signatures of John Vaughan to this document; one of them was of Plasgwyn, Carm., and another was of Trawscoed, Card.

3 Glanbran, Carm., H. S. for 1632. 4 Taliaris, Carm., H. S. for 1638.

5 Aberglasney, Bart., H. S. for Carm. 1637.

6 Probably Sir Walter Lloyd, of Llanfair Clydogau.

7 Query Trawscoed, Card. 8 Court Derllys, Carm., H. S. 1631.

9 Llettygariad or Strata Florida, Card.

10 Middleton Hall, Carm. 11 Of Prendergast, Knt. and Bart.

12 Intended for Sir Hugh Owen, of Orielton, but I question he ever signed it.

13 Criswell, Pemb., H. S. for that County 1640.

14 Trewern, Pemb., H. S. 1638. 15 Ffynongain, Pemb., H. S. 1637.

16 Of Picton Castle, Bart. 17 Of Gogerddan, Card., Bart.

18 From *Mercurius Aulicus*, 4th week (Jany. 26th, 1644), p. 796. (K. P. 142—17.)

XXXIX.

The Cavaliers defeated at Ellesmere by Col. Mytton, January 12th.

DOCUMENT XXXIX. A.D. 1644.

In the first place, I shall inform you that the cons[cient]ious and well-affected gentry in Shropshire, seeing the illegal proceedings of the Commissioners of Array, and daily feeling the grand oppressions that ensued therefrom, and being too sensible of the dangers which, like a deluge had overflown not only the most part of that county, but a great part of the Kingdom, some good patriots of them applied themselves to the honourable Houses of Parliament, propounding some remedies of redress, and obtained an order, intrusting some principal of the best affected gentry to be a Committee for the public good of that county,[1] to contribute, contrive, act, and do their best endeavours, as well for the clearing of the said county from their great oppressions, as also (as they saw need and convenient occasion) to assist Sir William Brereton, or any others, their good friends and fellow-sufferers, burdened with like grievances. To which purpose, and in pursuance of the relieving of their poor oppressed countrymen, they made choice of

[1] This Committee was appointed by an Ordinance of Parliament for the association of the Counties of Warwick, Stafford, and Salop, on the 10th April, 1643. The Shropshire Committee, therein nominated, comprised the following :—William Pierpoint, Sir John Corbet, Bart., Sir Gilbert Cornwall, Kt., Sir Morton Brigges, Bart., Richard Moore, Thomas Mytton (the above Col.), Robert Corbet, of Stanwardine in the Wood, Andrew Lloyd (the Master Lloyd mentioned above), Thomas Nichols, Humphrey Mackworth (the Master Mackworth above-named), John Corbet, of Aulston, Launcelot Lee, and Robert Talbot, Esquires, and Samuel Moore, Thomas Hunt (also above-named), Hercules Kinnersley, William Rowley, Thomas Knight, John Proud, and John Lloyd, gentlemen. Of these the Earl of Essex was recommended by the Ordinance to appoint Sir John Corbet to be Col.-General of the Shropshire forces. (K. P. 118—7.) I have not discovered whether he was so appointed or not. Col. Mytton's name figures hereafter as the chief mover for the Parliament in this county.

Wem, a town not far from Shrewsbury, which the enemy was possessed of. This town they began to fortify and garrison, but before they could complete their works, and had not scarce three hundred soldiers, and only Colonel Mytton, a gentleman of quality in that county and of approved courage and fidelity, now chosen high sheriff for that county. He, with Master Mackworth, Master Hunt, and Master Lloyd, three of the best-affected of that committee, and most zealous patriots, did valiantly, courageously, and resolutely defend this town, not then fully fortified against two days' several furious assaults of the Lord Capel and the malignant gentry of several counties, having at least 4,000 soldiers; and with an undaunted fortitude repulsed them, having slain or wounded most of the commanders and officers that led up their men to the assaults, as the enemy themselves then confessed.[1] But you shall see how God blesseth small beginnings that are laid upon good foundations. I will not repeat former actions of this valiant Colonel and garrison (exceeding worthy of a lasting memory); I shall only come to the present narration.

DOCUMENT XXXIX. A.D. 1644.

Lately a ship was sent from Bristol, with arms and ammunition, to furnish the rebels at Chester, and their adherents, the besiegers of Nantwich; but such was the loyalty and faithfulness of the fore-mast men to the good of the King and the Parliament (to their good be it spoken), that they forced the corrupt master and officers to tack about for Liverpool instead of Chester, and furnished the honest Lancashire men instead of the rebels at Chester.

Now, the rebels being thus disappointed and disfurnished, and the inhuman upstart, L. Byron, having besieged Nantwich, sent a strong convoy to Shrewsbury for arms and ammunition, both to supply themselves and Chester. The most vigilant and valiant commander, Col. Mytton, had by his espialls secret knowledge thereof, but prudently and providently made neither motion, nor took any seeming notice of it until they had been at Shrewsbury, where the rebels furnished themselves with eight large barrels of powder, seven hundred weight of match, and other ammunition. In their return they quartered the first night at Ellesmere, eight miles

[1] This was on the 17th and 18th of the preceding October. See Document xxv. ante, p. 86.

DOCUMENT XXXIX. A.D. 1644.

from the garrison of Wem; and within fourteen miles of that garrison four thousand more of the rebels were quartered, which I conceive made the convoy over-confident that the noble Colonel durst not peep beyond his works. But he that very night, being the 12th of this instant [January], with a party of horse and foot, in much silence, marched to Ellesmere, and undescried fell upon the enemy in his quarters, where besides what were slain, took prisoners Sir Nicholas Byron, Governor of Chester, Sir Richard Willis, Serjeant-Major-General of the horse (who once at Winchester, contrary to his engaged faith, made an escape to the Lord Grandison when they were taken by the Parliament's forces), together with his brother Major Willis, Capt. Offley, Capt. Hatton, Capt. Rixam [Dixon in another account], and one other captain, besides a hundred inferior officers and troopers, and two hundred and fifty horse and arms, 30 of these horse being the primest in these parts. He took also all the powder, match, and arms that the said convoy had furnished themselves withal at Shrewsbury, which renders the exploit more famous and of greater consequence, for in all probability the enemy is in want of powder, and if that noble Colonel were but timely furnished and supplied, and his most honourable Major-General competently dispatched and hastened away, those parts would (if the time and season be not neglected) be quickly cleared from those rapines and oppressions wherewith they are now deplorably infested.[1]

[1] From a pamphlet entitled "A True Relation of a notable Surprise and eminent Defeat given to the Rebels at Ellesmere, &c., by that vigilant . . commander . . Col. Mytton, commander-in-chief of the forces in Shropshire, under the Earl of Denbigh. Printed according to order for G. B. and R. W. (January 26, 164¾)." (K. P. 140—9.)

XL.

The Marquis of Ormond to Lord Byron—A further Transport of Forces from Ireland.

DOCUMENT XL. A.D. 1644.

My Lord,

His Majesty's choice of your Lordship to command in those parts, and over those men I had the good fortune to send so seasonably to his service, I find generally approved, and that approbation confirmed by the happy success of your conduct in the defeat of those rebellious forces that before your coming and the arrival of those men, had upon the matter possessed those counties and stricken fear into others. In all this I receive infinite satisfaction, and next to the prosperity of his Majesty's just arms, in nothing more than it hath pleased him to direct my endeavours into a hand that is so like to improve them into his service, and to whom I desire so much to be known by all the particular services and offices of friendship I shall be able to do.

There are some reasons that, notwithstanding the difficulty of providing for more men in those parts, induce me to send you two regiments more of foot and four troops of horse. The foot will not be much above 1,000, and the horse not many more than 160.

. . . . . .

Upon these grounds I shall, with all the speed I can, embark the aforesaid two regiments of foot and four troops of horse—the foot under the command of Col. Broughton and Col. Tylyer, the horse under the charge of Sir William Vaughan;[1] for all which your Lordship will be pleased to provide, as for men in want of all things, and so used to that want, that I doubt not any reasonable provision will satisfy them.[2]

. . . . . .

Your Lordship's most affectionate humble servant,

Dublin, 16th Jan., 164¾. Ormond.[3]

[1] Sir William Vaughan, afterwards commandant at Shrawardine Castle in Shropshire.

[2] They were sent about the beginning of February for Chester, as appears by a Letter from the Marquis to the Mayor of Chester, dated the 3rd February. Harl. MSS., 2135, fol. 8.

[3] Carte's "Life of Ormond." Ed. 1851. Vol. vi., 10.

XLI.

The Siege of Nantwich raised, and the forces that came from Ireland routed by Sir Thomas Fairfax and Brereton, January 25.

A.

Sir Thomas Fairfax's Account to the Earl of Essex.

DOCUMENT XLI. A. A.D. 1644.

MAY IT PLEASE YOUR EXCELLENCY,

I desire your pardon that I have not given your Excellency an account before this of the great mercy God hath showed in giving us a happy victory over the Irish army, to a total ruin of the foot and purchase of their chief commanders.

Upon the 21st of January I marched from Manchester to Nantwich, to relieve the town, with 2,500 foot and 28 troops of horse. The enemies' forces were above 3,000 foot and 1,800 horse. The first encounter we had was with a party of theirs in the Forest of Delamere, where about 30 were taken prisoners. About six miles further they maintained a pass against us, with about 200 men. I caused some foot and dragoons to be drawn out to force it, which, by God's assistance, they did in half-an-hour's space, and they took a major and some prisoners. Having advanced two miles further, we found a body of them in Acton Church, a mile from Nantwich. We drew up within cannon shot, which sometimes played upon us, but without hurt, God be thanked. We then understood that the Lord Byron, who had besieged the town on both sides of the river, was prevented, by overflowing of the water, from joining with that party at Acton Church; but heard that he was taking a compass to get over the river to join with it. We resolved to fall upon that party at the church before he should get up to it; but staying to bring up our rear and carriages, we gave him time to obtain what he sought for. Then we resolved to make way with pioneers through the hedges, and so to march to the town to relieve it; and by it, to add some more forces to ourselves, to enable us better to fight with them. But being a little advanced in our march, they told me the enemy was close upon the rear. So having about two regiments, being Col. Holland's and Col. Booth's, I marched not far before I came to be engaged with the greatest part of their army. The other part presently after assaulted our front. Then Sir William Brereton and Col. Ashton did very good service, and so did Col. Lambert and Major Copley with the horse. They were once in great danger, but that they being next to the town were assisted by forces which came to their succour in due time. We, in the other wing, were in as great distress, but that the horse, commanded by Sir Wm. Fairfax, did expose themselves to great danger to encourage the foot, though capable of little service in these narrow lanes. Yet, it pleased God, after two hours of hot fighting, they were forced by both wings to retreat to the church,[1] where they were caught as in a trap. A list of what we took I have here sent your Excellency.

DOCUMENT XLI. A.

A.D. 1614.

Thus the Lord of Hosts hath done great things for us, to whose name alone be ascribed all the glory—that nothing in the worthless creature may in anywise darken that which immediately appears herein of the Creator. Hoping still He will go along with us to prosper in this way, and make me, though unworthy, more capable to serve Him in it, and so to observe your Excellency's commands, as it may appear how much I am

Your Excellency's most humble servant,

THO. FAIRFAX.

Nantwich, Jan. 29, 1643.

The List of Prisoners taken.

Major-General Gibson.	Sir Ralph Done.
Sir Michael Ernely.	Major Hammond.
Sir Richard Fleetwood.	14 Captains.
Col. George Monk.	20 Lieutenants.
Col. Warren.	26 Ensigns.
Sir Francis Butten, Lieut.-Col.	2 Cornets.

[1] ActonCh urch.

DOCUMENT XLI. A.

A.D. 1644.

2 Quarter-Masters.
Mr. Sherlock, Chaplain to a Regiment.
41 Serjeants.
40 Drummers.
4 Canoneers.
22 Colours.
1,500 common Soldiers.
6 Ordnance, whereof five Brass.
20 Carriages and divers Wagons.
120 Women that followed the Camp; of whom many had long knives, with which they were said to have done mischief.[1]

B

Lord Byron's Account of it to the Marquis of Ormond.

DOCUMENT XLI. B.

A.D. 1644.

MY LORD,

By your Excellency's letter of the 16th of this month, I perceive that none of mine (except the first, which was written in great haste), are come to your Excellency's hands. In them I gave a larger account of what had passed in this army, but fear they are miscarried. It hath pleased God of late so to turn the tide of our good fortune here, that I cannot continue a relation in the same style; but however it be not pleasing, I am sure it is expedient I should faithfully relate to your Excellency as well our ill as our good success.

After the defeat we had given the rebels at Middlewich,[2] and that we had taken in two strong houses[3] possessed by them near Nantwich, it was thought fit that we should draw nearer the town and block it up, finding it to be of that importance, that unless we were masters of that town we could not assure ourselves of anything in the country. Within a few days after, some letters were intercepted from Sir Thomas Fairfax (who was then in Lanca-

[1] Rushworth, pt. iii., vol. ii., 302. A full account of the proceedings before Nantwich is given in a pamphlet, entitled "*Magnalia Dei*—a Relation of some of the remarkable passages in Cheshire before the Siege of Nantwich, &c." (K. P. 141—13.) There the names of the inferior officers are all given.

[2] See ante, p. 116.

[3] Crew Hall and Darfold Hall.

shire with 30 troops of horse) to Brereton, wherein he assured him to assist him with all that force, and to bring the foot of Staffordshire along with him to join with those of Lancashire. Whereupon I acquainted my Lord of Newcastle with the design, and desired him (his army then lying that way) to prevent Fairfax's march; which, if he had done, the town had within a few days been delivered up to me. But his occasions drawing him back to Yorkshire, Fairfax immediately advanced into Staffordshire, and being come as far as Newcastle with a good part of his horse, lest he should draw the foot of that county together, I immediately rose with almost all the horse I had, and a party of commanded musketeers, and fell into his quarter, not being above eight miles from me, took an hundred of his horse, with their colours and officers, killed and hurt as many more, and drove the rest away in such confusion that they rested not till they came into Lancashire, where they stayed some time ere Brereton could persuade any of that country to join with him. But at length, finding themselves secure from my Lord of Newcastle, and that the loss of Nantwich would make us absolute masters of Cheshire and thereby endanger Lancashire, the forces of that country were persuaded to join with Fairfax and Brereton, to the number of above 2,000 foot, besides a rabble of cudgellers, and immediately marched towards us.

So soon as I had intelligence of their approach (which in this ill-affected country I could never procure but by parties of horse, which I sent forth) it was resolved we should rise and fight with them, being equal with them in horse, and not far inferior in foot, as having 1,500 to meet their 2,000; withal our men being much impaired by sickness and hurt, and not a few run away. It fell out, unfortunately, that the night before we fought with them a small river[1] that ran betwixt our quarters swelled so upon the falling of rain and melting of snow, that one part of the army was forced to march six miles before it could join with the other; before which time the enemy had gained a pass upon us where we thought to have stopped him. Nevertheless, Col. Gibson, who had the ordering of the field as Major-General, in regard of Sir Michael Ernely's infirmity, was confident we had advantage

[1] The Weaver.

DOCUMENT XLI. B.

A.D. 1644.

enough over them, and Col. Monk[1] being at the same time come from Prince Rupert with a commission to raise a regiment, added great alacrity to the soldiers, especially Col. Warren's, with whom he marched as a volunteer. The place of the battle was in an enclosed field, where horse could do little service, and not above a mile from Nantwich; which I forewarned the Major-General of, and desired especial care might be taken lest we should receive prejudice by any sally out of the town, which he had assured me he had done. His own regiment had the right wing; my brother's the left; Warren's and Sir Michael Ernely's the battle; Hunke's regiment was to wait upon them that should attempt to sally out of the town.

At the first encounter we had much the better of them, both our wings clearly beating both theirs, and were possessed of many of their colours; and had given them a total defeat had not Col. Warren's men and Sir M. Ernely's at the same time (notwithstanding all the endeavours of their officers) retreated without almost fighting a stroke; so that the enemy's battle fell into the flanks of both our wings, and at the same time the enemy sallied out of the town with at least 600 men, and possessed themselves of a churchyard,[2] where all our carriages stood. Most of the officers retreated into the church, were they were all taken prisoners. Only my brother's regiment had the good fortune to bring off their colours with very little loss,[3] only Sir Francis Butler was taken by a mistake of the enemy's colours for his own. The ground was so enclosed the horse could do no service, and some of them, who were struck with a panic fear, so disordered the rest, that though they did not run away, yet it was impossible to make them charge. I staid above two hours after all the business of the foot was done, to try if anything could be done for the recovery of the cannon and carriages; but all was in vain. So that I was forced to retreat to Chester with what foot I could gather together of several

[1] This was no other than the afterwards famous General Monk—the chief instrument of Charles the Second's restoration. He and Col. Warren were taken prisoners here and sent up to London. Both were committed to the Tower; but Monk soon after accepted a Commission under the Parliament.

[2] Acton Churchyard.

[3] See the next letter.

regiments, which were betwixt 1,000 and 1,200, where now we are in a sad condition, the enemy braving us to the gates of the city, though with our horse we have hitherto beaten them back with loss to themselves.

DOCUMENT XLI. B. A.D. 1644.

All the comfort we have is the recruit that your E. is sending; but truly, my lord, the enemy is grown so strong upon their late success that without a larger supply we shall be able to do little good, and I could wish they were rather Irish than English, for the English we have already are very mutinous, and being for the most part these countrymen, are so poisoned by the ill-affected people here that they grow very cold in this service. And since the rebels here called in the Scots I know no reason why the King should make any scruple of calling in the Irish, or the Turks, if they would serve him. But this I shall humbly submit to your E.'s better judgment.

There is one Capt. Maynard who has offered his services very opportunely, and if it may stand with your E.'s good liking, will bring over a regiment for me. I shall desire your favour and assistance in it. As for the powder your E. sends I shall take care that either money or provision be returned for it; which I hope will be equivalent. There is nothing I am more ambitious of than your E.'s favour and good opinion, which, though my present misfortunes make me unworthy of, yet I hope they will not so far lessen me in your esteem, but that I may still be honoured with the reputation of being

Your Excellency's, &c.,

JOHN BYRON.[1]

Chester, Jan. 30, 1644.

C.

Sir Robert Byron's Letter to Ormond narrating their Defeat.

MAY IT PLEASE YOUR EXCELLENCY,

DOCUMENT XLI. C. A.D. 1644.

I gave your E. an account of our business at Middlewich, by a letter which I sent accompanied with one from my brother, which it seems was not come to your Excellency's hands.

[1] Carte's "Collection of Letters." Ed. 1739. Vol. i., p. 36.

DOCUMENT XLI. C.
A.D. 1644.

Since that day's good fortune our whole actions have been nothing but disasters. It began with my uncle Byron's surprizal coming from Shrewsbury to the army in company of Sir Richard Willis (who had the command of 400 horse), to convoy some ammunition to the army, quartering within four miles of Wem, a small garrison of the enemy's; they, with 120 horse and as many foot, seized upon them before any alarm was given, some of the officers got off and about 200 of the horse; the rest were all made prisoners.[1]

In the neck of this we received another great loss by storming the town; which being generally agreed upon by a Council of War, was accordingly put in execution. Some of the regiments did very gallantly, and not only entered their works, but my Lieut.-Col., with some of my regiment, got within the town; but for want of seconds, the enemy being very strong within, were forced to retreat to our great loss. Upon this service we lost Lieut.-Col. Boughton and Sandford,[2] with four captains more, many lieutenants and ensigns slain, and divers captains and other officers wounded—of soldiers hurt and slain, 400.

These were great losses, yet such as we were in hope in a short time to recover again. For all this ill-fortune our soldiers retained their courage still, which gave encouragement to the continuance of the siege, whilst the enemy left no way untried to enable themselves for the relief of the town. And on Thursday last Sir Thomas Fairfax, who was come to their relief with six regiments of foot, and some 1,200 horse, advanced where we had taken our ground. To oppose him our army was drawn in several enclosures, there our horse (which we were superior in) could do no good, nor we help one another, by reason of the great distance from one another. Yet Gibson's regiment and mine held them in very good play and lost nothing by them. Warren's regiment, though they had their beloved Col. Monk in the head of them, was no sooner charged but they broke, and being rallied

[1] See Document xxxix. ante, p. 122.

[2] This was "big letter" Sandford. He and Boughton were killed in scaling the mud-walls. Their bodies were brought to Chester, and with others deposited in one grave in the "great aisle of St. Wyburgh's." Harl. MSS., 2125, fol. 125.

DOCUMENT XLI. C.

A.D. 1644.

again, the next charge ran quite away. Some say they played foul-play and ran over to the enemy, at least 60 of them, and fired upon us. By this time they in the town had got 1,000 musketeers ready to fall out upon us. There was a bridge betwixt us and them, which they must pass. There, instead of 400 men my brother had appointed to make that pass good, Col. Gibson had appointed but 100, who were quickly beaten off and left the passage. Being over, the next regiment was Sir Michael Ernely's, who stood not long to dispute with them; but broke and ran. All this while Gibson's regiment and mine held entire, till being overcharged on all sides with horse and foot, were forced every man to shift for himself as well as he could. It was now high time for my men to think of a retreat, which they did against two regiments of the enemy, that pursued them, keeping them off with fire in the rear till they recovered the horse which secured them. Frank Butler was unfortunately taken in the coming off, by mistaking a regiment of theirs, thinking it had been ours. We lost all our artillery, munition and baggage, all our colonels taken prisoners, and most of the rest of the officers. We have rallied again of the soldiers about 1,300, and I believe many are yet straggling in the country.

We hear many of the soldiers taken prisoners, especially of Warren's, have taken conditions with them. Thus your Excellency sees what a desperate condition this country is in; which wholly relies upon such supplies as your Excellency shall think fit for our relief.

I rest, &c.,

Robt. Byron.[1]

Chester, this last of Jan., 1644.

[1] Carte's "Collection of Letters," vol. i., p. 40.

XLII.

Prince Rupert appointed to command in Shropshire, Cheshire, and North Wales.

A.

His Letter to Sir Francis Ottley, Governor of Shrewsbury.

DOCUMENT XLII. A.

A.D. 1644.

SIR,

His Majesty is pleased to entrust to my care his army in Shropshire and the countries adjacent, together with his interests there. In which command I cannot, but with very much apprehension, think upon Shrewsbury, [which is] in your government, and the safety thereof; especially, since I understand of a late design for the betraying thereof to the enemy, which you had divers persons in prison for; but I do not hear they are brought to justice by any proceeding against them, so that the punishment may go to some the example and terror to all. I must strictly require from you an account of that place, which is the head-quarter of those countries, and where I intend to make my own residence during the time of my stay in that command; and therefore must recommend to you the particulars following, and require you to call together the gentlemen and townsmen to assist you in such charges as will be requisite for the covering the castle of Shrewsbury, and the dividing and disposing thereof into rooms capable and fitting to receive the stores; so as such ammunition as from time to time shall be sent into those parts for his Majesty's service there may lie dry and safe. I desire this be done with all possible speed, for I have this day sent away fifty barrels of powder to begin your stores. Other proportions of that and all other kind of ammunition will be speedily brought thither, and for the better security of the stores which are the sinews of the King's business, I pray you, by the advice of Sir John

Mennes, to consider of an accommodation for such as shall be the guard of that place, by erecting of a court of guard and huts for the soldiers, for such number of men and in such manner as you and Sir John Mennes, shall think best, for his Majesty's service. I have no more to say to you at present, but shall willingly receive your letters, from time to time, concerning your affairs, and you shall be sure of all possible assistance and encouragement from me

DOCUMENT XLII. A. A.D. 1644.

Your very loving friend,

RUPERT.[1]

Oxon., 25th January, 1644.

B.

Sir Francis Ottley to Prince Rupert.

MAY IT PLEASE YOUR HIGHNESS,

DOCUMENT XLII. B. A.D. 1644.

Our country is heartily glad that his Majesty has entrusted the care of our county into your hands. I shall be obedient to perform your commands. All things shall be performed with all expedition, so far forth as the time will permit, against your Highness's coming. Justice hath been executed, and one of the corporals under my command hanged for neglect of duty in his place that night as the enemy approached. The huts and the court of guard shall be ready before your Highness's coming. There is one other condemned, but judgement is deferred till your Highness's coming hither. Our hearts do long for your presence to settle the distractions and complaints against us. I rest your servant, ready upon all occasions humbly to serve you,

FRANCIS OTTLEY.

Shrewsbury, this last day of January, 1644.[2]

[1] Owen and Blakeway's "Shrewsbury," vol. i.

[2] Warburton's "Prince Rupert," vol. ii., p. 368.

XLIII.

The State of Shrewsbury in February, great want of Money, and of the sending thither of forces from Chester, the latter place not being able to provide for them.

A.

Sir John Mennes to Prince Rupert.

DOCUMENT XLIII. A.

A.D. 1644.

But for my part I can do his Majesty no service here at all, being made useless by the insulting people who now tell us their power, and that three of the Commissioners of Array may question the best of us, from which power good Lord deliver me, and rather send me home from constable to constable to the parish I was born in. I have not heard from my Lord Byron since his loss, but by a letter written to the high sheriff and governor, which in effect bids us be careful of ourselves, as he will be of those parts, for that the gentlemen are somewhat troubled that they can expect no help from him. Money is a thing not spoken, neither do I perceive your Highness's last letter prevail at all with them. More than yesterday night they first proffered to give every troop 6d., and after some dispute they would have made it up to 12d., if it would have been received. I must crave your Highness's pardon if I quit the place, for I have not wherewithal to subsist any longer, having received but £22 now in eleven months, and lived upon my own without free quarters for horse or man. The fortune I have is all in the rebels' hands, or in such tenants as have forgot to pay. The ammunition is not as yet come from Worcester that I can hear of. This inclosed was sent me from Stafford, whence I hear they intend to draw more force this way from Coventry, which will soon make the neuters of these parts declare themselves, and I fear startle some that have been accounted friends. I hope your Highness will pardon this long scribble from the humblest of your servants,

JOHN MENNES.[1]

Hebb, two in the afternoon.

[1] Warburton's "Rupert," vol. ii., p. 371 n.

B.

MAY IT PLEASE YOUR HIGHNESS, DOCUMENT XLIII. B. A.D. 1644.

I have just now received a letter from my Lord Byron, which tells me that 1,700 foot are landed out of Ireland, under the command of Tillier and Broughton.[1] I hear his lordship intends to send hither, because they cannot make provision there. I shall endeavour here to make what shift I can to assist them, which must be in providing victuals, for money is a thing we hear not of. If your Highness be pleased to write to the high sheriff to command him to bespeak hose and shoes for them, I know that may be readily done, or any other thing that is not ready money. We have here about five hundred suits of clothes, which I have stayed for your Highness. They should have been sent to Chester, but their own clothes were good enough to run to the enemy. The rebels have forgot their late victory, and reassume their wonted fears and jealousies, which I hope will continue to their confusion, which I am sure will be much hastened by your Highness's presence, which we all greedily expect, though none more than

Your Highness's most humble Servant,

JOHN MENNES.[2]

Salop, Feb. 10th.

The foot will be here within five days.

[1] See Document xl. ante., p. 124.

[2] Warburton's "Prince Rupert," vol. ii., p. 374.

XLIV.

Parliamentary Party in Cheshire—An Intercepted Letter from Sir Thomas Fairfax to the Earl of Essex.

DOCUMENT XLIV.

A.D. 1644.

May it please your Excellency,

. . . .

I must confess I find the forces of Cheshire rise slowly, and a remissness in the gentry that are not active in the work. I hear Prince Rupert is raising some forces in Shropshire and shortly in Wales. Some Irish forces are newly landed, divers we hear are cast away. The work of Cheshire, for which your Excellency's commands were upon me, being through the mercy of God thus far despatched, I shall humbly desire your Excellency now to remand Sir William Brereton and Sir Thomas Myddelton, with their forces, to manage the rest of the business here, I being ordered by my father[1] to march into Yorkshire, thus hoping that I shall be able to render as good an account to your Excellency of my service there as by my stay here; and leaving these counties in so good a condition to defend themselves, if the gentlemen aforenamed be sent down. I humbly take leave, and rest

Your Excellency's most humble servant,

T. Fairfax.[2]

Manchester, 24th February, 164¾.

[1] Ferdinand's "Lord Fairfax."

[2] Warburton's "Prince Rupert," vol. ii., p. 38.

XLV.

The Lukewarmness of the Monmouthshire People to the King's cause—Capt. Dabridgecourt to Prince Rupert.

DOCUMENT XLV. A.D. 1644.

MAY IT PLEASE YOUR HIGHNESS,

I am very sorry I should be so unfortunate, these being the first commands you were pleased to honour me withal, as not to be able to perform them with that speed you expected; if your Highness shall be pleased to command me to the Turk, or Jew, or Gentile, I will go on my bare feet to serve you; but from the Welsh, good Lord deliver me. And I shall beseech you to send me no more into this country, if you intend I shall do you any service, without a strong party to compel them, not to entreat them. And then I will give them cause to put me into their Litany, as they have now given me cause to put them into mine. The ammunition hath been here these seven days for want of carriages, and I fear shall stay seven more unless I have some power to force the people. They value neither Sir John Winter, his warrants, nor mine, nor any. Some say they will not come; the rest come not and say nothing. All generally disaffected, and the force that is in Chepstow not able to compel them. I have sent to Colonel Holbye for what horse he hath; if they come to me I will try what may be done. Here be two or three constables deserve hanging, and I had done it ere this if I had but a party to defend me from their Welsh bills. I beseech you let me receive your commands that you may have no occasion to blame him who is, and ever will be,

Your Highness's humble servant,

THOMAS DABRIDGECOURT.

St. Pere, March 11th.

P.S.—Colonel Kirke writes on the 10th from Bridgenorth that Tuesday, the 14th, is a day on which cattle are usually driven out from Wales into the enemy's garrisons into Staffordshire, which he shall stop until he has command from the Prince.[1]

[1] Warburton's "Rupert," vol. ii., p. 385.

XLVI.

Great Successes of the Parliament Forces in Pembrokeshire, under Col. Laugharne, aided by Sea Forces under Vice-Admiral Swanley—Defeat of the Earl of Carbery—Haverfordwest, Tenby, Carew, Stackpool, and other places taken from the Royalists.

A.

Simon Thelwall's Letter to the Speaker of the House of Commons.

DOCUMENT XLVI. A. A.D. 1644.

For the Honourable William Lenthall, Esquire, Speaker of the Honourable House of Commons, now assembled in Parliament.

Sir,

Since I departed at Wrexham from my Major-General Sir Thomas Myddelton, being foreclosed towards Wem by Lord Byron's forces, and towards Nantwich by the Irish, and having knowledge both passages to be laid for me; it pleased God, I repaired about ten days before Christmas, through some difficulties, to the good town of Pembroke, which I then found environed almost on every side with adverse garrisons, under command of the Lord Carbery, who, confident in his party, great in respect of the small work that did resist him, did, sometimes without terror, and sometimes with fair plausible words, leave no means or opportunities unessayed, that might probably work the gentry there to a perfection. But I must be just to them in publishing to their much praise and honour, that after they had been publicly proclaimed traitors in the County Court, and in greatest, almost inevitable, extremities and danger, he could never prevail upon them in the least degree; wherupon, after he had garrisoned Tenby and Haverfordwest towns, with Carew and Roach Castles, he sent for ships to Bristol, which came to him with ordnance and other provisions wherewith to fortify Milford Harbour; for which performance he had brought with him from Oxford one Captain Richard Steel, a great talker, who pretended much to be an engineer. His purpose in this (which before had received mature consultation at Court) was conceived (by the concurrent conjecture of your friends that were likely to be distressed thereby), first to make good a very convenient landing place for Ireland, and there to interrupt any Parliament force that should come for the relief of Pembroke, whose security and support consisted merely in their expectation from sea. It pleased God to prevent this design, and certainly their success herein would have proved exceedingly pernicious to the State, because you have no harbour between that and Plymouth; and, consequently, the Irish (besides their landing place) had been much advantaged at and about their own home, when your great ships will not adventure long to ride, where they have not a place of refuge both to avoid the fury of storms and to supply themselves with necessaries. The gentry thereabouts (who are resolved to live and die in the cause you have undertaken) have commanded me, in their behalf, to beg your vigilant care and protection of that harbour, as a matter more important to the common, than their own particular safety.

The only notable exploits the Bristol ships performed was the surprisal of a little ship of Captain Poyer, our trusty and careful Mayor, fitted with eight pieces of ordnance and suitable accommodation for voyage to the Downs, to acquaint my Lord Admiral with the distress of those parts, and to implore aid. Within a little after Colonel Rowland Laugharne, the chief commander there, whose performances were ever ushered on with diligence and resolution (even when the enemy were in their high vapourings and insultings after their great conquest of the little ship), marched out with his troop and a few foot towards Carew Castle, two miles distant from Pembroke, where presently sallied out the Captain with his musketeers, on whom the Colonel (his company of horse and foot being then too much dispersed) charged, accompanied with seven horse only, and so effectually, that he routed all and took twenty with their arms, including the Lieutenant, whose name was Jones, who has since taken the covenant, and showed himself a gentleman, in faithful good service, at the taking of Tenby. This success was the

DOCUMENT XLVI. A. A.D. 1644. more remarkable because it was achieved between two garrisons of the enemy, not much more distant from each other than musket shot.

It pleased God within a small time after (where a daily siege was threatened) to send in the Parliament fleet under the command of Captain Swanley, Admiral, in the *Leopard Regis*, and Captain Smith, Vice-Admiral, in the *Swallow*, who being presently boarded by the Colonel, and next day by the Mayor, cheerfully promised all assistance necessary for the relief of the town, being commissioned so to do by my Lord Admiral, which afterwards they did really perform. The noise of their guns frightened the Bristol ships, the *Globe*, the *Providence*, with other small barques they had taken into a creek of the harbour, called the Pill, where they lay a great while impounded; for whose defence, and likewise for the annoyance of our fleet, Sir Henry Vaughan (the instrument of much mischief to those counties under his command), erects a strong fort and therein plants the two whole culverins, two demy culverins, two sacres, two minions, that were sent on purpose for fortification of the harbour, and likewise other proper ordnance of the ships, for security of which my Lord Carbery (as we were credibly informed) entered into a bond of ten thousand pounds to Sir John Pennington. These shot first at the fleet (a part of our nation's chief glory and strength), then the fleet mutually upon them, so that they were every day in constant agitation.

In the interim Colonel Laugharne borrowed from the Admiral and Vice-Admiral between seven and eight score men, under command of one Captain Whittey—a gentleman that in the ensuing action acted his part very well, and with these and his proper force, with some ordnance and necessary provision the Mayor furnished out of the castle, he assaulted a strong house of one Lort, a private gentleman [Stackpool], garrisoned for the King, which it pleased God to put into his hands with the loss of two men only. He rested not on this, but doubled the advantage of the success by the seasonable assailing (while men were busied with various cogitations of so sudden a victory) of another house, garrisoned by the enemy named Trefloyne, within a mile of Tenby, then the place of Lord Carbery's residence, who attempted a sally, but was over-awed with our horse and retreated, so that the house,

DOCUMENT XLVI. A.

A.D. 1644.

after some battery of it and firing of an out-house, was delivered up, on quarter of life and liberty to the besieged. There was found there forty good horses ready saddled and bridled, and one hundred arms. The conditions articled were generously performed by the Colonel, which deservedly improved both his and his men's reputation, that did no way violate their commander's promise. After this, without delay, it was debated whether the next attempt should be made on Carew and Tenby on the east side, or on the other side of the country on the fort at Pill and Haverfordwest, and it was resolved, in regard a repulse from either would be equally prejudicial, the first trial should be made on that place, the conquest whereof would produce the best advantage, and that was conceived to be Pill; whereupon the little army, consisting of about 250 foot, half seamen, part whereof under the command of Captain Richard Willoughby, and half landmen, with sixty horse, a demy-culverin, with a sacre, and five small field pieces, made a resolute adventure over the water, animated and encouraged by the presence of a good hearty old gentleman, Mr. John Laugharne, Colonel Laugharne's father, who had long before left his country habitation [St. Brides], and with his whole family, a few servants excepted, betaken himself to the Town of Pembroke. His interest and fair noble carriage had always engaged unto him the affections of many in that part of the country we were to set upon, called Roose. It was God's will our landing was not interrupted, and our horse immediately dispersing abroad to bring in men, cattle, and other necessaries to draw our carriages, found the country willing and ready; which so expedited the work that the demy-culverin and sacre were early in the evening planted in a hedge that within a short distance overlooked the fort, and presently played effectually upon it. Hereupon twenty musketeers were placed in Stainton, a steeple seated on a hill, that oversees most of that country, and thereabouts the horse presently ranged, to hinder correspondence between the Pill and Haverfordwest, and took some straggling soldiers and some messengers, and put them in the church. We saw no body of the enemy till a little before night. Sir Francis Lloyd, with about sixty horse and some foot, descended a hill from Johnson, but they being, as we conceived, afraid of our artillery, never touched the ascent of Stainton, where our horse were drawn, but

DOCUMENT XLVI. A.

A.D. 1644.

retreated to Haverford. Nothing worth report happened that night. Next morning very early the Colonel draws horse and foot towards an ambuscade the enemy had placed in a hedge a little distance on Stainton side from Pill, and having divided ourselves into three parts, the horse furiously and disorderly charged upon them, and routed the whole, took the officers and most of the soldiers—the rest fled into the fort; hereupon, we presently possessed the Pill village, and the ruins of an old chapel that stands above the fort within a stone's cast thereof. Upon this near approach to the sea, a demy-cannon of ours planted on the other side of the water, just opposite Pill fort, which that morning and the evening before had thundered incessantly, for fear of annoying us, grew silent. In the interim, while we were in preparation for a violent assault, the gentlemen in the fort hanged out a flag of truce, by which they obtained quarter, in rendering us possession of the fort, and themselves prisoners. There were taken there Mr. John Barlow, Master of the Ordnance, with five captains, and their inferior officers, 18 great ordnance, with six excellent field carriages, four whereof had been formerly employed against Gloucester, 300 common soldiers with their arms, the two Bristol ships, with the forementioned barques, wherein were 12 pieces of ordnance, and six barrels of powder. The news of the loss of this invincible fort was quickly at Haverford, where the great commanders, something amazed, presently called a council, and therein, as appeared by the event, resolved nothing but a full purpose on our nearer approach to run away. It seemed everything appeared to them in the shape of an enemy, so they ran away most disorderly in the beginning of the night, when nothing could occasion it, except a head of cattle that (perhaps a little frighted with the noise of guns) fled together on the top of a hill near the town; for Colonel Laugharne and the rest were settling the affairs of Pill, and desirous to confer with the Admiral and Vice-Admiral before their departure thence. Those of note that thus posted away were Sir Henry Vaughan, Major-General, Sir John Stepney, Governor of the Town, Sir Francis Lloyd (as we understood), Commander-in-Chief of the House, Lieut.-Colonel Butler, High Sheriff of the County, with two or three captains more. Colonel Laugharne succeeded them betimes next morning at Haverford, where they had left him

DOCUMENT XLVI. A.

A.D. 1644.

provision of some arms, meat, fire, and clothes, for his soldiers. I must not omit their most uncivil and ungentle usage of Sir Hugh Owen, still detained a prisoner (because he submitted not to those extremities proposed to him), contrary to the protestations and execrations of Lord Carbery. He was unbreasted and in his pantables, preparing for bed, at Haverford, when Sir Henry Vaughan, and another man with a mountier drawn over his face, takes him by the shoulders, and calling him "dissembling traitor"; some musketeers having presented their muskets at him, compelled him down stairs, and then on horseback, not permitting him time to put on his boots, nor his virtuous lady (a character justified in her pious resolution to share hand, fortune, and declines with her husband) suffered to have a pillion to ride upon behind him. All that I will say of this action is, that cowardice had totally and absolutely dispossessed their humanity. They stayed but little on their way, and were early next day at Carmarthen.

Within two days Roach Castle, about two miles distant from Haverford, and a very considerable stronghold, had it water, was summoned, and delivered. By this time, that part of the county being clear, our forces were withdrawn for Pembroke; and thence (having borrowed from the Admiral a brass demy-cannon, his master-gunner, with powder and other necessaries) we went for Tenby, whither, two or three days before, the High Sheriff with 80 men had repaired. There was come to this place about by sea, the Vice-Admiral in the *Swallow*, and Captain Gettensby in the *Prosperous*, with the *Crescent Frigate*. We shot very thick upon the town before the land forces appeared, our carriages being very heavy; who, so soon as they had arrived, placed their demy-cannon on a hill within musket shot, a demy-culverin within half a musket shot, the small field pieces being set to scour the guard-wings and hedges lined by the enemy; our footmen having also drawn down, and gained hedges and a good strong house within pistol shot. There continued, in this posture, hot pelting between the small shot from Thursday, two of the clock, till Saturday evening, during which space the sea, but especially the land, had shaked and battered many houses in the town, and done some execution on the men; but had not all this while impaired the town wall, except only the most necessary part

DOCUMENT XLVI. A.

A.D. 1644.

thereof, the great gate, our only place of entrance. This the Governor, Commissary Gwynne (who in his actions showed the metal and experience of a soldier), had strengthened with dung and rubbish, that grew hard and well compact, and on the outside had placed common baskets so close that a single man could but hale himself between them into a little wicket of the gate. Now all this while our forces, horse and foot, having quartered night and day in the fields, which course, if longer continued, might probably have discouraged the seamen, who are best at a hot and sudden action, the Colonel having consulted with the other officers and gentlemen present, resolved, in God's name, to adventure the storming of it that day, and all things prepared accordingly. The foot drew down and beat the enemy from their hedges, and quickly broke open a turnpike in the entrance of the suburbs; whereupon immediately advanced the horse, who with their proper noise, the noise of trumpets and the acclamations of our foot (who were good firemen, and secured their passage from annoyance out of windows), made the enemy, after about an hour's resistance, abandon the gate, when presently enters in the foot, and even as soon as they, the troop (wherein charged many gentlemen of quality, having alighted from their horseback) entered likewise. The prisoners taken of note were Commissary Gwynne, Colonel David Gwynne, the High Sheriff, Lieut.-Col. Butler, Captain George Lewis, and Captain Metholl, with their inferior officers; near upon 300 common soldiers, with their arms; so many ordnance there, at Haverford, Trefloyne, and after, at Carew, as made up the former number between fifty and sixty.

There were four accidents observed, that happened that morning very conducible to this great victory. First there was a breastwork of stone and lime within a small distance of the gate, on the outside thereof, wherein was an exceeding strong door, shot open with our ordnance; then their gunner, who was a good encourager to them, going to discharge his piece loaden with case-shot at our full body, already entered the suburbs, was shot dead. The third was the shooting in pieces the wicket of the Great Gate, through which all our men were obliged to enter one by one. And lastly, and of most efficacy, was the shooting of the Governor, with small shot, so dangerously that he was necessitated to retire, which gave very much discouragement to his soldiers. He is since dead.

The next business was the delivery up of Carew Castle (which was the only remaining garrison the enemy then had in Pembrokeshire), a very strong place, to the Mayor of Pembroke, to the use of and behoof of the gentry entrusted there by Parliament, on condition the officers to march away with their swords, and the common soldiers with their muskets and bags, and baggage, which was worth but little, God knows. By this time, which was cleansing week, the first week in Lent, the whole county was cleared of the malignant party that had long infested and almost ruined it. Those of the prisoners that took the covenant were entertained, others of the weaker sort, to the number of 200 and upwards, discharged and sent home, and some of the most refractory still detained prisoners.

The worthy gentlemen that were all this while mutually aiding and assisting each other both in action and counsel were Colonel Rowland Laugharne, Arthur Owen, Esquire, one of the Commissioners of the Militia, Captain Poyer, Mayor of Pembroke, Captain Rice Powell, a well experienced soldier that came from Ireland to endeavour the relief, and not like many other, the destruction of his bleeding country, Major Thomas Laugharne, Captain Walter Cuney, an honest real gentleman, Rowland Wogan, Lieutenant of the Horse, son to the worthy Commonwealth's man, Master John Wogan, of Wiston, and Captain John Powell. There was a gentleman likewise, one Master Gunter, that sustained much loss by plunder, and for his better defence maintained a constant garrison at a house of his Excellency's my Lord of Essex, near Carew. These were the men that were industrious on all opportunities to advance the cause, and had so far engaged themselves in the service, that they were resolved either to stand or fall with it. It pleased God, by their hands, with the assistance of the Royal Fleet (the Commanders whereof denied them nothing they stood in need of), to do wonderful things, to whom, and not to any human cause, must be ascribed the glory.

Shortly after Carmarthen town, not conceived tenantable by the enemy, was deserted, which deceived the inhabitants thereof, by some of their principal men, to make their addresses to Colonel

DOCUMENT XLVI. A, A.D. 1644.

Laugharne and the gentlemen joined with him, having confidence as they told him he would be constant to the expressions he made in his summons to them, which was, "That he would bring no detriment or violence upon them, in case they would join themselves, without coercion, in the service of King and Parliament." He ratified his words, and accepted them.

I left him the 27th of March in preparation to advance thither, which I pray God he may do successfully, in which he was the more dilatory, being desirous first to confirm Pembrokeshire. For which purpose, Captain Swanley and the Vice-Admiral had a meeting at Haverfordwest with most of the gentry and commonalty of the county, where the oath and covenant against the horrible plot at London was generally taken—the instructions for the administering of the National Covenant not having come down. I have written nothing but what I shall attest in any presence, being an eye-witness of most of the particulars, and though the narration may be imperfect in formalities of expression, yet, I dare justify it is not so in any truth or material circumstance; neither did I obtrude myself upon this work, but was wished and importuned unto it by the gentlemen of the county, wherin I conceived I was bound in duty, the best I could, to satisfy them, as having heretofore had the honour to sit in your house, for whose prosperity I shall ever pour forth my prayers to the Almighty, and in the interim remain,

Your servant in all sincerity to be commanded,

SIMON THELWALL.[1]

From aboard the *Globe*,

Dated the first of April, 1644.[2]

[1] Simon Thelwall, of Plasyward, Member for the Borough of Denbigh.

[2] "A True Relation of the routing his Majesty's forces in the County of Pembroke, under the command of the Earl of Carbery, by those valiant and courageous gentlemen, Colonel Rowland Laugharne, John Poyer, Simon Thelwall, Thomas Laugharne, and others well-affected, as it was sent in two several Relations of the Land Fight, and Sea Fight—the one to the Right Honourable Robert, Earl of Warwick, the other to the Honourable William Lenthall, Esquire, Speaker of the House of Commons, with the number of such ordnance, arms, ammunition, castles, commanders, and soldiers, as are taken, and that county, by God's blessing, cleared of the enemy. London: Printed for Edw. Husbands, April 12, 1644."

B.

Additional Particulars relating to the Fighting in Pembrokeshire, extracted from other Relations of the Proceedings.

The Names of the Ships.

DOCUMENT XLVI. B. A.D. 1644.

Leopard Regis, Admiral, Capt. Richard Swanley.
Swallow, Vice-Admiral, Capt. Wm. Smith.
Prosperous, Capt. Nicholas Gettonsby.
Leopard, merchant, Capt. John Guilson.
Providence, merchant, Capt. William Swanley.
Crescent, frigate, Capt. Peter Whittey, with two Liverpool vessels.[1]

[They started from Plymouth on the 18th January (must have been February), reached Milford, "after much foul weather and contrary winds, beating about the Land's End," on the 23rd of the same month.]

The next morning after we came to anchor in the Haven, Col. Laugharne and the Mayor of Pembroke came aboard the *Leopard*, and informed my Admiral of the feeble condition the well-affected party was in. As also of the strength, power, and insolency of the adverse party. For after the enemy had fortified the north side of the harbour, and intending to have fortified the south side within a day or two, had not our arrival frustrated that design, the enemy presuming on their strength, cast off their sheep's clothing, in which they had so long deluded the people, and demonstrated themselves to be like unto the rest of their confederates —ravening wolves (*sic*). The Earl of Carbery having voted, that after the harbour was fortified he would plunder the town of Pembroke, and the houses of the gentlemen who had adhered to that party, and that their persons should be put to death by cruel tortures. The Mayor of Pembroke, they said, should be put in a barrel of nails, and brought to Prick's-pill, and from the top of a hill should be rolled down into the sea.

[1] This list appears in Fenton's "Pembrokeshire, Appendix, No. 7." Also in King's Pamphlets, No. 152—13, and has been collated with another list in K. P. 152—14.

DOCUMENT XLVI. B. A.D. 1644.

This report so terrified the gentlemen that they fled from their houses and hid themselves in obscure places in disguise, and sent their wives and children to Tenby, where his Lordship [the Earl of Carbery] then lay, humbly to supplicate his Lordship to be pleased to grant them protection, that their houses might not be plundered, nor their persons abused by the rude soldiers; among whom there was a reverend, aged gentlewoman, the wife of Mr. Griffith White, who had in her house eight sons and eight daughters, who were virgins, and four small grand-children, in all twenty in number, with divers servants, both male and female. This gentlewoman pressing his Lordship to commiserate her sad state, in case her house should be plundered, desired his protection, assuring his Lordship that whensoever he would be pleased to give her husband leave to wait on him, she did not doubt but that her husband would give his Lordship ample satisfaction in all his lawful demands. His Lordship replied he would find a time to speak with her husband, but as for a protection he would grant her none. The gentlewoman, with tears in her eyes, desired his Lordship to look upon her children, who in point of honour he stood engaged to protect, as also the chastity of matrons and virgins, the which, without his Lordship's protection, she said, must be undoubtedly violated, and her family perish. To which his Lordship answered with divers reproaches and some jests, that it were better her children and family should perish than that the King should want means to perfect his design. To which she said, the King could not want, if his Majesty would be graciously pleased to be content with what God and the laws of the land have provided. At which his Lordship flung out of the room, leaving the gentlewoman with tears in her eyes, and so she departed to her house, full of grief and pensive thoughts. A passage from his Lordship of so barbarous a deportment, that I believe history can scarce parallel to have proceeded from any heathen. And if these be the loyal subjects who fight for the Gospel, the King's honour, and the subjects' liberty, I leave it to everyman's judgment to determine.

When the enemy was routed [at Prick's-pill] some of their soldiers fled to Haverfordwest, and informed the Commander

DOCUMENT XLVI. F. A.D. 1644.

there of the loss of the Fort, and that all their commanders and soldiers therein were taken prisoners. At which news it is reported Sir Henry Vaughan, with the rest of the commanders, began to rage and swear like mad-men, and as a bear robbed of her whelps, ran up and down the streets (crying) "Beat up our drums, gather our horse and foot together, for we will out this night and be revenged on the Round-headed Parliament dogs." And having with this bravado drawn their forces into a body, being about 450, Sir John Stepney, the governor of that town, like a prudent overseer, went into the churchyard to see if he could discern our forces approach towards Haverfordwest. About half a mile from the town he discovered a herd of young black bullocks coming towards him.[1] Those horned beasts so amazed the Knight, that being afraid of his own shadow his worship ran to the head of their forces and swore "God's wounds" the Roundhead Dogs were coming; at which report they marched out of the town, and calling to mind the valiant example of their Lieut.-General Carbery[2] they wheeled about and ran away. The boys of the town perceiving them running, fell on their rear, and took from them sixty muskets. This disorder in the rear made those in the front believe that the Roundheads were at their heels indeed: the fear thereof metamorphosed all her cousin Taffies into mercuries, and with winged speed every man fled for his life, some threw away their arms, and those that had charge of the powder flung it into the river; and in this manner was the town of Haverfordwest surrendered, verifying that saying of the Kingly Prophet David: *The wicked fleeth when no man pursueth.* When the enemy fled, they left behind them in Haverfordwest one hundred red coats which were never worn, a quantity of victuals, and ten pieces of ordnance, all which argued they wanted nothing but a good cause to maintain.[3]

[1] In another account this historical herd of bullocks is said to have belonged to one Wheeler, a grazier.

[2] Alluding to the Earl's quitting the county after the attack upon Trefloyne, under the pretence of going to seek aid for the defence of Haverfordwest.

[3] From a pamphlet, entitled "An Exact Relation of that famous and notable victory obtained at Milford Haven, &c., written by Capt. Wm. Smith, Vice-Admiral, &c. London: Printed by Moses Bell, 25 July, 1644." (K. P. 167—12.) There was an earlier printed copy of this. (K. P. 152—14.)

C.

DOCUMENT XLVI. C. A.D. 1644.

A list of the names of the worthy valiant Commanders now in action in the County of Pembroke, in the service of the King and Parliament, who opposed the Earl of Carbery.

Rowland Laugharne, Colonel and Commander-in-Chief
Simon Thelwall, Colonel and Volunteer
Thomas Laugharne, Sergeant-Major
Capt. Rice Powell
Capt. Walter Cuney
Capt. John Poyer
Capt. Peter Whittey
Lieut. Wogan
Lieut. Richard Jones
Coronet Powell

A list of the malignant Commanders taken prisoners at the Pill with their inferior officers.

John Barlow, Esquire, Master of the Ordnance, and Captain of a troop of horse—"a church Papist"
Capt. Edmund Bradshaw
Capt. John Bradshaw
Capt. John Butler
Capt. Arnold Butler
Capt. William Marychurch
Capt. John Price
Captain Francis Edmunds

The names of the Commanders who ran away from Haverfordwest.

Sir Henry Vaughan, Major General of the Army.
Sir John Stepney, Knight and Baronet, Governor of Haverfordwest
Sir Francis Lloyd, Knight, Commander-in-chief of the Horse
Lieut.-Col. Butler, High Sheriff of the County
James Martin, Captain of a troop of horse
Capt. John Edwardes, Commissioner of Array
Capt. Hull of Bristol, with 100 seamen who ran away

Prisoners of note taken at Tenby.

DOCUMENT XLVI. C.

A.D. 1644.

John Gwynne, Governor of Tenby
Colonel David Gwynne
Lieut.-Col. Thomas Butler, High Sheriff, who ran away from Haverfordwest.
Capt. George Lewis
Capt. Metholl or Mitchell
Capt. Rice Prichard
Archdeacon Rudd, a malignant priest.[1]

[1] He had long been "wanted." See Commons' Journals for April 19, 1643. These lists have been prepared by a collating of the list published in the pamphlet reprinted in Fenton's Pembrokeshire, with that published as a schedule to Capt. Wm. Smith's narration.

XLVII.

Three Letters from Mr. John Vaughan, of Trawscoed, relating to affairs in Pembrokeshire, Cardiganshire, and Carmarthenshire.

A.

"Trawscoed," 12th March, 1644.

SIR,

DOCUMENT XLVII. A. A.D. 1644.

The news is very sad, and of as much consequence to the King's affairs as any accident that hath happened almost since these troubles began. The shipping upon Wednesday, in the evening, appeared before Tenby, and summoned them to yield the town; which, they refusing, they continued before it until Thursday morning, and then began to storm it violently from sea with their ordnance. The same morning their land forces likewise set down before the town, and played it hotly with their cannon, continuing for the most part day and night, until Saturday, about 5 of the clock, at which time their shot forced the very gate, and no where else as I learn, and gained the town, plundering to the utmost, but gave quarter for life. There were taken prisoners of them that commanded Colonel David Gwynne, Commissary Gwynne, Captains George Lewis and Butler, the now Sheriff of Pembrokeshire. No relief came for want of horse, and the truth is that all the mischances happened for want of a moving reserve of strength to relieve the garrisons that should happen to be distressed, whereof there was none; the ammunition, as is reported, was very scarce in the town. It was absolutely the strongest hold in South Wales, and of greatest consequence to the King. Had it been provided for with knowing care, it was scarcely forceable; and to regain it will require a mighty strength and knowing soldiers, whereof there was little afore in my poor judgment. It sweeps with it these countries . . . . and powerful all the arms of Carmarthenshire, few excepted, and a few in the hands of the trained men here besides those sent into the country by Mr. Bushell,[1] which are all fixed now, were lost. The people

[1] Bushell, working the Cardiganshire lead mines, would naturally take an interest in these parts.

DOCUMENT XLVII. A.
A.D. 1644.

are disheartened by the greatness of the loss, that it will require no less a name than the Prince[1] to new spirit them, being yet for the most part (I am confident) loyal. But additional success which threatens the vulgar with present danger for the most part governs the actions of the common sort. They would hear of no treaty at all from the Earl. What further resources they have I know not; but am certain that the greatness of events raises men into attempts they durst not have thought of before. We are all ruined by this mischance without a timely rescue. There is universal complaint against the conduct of things here, and certainly not without cause. A seasonable and resolved crossing of their current would bring them to other and more temperate considerations, which cannot be done by the soldiery of these parts only. Some ammunition that came from Bristol and ventured to relieve the town, was chased by a frigate of Swanley's and hardly escaped, putting into a creek at Llanelly, and is safe. Which is upon the matter all with these counties, the arms and stores of both being used in these late unfortunate actions. What is intended must be with great secrecy and speed; and the action is of much more difficulty than it was before. Had Tenby been saved the country had been easily commanded with horse; but now they have all the holds, Pembroke, Tenby, and Haverford, and by this time, I believe, Carew Castle, which was garrisoned, as I hear, but with fifty men. They are numerous in ordnance of what nature they please. By the shipping all their successes were performed, by marines, who being promised the plunder, adventured boldly upon attempts near the water. That country is wholly theirs, and the other two unfurnished with arms or ammunition, nor have the people will (because they want hopes) to do anything under that military conduct which brought them to these extremities. It were well if his Highness intends to redeem this mischief, that he had more particulars and sincere advertisement on every point.

Yours, &c.,

Jo. Vaughan.

To my worthy friend,

Morgan Herbert, Esq.

[1] Prince Rupert is the saviour here alluded to.

B.

DOCUMENT XLVII. B.

A.D. 1644.

SIR,

The news I have since I saw you out of Pembrokeshire is, that they intend, with some speed, to advance into Carmarthen or Cardiganshire, thereby to interest themselves, as well as they may, in the country, before any of the King's forces prevent them; nor is that consideration without probability of advantage to them. Those countries, as now they stand, being, in the general, like to yield themselves to the first danger, or to fall in with the first protection, being very impotent for resistance in themselves. If you shall think it fit to advance, as you intended, either to Cardigan or Carmarthen, or into their country, acquaint me with full directions, as you will have me serve you in. Little will be effected in general here until by some appearance of strength men be more emboldened to declare themselves. You may, as I am informed, if you decline Carmarthen, march from Llanymdovery, a private way, to a place called Llanybyther, where, partly in Cardiganshire and partly in Carmarthenshire, the river dividing only, you may have tolerable quarter for a night at the houses of Jenkin Lloyd, the widow Powell, and others near together, besides the village; and thence to Cardigan. I expect your resolution and direction with all speed by the bearer, being most entirely,

Your affectionate friend and servant,

JO. VAUGHAN.

Trawscoed, in Cardiganshire, April 10th, Wednesday.

For my worthy and honoured friend Colonel
Herbert Price, at Brecon, and in his absence
for Serjeant-Major Morgan.[1]

C.

April 11th.

DOCUMENT XLVII. C.

A.D. 1644.

DEAR SIR,

I received your letter this Thursday morning by the break of day, but had yesternight dispatched one to you which you will timely receive this day. I was doubtful of your being at home, and therefore wrote not so fully. My intelligence is here that in Pembrokeshire they were much moved by the answer

[1] Evidently Major Turberville Morgan, the Deputy-Governor of Brecknock.

returned them from this county to their letter, inasmuch that it being proposed among them that they should summon us once more; it was answered by Laugharne he would not, but with his sword in his hand. This day they have convened all the country to a muster at Colby Moor, about 13 miles from Carmarthen, whence it is imagined they will march for this or Carmarthenshire, that country within itself appears in good number as the manner is; but the body of the country absolutely refuses any attempt abroad with them, as I am informed, so as their action must depend upon their strength, not being, as I hear, but between three or four hundred foot, and about seven score horse. Here will no great good be done until some force appears. I prepare what may be, having these some days fixed the trained band of this quarter, who are altogether undisciplined in the nature of a garrison, where they are diligently exercised, and will become of use signifying nothing before. I collect what volunteers I can to arm with the arms in my power as dragoons, and what horse can be prepared; but these will come in presently upon your appearance and summons. Direct your letter to the Sheriff, that you require by the direction of the Prince the appearance of all horse and other strength of this county at the place and time you shall think fit, and I doubt not we shall be entire. I think it requisite you should hasten your march with what speed you can, and send to Major Butler that his horse remove not but with yours, that your attempt may be the entirer. It will not be amiss that you send the letter I propose you should send to the Sheriff to me, with notice of the meeting you determine to have with us, that it may be certain and prepared with some industry. I am glad Sir Hugh Owen is for conditions. He may prove of great use, but I am truly sorry that articles of such nature as your letter intimates are preferred against the Earl of Carbery, for upon my soul he was free from the least falsehood, whatever else was amiss. The command is now, I hope, happily disposed of into his Highness Prince Rupert's hands.

DOCUMENT XLVII. C. A.D. 1644.

Jo. V.

For my much honoured friend,

COLONEL HERBERT PRICE.[1]

[1] These letters formed part of the collection made by Bennett, Secretary to Prince Rupert. They became afterwards the property of Mr. Bentley, the publisher, and the whole collection was sold in 1852. These are from the *Arch. Camb.*, vol. iv., N.S., p. 66.

XLVIII.

Swansea Summoned by the Parliament Forces.

DOCUMENT XLVIII. A.D. 1644.

In the meantime, the fidelity and courage of the loyal Welsh, whereof we were this day advertised deserve place here. His Majesty had caused a garrison to be placed at Swansea, a town of good note in Glamorganshire, under the command of the High Sheriff of the county, who kept there in person, which being a great eyesore to the rebels, whom the prevailing faction which remains at Westminster entertained in pay to disturb, and if it may be possible to subdue that country, they caused a summons to be sent to the Mayor of the town and others of the principal gentry who were there residing, subscribed by Robert Moulton, one of the chieftains of the rebels, which, with the answer to it, I shall here put down, that you may see as well the insolence of the saucy rebels, as the courageous gallantry of those noble gentlemen.

The letter or summons was as followeth:—

To the Mayor and Gentlemen of Swansea.

GENTLEMEN,

These are to will and require you, in the name of the Right Honourable Robert, Earl of Warwick, Lord High Admiral of England, Wales, and Ireland, and his Majesty's Navy Royal at Sea, that you forthwith yield the town and garrison into the obedience of the King and Parliament, and in so doing you shall be received into the protection and the associated Covenant, and shall be defended against all Irish rebels, Papists, and those that seek to subvert liberties, and to destroy religion, which, at this time, all the Papists and rebels in the three Kingdoms are in arms to overthrow. Therefore, consider of it, and submit; for if you shall be obstinate, and spill any blood in resisting, you may not expect such favour as your neighbours have had. And this is the advice of your friend, who endeavours to preserve you, if you accept of his profer; if not, I shall endeavour to keep you without trade till your forced obedience bring you to the mercy of him that tendereth you grace and favour. I shall expect your answer by the bearer.

ROB. MOULTON.

Milford Haven, from his Majesty's ship the *Lion*,
the 15th of May, 1644.

Which saucy paper being received, the High Sheriff and the rest of the gentlemen, full of just disdain, returned this sudden answer to it, which, for the ingenuity and spirit, is well worth the reading, and not the reading only, but the imitation of all loyal subjects, who shall at any time be tempted by the like allurements to an apostacy from their allegiance to their Sovereign Lord. Now for the answer; it was thus:—

To Robert Moulton, Subscriber to the Paper directed to the Mayor and Gentlemen of Swansea.

We cannot understand how we may, with any justice or loyalty, return you the name of gentleman to your rude and rebellious paper, in the front whereof you have the boldness and presumption, in the name of the right honourable (as you term him) (whom we do and must account a dishonourable and most insulting rebel) Robert, Earl of Warwick, (by you styled) High Admiral of England, Wales, and Ireland, and his Majesty's Navy Royal at Sea (the which we do and ought to protest he hath most traitorously betrayed and rebelliously possessed) to will and require us forthwith to yield the town and garrison of Swansea into the obedience of the King and Parliament (a most foul treason, masked under a fair and specious show of a most loyal and just adherency and subjection to his Majesty and his Parliament at Oxford), in defiance of which your traitorous summons we send you this our fixed

DOCUMENT XLVIII. A.D. 1644.

resolution, that we will neither yield town nor garrison, nor any the least interest we hold of life or fortune (under the protection of his sacred Majesty), but will defend the same and our country against any your proud and insolent menacings (wherein your proper trade is exhibited), and in the account of a rebel and traitor we leave you to your fearful destruction.

Subcribed by the High Sheriff, and most of the
Gentlemen of Glamorganshire.[1]

[1] *Mercurius Aulicus* for the 21st week, ending May 25. (K. P. 161—7.)

XLIX.

Charge of Inhumanity against Admiral Swanley, at Milford, in a Letter from the Marquis of Ormond to the Archbishop of York.

MAY IT PLEASE YOUR GRACE, DOCUMENT XLIX. A.D. 1644.

When Colonel Trafford was ready to embark, himself and 300 good well-armed men, above 20 barrel of powder, with match proportionable, and six pieces of iron-ordnance well-fitted, being aboard of Capt. John Bartlett, all for the defence of Anglesey, here arrived two Parliament ships and a frigate to hinder this preparation made at my very great and particular charge. I have since tried from other ports to send them away, but the too good intelligence those ships have from their friends on shore of all our motions makes me unwilling to hazard so good men and provisions. The unfortunate taking of Col. Willoughby with about 150 men bound for Bristol, by their fellows, and their inhuman throwing over board of 70 men and two women, under the name of Irish rebels, making the men also very fearful to venture upon the voyage, it being very well known to them that most of the men so murdered had served with them against the Irish, and all of them lived during the war in our quarters.[1] In addition to these difficulties we are here threatened with an invasion of the Scots out of the North who have treacherously surprised Belfast, and attempted other English garrisons, so that until these seas be clearer and the

[1] This is no story; for in the "*Perfect Diurnal*" (No. 41, under date May 8th) it is confirmed. There it is stated of Capt. Swanley, and to his praise, for that newspaper was a Parliament advocate, "that such Irish rebels as he took in a ship intended for Wales he made water rats of, and cast them into the sea." There must have been some grounds for the belief that they were Irish, whether they were rebels or not, for we are told by the same authority that such as were English he entertained, and having prevailed upon them to take the covenant, they fought stoutly with him, and assisted in the taking of Carmarthen *Merc. Aulicus* raged very much on this.

DOCUMENT XLIX. A.D. 1644.

danger of the Scots over, Anglesey can expect little (indeed no) succour out of Ireland.

I had a message delivered me from your Grace by Mr. Lutterell, and some intimation of the same thing from my good friend, Mr. Trevor,[1] whereupon I humbly besought your Grace's leave to take notice of and vindicate myself from that very false and malicious scandal cast upon me by a person that I never injured, unless he understood my preventing the seduction of the army here from his Majesty's obedience by his instruments and sons, to be injury to him; but my part being to justify myself by other means than recrimination, I humbly desire it may go no further, unless your Grace will be pleased to tell it my accuser to heighten his malice, which out of the clearness of my soul I do more desire than I wish to revenge. In this I most earnestly beg your Grace's speedy leave that I may prove myself in some degree (at least as far as innocency from so black a crime will make me), worthy the continuance of your favour, and the name of

Your Grace's most faithful humble servant,

ORMONDE.[2]

Dublin Castle, 27 May, 1644.

(*Indorsed*). A Copy of a letter to the Lord Archbishop of York, dated the 27 of May, 1644.

[1] This was Mr. Arthur Trevor, a great friend of Prince Rupert, whose agent he was at the Royal head quarters. He was also a voluminous and an especially interesting correspondent of the Marquis of Ormond.

[2] From the Carte's Papers in the Bodleian Library. This letter was published in the *Arch. Cambrensis*, vol. xv., 3rd series, p. 313, where it was stated that it was printed for the first time. This, however, was a mistake, for it was published in Carte's "Collection of Letters," Lond., 1739, vol. i., p. 48.

L.

An Ordinance of the Lords and Commons assembled in Parliament for the Association of the Counties of Pembroke, Carmarthen, and Cardigan. June, 1644.

The Lords and Commons assembled in Parliament, taking into their consideration the present condition of the County of Pembroke, which, by the wonderful power of Almighty God, manifested in weak means, is delivered from the tyranny and intolerable oppression of the forces raised against the Parliament and Kingdom under the command of the Earl of Carbery, and that by the further assistance and blessing of God, if timely care be taken, for the maintaining and prosecuting of the said great work, the rest of the Counties of South Wales may be reduced to the obedience of the King and Parliament, who cannot but be deeply sensible of the great miseries they have in like manner sustained under the same tyranny, and how great a benefit and comfort it will be to them to be also delivered from the same, have thought it necessary that over and above such provisions of arms and ammunition as have been already ordered to be made for the said County of Pembroke, such further competent supplies and provision be had and established for the maintenance of such officers and soldiers as shall be employed in the preservation of the peace of the said County of Pembroke, and in the reducing of the rest of the said counties, as during the time of the said service shall be requisite. And do further order and ordain, and be it ordered and ordained by the authority aforesaid, that the three Counties of Pembroke, Carmarthen, and Cardigan shall enter into an association, and are hereby associated, for the mutual defence and safety of each other; and that Herbert Perrot, Rice Vaughan, Thomas Barlow, gent., Griffith White, Sampson Lort, Esquires, Thomas Powell, gent., DOCUMENT L. A.D. 1644.

DOCUMENT L. A.D. 1644.

John Elliot, Esquire, George Adams, gent., Thomas Bowen, of Treloyn, John Phillips, Esquire, John Lort, George Hayward, William Laugharne, Thomas Wogan, John Mathias, gent., Thomas Warren, Esquire, James Bowen, George William Griffith, John Lloyd, of Kilrhue, David Morgan, and Thomas Jones, of Newport, gentlemen,[1] shall be, and are hereby named to be a committee, to meet at such times and places as they shall think fit, for raising of men, money, horses, arms, and ammunition, upon the proposition formerly agreed on by both Houses of Parliament, or by any other way that they shall judge convenient, for the suppressing of the rebellion, stirred up by the malignant persons, who desire and endeavour to subvert the happiness of this Kingdom, and shall have power to do all things necessary thereunto upon all occasions, and to join with any other forces raised or to be raised by the authority of Parliament, and that the Earl of Essex, Lord-General, be desired to grant a commission to the said Rowland Laugharne, to command in chief as Major-General of the forces raised, and to be so raised within the said three counties, and carry the said forces to such places as he shall think fit, and subdue, fight with, kill, slay, and imprison all such persons as shall levy war without the consent of both Houses of Parliament; and that what money, horses, arms, or ammunition, shall be contributed by any person towards this service, shall be secured to be repaid with interest after eight pounds per cent., by the public faith of both Houses of Parliament, upon the showing an acquittance or certificate, under the hands of any four of the said committee, of the receipt of the said moneys or appraisement of the said horses, arms, or ammunition, and the said moneys so brought in shall be issued in every of the said counties by the appointment of any four of the said committee.

And be it further ordained by the said Lords and Commons, that

[1] On the 26th July following, the following new names were added to the committee, viz.:—Sir Richard Phillipps, Bart., John Laugharne, Arthur Owen, Roger Lort, Lewis Barlow, Esquires, Capt. Richard Swanley, and Capt. William Smith, and Thomas Wogan, John Lloyd, and David Morgan, were expunged, because they had gone over to the other side. Again, on the 24th January, 1645, the following new names were added, viz., James Lewis, of Cardigan, Esq.; David Lewis, of Gernos, Thomas Evans, Thomas Lloyd, of Gwemoilig, and John Lloyd, of Vaerdref, gentlemen. See *Commons' Journals.*

the said committee, or any four or more of them, shall have full power and authority to put in execution within the said County of Pembroke, and the said other counties, when the same shall be reduced, the ordinances of this present Parliament hereafter mentioned, that is to say, the ordinances for sequestration of malignants', delinquents', and Papists' estates, and the ordinance for weekly assessments. And shall have full power and authority to set and let the lands, tenements, and hereditaments of all Papists and delinquents which are or shall be seized and sequestered, according to the ordinance of Parliament for sequestration within the said several counties, or either of them, from year to year, or by lease or leases, for the intents and purposes aforesaid, so long as the said sequestration shall continue; and shall have power and authority, and are hereby required to administer the Covenant appointed to be taken by the three Kingdoms of England, Scotland, and Ireland, to all persons within the said three counties, and every of them who ought to take the same by the late ordinance and instructions for that purpose, and have not already taken it.[1]

[1] From a copy printed for Edward Husbands, June 14, 1644. (K. P. 161—1.)

LI.

Shropshire and Cheshire in Danger—Prince Rupert's Power increasing—Letter from the Earl of Denbigh, Sir W. Brereton, Col. Mytton, and others, to the Committee of both Kingdoms. June 15.

DOCUMENT LI. A.D. 1644.

RIGHT HONOURABLE,

We have this day, with Sir William Waller, seen your vote for his return and marching into the West, which appears to us to be of sad consequence to all these parts, and to the whole Kingdom as things stand at present. The power of Prince Rupert's army in Lancashire, with their dailie encrease of numbers and confidence, is such that that county, with the strength of all friends adjacent, is not able to bear (had we no other enemy). But to add to the sufferings of these poor countyes, all the King's forces by Sir W. Waller's prosecution of him, are driven upon us, and as we hear are quartered neer Shrewsburie, on the West side of the Severn, with a purpose to joyne with Prince Rupert, w^{ch}, had Sir William Waller proceeded in his pursuit of them, might probably be prevented, or if by speedy and hazardous marches the King's forces should joyne with P. Rupert, Sir W. Waller, by taking in the general forces of this association with those of Sir Thomas Myddelton's, and Cheshire may be enabled to give them both opposition, or at the least preserve these countyes and block up the united enemy on this side, until God may please to give the Northern forces opportunity to fall down upon them upon the other, to bring them to certain straights, and our miseries to a speedy end, which (were there nothing else) seemed to us of weight to carry on S^{r} W^{m} in his advance forward with a fair probability. But if these advantages be compared with the ill-effects either of his delay or return we conceive will represent his moving forward to be of urgent necessitie.

The Kinge and Prince's forces left without an army to oppose them will speedily destroy the whole remainder of Lancashire, deprive us of that great strength of foot and those numbers of arms that yet we have in Manchester and Warrington. The encouragement the ill-affected within the counties of Salop, Cheshire, and Staffordshire will receive by the presence of the King's person and his forces, with the discouragements that will fall upon your friends by the retreat and absence of that power [which] might preserve them, will lay necessity upon those in Wem, Nantwich, and Stafford, to quit their garrisons as not able (after ten weeks' lying under the power of a strong army in the field) to bear the shock of their assaults. These are not the conjectures of fear but of the knowledge we have of the condition of these parts. And what an increase of power will be added to the Kinge by this means, what a prolonging of our miseries, what an admiracon it will beget in the heartes of the people that soe many armies are in the Kingdom for us, and none disposed of to coape with the greatest strength of the enemy, we refer to your wisdomes, humbly beseeching you to give speedy order for Sir W$^{m.}$ Waller's advance, or for his stay here until his Excellency come up for our relief, wch as it is extremely wanted by these counties, soe it is earnestly desired by

DOCUMENT LI. A.D. 1644.

Your hono^{rs} faithfull humble Servants,

B. Denbigh,
Will. Brereton.

St. Rugeley. Henry Brooke.

Thomas Mytton,
Edward Leigh,
Sa. Rooper,
Chidly Coote.

Sturbridge,
June 15, 1644.

To the Right Honorable y^{e} Comittee of
both y^{e} Kingdomes sittinge
at Darby House in
Westm$^{r.}$
speed these
pr'sent.[1]

[1] State Papers Domestic, (Charles I.), No. 316, fol. 88.

LII.

The Archbishop of York to the Marquis of Ormond, relating to the Appointment of Sir John Mennes to the Governorship of Beaumaris, &c. June 19.

DOCUMENT LII. A.D. 1644.

MAY IT PLEASE YOUR EXCELLENCY,

I humbly thank your Excellency for your great care of this poor country from time to time, and especially for this great provision, prepared under Colonel Trafford, for whose person I am particularly obliged to your Excellency.

Sir John Mennes is appointed Governor by Prince Rupert of these three counties, and abides as yet at Beaumaris. But hath no force at all in readiness, nor hath hitherto so much as taken a general and particular muster, and seems not to like well of the employment; nor the people much of him. I received but even now a letter from his Majesty to go and piece up if I can some breaches between him and his subjects of Anglesey, which I must go understand from him as soon as I can.

I found by his Highness Prince Rupert, as he was putting into the field, that he expected, and had some design upon the 300 men and Colonel Trafford, and more particulars I do not understand in that business. Whether his Highness intended to have him along with him this voyage, or to place him here (for he is not too much in love with Mennes I know not).

But if your Excellency shall detain the men by reason of these occasions in the north of Ireland, if you shall be pleased to let Capt. Bartlett bring hither the cannon and ammunition, and to trust them at Conway, the cannon shall be safe, and the ammunition paid for with due acknowledgement of these great favours.

I have likewise presumed to be an humble suitor unto your Excellency for the greater of some four or five skiffs or frigates, which lie there unused, and two pieces of ordnance to be used in her, in hope Captain Bartlett (if this taking of Liverpool shall call away the ships which guard him) will do me the favour to hail her to Beaumaris after his ship. And it shall be kept ready to serve your Excellency from time to time.

My most noble Lord, for Mr. Lutterell, his relation, I have already written unto your Excellency by Mr. Arthur Trevor, from Worcester, and since by the Lord Dillon, that without wronging that Lord (with whom I desire to have neither friendship nor enmity), I cannot justify upon him any words to that effect, mentioned in your Lordship's letters, to wit, that he should ever say in my hearing that your Excellency was the cause of that rebellion, or the first mover in this same. Had he said any thing of that nature unto me, I had undoubtedly acquainted his Majesty with the same, being sworn of his council as well as his Lordship.

But Mr. Lutterell might be mistaken in my words or relation; because I told him indeed that the lord did no way love your Excellency, and that your Excellency has no account of him accordingly. That his Lordship said your Excellency had lost nothing in point of private estate by the war (wherein he was contradicted openly by myself and another gentleman), and that your Excellency brought not ten men of all your retainers to aid the King, but raised your Excellency's reputation by his, the said Lord's, forces and preparation, to which he was so roundly answered upon the place, as in truth, most noble Lord, it needs no further expostulation, especially it being but table talk.

I am not so punctually informed of the occurrences of the times, as to presume to give your Excellency any taste of them. Prince Rupert, after the taking of Liverpool (but not nine of the great ships which are fallen upon the North of England or Ireland), is gone in full speed to relieve the Marquis of Newcastle at York, if the ill-conduct of the Court army do not call him thither (the words of the letter I now received from his camp near Warrington).

His Majesty seemeth to be drawing back again to Oxford; my Lord of Londonderry writes that he hears the Scots were repelled in three assaults they made upon York, with the loss of 3,000 men. And that they have raised the siege.

DOCUMENT LII.
A.D. 1644.

I would there were as much truth in this as in other parts of the news, that those rogues are got into Hull. Prince Maurice is still at Lime, which is all I can add to what I formerly wrote unto your Excellency. I beseech your Excellency to extend your favour to one Mr. Evan Lloyd, a prebendary of one of the Cathedrals in Dublin, and one whose honesty and good parts I have known from a child, he having been my pupil. His Majesty had given him the poor Bishopric of Kilphanore, in that Kingdom, but because he stopt upon his *commendam* I returned it back to his Majesty again, because it had been much to his loss.

God Almighty ever bless and preserve your Excellency.

Your Excellency's most humble and devoted servant,

Jo. Eborac.

Conway, 19th June, 1644.

To his Excellency the Lord Marquis of Ormond, Lord-Lieutenant of Ireland, present these.[1]

[1] Carte's "Collection of Original Letters," vol. i., p. 49; and *Arch. Cambrensis* for 1869, p. 317.

LIII.

Victory at Duddleston by Col. Mytton; and Oswestry taken from the Royalists by the Earl of Denbigh. June 19 *and* 23.

Letters sent from Colonel Mytton. DOCUMENT LIII. A.D. 1644.

Sir,

I came hither about eleven of the clock on Tuesday night; I had not been in bed a quarter of an hour but a friend came to me and informed me that there were carriages summoned to be in Oswestry by nine of the clock yesterday to carry ammunition to Prince Rupert, which we hear he standeth in need of very much. I drew out all the small forces could be spared hence, and marched towards Chirk to surprise it. I went on with the horse to a place so appointed, one to meet me to give further intelligence, who, when he came, did assure me that a party was gone out of Oswestry that morning to convey it thither. I cannot learn that it is yet gone past. I have sent to the Earl of Denbigh to give him notice hereof, who as I even now received intelligence that he hath sent forces towards me. If they come before the ammunition be past, I intend by God's help to fall upon the town which they are about to fortify very strongly. Yesterday I took two of Major Sacheverel's troopers, who, upon examination, confessed that a Lieutenant of foot with 20 musqueteers were gone a mile past us, we being at St. Martin's, they going towards Bangor. I followed them as fast as I could with 25 horse, and as many dragoons; when we came in sight of them, they not seeing us, the dragoons alighted to charge them in the rear, the place being enclosed ground, full of woods and very uneven. Instead of 20 we found 54. One of our troopers discharged a pistol, how or wherefore I cannot learn, but it gave them such an alarm, whereupon we charged them with our horse, routed them, took prisoners according to the note enclosed.

DOCUMENT LIII. A.D. 1644.

Blessed be God for all his mercies. He is the only giver of all victories, and whom I trust will never forget them that are faithful in His services. I thank my God I have not one man slain in any fight since I parted last from you.

Dated June 20, 1644.

A list of the Prisoners taken at Duddleston June 19, 1644.

Bartholomew Fuller, Marshall
Owen Jones, Quarter Master
Richard Foulks, Serjeant
Robert Jones
Joseph Jones
Owen Lewis
Richard ap David
Richard ap Thomas
Thomas Owen
Richard Trevard
Morgan ap Richard
Hugh ap Thomas
John Henry
Richard Jones
Robert Davies
Morgan ap Robert
Edward Jones
Thomas Rogers
John Steel
Thomas ap Thomas
Robert Jones
Randby Stocton
Edward Philip
John Roberts
Richard Davies
Edward Williams
John Owen

Upon Saturday last, about two of the clock in the afternoon, my Lord, with his horse and 200 foot, fell upon this town. My Lord, by reason of his command into Lancashire, could not spare any of his foot, therefore we are constrained to take this small force out of Wem, which God so blessed, that before five of the clock we entered the town. We were forced first to take the church wherein there was 25. The next morning the castle was surrendered, the particulars I refer to my Lord's relation.

"Ossastree," 24 of June, 1644.

Thus far the letters from that heroic conqueror, Col. Mytton.

Now followeth other Letters from the Earl of Denbigh's quarters, of the particulars of the Victory at Oswestry:— DOCUMENT LIII. A.D. 1644.

SIR,

I desire you to join with us and for us in praises to God, who hath done great things for us and by us.

Upon Thursday last we came out of Stafford, horse and foot, to intercept some ammunition going to Prince Rupert, by way of Wales, over the river Gomerah (?) That night we marched not far by reason of great rain; but my Lord of Denbigh, early the next day, got to horse, and leaving all our foot at Drayton, we marched to Wem, and our horse to Ellesmere, and 200 foot and a troop of horse under the command of Colonel Mytton. Early next day we overtook our horse and those foot, and by 12 o'clock on Saturday, we beleagured the enemy's garrison town of Oswestry, which is a walled town, and in it the church well manned, and the castle.

They gave us a hot salute, and our men as gallantly entertained it and returned an answer.

Captain Keme undertook to make good the Chester passage and the Chirk Castle road with these troops, viz., Captain Keme's own troop, Colonel Barton's, Captain Noakes's, Captain Tompson's, and Captain Broother's.

Captain Keme immediately fixed his guards and sent out parties into the mountains and scouts everyway, who returned with news of one Colonel Marrow's appearing with a body of horse, but they never came up, though expected.

My Lord's horse, commanded by Major Frazer, had the guard of the Shrewsbury road and Morton. Our foot made an onslaught on the church, being but 200, and after half an hour's sore fight entered the church. The enemy fled into the steeple, thence they fetched them down with powder. There we took 27 prisoners. Then we brought up a sacre to the gate through the suburbs, and a party of horse was called off the guards, both of my Lord's and ours, and my Lord's lifeguard. We shot the gate through at two shots, and they fired from the gate at our men. But one of our shot striking a woman's bowels out, and wounding two or three, put them in fear, that they betook themselves to the castle. We forced open the gates, and the horse entered resolutely, and by three o'clock were possessed of the town—as good a piece of service (God

DOCUMENT LIII. A.D. 1644.

have all praise) as this year hath produced. My Lord himself entered the town, with the horse, neglecting thoughts of his own safety. Our men minded not the plundering of the town (which was their right in taking it in this way), but followed us to the castle, where they fiercely fired upon us—every way being well manned. We made some shot with the great sacre, but they took little effect.

Only some timorous men got over the walls, one broke his arm falling, others, Captain Keme's horse lighted upon and took them prisoners. Captain Keme sent my Lord from his guard 14 prisoners into the town, besides one Captain, which his scout took by Chirk Castle, with his commission under his Majesty's hand, and sent it to my Lord also.

My Lord at night called a Council of War, and ordered a strong guard, and designed a party of troopers to venture to fire the castle gates with pitch, but our men wearied out slipped the opportunity. My Lord, by break of day waking, came to Captain Keme in the same house with him, and designed him to go forward with the design; but on his way there met him a party of women of all sorts down on their knees confounding him with their Welsh howlings, that he was fain to get an interpreter, which was to beseech me to entreat my Lord, before he blew up the Castle, they might go up and speak to their husbands, children, and the officers, which he moved, and my Lord condescended to, so that Captain Keme might go with them and a trumpet, which he did courageously, and carried this message. Then my Lord, to avoid the effusion of blood, offered them mercy, if they would accept of it, whereupon they threw down this paper :—

To the Right Honourable the Earl of Denbigh.

Propositions propounded by us for the delivering up of the Castle of Oswestry:

First, to march away with our arms, bag and baggage, officers and soldiers, and all other persons whatsoever being in the said Castle, and

Secondly, that we, the said officers, and all other persons whatsoever, being within the said Castle, may be guarded through your quarters to Montford Bridge, or quietly to abide in our own habitations.

Thirdly, that we, may march out of the said Castle, over the said bridge, with our muskets charged, lighted matches, and balls in our mouths. DOCUMENT LIII. A.D. 1644.

These propositions being granted, the Castle shall be delivered by the officers subscribed.

JOHN BIRDWELL, Lieutenant-Colonel.
JOHN WARREN, Captain.
NICHS. HOOKS, Lieutenant.
THOMAS DAVENPORT, Lieutenant.
HUGH LLOYD, Ancient.
LEWIS MORGAN, Ancient.

Capt. Keme returned leaving the women. My Lord refused to condescend. At last the women prevailed, and cried to me to come up. Then the two brave champions, Colonel Mytton and Captain Keme, went up, and they said they would repose themselves on such quarters as my Lord would sign to, which was their lives only.

So they marched out, and we found 100 good muskets, besides others stolen away, eight halberts and officers to them, one barrel of powder and suitable match, many swords, and some few pistols, 20 gentlemen of Wales and Shropshire, divers officers, and 200 prisoners, besides what were lost.

Immediately (it being the Lord's day) my Lord called away all to go to church to praise God, which was done, and our dead buried.

In all this service we had but two slain and one horse, and but four wounded, blessed be God.

This town is of great concernment. We had a Council of War at 10 o'clock, at which my Lord-General (the Earl of Denbigh) made Colonel Mytton Governor of Oswestry. And we have resolved upon a great design, which is to join with the Cheshire Forces, where Sir Thomas Myddelton is now at Nantwich, and hath been there four days, and go against Prince Rupert into Lancashire. I pray commend us especially now in your constant prayers to the Lord. Be doing as well as we; and praise God for his miraculous love by us a poor weak army.

This day my Lord received thanks from the Committee of both Kingdoms for the last service at Tipton Green. It is a sad sight

DOCUMENT LIII. A.D. 1644.

to behold the ignorance of these Welsh in these parts, and how they are enslaved to serve. We shall leave a garrison here and Colonel Mytton, and march to our foot on Wednesday next with our body of horse. Colonel Fox is with us here; our men fetched in 300 cows and salt runts of the mountains, and sell good pennyworths. This town to avoid plundering are to give 500 pounds to the soldiers.[1]

List of Prisoners taken at Oswestry.

Lieut.-Col. Bledwyn[2]
Sir Abraham Shipman, the Governor then at Shrewsbury
Capt. John Farrell
Capt. John Madrin
Capt. Thomas Tenet
Capt. Phillips
Lieut. Nicholas Hooke
Lieut. Richard Franklin
Lieut. Thomas Davenport
Cornet Leonard
Cornet Lloyd
Ensign Morgan
Ensign Wynne
Commissary Richard Edwards, with nine sergeants, nine corporals, one drum-major, 305 common soldiers, eighty townsmen in arms. Also 200 muskets, 100 pikes, and other weapons, and forty-five barrels of powder.[3]

[1] From a pamphlet, entitled "Two Great Victories: one obtained by the Earl of Denbigh at Oswestry, &c., certified by letters from the Earl of Denbigh's quarters; the other victory by Colonel Mitton, with a list of the prisoners by him taken. Pub. according to order. London: Printed by T. Coe, 1644." (K. P. 163—3.)

[2] This is the Lieut.-Col. who signed the conditions in preceding page as Birdwell. Bledwyn, or Baldwin was the right name.

[3] *The Kingdom's Weekly Intelligencer*, No. 61, p. 490.

LIV.

The Earl of Denbigh to the Committee of both Kingdoms—as to Rumours of a Design to Besiege Oswestry.

A.

DOCUMENT LIV. A. A.D. 1644.

MY LORDS AND GENTLEMEN,

Upon my march to the rendevous at Knotsford to follow those commands you have laid upon me, Coll[ll] Mytton hath sent me word of the enemies' gathering into a great body in Wales, Shrewsbury, and Chester to regaine Oswaldstre. Upon my leaving that place I ordered a good quantity of ammunition and three companies of S[r] W. Middleton's to be sent to reinforce that garrison, w[ch] by my horse weare safely convaid into the towne, so that now there are neare upon 400 musquetteers fitted with all necessaries, and a good ingenier to secure that garrison, and a full troope of horse, yett in regard the enemy is now emptying all their garrisons and will venture all rather than not recover that place, w[ch] they conceave to bee of so great concernment to their affairs, I shall humbly beseech your lo[ps] to order that some forces may undertake the reliefe and defence of these parts in my absence, and that whilst I am executing your lo[ps] commands in other places my honor may not suffer, nor the advantages be lost where a more immediate charge and trust is conferred upon me. This I thought fitt to represent to your lo[ps] wisdome, and remaine,

My Lords and Gentlemen,

Your most humble and affectionate servant,

B. DENBIGH.[1]

Wem,
27 June, 1644.

[1] State Papers Dom., Charles I. Bundle 316, fol. 109.

B.

DOCUMENT LIV. B.

A.D. 1644.

MY LORD AND GENTLEMEN,

To-morrow night I hope to quarter with the force I have bene able to gett togeather att Manchester, but the number comes farr short of those assigned me by your lopps, for Nottingham and Derbie have sent me 9 troopes of horse but no foote; from Leicester I have received neither horse nor foote. My regiment of foote and Sr Thomas Middleton's are grown so weake that they are not able to guard theire colours, and therefore wee thought fitt to leave them for the defence of Wem and Oswaldstre. This day I had the honour to receave your lops of the 24 of this present att 9 o'clock in the morning, by which itt doth appeare your lops design of ioyning these forces was principally intended to hinder Prince Rupert's returne, and falling into these parts, and to give opposition in his march towards Sr W. Waller in case hee should bend that way. Now advertisement is come from the Lord Fairfax from Yorke, that part of his forces are allreadie advanced as farr as Skipton-in-Craven, and that the body of his army is to follow to raise the siege att Yorke, wch the Generalls there are resolv'd both to continue and to fight with him att the same time. Whereupon Sr John Meldrum is called away with all the forces hee can carry with him into Yorkshire, and itt is expected I should do the like, wch neither my instructions give anie power or capacity for, nor is itt safe for me to venture those forces att so great a distance without order, wch might be in this coniuncture emploid with as great advantage in the places of my owne trust and charge. Yett I shall not be wanting to serve the Kingdome in anie place where I may give assistance to this great worke now in hand; but with relation and respect still to your lops' orders and commands upon

Your Lops'

Nantwich,
June 28, att
three o'clocke
in the afternoone,
1644.

Most humble and
affectionat servant,
B. DENBIGH.

I humbly desire your lopps would bee pleased to send me your instructions in this businesse with all the speede that may bee.[1]

[1] State Papers Dom. Char. I., 316, fol. 112.

LV.

Oswestry, besieged by the Royalists, is relieved by Sir Thomas Myddelton and the Earl of Denbigh.

A.

Sir Thomas Myddelton's Account.

To the Honourable William Lenthal, Esquire, Speaker of the House of Commons. DOCUMENT LV. A. A.D. 1644.

HONOURED SIR,

Not to trouble you with vain relations whereby to hinder the other serious employment for the Kingdom's good, may it please you to be advertised that the Town of Oswestry, late taken by the forces of Parliament, under my brother, Col. Mytton's command, was upon Saturday last begun to be begirt, and since strictly besieged by the King's forces, consisting of about 1,500 horse and 3,500 foot, under the command of Col. Marrow. And that thereupon, in pursuance of a Council of War's determination, occasioned by an earnest and importunate letter from my brother, Col. Mytton, directed to me for speedy relief and raising of the siege of the said town, I did upon the Lord's day last past, with such forces of horse and foot as I then had with me, and the foot forces of Cheshire, all of us then at Knutsford (intending to have marched for Manchester, and then for the service in the north, according to enjoinment of the Committee of both Kingdoms), return and readvance with all my said forces unto a place called Spurstow Heath, where that night we quartered, and thence advanced upon Monday towards Whitchurch. We quartered that night likewise in the open fields, at a place called the Fens,[1] in Flintshire, whence yesterday we marched towards Ellesmere, and

[1] Fen's Hall.

DOCUMENT LV. A. A.D. 1644.

so to Oswestry, where the enemy endeavoured, by battering and storming of the same, violently to have carried it. About two o'clock in the afternoon we came in sight of the town, and within three miles of it, where the enemy having got intelligence of our approach were prepared to receive us. The chief forces of our enemy consisted of the most valiant commanders and soldiers drawn out of the garrisons of Chester, Cheshire, Shrewsbury, Shropshire, Ludlow, Derbyshire, and Flintshire, and other places. The enemy had taken up the passage of water near Whittington, and very furiously assaulted and charged us, but were repulsed, and forced to retire through the courage of our horse, who most courageously entertained the enemy. Three several times the skirmish was doubtful, either side being forced so often to retreat; but in the end, our foot forces coming up relieved the horse, beat back the enemy, and pursued them with such force that the horse, thereby encouraged, which indeed was formerly weary, joining with the foot, they put the enemy to an absolute flight, in which we pursued them five miles towards Shrewsbury, to a place called Felton Heath, and where we remained after their flight again masters of the field.

In the skirmish with the enemy, and in the pursuit, we lost several of our horse, some of our troops, but never a footman which I am yet informed of. Many of the troopers are hurt, but I hope they will recover. I lost one Captain Williams; and one Capt.-Lieut. Fletcher, a very courageous man, being Capt.-Lieut. to Col. Barton, in my brigade, was dangerously shot, but I hope not mortally. As for the enemy, they lost many stout men, had many of them taken prisoners; the number whereof the enclosed will manifest, some of them being of great quality, as the Lord Newport's eldest son. And, besides, such was their haste in their flight, that we found in the way of our pursuit, the highway, as it were, strewn with store of bread, cheese, bacon, and other good provisions, clothes, and else such necessary appurtenances to an army, besides some whole veals and muttons newly killed. The enemy before the relief came had taken the church, the strongest hold about the town. Upon the approach of the relief they suddenly deserted it, and sent their two battering pieces unto Shrewsbury. In the way also were taken by our forces seven carts

DOCUMENT LV. A.

A.D. 1644.

and wagons, laden with provisions, such as beer, bread, and other necessaries, and one was laden with powder and other ammunition.

The Town of Oswestry I find to be a very strong town, and if once fortified, of great concernment, and the key that lets us into Wales.

Sir, I had to my aid three regiments of foot, viz., Col. George Boothe's regiment, a gallant regiment, led by himself on foot to the face of the enemy. Another by Col. Mainwaring, and the third by Col. Croxon; all of them stout and gallant commanders, and the rest of the officers and soldiers full of courage and resolution. Major Louthiane, Adjutant-General, that brave and faithful commander, to whom I cannot ascribe too much honour, brought up the rear that day.

Sir, I rest, yours, &c.,

THO. MYDDELTON.

[ENCLOSURE.]

Prisoners taken at Oswestry July 3, 1644.

Francis Newport, heir to the Lord Newport Capt. Swynerton	Captains of a Troop of Horse
Twenty Welsh and Shropshire gentlemen	Two pieces of artillery to come up to the walls to save the Musketeers
One Cornet of Horse, who had no command	Seven carriages, whereof one of powder
Lieut. Nowell	200 common soldiers, most of them Welsh
One Quartermaster	100 horse
Two corporals	Great store of arms found in the corn and ditches.
Thirty-two troopers	

There is since taken Major Manlye[1] and Major Whirney, under the walls of Shrewsbury.[2]

[1] Major Manly was Governor of Bangor, Flintshire.

[2] From a pamphlet, entitled "A Copy of a Letter sent from Sir Thos. Myddelton, &c. London: Printed for Edward Husbands, July 10, 1644." (K. P. 164—16.)

B.

The Earl of Denbigh's Account to the Committee at Derby House.

DOCUMENT LV. B.

A.D. 1644.

MY LORDS AND GENTLEMEN,

I advanced with these united for
Knotsford, in prosecution of yo
for Lancashire and being
the news of a
walstre with 2,000 foote and 600 horsemen
gathered together, besides some small forces taken out of garrisons, to take advantage of the absence of ours. Upon mature deliberation, and with the advice of the Councill of War, I desired Sr Thomas Middleton to take with him his owne horse, and the Cheshire foote, and to ioyne with the foote in Wem, to raise the seige. Att the same time I went to Manchester, to advise with Sr John Meldrum, about the affairs of those parts, and finding it unsafe for me to passe into Yorkshire, whilst my own association lay under so great a danger, and that my instructions had not such a latitude, and unwilling to give the enemy the opportunity of raising a considerable body in Wales and Shropshire, wch they were endeavouring to doe, as by sadd experience in Lancashire, they weare suffer'd to perfect theire leavies there. I assign'd over to Sr John Meldrum, the nine troopes of Nottingham and Derbie, in all 500 horse, to ioyne with Sr W. Brereton's horse, and the horse and foote of Lancashire, to give their assistance
before Yorke, and with my own re-
horse and the Staffordshire horse and
rch'd back towards Oswaldstre and sent to
as Middleton to acquaint him with my
of ioyning with him, but hee finding his oppor-
thought itt not fitt to stay for me; and the day before I came to Oswaldstre, had the good successe to raise the siege. For the particulars of that action I shall refer your lo^ps^ to Sr Thomas Middleton's relation, and shall only add thus much, that my regiment of foote, seconded by Sr Thomas Middleton, and

DOCUMENT LV. B. A.D. 1644.

his horse, had the honour to beate backe the enemy three miles to Oswaldstre, and a little beyond that towne, till the Cheshire foote tooke their places, and followed the execution, and if I could have advanc'd in a convenient time, or the action had bene deferr'd till our forces had been united (wch the Councill of Warr enclined unto, and the attempt had bene putt off if the letters sent to give advertisement of my approach had not bene conceal'd), though God was pleased to give great testimonies of his goodnesse and favor in what was done, the victory had been more compleate, and in all probabilitie wee had bene masters of theire cannon and of theire best men, wch did belong to the garrisons of Shrewsbury and the adiacent parts, wch would consequently have placed us in faire hopes of gaining these parts of the Kingdome. Upon my arrival at Oswaldstre, with the advice of the Councill of Warr, I order'd our march the same day towards Shrewsbury, as well to pursue as to take them unprovided upon their route, wch happened but the day before, as in hope of drawing in the country, and giveing opportunity to a party in Shrewsbury, wch the committee at Wem had often assur'd me would upon anie advantage declare themselves in our favor. Upon Thursday, the 4 of this month, I appointed a rendevous for all our forces upon Knocking Heath, from thence wee advanc'd to Montford Bridge, upon the Severne, where the enemy had made a drawbridge, and placed about 40 musquetteers with some horse for a guard. We gain'd the bridge with little dispute, and the horse pass'd the ford close by the bridge. Their foote was pursued with great vigour, and theire horse was followed within a mile and a half of Shrewsbury, where we tooke Major Fisher in his quarters, major to Coll^ll^ Egerton, with some troopers. But being in some apprehension of some ambush, I caus'd a retreate to be sounded, and drew upp the horse upon a heath within a mile of the towne. By that time the reare came upp wee had intelligence that Marrow was issued out of the towne with his horse, and had lined all the hedges betwixt that heath and Shrewsbury with musquetteers: immediately I order'd the horse and foote to give on, who kill'd some upon the place, drove the rest into the gates of the towne, and my troope wch ledd the van took Major Manley, major to the Lord Byron, and Governor of Bangor, within little more than pistoll shott of their workes.

DOCUMENT LV. B. A.D. 1644.

Wee tooke that day other officers, 20 troopers and common soldiers. Coll[ll] Marrow was farr engaged and had bene taken, but for the goodnesse of his horse. Upon facing of the towne, and viewing the large circumference, and the strength of theire workes (from where itt did appeare they did not want men by theire shooting of 100 musquetts in a volley severall times), and our forces no way proportionable in number to the greatnesse of the designe, I held it unsafe to engage these forces in a siege, and so drew off back to the heath, where wee quartered that night; but with much difficulty brought off the Cheshire foote, who could by no order be withdraune from firing against the towne. That evening one foote colours was brought me from a house neere Montford Bridge. The next day wee march'd to Wem where upon the receipt of your lo[ps'] instructions, w[ch] gave me the liberty I formerly desired of your lo[ps], I press'd the returning back to the assistance of the armies in Yorkshire, reports being then various and doubtfull concerning the late greate victory itt hath pleas'd God to blesse theire endeavours with in those parts.[1] S[r] Thomas Middleton, though desirous to imploy his forces in Wales was, notwithstanding, persuaded to joyne with me in pursuance of your lo[ps'] orders. Att Whitchurch, Major Louthiane, mov'd me from the Cheshire commanders to take Chomley House in my way, w[ch] I willingly consented unto, and upon Sunday last, the 7 of this month, in the night, lay down before that place. By the next morning wee had rais'd two batteries w[ch] did not worke the effect that was expected, whereupon I ordered the giveing on in severall places to storme itt, haveing intelligence they had but few men to maintaine the workes. But finding the Cheshire commanders who had engag'd me verie backward, some absent, and those that were present not unmindfull of a former disgrace and repulse they had receaved there with great losse, could not, except Major Louthiane, be persuaded that the attempt was faisable. In the end I declar'd if they would not assist me in the service of theire owne county, I would make a tryall only with the Staffordshire regiment of foote, w[ch] consisted but of 200 musquetteers w[ch] by way of emulation brought back the Cheshire foot to theire accustomed forwardnesse and valour w[ch] they have express'd on all

[1] Marston Moor, 2nd July.

DOCUMENT LV. B. A.D. 1644.

occasions. The Staffordshire foote ledd the way, seconded by some Cheshire foote, and the rest of the Cheshire foote weare dispos'd of to give on in two other severall parts, and in places where the mote was conceiv'd most fordable. The assault was so fierce upon their workes, and att the same time our men endeavouring to gett down the drawbridge behind those workes, bredd such a distraction in the enemy that they quitt their workes and retired into the house, and the Governor himself looking out of the window demanded quarter, w[ch] being then granted by Major Louthiane, and after by me, inform'd the Governour, caus'd the bridge to be lett down, and our men entred. Wee tooke in the house of the Governour, L. Coll[ll] Horton (who but two howers before return'd a scornefull answere to the summons I sent that he would begine to parley a month after) with 65 prisoners, their armes, and two barrells of powder, one foote coulors, great store of provisions, and about 20 horse, some whereof weare of great valew. The house is surrounded with a large deepe mote, and with small addition may be rendered verie considerable and of great strength. Upon my retiring into a convenient place, whither I had call'd a Councill of Warr before wee weare assembled, both horse and foote and traine of artillery march'd away without order, and I forc'd to follow after to Nantwich. This may give your lo[ps] some testimony both of the danger and trouble incident to those who command forces of severall qualities and dependencies, and unlesse your lo[ps] will bee pleas'd to right me in my power that I may raise forces to make mee more considerable to those who are appointed to ioyne with me and are in no other relation to me than upon the occasion of some speciall service, I shall not only bee disabled from doing your lo[ps]' service, when by the computation of forces assign'd unto me there may be much expected of me, but even those forces by such disorder and variety of commands will be subiect to dishonour, ruine, and destruction. I had appointed Knotsford for a rendevous to all our forces, but receavinge the enclosed letter from S[r] William Brereton wherein I am advis'd by the Generalls before Yorke to hold intelligence with S[r] W. Waller with intimation of their sending 5,000 horse, under the command of Maior-Generall Cromwell, to disperse the remainder of Prince Rupert's forces, and S[r.] Thomas Middleton lying under no command to ioyne with me against the

DOCUMENT LV. B. A.D. 1644.

King's army, and now conceiving himself free is loth to loose the opportunity of entring Wales and settling himself there in some place of advantage, wch Sr T. Middleton, who hath great interest in the Cheshire gentlemen, doth press verie much; and the Staffordshire committee declaring their want of foote to defend Stafford upon the approach of the King's army upon those confines, my regiment of horse much discontented as will appeare by the enclos'd petition of some of the chiefe commanders in the name of the rest. All these considerations do necessitate me to retire to Stafford as being of no use heere, and intend to remaine there as long as I shall finde myself usefull to the service of the Kingdome and of that association, or anie way capable of performing your lo^ps'^ commands; but when I shall finde myself destitute of forces I must repaire to your lo^ps^ to be enabled for that service wch you have further engag'd me in by setting a valew and esteeme upon those act ons wch itt hath pleas'd God to blesse me in, a favor wch I must ever acknowledge with all humble respect and thankfulnesse, and for ever remaine

Your lo^ps'^

Nantwich, July 11, 1644.

Most humble and most affectionat servant,
B. Denbigh.

In the margin.

I would willingly have omitted the giveing your lo^ps'^ account of the losse of Major Pinkeney, Major to Coll^u^ Rugelay in the takeing of Chomley House. Hee was a gallant gentleman and a good soldier, but hazarded himself in this occasion beyond my orders. I lost no other officer, 2 serjeants, 4 common soldiers, and about 20 wounded.[1]

C.

Sir Fulke Hunke's Account of it to Prince Rupert.

DOCUMENT LV. C. A.D. 1644.

May it please your Highness,

Upon Tuesday, July the 2d., I was drawn out, with what force I could, to ioyne with Coll. Marrow for the regaining of Oswestrie, where having intelligence of the approach of the enemy,

[1] State Papers Dom., Char. I., 316, fol. 120.

DOCUMENT LV. C.

A.D. 1644.

I commanded Collonel Marrow to send out a party of horse to discover their strength, but expressly forbad him to engage himself; yet contrarie to my knowledge or direction, he tooke with him the whole bodie of horse, and engaged himself so farre, that he was routed before I knew anything of it. As soon as I had notice thereof, by a messeng from himself, who desired mee to drawe off, his horse being wholly routed, I put myself in a posture for the security of the cannon, and drawing them off, the first man I mett withal was Marrow all alone. And perceiving that the enemy was like to cutt between us and Shrewsbury, wee drew what strength wee could together, and with small losse made a retreat, and brought off our cannon to Shrewsbury, where wee quartered the remainder of Marrow's troopes. The Thursday following, the enemy advanc'd up to this town, the Lord Denbigh commanding-in-chiefe, thinking to have surprised it out of a confidence of a good partie hee had of the towne; but the outworkes were so well defended, and Marrow falling out with some horse, his Lordship was forced to retire with some losse, and being past over Montford

                                                                                to
Bridge, hee sett it on fire and retired, dividing his troopes 51 . 4 .

O s w e s t r y where he t a r
65 . 3 . 49 . 53 . 8 . 49 . 51 . 47 . 57 66 . 112 52 . 10 . 47 .

r i e d not long but
47 . 6 . 25 . 35 131 97 100 borrowed 110 . 39 and with

his own troopes he went to Cholmondly, which iust now I heare

to goe a b
he hath taken. Marrow is now returning 51 . 4 79 10 . 23 .

o u t C h i r d e to to
4 . 2 . 51. 24 . 33 . 6 . 47 . 35 . 8 51 . 4 seeke 51 . 4 get

his horse a g a i n e This c o u
116 125 togither 10 . 31 . 10 . 6 . 41 . 8 111 2 . 4 . 4 .

n t r i e in b a d c o
2 . 41 . 51 . 47 . 57 is 101 a very 23 . 10 . 27 94 . 27 .

n di ti on, and men are s l o w
6 . 51 . 4 . 41 112 110 72 heere very 49 . 37 . 4 . 53

your Highnesse c o
in fulfilling 84 . 47 32 . 6 . 31 . 33 . 41 . 8 . 49 95 . 10 .

m ands H e e r e is very to
41 . 27 . 49 33 . 8 . 8 . 47 . 8 81 . 93 little added 51 . 4

what your H ighness
96 84 . 47 32 . 6 . 31 . 33 . 41 . 8 . 49 left, nor was

DOCUMENT LV. C.

A.D. 1644.

e v e r | a n y | m a n | | so
8 . 2 . 8 . 47 | 10 . 41 . 57 | 39 . 10 . 41 | amongst | 114

m a n y | | as | I | am, | and
39 . 10 . 41 . 57 | caterpillars | 10 . 49 | 5 | 10 . 39 | 112

s e e | not | any | | to | a m e n d
49 . 8 . 8 | 93 | 91 | possibility | 131 | 10 . 39 . 8 . 41 . 27 .

m e n t | in | your | | a b
39 . 8 . 41 . 51 | 101 | 84 . 47 | Highness | 10 . 23 .

s e n c e.
49 . 8 . 41 . 25 . 8 I shall most humbly desire your Highness to

con s i d e r | what | | h a v e
94 . 49 . 6 . 27 . 8 . 47 | 90 | good intelligence I | 33 . 10 . 2 . 8

where | by | | they
151 | 97 | I am informed that having taken Cholmondly | 85

in t e n d | f o r | M o r t o n
101 . 51 . 8 . 41 . 27 | 29 . 4 . 47 | 38 . 4 . 47 . 51 . 4 . 41

C o r b e t, | f r o m | the n c e
24 . 4 . 47 . 23 . 8 . 51 | 29 . 47 . 4 . 39 | 110 . 41 . 25 . 8

to | A r t l y, | and | so | to | us
51 . 4 | 9 . 47 . 51 . 37 . 57 | 112 | 114 | 51 . 4 | 67 if

| are | not | p r e v e n t e d.
they | 81 | 92 | 43 . 47 . 8 . 2 . 8 . 41 . 51 . 8 . 27 | If your

| not | c a s t | | e y e | upon
Highness doe | 92 | 25 . 10 . 48 . 51 | an | 8 . 57 . 8 | 103

the | forces | as | are | here.
90 | 115 | 82 | 81 | 105

The news is better from the King's army from whence wee receive intelligence that his forces have brought off ten pieces of Waller's ordnance and many prisoners with the Generall of the artillery. In this action the Lord Wilmot was taken prisoner, and by the same party that tooke him brought into the King's guards unknown to them that brought him, whereby they became prisoners themselves, and hee rescued, having only received a slight hurt. Sr William Waller who commanded reported to be hurt and retired to Northampton. The King is now at Evesham. . . .

. . more as to overthrow of the ungratefull Scot.

Your Highness

most humble servant,

Salop, July 10th, 1644. F. Hunkes.[1]

Addressed—ffor his Highness Prince Rupert.

[1] State Papers Dom., vol. 316, fol. 132.

LVI.

Glimpses of Col. Charles Gerard[1] *in South Wales, and of the Success of the Cavaliers there.*

A.

We told you this day month of the rebels murder at Milford Haven,[2] which hath prospered so equally that now that bloody mariner begins to fear he may ere long be brought to reckon for it. For Swanley, not satisfied with piracy and sea-villanies, did practise by land also, in Pembrokeshire, Carmarthenshire, and Glamorganshire, till that gallant gentleman, Col. Charles Gerard made him face about, driving the barbarous felon back to the place from whence he came. Two of the three counties are perfectly cleared, and the third so chastised that the rebels are already at the water-side. The Welsh gentlemen and commons were so much startled at the horror of the fact [the water rats again] that they now rise as one man to punish the malefactors.[3] DOCUMENT LVI. A. A.D. 1644.

B.

How Swanley hath since prospered [since the water rats business] you may know of the inhabitants of Monmouthshire, Glamorganshire, Carmarthenshire, Cardiganshire, and Pembrokeshire, in all which counties those rebels had got footing, but are now chased thence to their last reserve in Pembrokeshire by that valiant brave gentleman, Colonel Charles Gerard, General of his Majesty's forces in those parts; who since his late landing at the DOCUMENT LVI. B. A.D. 1644.

[1] Col. Gerard, a great favourite of Rupert, was made General of South Wales when the command was given up by the Earl Carbery.

[2] This refers to Swanley making "water rats" of the Irish.

[3] *Merc. Aulicus*, 26th week, June 29th. (K. P. 166—6.)

DOCUMENT LVI. B. A.D. 1644.

Black Rock, in Monmouthshire, unto Saint David's, in Pembrokeshire, hath made an impression of above 100 miles; hath taken Cardiff, where the rebels had placed a strong garrison, which much annoyed all that county of Glamorgan. This done he advanced into Carmarthenshire, and took Kidwelly, a strong haven town, where he left a good garrison, and then fell on the Town and Castle of Carmarthen, which he presently mastered, and there he placed another good garrison, under Colonel Lovelace, and left a garrison also at Abermarlais. After he had totally cleared that county also, he marched into Cardiganshire, which was much distressed by the Pembrokeshire rebels; and at Cardigan he killed and took prisoners above two hundred rebels, having beaten, cut off, and taken all the rebels got into that county. He strongly garrisoned Cardigan Castle, and then advanced into Pembrokeshire (the most seditious county of all Wales, or rather of England, for the inhabitants live like English Corporations, very unlike the loyal Welshmen), and here he took Emlyn Castle, Laugharne Castle, with two other garrisons. And on Sunday was sennight he assaulted and took Roch Castle, a very considerable place, with a booty of 500 head of oxen and 2,000 sheep, all which the rebels had ordained for themselves and their brethren. So that of the seven hundreds in Pembrokeshire the rebels have lost five, being driven down to the water side, where they lie close and by no means can be invited forth to fight, though his Majesty's forces have lain already eighteen days in the field, in all which time the rebels have not dared to attempt anything against them, only they have valiantly forged some slanders in tickets and warrants to abuse the people, one of which came lately to our hands, whereof this is a true copy:—

To the Petty Constables of Walton, and to either of them.

Whereas I have received a warrant from the Gentlemen Commissioners appointed for this County of Pembroke, to me and my fellow High Constable directed, importing that whereas the neighbouring County of Carmarthen is at this present intolerably annoyed by powerful forces, both of horse and foot, who have lately invaded the same, their army consisting for the most part of Papists and Irish rebels, who were actors in the bloody and barbarous massacres, and exceeding great effusion of Protestant blood in Ireland, and frequently vow the slaughter and destruction of all true Protestants in these three counties of Carmarthen, Cardigan, and Pembroke, men, women, and children; and so utterly to spoil and make desolate this whole country. These are therefore in his Majesty's name to will and require you forthwith, upon receipt hereof, to raise all the strength and power within your parish, both horse and foot, and to bring them all, as well gentry, trained bands, dragooners, and all able-bodied men, above the age of 16 to 60, with all manner of offensive and defensive arms, and all horses fit for service or carriage, that are within your parish, to appear before the said Commissioners upon Friday next, by 8 of the clock in the morning, for his Majesty and the honourable Houses of Parliament, and in the just defence of our and their religion, lives, liberties, and posterity, every man bringing with him six days' provision in victuals and money, and to submit to such orders as to that purpose they shall receive from such Commissioners, letting all such persons who shall disobey this summons to wit they shall be esteemed rebels and traitors against the King and Parliament, and wicked subverters of their religion, liberties, and country, and that you fail not the execution and due return hereof at your perils.

DOCUMENT LVI. B. A.D. 1644.

HUGH CARROW.[1]

Dated 12th June, 1644.

C.

Pembrokeshire.

The last week I[2] gave you an account of the good success of Colonel Lohun [Laugharne], and Captain Moulton, who with the soldiers under his command performed a gallant exploit against Colonel Gerard, that grand Papist, by routing and dispersing his forces, they killed and took 500 of them, and so stopped their

DOCUMENT LVI. C. A.D. 1644.

[1] *Merc. Aulicus*, 29th week, July 20. (K. P. 168.)

[2] *True Reformer*, No. 41. Aug. 3. (K. P. 168—11.)

DOCUMENT LVI. C. A.D. 1644.

intended progress into Pembrokeshire, which they would have plundered and spoiled, as they had before done in Monmouthshire, Glamorganshire, Carmarthenshire, and Cardiganshire, in all which places they had done much mischief, and had taken several forts and castles, viz., Cardigan, Emlyn, and Laugharne Castle, since the landing of Col. Gerard, and his Irish and Popish forces at the Black Rock, in Monmouthshire. Our commanders there [in Pembrokeshire], to hinder their further progress, have sent out several warrants into the said counties [for a copy of which see preceding Extract B.]

Since the before-mentioned action, it is also certified by some from the Lord Admiral's Navy, that Capt. Moulton hath taken nine ships near Milford Haven, which were laden with wine and tobacco, going from the West, and had in them above 100 pieces of ordnance, all which will be now employed for the use of the Parliament soldiers.

D.

DOCUMENT LVI. D. A.D. 1644.

We must desire you to recall one passage in the last week save one, where we told you Haverfordwest, in Pembrokeshire, was surrendered up to Colonel Charles Gerard, which (as appears now) was said somewhat too early, for we have since received certain intelligence that the rebels kept it till the 22 of this instant, on which day they were forced thence, and Colonel Gerard took possession of the town; the frightened rebels hasting into their two only holes, Tenby and Pembroke Castle, one whereof we hope will not be long lived, for this last week his Majesty's forces took the Governor of Tenby (brother to Laugharne the chief rebel), and followed it so close, that they took that night a whole troop of horse belonging to Tenby garrison—the loyal Welshmen of Monmouthshire, Glamorganshire, Carmarthenshire, and Cardiganshire, being all up to reduce the rebels of Tenby and Pembroke, which makes all the Londoners in their last week's pamphlet fall so foul

DOCUMENT LVI. D.

A.D. 1644.

on the Welshmen, saying "the word of God hath scarce appeared to the Welsh mountaineers, much of their counties being little better than downright heathens." 'Tis of late pretty welcome to us to hear the rebels rail, for we find they gape widest when they have been best beaten.[1]

[1] *Merc. Aulicus*, 35th week, August 31.

LVII.

Capture of Royalist Horse at Welshpool by Sir Thomas Myddelton. August 5.

DOCUMENT LVII. A.D. 1644.

By letters out of Cheshire, dated the 7th of this instant August, it is advertised—That Col. Mytton lately faced Shrewsbury with his horse, and with another party kept Montford Bridge towards the Welsh gate, within three miles of Shrewsbury, and wheeled about the town with another party through Crow-Meole and Brase-Meole, to Atcham Bridge, where Col. Hunke, the Governor of Shrewsbury lies, and drove away many of his horse, calves, and sheep, and did much hinder Shrewsbury fair, which was that day; whereupon Col. Hunke sent out a party of horse against Col. Mytton's forces, which, being driven into a lane, our forces fell upon them on both sides, whereupon the enemy's forces fled through hedges and ditches, and left above forty horse.

From thence, having intelligence of the enemy's horse quartering at Welshpool, Colonel Mytton's forces marched that way, and in their march Sir Thomas Myddelton joined with them on Saturday, August 3, with two colours of Nantwich foot and his own horse; and on the Lord's day, at night, having made a body of 550 horse and foot, beat up the enemy's quarters (being Prince Rupert's own regiments), took 346 horse, with most of their arms, three horse colours, whereof one was Sir Thomas Dallison's (brother to popish Dallison, the lawyer), three captains, and twelve other commanders and officers, and forty common soldiers, with much riches and treasure. Prince Rupert's own cornet was slain. Sir Thomas Dallison fled away without his breeches, in which was found a letter which he intended to send to Prince Rupert the next day. After this our forces drove away 200 head of cattle of Sir Pierce[1] Herbert close from the walls of Red Castle.[2] Also an hundred and twenty of Prince Rupert's horse

[1] Percy.

[2] Red Castle is another name for Powis Castle.

are lately come into Nantwich, and to Col. Mytton, and many others, come in daily to the Parliament's garrisons of Oswestry and Wem.[1] DOCUMENT LVII. A.D. 1644.

Sir Thomas Dallison's Letter.

SIR,

I have had 113 coats and caps for foot soldiers in the house of my Lord Powis, an 100 of which are blue, which will serve very well for your Highness's regiment of foot. The rest are green, which may serve for Col. Tylyer's.[2] There was also three or four hundred yards of cloth, which may serve to make coats or cloaks for your Highness's regiment of horse. I am requested to let your Highness know that he[3] will dispose both of the coats and cloaks at your pleasure. He makes expression to be exceedingly desirous to serve your Highness, and he assures me he will employ all his power to that purpose. The general rendezvous of the gentlemen of the county shall be to-morrow, about our arrears and for the providing our quarters. The regiment of your Highness is for the present very weak in horse, and we have lost many by reason of the great march which we have had. There are four troops quartered within Welshpool, and the rest as commodiously as they can thereabouts, without being exempted from keeping guard or standing sentinel. I fear to receive the like blow suddenly as those did lately that were at Shrewsbury. All our horses are at grass in the day time, and in the night we fetch them in, with many other services, which we are constrained to continue, notwithstanding our weak estate where we are. We do daily expect supplies from your Highness, which I beseech you most humbly to consider, and so remain in the quality of

A most humble servant and officer to your Highness,

THOMAS DALLISON.[4]

Pool, August 4.

[1] *Mercurius Civicus*, No. 64, Aug. 15, 1644. (K. P. 170—15.)
[2] Sylier's in copy. [3] The Lord Powis.
[4] *The True Informer*, No. 43, Aug. 17, 1644. (K. P. 170—23.)

LVIII.

A Contest at Tarvin, near Chester, Aug. 21, 1644.

DOCUMENT LVIII.

A.D. 1644.

SIR,

In my last I gave you an account of the skirmish in Lancashire, where the Lord Ogleby, Col. Mynn, and divers other persons of quality, Scotch-commanders and gentlemen, were taken prisoners. Since which, upon Sabbath-day last, some of our forces from Northwich skirmished with Col. Marrow, near Crowton House,[1] wherein we had a garrison kept, where we lost 14 men, who were taken prisoners. But the enemy's loss was far greater, for Colonel Marrow, a second Nimrod, received his mortal wound, upon which he is since dead in Chester. Both he and his regiment of horse die (*sic*) at one time. And it is reported by some that the bloody Prince Rupert is going towards the King.

I shall now acquaint you with God's continued goodness unto us. Upon Wednesday, the 21st of August, Sir Wm. Brereton, that active and faithful patriot, sent forth a party of horse and foot from Nantwich in Cheshire, who marched from thence to Frodsham, hoping to have found the enemy there. From thence they marched over the Forest of Delamere to Ashton,[2] (where we heard they quartered), to have met with them there, but having intelligence that they were at Tarvin, within four miles of Chester, marched towards them, and meeting some of their scouts pursued them into Tarvin, and there fell upon the enemy and soon routed them.

Some fled into the church, others out of the town towards Chester, but were pursued gallantly by that valiant Captain Sankey who commands Sir William Brereton's own troop within pistol shot of the walls of Chester. A gentleman of Sir William Brereton's

[1] In the parish of Weaverham.

[2] A village on the North-west border of the Forest.

troop, named Mr. Dury, killed one of the enemy close at the works of Chester. And while these were in pursuit of the enemy towards Chester, the rest were not idle in Tarvin; for that worthy and valiant Lieut.-Colonel Jones, who commanded the horse, behaved himself gallantly, and so did the valiant Major Trevors who commanded the foot. The enemy fired very fast out of the church; they took some horses into the church. The service being very hot there was one brave horse they could not get in, but one of the enemy held him in his hand under the church wall. A corporal of Sir Wm. Brereton's troop, named John Cooper, seeing the horse, ventured to fetch him; but they fired so fast out of the church that he retreated twice, but the third time he ventured up, he pistol'd the enemy and brought away the horse, which horse was valued worth four score pounds. There was taken at the same time between forty and fifty prisoners and about three hundred horse, some very gallant ones. When they had done they marched away with their prisoners and horses and lost but two men. Had not the enemy at Chester had such an alarm and made such haste towards us we should have taken the church.[1]

[A list of the prisoners taken is given—comprising Capt. Ed. Gibson, Cornet Clements, thirteen of Col. Chalcross's regiment, eight of Capt. Swinnington's men, four of Lieut.-Col. Grosvenor's men, seven under Lieut.-Col. Leigh, four of Capt. Phillips's troop, one of Capt. Woodhas's, one under Capt. Richard, and one of no company.]

[1] From a pamphlet, entitled "A True Relation of two great Victories obtained of the enemy: the one by Sir William Brereton in Cheshire, &c. London: Printed for Thomas Underhill, at the sign of the Bible in Woodstreet (August 30th), 1644." (K. P. 171—25.)

LIX.

Defeat of the Royalist Army of the North on its march to the King, at Malpas, in Cheshire, August 26.

DOCUMENT LIX.

A.D. 1644.

Sir,

As you have been frequent in your addresses to God in our behalf, so you may look upon a wonderful and extraordinary deliverance and victory as a return of your prayers, for which I desire such return of thanks may be made, as shall be thought fit, for so great a mercy which God gave us upon Monday morning, being August 26th. Upon Saturday evening intelligence came to Nantwich of the enemies passing by us towards the King, and quartering about Whitchurch, whereof I met with the news at my coming out of Lancashire, where I had leave to meet Sir John Meldrum and the Lancashire gentlemen. And my horse were not (since they had the fight at Tarvin) returned hither, but were quartered about Middlewich. Two or three of our troops came not in, which made the assault heavier upon the rest; which, together with some seven companies of foot (whereof three or four were of my own regiment, one of Colonel Brooke's, and the rest of Col. Duckenfield's regiments), marched out of Nantwich upon Sabbath-day, in the evening, about six of the clock, and came to Malpas the next morning about the spring of day, where my troop charged the enemy three or four times, the other troops which followed, not being able to come up in the narrow lanes.

The enemy were judged to be about forty colours, and betwixt two thousand and three thousand in number. The commanders thereof, being many of them Papists (for this was the remainder of the Earl of Newcastle's army, sometime commanded by Goring), did fight, and come on very gallantly, but their leaders never went back again. There was in the front of my troops divers officers, who behaved themselves very gallantly, as Lieut.-Col. Jones, Capt. Sankey, Capt. Finch, Capt. Church, Lieut. Burroughs, and divers others. When we came to the top of the hill we discovered the enemy to stand in six or seven several bodies, or divisions, in very good order. But before this time we had killed divers of their colonels and great officers. It was not thought fit to pursue any farther, we having beaten two strong parties of them, and followed them through Malpas town. Nor was it safe to engage a handful against so great a number, and we could not retreat without danger of losing all. Therefore, it was resolved that we should stand in the mouth of the lane till the foot came up to relieve them, which were commanded by Major Lanchane (?) and Col. Venables, which was accordingly done. But before the foot came up, our horse were very much spent, having received three or four fresh charges by several fresh brigades or divisions, wherein was neither man nor one foot of ground lost, but rather gained every charge. And when the foot came up they performed very good execution; yet they were all in danger to be surrounded by the enemy, who, as they were sufficiently strong, so they wanted not opportunity, when God delivered up so many of their commanders into our hands, who were killed, wounded, and taken prisoners, as will appear by the enclosed.

Their common soldiers, upon the loss of so many of their commanders, retreated, and we were not able to pursue them far. But had we had five hundred horse, we might (by God's blessing) have wholly destroyed this army, whereof there may be still about 2,000 remaining, which, with the addition of Sir William Vaughan's regiment, and Colonel Trevor's, and the remainder of the Prince's regiment of horse, they cannot be but above 3,000 strong. They were then upon their march towards Shrewsbury, and so to the King; but fled back towards Chester, where they could not be admitted, but were looked upon very scornfully, because they were beaten back by so inconsiderable a number, which they exceeded above ten to one.

The enemy being still an overmatch to us, it is not improbable they may force their passage to join with the King's army; therefore, it were much to be desired that what horse and foot is intended us might be speeded unto these parts. It is uncertain where the Prince [Rupert] is, but some say he is gone towards Shrewsbury, some say towards the King, but it is not known to very many in Chester. Lieut.-Col. Jones, Capt. Zanchy [or Sankey], Capt. Finch, Capt. Church, and others, showed much courage and

DOCUMENT LIX. A.D. 1644.

resolution in standing so valiantly, not shrinking a foot at several charges by the enemy, which did so much amaze the enemy that some of them swore "they were devils and not men." Hereof, I desire God may have the glory. I have no more to add, but, with my respects to you, desiring the continuance of your prayers, subscribe myself

Your assured friend,

WILL. BRERETON.

[INCLOSURE.]

A list of prisoners taken by the Cheshire forces for the Parliament at Malpas, Aug. 26, 1644.

1. Major Cromwell, who commanded as Major to the Duke of York's regiment of horse.
2. Major Maxie, Major of Sir Charles Lucas's regiment, of which regiment there is no field commander left, Sir Charles himself (who was Lieut.-General to the Prince) being taken at York, and his Lieut.-Col. also.
3. Major Craulthorn of Col. Forier's regiment (formerly Clavering's regiment).
4. Capt. Thomas Clavering, brother to Col. Clavering of the North, who is dead at Kendal.
5. Capt. Barker and Lieut. Mountain, with some other inferior officers, and about 20 common soldiers. The two Majors and the Lieutenant are dangerously wounded.

At the same time there were slain Col. Conyers, Col. Baynes, Col. Hesketh, and 'tis said three other majors, and other officers about 40;—others say an hundred slain more. Sir Marmaduke Langdale, as is reported by a trumpeter (whom he sent to Mr. Brereton for a list of prisoners), is wounded in the back, so is Capt. Harris, and both lie wounded at Chester. But on our part we lost not one man, neither taken nor killed, nor any dangerously wounded. Lieut.-Col. Jones (who behaved himself most gallantly) being shot in the thigh, but I hope but slightly, and some other officers and soldiers of Sir W. Brereton's own troop (who were in the van) very slightly wounded.[1]

[1] From a pamphlet, entitled "The Successes of our Cheshire Forces, as related by Sir W. Brereton's own pen to a Minister of note in the City, &c. London: Printed for Thomas Underhill (Sep. 4), 1644." (K.P. 172—8.)

LX.

Montgomery, having been delivered up to the Parliament, is besieged by Lord Byron—Brereton and Myddelton, assisted by Sir John Meldrum, raise the Siege and rout the Cavaliers.

A.

Sir William Brereton's Account of the Victory, to the Committee of both Kingdoms.

RIGHT HONOURABLES,

That God who is most glorified by working by the weakest and unworthiest instruments hath this day given a most glorious victory, and as much manifested his power therein, as in any day I have been engaged since the beginning of these Wars. DOCUMENT LX. A. A.D. 1644.

We have relieved Montgomery Castle, wherein there was closely besieged and much distressed the Lord Herbert of Cherbury, Col. Price, and most of Sir Thomas Myddelton's officers, and near 500 soldiers.

We were so very hard taxed by the multitude of our enemies (who did much exceed us in number), as that if the commanders and soldiers had not engaged and behaved themselves very gallantly, or if we had wanted any part of our forces, it might have hazarded our army, for it was very dubious and uncertain which way the Lord would incline the victory. It came to push of pike, wherein they were much too hard for us, having many more pikes. Our horse also at the beginning of the battle were worsted and retreated, but there was, I do believe, an unanimous resolution, both in horse and foot, to fight it out to the last man. Indeed, there could be no other hope nor expectation of safety or escape, there remaining no way of retreat, all passages being entirely in the enemy's power (if masters of the field), and truly, if God had not infatuated, they might easily have interrupted our passage,

DOCUMENT LX. A.

A.D. 1644.

and made good divers passes against us. But our extremity was God's opportunity to magnify His power, for when it was most dubious, the Lord so guided and encouraged our men, that with a fresh valiant charge we routed and put to retreat and flight their whole army, pursued them many miles, even in the mountains, and did perform great execution upon them; slew (I do believe) 500, wounded many more, took near 1,500 prisoners, and amongst them Colonel Broughton and Col. Tilsley, who they report to be General-Majors. There were also taken Lieutenant-Colonels, Majors, and Captains more than twenty, and all their carriages, and near 20 barrels of powder, wherewith they were furnished the night before the battle. We took also (as was conceived) near 1,500 or 2,000 arms, most for foot. Most of their horse escaped towards Shrewsbury and Chester.

The enemy's army was reported (and I do believe it) no less than 4,000,—the foot being the old Irish, who came out of Ireland with Col. Broughton, Warren, Tillier, and some of Col. Ellis, and some of Col. Sir Michael Woodhouse's and Sir Michael Ernely's regiment from Shrewsbury, Chester, and Ludlow. Our army consisted of about 1,500 foot, and 1,500 horse. We lost not 40 men slain, and I do believe there were not 60 wounded. Our greatest loss was of Sir William Fairfax and Major Fitz Simons, most gallant men. Sir John Meldrum did with much judgment order and command these forces, and therefore deserves a large share in the honour of this day's success. But, indeed, the whole honour and glory is to be given and ascribed to God, the giver of victories, and who is most deservedly styled the Lord of Hosts.

What remains further to be done in prosecution of this victory shall not be omitted, and if it please God that Newcastle be delivered, and some Scottish forces assigned to assist in the taking of Chester, I hope through God's mercy there may be a good account given of all these parts of the Kingdom. To effect which no man shall serve you with more faithfulness than

Your humble servant,

WILLIAM BRERETON.

Montgomery,

September 18, 1644.

We know not how to dispose of these common prisoners, unless it would please you to order some of them that will take the Covenant to be shipped (if God give us Liverpool) and transported over into Ireland to serve you there. DOCUMENT LX. A. A.D. 1644.

We have left Sir Thomas Myddelton in a good condition in Montgomery Castle, and the gentlemen of the country begin to come in unto him. Sir John Price is already come unto him before I came thence. The L. Herbert is come away with us towards Oswestry.

B.

Sir Thomas Myddelton's Account of it.

My Lords and Gentlemen,

I formerly acquainted you of our coming hither, and of our proceedings in these parts, and also of the good success it pleased God to bestow upon us. Since which time the enemy hastened to come upon us before we could bring in provisions for our garrison, by reason whereof I was enforced to retreat with my horse unto Oswestry, with some small loss only of stragglers that lay loitering behind, leaving all my foot in the castle, and hastened into Cheshire to procure relief, and likewise into Lancashire to Sir John Meldrum, from whom I found a great deal of readiness to relieve us in our distress, and to preserve what we had gotten from the enemy, being 37 barrels of powder and 12 of brimstone, both of which they exceedingly wanted. Sir John Meldrum, with Sir William Brereton and Sir William Fairfax, marched with 3,000 horse and foot towards Montgomery, and came thither on the 17th of this instant September, where we lay that night in the field that was most advantageous for us, which the enemy had possessed themselves of before, and deserted at our coming thither, placing themselves upon the mountain above the castle, a place of great advantage for them. We resolved not to go to them but to endeavour the victualling of the castle, whereupon we sent out parties DOCUMENT LX. B. A.D. 1644

DOCUMENT LX. B. A.D. 1644. for the bringing in of provisions, which the enemy perceiving they marched down in a body, both horse and foot, being in number about 5,000, and came up to our ground and gave us battle, wherein, after an hour's fight, it pleased God, we obtained a glorious victory, having taken many officers, 1,400 common soldiers, slain 400, and taken their ammunition, with a great part of their arms and some few horse, the rest all flying away. The Lord Byron commanded in chief the enemy's forces, and Sir John Meldrum the Parliament's forces, who behaved himself most bravely and gallantly; and Sir William Fairfax, who had the command of the horse, did most valiantly set upon their horse, and engaged himself so far that he was taken prisoner, but presently fetched off by the valour of our men, but sore wounded. Our men issued also out of the castle, and fell upon the enemies in their trenches, and took divers of their officers and soldiers which they had left to keep their walls. Sir William Brereton with the Cheshire foot did most bravely behave themselves that day, and did beat the best foot in England, as they the very enemies confess, being all Prince Rupert's foot, and the chosen foot out of all their garrisons. I shall make it still my humble suit that you will please to afford me some speedy course for present money for the payment of my soldiers, for without that I shall not be able to keep them together. And for the present I shall take upon me the boldness to subscribe myself,

My Lords and Gentlemen,

Your humble servant,

THOMAS MYDDELTON.

Mountgomery Castle,

September 19, 1644.

Since the writing of this letter it hath pleased God to take to His mercy Sir William Fairfax, who is even now dead.

C.

Sir John Meldrum's Letter to the Committee of Safety.

DOCUMENT LX. C. A.D. 1644. MY LORDS,

I have thought fit to give your Lordships a brief account of some passages of business here in Wales, forbearing a larger

DOCUMENT LX. C. A.D. 1644.

relation till I shall have further time and a larger subject, which in all probability, by God's assistance, may offer itself within a short time. I was by the earnest invitations of Sir William Brereton and Sir Thomas Myddelton easily persuaded to concur with them for the relief of Montgomery Castle, besieged by the King's forces. I resolved to contribute my best endeavours in that expedition, as well in regard of the importance of the service as that Liverpool was not to be attempted suddenly by such forces as I had (being in number inferior to the forces within the town), whereupon I went along with the Yorkshire, Lancashire, Cheshire, and Staffordshire forces (amounting to 3,000 horse and foot), and marched to Montgomery Castle, in Wales, which was by a great deal of industry and resolution taken by Sir Thomas Myddelton, together with a great deal of powder, match, and brimstone, which (coming from Bristol) was prepared for the relief of Shrewsbury, Chester, and Liverpool. Upon our approach towards the castle the enemy did withdraw themselves in some disorder; the next day after, being the 18th of September, they did take advantage of the weakness of our quarters, the third part of our horse being employed abroad for victuals and forage. Their horse and foot came on with great courage, resolving to break through our forces and to make themselves masters of a bridge we had gained the night before, which would have cut off the passage of our retreat. It pleased God to dispose so of the issue of the business that (by the resolution of the officers and soldiers of horse and foot) the enemy did lose the advantage they had in the beginning, and were shamefully routed, by the pursuit of the victory, which continued for the space of three miles. There are found dead upon the place 500, besides many officers of quality killed and wounded, and 1,200 prisoners. Sir William Fairfax and Major Fitz Simons (who carried themselves most bravely) are deadly wounded, without great hope of recovery, with some other captains and officers of our horse. The Cheshire foot, with their officers, carried themselves more like lions than men, especially Major Lowthian, who commanded as Major-General. The castle is relieved with victuals. Sir Thomas Myddelton's soldiers, who were before as prisoners, are made free, together with the Lord Herbert of Cherbury. Amongst the prisoners are Major-General Tilsley,

DOCUMENT LX. C. A.D. 1644. Col. Broughton, and divers Lieut.-Colonels and Majors, with many Captains and Lieutenants, so that by the blow given here the best of their foot are taken away. Shrewsbury, Chester, and Liverpool, unfurnished with ammunition, and North Wales (which formerly hath been the nursery for the King's armies), in all likelihood will shake off that yoke of servitude which formerly did lie upon their necks, and will be reduced to the obedience of the King and Parliament by the example of Montgomery Castle, which is one of the goodliest and strongest places that ever I looked upon. The personal carriage and endeavours of Sir William Brereton and Sir Thomas Myddelton hath been exceeding great in the advancement of this service. There is good hope that Liverpool, by famine, will be soon reduced, and that Shrewsbury and Chester will be at the last gasp, whereof, by God's assistance, there shall be a short trial made. So having no further for the present to impart to your Lordships, I shall cherish all occasions wherein I may approve myself

Your Lordships' most humble servant,

JOHN MELDRUM.

Montgomery Castle,
September 19, 1644.

MY LORDS,

The intelligence I have had since the closing of my letter, of a body of horse and Col. Hunke's regiment of foot, that are marched to Shrewsbury, and that the Lord Byron and Molyneux are gone back to Chester, I have altered my resolution touching Shrewsbury, which at the best had no other inducement but the hope of a party within the town and the scarcity of soldiers there.

I am, your Lordships' most humble servant,

JOHN MELDRUM.

D.

A List of the Prisoners taken and slain at the Battle near Montgomery, upon the 18th of September, 1644.

DOCUMENT LX. D. A.D. 1644.

Col. Broughton	Major Williams	Capt. Bellamy
Sir Tho. Tilsley, Col.	Capt. Boulton	Capt. Floyd
Lieut.-Col. Bladwell	Capt. Egerton	Capt. Dolebin

DOCUMENT LX. D.
A.D. 1644.

Capt. Congreve	Ensign Host	Samuel Day
Capt. Bowman	Ensign Lagden	Will. Williams
Capt. Right	Ensign Jones	Jo. Davies
Capt. Morgan	Ensign Barker	Peter Lee
Lieut. Sydney	Ensign Price	Will. Manning
Lieut. Rowes	Ensign Roberts	Ed. Phillips
Lieut. Griffith	Ensign Richardson	Jo. Hin
Lieut. Morgan	Ensign Prichard	Ralph Aston
Lieut. Thurland	Ensign Winn	Roger Stanton
Lieut. Wilson	Ensign Johnson	Griffith Davies
Lieut. Lloyd	Ensign Roe	John Smith
Lieut. Lewis	Ensign-Right	John Paster
Lieut. Bowen	Ensign Erwin	Will. Pasley
Lieut. Bricham	*Serjeants.*	Thomas Colston
Lieut. Hager	Simeon Day	Rob. Stanford
Lieut. Minchley	Francis West	Isaac Guy
Lieut. Lloyd	Richard Watson	Thomas Lattham
Lieut. Olliver	Francis Gough	John Brown
Lieut. Kavanagh	John Morgan	John Knowles
Lieut. Perkins	John Sprigman	Robert Barber
Lieut. Aldersay	Will. Hughes	Sam. Rode
Quart.-Mr. Snelling	John Davies	Rob. Feade
Cornet Persons	Tho. Ward	Roger Pyer
Cornet Hackkison	Ja. Newin	Nath. Dale
Cornet Stagge	Edward Badcocke	Will. Compton
Ensign Wallis	Richard Elty	Ralph Williams
Ensign Williams	Morris Jones	Rob. Baccot
Ensign Dutton	Rand. Griffith	John Hunston
Ensign Lampley	Ralph Smith	Rob. Jones
Ensign Parr	Will. Jackson	Cornelius Segel
Ensign Edwards	Ralph Herley	Edward Jones
Ensign Clanton	Jam. Jeffries	Edw. Suebourne
Ensign Harrison	Rich. Morgan	57 Corporals by name
Ensign Coutry	Griffith Lloyd	11 Drummers[1] ,,

[1] The foregoing letters are from a pamphlet, entitled "Letters from Sir Wm. Brereton, &c., of the great victory, by God's providence, given them in raising the Siege before Montgomery Castle, &c. Printed for John Wright, &c." (K P. 174—4.)

E.

Sir Michael Ernely's Letter to Prince Rupert.

DOCUMENT LX. E.

A.D. 1644.

May it please your Highness,

I am very sorry that I have not better news to present you withal. Upon the delivery of the Castle of Montgomery to the enemy by that treacherous Lord of Cherbury, for the regaining of it, and your Highness's powder, which was taken at Newtown, and brought thither, I drew out a considerable force of horse and foot, who marched thither, where they beat Sir Thomas Myddelton, and forced both his horse and foot into the castle, and kept them in ten days, and upon intelligence of the enemy's drawing thither for their relief, my Lord Byron came thither with a considerable force upon Tuesday last, where it was our hap to be beaten yesterday, and the castle relieved. The enemy's forces that came to relieve the castle were commanded by Sir William Brereton, Sir John Meldrum, and Sir William Fairfax, who was there slain.

I rest, your Highness's most obedient servant,

Mic. Ernely.[1]

Shrewsbury, 19th September, 1644.

F.

Arthur Trevor's Account of the Defeat at Montgomery in a Letter, to the Marquis of Ormond.

DOCUMENT LX. F.

A.D. 1644

May it please your Excellency,

My last letter to your Excellency left the business before Montgomery in the balance, and this will inform your Lordship that, both parties being weighed, we were found too light (of foot at least), for, in plain English, our men ran shamefully when they had no cause of so great fear, so that we here are ordained to be the mocking-stock of the War.

[1] Warburton's "Prince Rupert," vol iii., 25.

DOCUMENT LX. F. A.D. 1644.

The first charge was made by my brother upon all their horse, who killed Sir William Fairfax at the head of them, and put them all in disorder. Broughton and Washington did as well with the foot. Sir William Vaughan was the occasion of fighting the enemy in that place; but as my Lord Byron tells me, contributed not much to the action. All the Lancashire horse ran without a blow struck, which disheartened the foot so infinitely that, being in disorder with the pursuit of the enemy, they could not be persuaded to rally again; which the rebels did, and advanced and made good the place, relieved the castle, being the work they came for, and took some prisoners. Our party consisted of 1,500 horse, and 2,000 foot, being the regiments of Broughton, Tylyer, Warren, Hunke, Ernely, and the Prince of Wales, and are all taken. There are not 100 foot come off, and all their officers which were not taken before, killed or taken. Col. Broughton was there shot and taken prisoner. But I here Col. Washington is well. What horse was lost in the action were out of my brother's regiment, and not many; but amongst them his jewel *Bay Squire*, whose solemn mourner he now is. My Lord Byron is infinitely unfortunate, and hath now finished with your Excellency, that is to say, made an end of all your Lordship's army unto a man, without any the least service; and truly, my Lord, people now begin to speak out, and say those forces were trifled away by my Lord Byron, who is here observed never to have prospered since his practice to supplant Capel, who is as prudent and valiant a person as the nation affords. I am only sorry that our good King is punished for the ill-nature or conscience of his people.

This last night the enemy possessed themselves of Birket House, in Worrall, wherein we had a small garrison for securing the passage hence to Liverpool, which will now be much more straightened than formerly, and I am afraid will not long hold out. By this your Excellency will soon make your own judgment of Chester and the parts adjacent, being upon the matter on all hands besieged. We reckon upon no friend but the Marquis of Ormond. . . . . . .

A. Trevor.

Chester, Sept. 23, 1644.[1]

[1] Carte's "Collection of Original Letters," vol. i., p. 64.

LXI.

Monmouth taken by Col. Massey for the Parliament, Sept. 26, 1644.

DOCUMENT LXI.
A.D. 1644.

[After obstructing the erection of works at Beachley to cover a passage for the Royalists across the Severn], Massey's next work was the taking of Monmouth, which indeed was betrayed unto him by Lieut.-Col. Kyrle, one that revolted from the Parliament party upon the loss of Bristol, and now had a mind to tack about again and purchase his peace with them at the price of this town. In order to which, Massey quartering his horse and foot near thereunto on the forest side, after the action of Beachley, Kyrle propounded this method (which was followed) to accomplish the business, viz.: That Massey should pretend a sudden return to Gloucester with his forces, and Kyrle would come out as if to fall upon his rear, and carrying them back with him [as if they were prisoners], let them into Monmouth. Accordingly, Massey gave out necessity of a retreat, and having marched back three miles, lodged his forces in a thicket of the forest, and sent his scouts abroad to prevent discovery. The intelligence soon reaches Monmouth, and Lieut. Kyrle draws out, whom Massey surprises at High-Meadow House about midnight, with his troop of about 30 horse, and with as little noise as might be, advanced thence to Monmouth. Yet the alarm was given, for Kyrle's cornet escaped the surprise, and was got thither, so that the town stood upon their guard, expecting an enemy. Yet Kyrle, arriving at the town's end with a hundred selected horse, confidently came up to the draw-bridge, pretended a return with many prisoners taken, persuaded the guards, and prevailed with Col. Holtby, the Governor, by the means of the officers of the guard, to let down the draw-bridge, which was done, but with much jealousy [*i.e.*, suspicion], and a strong guard, and the bridge presently drawn up again, insomuch that this first party was likely to be held prisoners, and began to suspect that Kyrle, instead of betraying the town, had betrayed them. However, they declare themselves, fall on, overpower the guard, and make good the bridge, keeping an eye to Kyrle's deportment, who fought as heartily as any of them, and so let in the main body, and soon mastered the town; but by favour of the night [which was] dark and rainy, the Governor and most of the garrison made the escape over the dry graft.

DOCUMENT LXI.

A.D. 1644.

This surprise of Monmouth, the key of South Wales, and the only safe intercourse for the King's army between the West, Wales, and the northern parts, alarmed all the King's party thereabouts, especially the Marquis of Worcester, at Raglan Castle, who raised the country, and called in some of Prince Rupert's horse to their assistance, who, with Sir Wm. Blaxton's brigade, making as was reported 500 horse and above 1,000 foot, marched thither, and beat up some of Massey's out-quarters; but after a brisk skirmish were repulsed, a major of horse and two captains slain, Sir Wm. Blaxton wounded, and divers prisoners taken, of whom, such as were Welsh, Massey used very kindly, and soon after sent them to their homes, everyone with a little note directed to his master, or to the parish where he lived, to signify to them "That the intention of the Parliament, and of Massey in coming thither, was not to destroy or enslave their persons, or take away their goods or livelihoods; but to preserve their lives and fortunes, to open the cause of justice, and free them of their heavy burthens under the forces of Rupert, a German." By which artifice, and free discharge of the prisoners, the Welsh people began to entertain better thoughts of the Parliament's party than formerly.[1]

[1] "Rushworth," vol. ii., part iii., 742. See also *The Kingdom's Weekly Intelligencer*, No. 74, and *The London Post*, No. 7. (K. P. 172—22, 23.)

LXII.

Powis Castle taken by Sir Thomas Myddelton. Oct. 2.

DOCUMENT LXII. A.D. 1644.

By letters from Welshpool, in Montgomeryshire, brought to Town on Thursday last, it was advertised that Sir Thomas Myddelton had taken Red Castle, a place of very great consequence, and one of the strongest of the enemy's holds in North Wales. The manner of the taking thereof is related to be thus: The enemy in this castle (the Lord Powis, a grand Papist, being Governor and owner thereof) did often oppose and interrupt the bringing in of provisions unto our forces at Montgomery Castle, whereupon Sir Thomas Myddelton summoned the whole country thereabouts to come in unto him; and on Monday, the last of September, advanced from Montgomery unto Pool, with 300 foot and 200 horse, where they quartered Monday and Tuesday night. And on Wednesday morning, at two, Mr. John Arundell, master-gunner to Sir Thomas Myddelton, placed a petarre against the outer gate, which burst the gate in pieces, and (notwithstanding the many showers of stones thrown from the castle by the enemy) Sir Thomas Myddelton's foot, commanded by Capt. Hugh Massey and Major Henry Ket, rushed into the works, got into the porch of the castle, and so stormed the castle-gate, entered it, and possessed themselves both of the old and new castle, and of all the plate, provisions, and goods there, which was great store that had been brought in from all parts thereabouts. They took therein prisoners the Lord Powis and his brother, with his two sons, three captains, one lieutenant, eighty officers and common soldiers. The place is of very great concernment, for before the taking thereof it did much mischief to the country, and almost blocked up the passages to Montgomery Castle from Oswestry, so that now the strongest forts in all North Wales are in the possession of the Parliament; this being conceived of sufficient strength to hold out a year's siege, and to be able to keep out ten thousand men for a year,

DOCUMENT LXII. A.D. 1644.

it having at present sufficient provisions in it of all sorts for that continuance. Besides, Sir Thomas Myddelton hath now the command of all North Wales, and can raise men there at his pleasure.[1]

Another Account.

Sir Thomas Myddelton marched by moonlight towards the place, with 300 foot and 40 horse, and forbore his approach to the castle till the moon was down. Then his master-gunner fixed a petard on the gate, blew it open, and our soldiers rushed in, and after some few hours' dispute, though the enemy showered down stones from the top of the castle, yet our men got over the walls and became masters of the place, and took prisoner the said Lord Powis, the greatest blasphemer in the world (this is for the honour of the Cavaliers), and his brother, and a seminary priest, whom they at Oxford will tell you is employed to settle the Protestant religion. Also, they took forty horse, 200 arms, and about fifty prisoners, an hundred of them escaping out of the castle in the dark.

Sir John Price, a Parliament man (whose heart was always with the Parliament, but was so over-mastered by the enemy that he durst not appear), writes that the country do come in cheerfully. They only want arms to defend themselves, and he hopes to help his neighbours' counties in Pembrokeshire.[2]

[1] *True Informer*, No. 49, p. 363. (K. P. 176—17.)

[2] *The Kingdom's Weekly Intelligencer*, No. 76. (K. P. 176—23.)

LXIII.

The Archbishop of York to the Marquis of Ormond—Of North Wales and General News. October 30.

DOCUMENT LXIII. A.D. 1644.

MAY IT PLEASE YOUR EXCELLENCY,

When I last heard from your Excellency about trading in corn and coals, before I could get ships laden for this latter commodity, a great many of the rebels were come to Liverpool, and so little supply could be sent in that kind. Corn from this harbour is gone out hitherto in great abundance, but if your Excellency does not provide for it from the court, it is not likely to do so hereafter. The Sheriff of this county (one Johnes,[1] of more boldness than wit), doing what he can to hinder corn to be carried thither without a license from the Lord Byron (that is, some sharking profit to himself), upon pretence the King's Proclamation for exportation to that Kingdom should be determined, which is more than I knew, and more (I am sure) than the King and Council intended, when I came from Oxenford (*sic*). This Johnes (as Chedle[2] heretofore) hath seized the last week upon a Scottish bark which came to Carnarvon with salt, with a pass from your Excellency, imprisoned the poor men, and sold their salt without consulting your Excellency, as will appear unto your Excellency, I conceive, by their cries and supplications. And I feared me much this heady man (linked in faction with Sir John Mennes) will utterly destroy all trading in these parts. Howbeit, I do and will (as long as I am entrusted) keep this port free from these concussions. Your Excellency's undeserved favour towards me puts me to this boldness, and your Excellency to this trouble, that I presume to become a suitor unto your Excellency in the behalf of the bearer, Mr. Malorye, who intends to live

[1] Robert Jones, of Castellmarch, H. S. 1644.

[2] Thomas Cheadle, of Beaumaris, H. S. 1642.

DOCUMENT LXIII. A.D. 1644.

in Ireland. [He] is a kinsman of mine by the mother's side, and by the father's descended from an ancient and noble house of that name in Yorkshire, where I am no real but a nominal bishop only. What favour or encouragement your Excellency shall vouchsafe to afford him according to his parts and calling in the ministry I shall account it as done to myself.

I had not been silent thus long, noble Lord, if I had any certainty at all of our informations, coined for the most part at Shrewsbury or Chester, for the meridian of this poor country, in a manner abandoned and deserted.

. . . .

The Prince,[1] our Governor, is at Bristol, or thereabouts, much discouraged with the bad success in Yorkshire, and the worse (for so it was) at Montgomery. Yet, if your Excellency will believe Chester news, he is coming down with 3,000 men, and Charles Gerard with 5,000; but if your Excellency will consult our fears, who sees his regiment called away to go to his Highness, he is not in that forwardness to come to these parts, but is rather drawing towards his Majesty.

Of ourselves and neighbourhood I can write no good news. Liverpool remains sore besieged, and the Governor and I have made bold with your Excellency's pinnace and servant, Capt. Lloyd, to attempt the relieving thereof with victuals from Beaumaris. God Almighty speed him! For from Chester there is little hope. Worrall is all lost to the enemy, and plundered to the ground by Sir Wm. Brereton. Myddelton (quietly possessed of Montgomeryshire by the help of Sir John Price[2]) did enter Ruthin, near Denbigh, the 19th of this month, at two of the clock, admitted into the town by Trevor[3] and his horse, who ran away, but Sword putting himself into the castle with some 80 men (the place being but in repairing), did beat him away with stones and shot, that upon two of the clock upon Monday he retired to Wem, and left 100 men slain behind him. Whether he will advance from thence into Merionethshire, or make once more

[1] Prince Rupert.

[2] Sir John Price of Newton, originally for the King, but had just turned round. Ante p. 213.

[3] A brother of Arthur Trevor, the news-writer.

DOCUMENT LXIII. A.D. 1644.

for Denbighshire, is the dispute of your Excellency's servants in these parts. . . . .

Chester was set upon on Monday last, and the outworks entered, but regained again. Fourteen of the enemies killed, [but they] are not retired far from the works. It is thought that that city is full of disaffected persons, and certain [it is] that they do not love their present Governor,[1] as it is also that the enemy knows too well what little accord there is between Legge and the Prince's creatures with that poor Lord,[2] who commands, or should command in chief in these parts. A most worthy man, but unfortunately matched in his Government.

God Almighty bless your Excellency in all your endeavours, and I do, and shall ever, remain

Your Excellency's most humble and obliged servant,

JO. EBORAC.[3]

Conway, this 30th day of October, 1644.

[1] William Legge was appointed by Prince Rupert Governor of Chester on the 19th day of May, 1644. Harl. MSS., 2135 fol. 26.

[2] Lord Capel. Lord Byron endeavoured all he could to supplant him, and ultimately succeeded. See ante p. 209.

[3] Carte's "Collection of Letters," vol. i., p. 67. Also *Arch. Camb.* for 1869, p. 324.

LXIV.

Monmouth re-taken by the Royalists, and also Pembridge Castle. November, 1644.

DOCUMENT LXIV. A.D. 1644.

At Monmouth Col. Broughton's Captain-Lieutenant, in Massey's absence, undertook to garrison a house near Goodrich Castle; but within a few days the house was fired about his ears, and he and all his company carried prisoners to Hereford. But this was but the omen of a greater loss to Massey, for he being, by an express, Nov. the 10th, ordered by the Committee of both Kingdoms to march with all the strength he could make into the borders of Oxfordshire, to prevent the Welsh forces, under the conduct of Col. Gerard, from joining with the rest of his Majesty's army, or that he should join with the Parliament's forces as occasion should require, called off his own regiment of horse from about Monmouth and marched to Evesham, but Gerard was arrived there before, nor could he retard his march, being too weak to encounter him. In his absence he committed the charge of the town to Major Throgmorton, serjeant-major to Col. Harley, who, that he might have the honour of doing somewhat, marched out with 1,300 men to Chepstow, on Sunday, November 17, intending to attack that castle; but some Royalists in Monmouth, tenants to the Lord Herbert, sent his Lordship notice to Raglan Castle how weak they had left the town, and that it would not be difficult to regain it, who presently sent to Col. Progers[1] and to Sir Trevor Williams, who kept a garrison at his own house at Llangibby, to send what forces could be spared; and his Lordship himself sent 150 horse and foot from Raglan, commanded by his brother, the Lord Charles Somerset,[2] and all met at an appointed rendezvous near Monmouth, on Tuesday, the 19th, by five o'clock in the morning, and instantly made their

[1] Or Proger, of Wernddu, Monmouthshire.
[2] The same who led the horse at the disaster at Highnam.

DOCUMENT LXIV. A.D. 1644.

approach to the higher side of the town that looketh towards Hereford, having only a sloping bank cast up with a dry graft of no depth. Lieut.-Col. Somerset (a kinsman of his Lordship) got over with a party of about 40 horse, without any opposition, and came to Dixon's gate,[1] where they found but six men, who fled at their approach, whereupon one took an iron bar with which he broke the chain, forced open the gate, and so let in their whole body of horse, who rid up the town in full career, seized upon the main-guard, and surprised the rest of the garrison, for the most part in their beds. Amongst the prisoners they took were the Committee of South Wales, consisting of Col. Broughton, Col. Stephens, Mr. Catching of Trelech, and Mr. Jones of Usk, together with four captains, about 150 common soldiers, 14 pieces of ordnance, 15 barrels of gunpowder, with bullet and match proportionable, and a store of good arms.

Massey, receiving advice hereof at Barford, hasted back to the relief of the party gone against Chepstow; but they hearing of the loss, without effecting anything against Chepstow, got over at Tintern-ferry, over the Wye, and were met by Massey in the forest, who marched to Ross, designing to have gone over to the relief of Pembridge Castle (an out-guard to Monmouth), but found the bridge broken down, so that those in the castle were forced to surrender upon quarter; and most of them took up arms for the King, having formerly been of his side, and taken prisoners.[2]

[1] The entrance to the town from Ross.

[2] Rushworth, part iii., vol. ii., p. 743. The Lord Herbert, hearing that there was but a small party left in Monmouth, first sent out seven or eight of his soldiers, who came to Monmouth like countrymen, and fell into discourse with the sentinels, feigning themselves to be of the Parliament party; but at last, when the sentinels were most secure, two troops of horse were ready, who, watching the fittest opportunity, broke through the sentinels, and the bridge being down, broke into the castle, mastered it, and have now possessed themselves thereof. *True Informer*, No. 56. (K. P. 183—9.)

LXV.

Abbey Cwm-Hir, Radnorshire, a Royalist Garrison, taken by the Parliament Forces under Myddelton. December.

SIR,

Our forces being so small in number we cannot but see the mighty hand of God in blessing our proceedings, as I have formerly showed. And now again, our General, Sir Thomas Myddelton (since the taking of Mr. Pugh's house[1]), having intelligence that the enemy had made them a garrison at Abbey Cwm-Hir, a very strong house, and built with stone of a great thickness, and the walls and outworks all very strong, the house having been in former times an Abbey of the Papists, which is situated upon the borders of Montgomeryshire, within twelve miles of Montgomery, or thereabouts; and the country, by reason of the cruelties, plunder, and unchristian usage of the cruel and merciless enemy towards them, as far as Kery, Newtown, and other places, and some miles distant, suffered exceedingly, and were almost utterly undone; which, notwithstanding the great strength of the enemy, our General being troubled to hear of the cruelties against the poor people by the enemy, put on a brave resolution, trusting in the Lord, and went against them and marched thither. We came before them on Wednesday last with our old forces, and Col. Beales and Lieut.-Col. Carter, who came to him out of South Wales.[2] Our general being resolved to do his utmost for the gaining of it, summoned the Castle, but the Governor

DOCUMENT LXV. A.D. 1644.

[1] Mathafarn, the House of Mr. Rowland Pugh, which was burnt to the ground. See *Cambrian Quarterly Magazine*, vol. i., p. 70.

[2] Capt. Beal or Beales had been sent from London by sea with foot forces and ammunition, to assist Sir Thomas Myddelton. Landing at Milford Haven, where he was driven by stress of weather, he assisted Laugharne for a while, and then pushed his way through Cardiganshire, and near Lampeter was met by a party of Myddelton's soldiers, on the 2nd day of November. *Perfect Passages*, No. 7; *Cambrian Quarterly Magazine*, vol. i., sup.

DOCUMENT LXV. A.D. 1644.

returned a flat denial, and said that he would not deliver up the said garrison to us; whereupon we immediately stormed it, and that with such violence that we soon took it by force. I have sent you a list of the particulars that you may see and know the great things that God hath done for us. To Him be praise. This garrison of theirs is Master Fowler's[1] house, which began to be a great annoyance to us. But God be blessed, we are now free from it, and that which is most of all to be admired is the great providence of Almighty God to us in this particular, which I can assure you is true, that we lost not one man in all this that was slain, though some were wounded. Since which our General having thrown down the enemy's works, and made the garrison unserviceable for the future, we made entrance [return] and marched away from thence to Flintshire, where our General took great care for the securing of those parts and placed a garrison there. At Wellington there is a garrison put within Mr. Dymack's house, which will do the enemy, we hope, some detriment and hinder their projects. The enemy are grown so desperate in their proceedings that they care not what hurt they do to honest godly men, such as are firm Protestants; but my General's resolution is such that we hope to give a very good account in short time of our proceeding against all their power.

So for the present I rest,

—— ——.

Red Castle, the 9th of December, 1644.

A list of particulars of what was taken by Sir Thomas Myddelton and Col. Mytton at Abbey Cwm-Hir.

Col. Barnard, the Governor of the said garrison, Hugh Lloyd, Esquire,[2] Commissioner of Array, and High Sheriff for that county,

[1] Richard Fowler, afterwards, under Cromwell in 1655, High Sheriff for Radnorshire, the richest man in the county, if there is any truth in the old rhyme—

"Alas! alas! poor Radnorshire,
Never a park, nor ever a deer,
Nor ever a Squire of five hundred a year,
Save Richard Fowler of Abbey Cwm-Hir."

Llyfryddiaeth y Cymry, p. 195.

[2] Of Caerfagu.

2 Captains of Foot, 1 Captain of Horse, 1 Capt.-Lieut, 3 Lieutenants, 2 Foot Colours, 1 Cornet of Horse, 4 Sergeants, 8 Corporals, 2 Trumpeters, 4 drums, 60 common soldiers, 3 barrels of powder, 60 fire locks, 40 horse, 40 horse-arms, besides 200 musketeers, many arms and other ammunition.[3]

DOCUMENT LXV.

A.D. 1644.

[3] *Perfect Occurrences*, No. 20; 20-27 Dec., 1644. (K. P. large 4to., 15—6.)

LXVI.

Major-General Laugharne takes Cardigan Town and Castle.
December, 1644.

DOCUMENT LXVI.
A.D. 1644.

Right Honourables,

Since my last of the 20th November, by Capt. Green, in the *Doggerboat*, Major-General Laugharne keeping the field, with such forces as the indigence of the county gave a possibility of subsistence, pretending for Carmarthen, lying still, working by double policy to draw the heart of the inhabitants of Cardiganshire to the State and the force of Carmarthen, with their adherents into the said town, for their defence, and the indemnity of their adjacent garrisons, opportunely rose and advanced from his quarters to the town of Cardigan, where the country, formerly invited, made a party to assist the General to complete the design in agitation, and the town (faced at distance) willingly surrendered and complied. The castle, being a considerable place, ably manned, having the ordnance of the *Convert* frigate (there shipwrecked), most obstinately held out till a demi-culverin of brass, belonging to the *Leopard*, was mounted, and played three days upon them, forcing a breach, which was gallantly entered and made good by our party, and the castle stormed, wherein were 100 commanders and soldiers, with their arms and good plunder, not forgetting the *Convert's* ordnance, returned by Divine Providence; and works of mercy in a Commander adding honour to acts of chivalry, invited the General to give the steward life, who contemned quarter. The town and castle reduced, and the country in the major part (as conceived), well-affected. Our army is advancing towards New Castle, the enemy's next garrison, which (as conceived) will be slighted or acquitted by the enemy, and that country brought to a right understanding of their duties, and Parliament's just and honourable proceedings. To God be rendered the due praises of his mercies. Vessels of late have been designed to the well-affected garrisons in Ireland, but none (in regard to contrary winds) returned, and shipping to ply up the channel as high as Miniard [Minehead], have also been commissioned to give intelligence and assistance to our forces in those parts. Sir Thos. Myddelton's magazine of ammunition is since disposed of to Liverpool. Nothing that integrity and action may add life to the public good, shall by God's assistance be wanting, and my faithful endeavours shall comply with your Honour's great trust, whose happiness shall ever consist, my very good Lord, to be

DOCUMENT LXVI. A.D. 1644.

Your most humble and faithful servant,

RICH. SWANLEY.[1]

1 January, 164$\frac{3}{4}$.

[1] A letter sent to the Right Honourable the Earl of Warwick, from Capt. Richard Swanley. Published by Authority. Printed for John Thomas, 1644 (K. P. 189 – 1.)

LXVII.

An Attempt to Besiege Chirk Castle by Sir Thomas Myddelton, its owner. Christmas, 1644.

DOCUMENT LXVII. A.D. 1644.

MAY IT PLEASE YOUR HIGHNESS,

This gentleman, journeying towards Oxford, I most humbly beseech leave to present to your Highness by him an account of a late action of the rebels. They lately besieged me for three days; their engineers attempted to work into the castle with iron crows and pickers, under great planks and tables which they had erected against the castle-side for their shelter, but my stones beat them off. They acknowledged in Oswestry they had 31 slain by the castle, and 43 others hurt; their prime engineer was slain by the castle-side; they are very sad for him. If your Highness please, this gentleman will fully impart all the passages during the siege to your Highness; he was in the castle with me. I shall not presume to be further tedious. I most humbly kiss your Highness's sweet hands, and will ever be

Your Highness's most humble
And assuredly faithful servant,
JOHN WATTS.[1]

Chirk Castle, December 25, 1644.
To his Highness Prince Rupert, humbly present this.

[1] The original is at Chirk Castle, in the possession of Mrs. Myddelton-Biddulph. *Mercurius Aulicus,* referring to this event, states that it was Sir Thomas's intention to keep Christmas in one of his own houses. "He came therefore before Chirk four days before Christmas, with his two brothers, Cols. Mytton and Powell. He would not abuse the castle with ordnance (because it was his own house), but fell on with fire-locks at a sink-hole where the Governor, Col. Watts, was ready to receive him; and gave a pretty number admittance (having an inner work within that hole), but when he saw his opportunity, he knocked them all down that came in, and with muskets killed of the rebels 67, wounded many more, and beat off Sir Thomas, who became so enraged that he plundered his own tenants." January 5-12, 164$\frac{4}{5}$, p. 1324. (K. P. 191-7.)

DOCUMENTS

ILLUSTRATING TRANSACTIONS

IN THE YEAR 1645.

LXVIII.

Defeat of an attempt by the Lord Byron to relieve Beeston Castle, besieged by Brereton's Forces. January 18.

SIR,

These lines may give you this account of this day's success, wherein it hath pleased God wonderfully to work and to fight for us, to the great amazement of the enemy. This day twelvemonth the Lord was pleased to do great things for us, when this town of Nantwich was fiercely assaulted, and the enemy were repulsed with the loss of near 500 slain and wounded, and near 1,000 more ran away, which was done with very little loss on our part. And this day, about two of the clock, the enemy, with about 800 foot and 300 horse, issued out of Chester, intending to fall upon our quarters at Christleton, within a mile or little more of the city, and had prepared a strong ambushment, through which our horse charging very resolutely fell fiercely upon the enemy's horse, which were placed in the rear of their ambuscade, routing them, slaying many, and taking above 200 prisoners, amongst which are two colonels, one lieut.-colonel, two sergeant-majors, and ten other eminent officers. [We] took good store of

DOCUMENT LXVIII.

A.D. 1645.

DOCUMENT LXVIII. A.D. 1645.

horse and arms, and did great execution upon them until their entering within the gate.

The foot (who were led on and commanded by Adjutant Louthian) performed a gallant service, came on valiantly, and beat the enemy from their ambuscades; and slew many of them, who, being under the protection of our own cannon, could not be so totally slain and taken as otherwise.

Lieutenant-Colonel Jones led on and commanded the horse with judgment, and the Lord's mercy and goodness is much magnified in the preservation of our men. I do not know of any of our commanders that are slain, only Capt. Blackwell is wanting,[1] and Capt. Zanchy (who is a very valiant man, and commands my own troop), being without his armour, wounded in the body, but we hope not mortally.

That we may have a good effect upon Beeston Castle, we shall neglect no endeavours to improve time and advantage so far as remains in our power; and do desire that such a prudent respect may be had of us as that we may not be oppressed with fresh supplies of horse from the King's army.

I have not time to enlarge myself, but with my kindest respects to you, conclude in haste, and remain

Your assured friend and servant,

WILL. BRERETON.

January 18th, 1645.

Postscript.—There were about 500 or 600 of Cheshire foot, and some few of Sir Thomas Myddelton's own regiment of horse, and Sir William Myddelton's horse, which (I take it) were not 100. Those foot which came out of Liverpool, and now are under my Lieut.-Col. Jones (some of which served in Ireland), did perform good service this day.

A List of the Prisoners that were taken.

Col. Wereden[2]	Lieut.-Col. Gough[3]
Col. Vane[3]	Sergt.-Major Grey[3]

[1] He was taken prisoner, but allowed afterwards to return on his parole.

[2] Succeeded Col. Marrow,—was son of a Chester attorney.

[3] Vane, Grey, and Gough, had served in Ireland

DOCUMENT LXVIII.

A.D. 1645.

Sergt.-Major Deane
Capt. Rory O'Neale[1]
Capt. Harrington
Capt. Ware
Capt. Pool of Pool
Capt. Ravenscroft
Capt.-Lieut. Marrow-Hagan
Lieut. Humphreys
Lieut. Goulbourne
Lieut. Wright
Lieut. Davies
Lieut. Dowdall
Lieut. Balls
Lieut. Castleton
Lieut. Brookes
Lieut. Bryan
Lieut. Dering
Ensigns Musgrave, Gorse, George, and Chute
Serjeants Price, Moulton, and Corporal Jackson.

Of Major Mainwaring's regiment were taken 36 men, 1 of Col. Trevor's, 25 of Col. Gibsons, 5 of Sir Robert Byron's, 33 of Col. Warden's [Warren's probably], 1 of Capt. Smith's, 11 of Capt. Morgan's, 2 of Lieut.-Col. Grosvenor, 6 of Capt. Lloyd, 1 of Capt. Rews', 2 of Capt. Prichard's, 2 of Col. Russell's; and of Legge, the Governor's own troop, 4.[2]

[1] A notorious Irish rebel.

[2] *Perfect Passages*, No. 14, January 22, 1645. (K. P. 190—9). From which the foot notes also are taken.

LXIX.

A.

Touching the taking of Cardigan Castle and Town, and of the Defeat of an Attempt to Regain it—An Extract out of a Letter written by Captain William Smith to the Lord High Admiral from aboard the ship called the "Swallow," in Milford Haven. Dated the 5th of February, 1645.

DOCUMENT LXIX. A. A.D. 1645.

After many great rains which have fallen in these parts (which was no invitation for a soldier to lye in the fields), yet such was the gallantry of Major-General Laugharne to promote the cause in hand, that the Almighty no sooner crowned his desires with a happy season, but in a grateful acknowledgement he placed a garrison in Laugharne Castle, and from thence marched towards Cardigan with about five hundred horse and two hundred foot, and on the 21st December, 1644, he sate down before Cardigan Castle demanding the surrender thereof for the service of the King and Parliament. But Major Slaughter, who commanded in chief, replied he held that castle for the service of the King, and so long as he had life he would keep it for his Majesty (though therein he was not a man of his word). After three days' siege, the Major-General perceiving all further attempts would be in vain unless a breach could be forced, and having no artillery with him, he forthwith gave order the demy-culverin should be brought from Laugharne, which with much difficulty and industry came safe to Cardigan, and being placed to the best advantage he fell to battery.

The enemy within the castle-yard cast up a half-moon some distance from the place, on which the demy-culverin played, in which they placed their great guns laden with case shot, that in case a breach should be made those guns might disanimate our men in entering, or perform sudden execution on them. Our men plying the demy-culverin forced a breach, and being full of resolution entered, running in the mouth of their guns recovered the half-moon, where the enemy, as men bereft of all sense, having not the power to give fire to their guns, although the linstocks were in their hands ready lighted, cast down their arms and cried for quarter, the which was granted; from thence we entered the castle and took prisoner Major Slaughter and his wife, one Captain Vaughan, with their Lieutenant and Ensign, one Doctor Taylor, a Divine, with about an hundred common soldiers, six great guns, a hundred and fifty arms, a quantity of powder, ball, and other provisions, and this was done the 29th of December last. On the 4th of January, General Gerard sat down before the castle with about 1,200 horse and 1,300 foot; Major-General Laugharne recruited his forces to about 600 horse and 300 foot, and advanced towards Cardigan to redeem his friends who were in the castle out of the power of the enemy. Lieutenant-Colonel Powell in the night sent a soldier, who swam through the river, and informed Major-General Laugharne that unless he would relieve the castle within eight days he should be enforced to surrender it for want of victuals and ammunition, which he believed might be supplied if some seamen versed in managing a water fight and climbing up rocks were employed. So 120 seamen were sent, who, after a view had of the place, undertook it, which was performed in this wise—A boat laden with provisions was placed in the middle between four boats on each side, two of which were manned with seamen, who in flanks faced both ways, playing with their muskets on the enemy, who from the shore played on them with about 300 musketeers, yet our seamen gallantly proceeded, put all the provisions in the castle, and returned without the loss of one man, only two slightly wounded. After this Col. Laugharne, having drawn his foot into a body, being without seamen, in all about 350, he encouraged them to give an assault on the town, which, after some debate, was attempted, and on the 22nd of January last our foot forced their passage over the bridge, in which we lost but one man; and having beaten the enemy from their first guard, they pressed on to the second, which they also took, and pursuing the victory beat them out of their main guard, which was at the market-place, and then out of the church,

DOCUMENT LXIX. A. A.D. 1645.

where our forces took two brass demy-culverins which Gerard brought from Bristol, with some powder, ball, and other provisions, and following the enemy beat them all out of the town, and so we are now masters both of the town and castle. Of the enemy were slain in the place 85, besides those that were slain before the castle; 100 prisoners were taken and their whole forces routed, and I believe in their flight they never looked behind them until they came to Castle Emlyn, which is six (*sic*) miles from Cardigan. In the town we also took 250 arms. I have not heard since these unhappy differences begun in this Kingdom that the hand of the Almighty hath more visibly appeared in giving so great victories to so small a handful than hath been manifested in these parts, and to His own power we attribute all the praise and glory.[1]

B.

Further particulars of the Attempt to Regain Cardigan Castle by the Royalists under Gerard. January 22.

DOCUMENT LXIX. B. A.D. 1645.

The most considerable exploit that hath been performed in any of our armies since my last was by Lieut.-Col. Powell and Col. Laugharne, near Cardigan Castle, in Wales, against Gen. Gerard, the particulars whereof on Thursday, Feb. 6, was thus advertised.

The enemy having intelligence that there was great want of provisions in the castle, whereof Lieut.-Col. Powell was Governor, Col. Gerard having gathered all the forces he could to besiege it, for that purpose marched towards it with a great party, and in his march intercepted some boats of provisions that were going for their relief. Upon his approach and sitting down before the castle, having by a stratagem got possession of the town, he sent in by a trumpet a menacing summons to the Governor, requiring him in his Majesty's name to surrender the castle, with all the ordnance, arms, and ammunition therein, unto him, together with

[1] From a pamphlet, entitled "God appearing for the Parliament in sundry late Victories bestowed upon their forces, &c. Printed at London for Edw. Husbands, March 10, 164$\frac{4}{5}$." (K. P. 195—22.)

the provisions [prisoners] therein, for the prisoners who were taken therein of Col. Gerard's, whereof I gave you an account some weeks since, remained there; and further threatened the Governor that if he would not surrender it by a day which he named, he would not give quarter to him or any of his soldiers, with some other haughty and lofty expressions to that purpose. Upon the reading of this summons, the gallant Lieut.-Colonel called his officers and soldiers together, and used many notable encouragements unto them to behave themselves like brave spirits, further telling them that whereas Col. Gerard threatened to give no quarter, he would neither give nor take quarter, adding that he would rather feed upon those hides (there being 300 in the room which he pointed to) before he would starve, and that those who loved him would do the like before they would yield to the enemy, and thereupon, by the concurrence of his officers and soldiers, he sent the enemy an absolute denial, and in the meantime got an opportunity to send to Col. Gough [must be Laugharne] to come with a party to his relief.

Upon this the enemy broke down the bridge between Cardigan and Pembrokeshire, that so no relief might come, and fell to making their batteries and planting their ordnance against it [the castle], for the storming of it, which they endeavoured to do oftentimes, but were still repulsed, losing about 150 men upon their several onsets. While the enemy were in this posture, Col. Laugharne came out of Pembrokeshire to the relief of the castle, but when he came to the bridge, he found it was broken down, which was some impediment unto him; whereupon he caused an arrow with a letter to be shot into the castle, to give them notice he was coming, and that they might sally out upon the enemy the same time he fell on. After this, leaving the horse behind them, the foot soldiers (being led by this their valiant Commander, who told them that if but an hundred went he would lead them on) making use of faggots and other pieces of wood, got over the river and fell upon the rear of the enemy, and those in the castle falling upon them at the same time, the enemy were quickly put to the rout; 200 of them slain on the place, four brass pieces of ordnance, 600 arms, and 150 prisoners taken. The chief of the prisoners were Major William Slaughter, Capt. Nicholas Butler, Capt. Richard

DOCUMENT LXIX. B. A.D. 1645.

Pryse, Dr. Jeremy Taylor,[1] Lieut. Thomas Barrow (? Barlow), Lieut. Morgan Mathewes, Ensign Edward Barrow, and others.

I have been more particular in this success, in regard the malignants did the beginning of this week report with much confidence that Col. Gerard had totally routed Col. Laugharne's forces, taken Cardigan Castle, and reduced several places in Wales: *cujus contrarium verum est.*[2]

There were some reports about the beginning of this week spread abroad by some malignants, which they had from their friends, the Cavaliers, of the retaking again of Cardigan Castle, in Wales, and some other famous exploits done by Col. Gerard's forces, which they boasted to be very numerous and strong in those parts of Wales; but the falsity of this relation being apparent (Gerard being, as we hear, yet about Ceciter [Cirencester] with his forces, where we hear they have miserably plundered the town), a course will be taken to find out the first publishers thereof, as also of some other fictions, that so they may receive condign punishment for the present, and be taken notice of for the future.[3]

From Wales it is certified of truth that Col. Gerard, with all his strength, came against Cardigan and besieged the castle, which was kept by Col. Jones, and by a stratagem got to the town and broke down the bridge between it and Pembrokeshire, which was near the Town and Castle of Cardigan, that no relief might come, and by a trumpet he sent summons to the castle. Col. Jones returned answer that he had in the castle divers raw hides, and

[1] A Doctor whom, because I know very well, I cannot but name Doctor Jeremy Taylor, a most spruce neat formalist, a very ginger-bread Idol, an Arminian in print. No. 69, *Merc. Britanicus.* (K. P. 193—6.)

[2] *The True Informer.* No. 65, 1-8, February, p. 491. (K. P. 193—4.)

[3] *Merc. Civicus*, No. 89, Feb. 6, p. 811. (K. P. 192—9.)

DOCUMENT LXIX. B. A.D. 1645.

when necessaries failed they would eat them, and when these were spent they would come out and fight for their lives, but would not deliver the castle. In the meantime Col. Jones sent to Col. Laugharne to come to relieve him, which he promised and did, but when he came to the bridge he found it broken down, which was some impediment; yet he, like a brave soldier, made way to pass the river, and while he was getting over, he sent an arrow into the castle with a letter, to give them notice he was coming, and did come, and fell upon the enemy. At the same time they in the castle issued out, and wholly routed all Gerard's forces, took and slew 350; 200 were dead on the place. They also took 200 arms and four pieces of brass ordnance.[1]

The forgery they (the parliamentary press) most insist on is their victory over General Gerard, wherein they'll abate nothing of 800 kill'd and taken, with four pieces of cannon. The truth whereof was impartially thus: The rebels of Pembrokeshire having besieged Cardigan Castle above a fortnight despaired to master it, for they heard General Gerard was on his march to relieve it, therefore in haste they bribed a sergeant to betray a sally port, which was done accordingly, and the castle surprised without a blow struck. General Gerard (who came the next day after this treachery) presently sate down and laid siege to the castle, wherein, having continued fifteen days, intelligence came (from some pretended friends) that Myddelton and his fellows were coming upon him; hereupon he left a strength to continue the siege, and keep them of Pembrokeshire from passing the river at Cardigan, and marched with the rest to meet Myddelton; but when he had marched twenty miles he found his friends' letters had betrayed him into a false alarm, and therefore returned back to Cardigan, where the rebels that very day had made a pass over the river, relieved the castle, fallen upon his force in the town, and mastered four pieces of cannon; whereupon, with his own troop, he charged

[1] *The Scottish Dove*, No. 68, 7th February. (K. P. 193—3.)

DOCUMENT LXIX. B. A.D. 1645.

into them and rescued his cannon; the sum of the rebels' victory being twelve men killed, twenty taken, with two drakes. This action happened yesterday was sennight; but next night he fell into the rebels' quarters, regained most of his prisoners, and took a whole troop of horse, both officers and common soldiers, which done, he marched after the rebels into Pembrokeshire, to bid them battle if they durst draw out.[1]

There came further news out of Wales that in the pursuit of Gerard, whom Col. Laugharne routed, as you have formerly heard, at the raising of the siege before Cardigan, Col. Laugharne hath met with Col. Pet, who retreated with his foot into a church,[2] where Col. Laugharne beset him with so many of his forces as came up to him thither that night. But the church being large, and the ways into it at several distances, passing several ways, Col. Pet got away out of the church by a private way, with all his men, in the night; and the next morning Col. Laugharne possessed himself of the said church, but the Cavaliers were fled, and had strewed their gunpowder all over the church, up and down the ground, to spoil it from doing any service to us. There were many barrels, but all so spoilt. There were taken in the church between 200 and 300 arms, but Col. Pet and the Cavaliers fled.[3]

Gerard is at Carmarthen, recruiting as fast as he can with the Welsh, who come to him with very little affection, but they are forced; and so he, as some say, increaseth his number again; but Col. Laugharne is very vigilant, who hath refreshed Lieut.-Col. Powell, who so bravely kept Gerard out of Cardigan, and hath supplied that garrison with provisions and ammunition, and we hope they are now in a good condition.[4]

[1] *Merc. Aulicus*, February 2-9, 1645. (K. P. 195—4, under date February 6.)

[2] I am sorry that I have not been able to discover what church this was.

[3] *Perfect Occurrences*, the 7th week. (K. P., large 4to., 15—24, under date Tuesday, February 11.)

[4] *Ibid.* 9th week, under date Friday, Feb. 21. (K. P. 15—28.)

LXX.

Shrewsbury taken by the Parliament. February 22, 1645.

Sir,

On the 21st of this instant [February], by order of the Committee [for Shropshire], there were drawn out of the garrisons of Wem, Morton Corbet, and Stoke, 250 foot and 250 horse. From our good friend Sir William Brereton we were assisted with 250 foot, and 350 horse of the Staffordshire forces, under the command of Colonel Bowyer. All the foot being, by order from the Committee, placed under the command of Lieut.-Col. Reinking, an able soldier, who for his discreet managing this business deserves much honour. Our horse were commanded by Colonel Mytton. Things being thus ordered, we marched towards Shrewsbury, which is a very strong town, well-walled and compassed about with a navigable river in the form of an horse-shoe—the neck of land at the opening of the horse-shoe being not a bow-shot over, in which stands (on the east-side on the top of a high hill) a strong castle, the river running directly along close under the side of the hill. From the north-west side of the hill there runs a strong wall, and a great ditch to the river on that side. Notwithstanding the strength of the place we were not discouraged, but marched on, and came to Shrewsbury about three o'clock on Saturday morning.[1] How to get over the work was both dangerous and difficult, being strongly pallisadoed and well fortified. We, therefore, in a little boat that was provided for the purpose, conveyed eight carpenters up the river, and landed them within the enemy's breast-work under the castle-hill. On the east-side were the sentinels [who] after some pause gave fire upon them, but they soon sawed down so many of the pallisades as gave our men free

DOCUMENT LXX. A.D. 1645.

[1] February 22nd

DOCUMENT LXX. A.D. 1645.

passage. The first that stormed were 40 troopers, dismounted, with their pistols and about as many fire-locks, who were led on by one Mr. Huson, a minister,[1] Capt. Willers, and Lieut. Benbow.[2] After these followed some other musketeers along Severn side, under Castle-hill, and near Sir William Owen's house,[3] entered the town. After these marched 350 more foot under the command of Lieut.-Col. Reinking. These having gained the streets, part of them marched to the market-place, who after some exchange of shot gained the main court of guard there. The rest marched to the castle-forward-gate [foregate] which within a quarter of an hour was gained, the gates opened, the draw-bridge let down, at which our horse, under the command of Col. Mytton and Col. Bowyer, with the gentlemen of the Committee,[4] entered. It was now about break of day. The scriks [shrieks, Welsh *screch*] in the town was such strange kind of cock-crowing as I believe you never heard the like.[5] Being thus entered, the castle and a strong out-work at Frankwell held out, but by twelve o'clock the castle was delivered upon these conditions: "That the English should march to Ludlow, but the Irish to be delivered up,"[6] which we shall hang with authority. The strong work at Frankwell was surrendered upon bare quarter.

And thus it pleased God of his great goodness to deliver so strong a hold into our hands, with the loss only of two common soldiers. We cannot be sufficiently thankful, for it is a place of

[1] A native of Ireland who acted, it is supposed, for some time in Shrewsbury as a Parliament spy.

[2] On October 15th, 1651, Benbow once more appeared in the Cabbage-garden, where we see he has just distinguished himself. Then it was however to meet his doom by an order of a Military Tribunal, for having, along with others, attempted to seize Shrewsbury for Charles II.

[3] Sir William Owen of Condover, then residing at the Council House.

[4] The Committee were Samuel Moore, Robert Clyve, Robert Charleton, Thomas Hunt, Andrew Lloyd, and Leigh Bruen [or Owen.]

[5] Most of the officers and gentry were taken in their beds. (K. P. 194—26.)

[6] Another account states the conditions to have been that the officers and soldiers should march out with their arms, but to leave the arms and ammunition in the castle behind them, as also such officers and soldiers as had been taken in the town. *Ibid.*

great concernment. And now many honest people are delivered out of an Egyptian slavery. DOCUMENT LXX. A.D. 1645.

Your friend to serve you,[1]

—— ——.

Salop, Feb. 22, 164⅘.

Prisoners taken at Shrewsbury.

Knights and Baronets.

Sir Michael Ernely, Governor, and his brother.

Sir Richard Lee [Lee Hall], Bart

Sir Thos. Harris [Borealton], Bart

Sir Henry F. Thynn [Caus Castle] Bart.

Sir William Owen [Condover].

Sir John Weld, senior.

Sir John Weld, junior

Sir Thomas Lyster [Routon].

Doctor Lewin, P. Rupert's advocate.

Doctor Arneway.

Esquires of £1,500 and £2,000 a year.

Francis Thomas [Shelvocke].

Herbert Vaughan.

Thomas Owen [Town Clerk].

Edward Kynaston [Otely].

Robert Ireland [Adbrighton].

Richard Trevis.

Thomas Morris.

Arthur Sandford [Sandford].

Robert Sandford

Pelham Corbet [Leigh].

Thomas Jones [Chief Justice afterwards].

Lieut.-Col. Edward Owen, Lieut.-Col. Thomas Owen, Major Ranger, Captains Rainsford, Lucas, Cressy, Collins, Long, Pontesbury Owen [Eton Mascot], and Henry Harrison.

John Pey, Feodary; Cassey Benthall, Edward Talbot, Rich. Lee, Ed. Stanley, F. Mainwaring, John Jones, John Bradshaw, Ed. Littleton, Peter Dorrington, Thos. Barker, John Whitaker, Joseph Taylor, Fr. Sandford, Richard Gibbons, George Mainwaring, and Charles Smith, gentlemen, and 200 other prisoners, of whom 49 were Irish.

There was also taken fifteen pieces of ordnance, many hundreds of arms, divers barrels of gunpowder, Prince Maurice's magazine,

[1] From a pamphlet, entitled "A True Relation of the Taking of Shrewsbury, &c." (K. P. 192—2.)

DOCUMENT LXX. A.D. 1645.

divers carriages, bag and baggage of the Prince, besides other prisoners, and purchase not yet discovered.

The reason we found no more commanders was because Prince Maurice had drawn them out for his design at Chester.[1]

[1] The above list of prisoners, with particulars, has been made out by a comparison of several lists published at the time, and for the residences I am indebted to Owen and Blakeway's "Shrewsbury," vol. i., p. 455.

LXXI.

An Intercession on behalf of Lord Powis and Mr. Herbert Vaughan, imprisoned by the Parliament.

DOCUMENT LXXI. A.D. 1645.

My Lo.,

I p'sume to take the occasion of the Duch Embassador's returne to conveye my humble service to y^r^ Lo. a present that heretofore hath beene acceptable to y^r^ Lo., and knowinge noe cause why it should not be so still (on my part) I am hopefull of y^r^ wonted favour: and if it be not a tyme for y^r^ Lo. to owne a servant (though never deservinge ill) att London, yett I cann with confidence avowe my fidelity to y^r^ Lo. Yea, even in the court at Oxford, and shall live and dye with that resolution. I hope I shall have so much virtue and religion to keep my professions to y^r^ Lo., and if my fortune cast me upon never so hard a rock I shall not save my selfe to shipwrack my friends, and therefore y^r^ Lo. may receyve my letters w^h^out the feare of readinge them; all that I desire for the present is that the bond w^h^ was in my iron chest, w^h^ Sr Percy Herbert was bownd in to pay Nell Vaughan's portion may be kept saulfe since I was trusted wh it, and I would be exceedinge sorrie that what concerns another should miscarrie.

I doe also recomend the distressed estate of my Lo. Powys, who is a prisoner at Stafford; and Herbert Vaughan, y^r^ Lo. ward taken at the surprise of Shrewsbury—not an enemie, but only livinge there, and had nothing to doe in this warr. They both are so near y^r^ Lo. consideration that I hope y^u^ will not thinke it amisse in me to remember them to y^r^ care. Y^r^ Lo. knows what enemies y^r^ ward hath, who will be glad to have th^r^ private ends under publicke p^r^tences, and therefore submit it to y^r^ Lo. noble consideration. For myselfe I hope to live yett to doe y^r^ Lo. as much service as I have ever donne, and I doe rest to y^r^ Lo and to all y^r^ family an

Humble servant,

JAMES PALMER.

Oxford, this 25 of March.

To the Right Ho^ble^ my singular good Lo., my Lo. the Earle of Pembrock and Montgomery, at Whitehall these.[1]

[1] State Papers Dom., Car. I., 1645, vol. cccxix., fol. 249b.

LXXII.

Of the Ravages committed by the Royalist Armies of Prince Rupert and Prince Maurice upon their coming to relieve Beeston Castle, and in their Retreat—Gerard gone to fight Laugharne.

DOCUMENT LXXII.

A.D. 1645.

SIR,

Since the King's great army lay in these parts the country hath suffered much, and they have been as barbarous in their retreat; for they have not only plundered about Flintshire, Denbighshire, and the borders of Shropshire and Cheshire, but have committed so many murders and rapines, both in these parts, as also in Herefordshire, Worcestershire, and the rest of those places they have been, that the like hath not been heard of. In Cheshire they have not only plundered about Churton, Barton, and Crew, but burnt Farndon, where we kept the pass at Holt Bridge. The Irish and Papists have been at Broughton, and carried away divers Protestants of the town prisoners, and burnt down all the houses in that town. From thence they went to Christleton, and burnt down all that town, the minister's house and the church also. Sir W. Brereton hath sent a party to block up the ways to Chester to keep provisions from the enemy, who we hear have but short commons in Chester. The Lord Byron nor any of the officers dare give any distaste to any Papist or Irish rebel, who bear all the sway in Chester, to their faces tell the Protestants there that they are the rebels, and that themselves are the good subjects that fight for God and King Charles.

Gerard, we hear, hath received an express, and is gone back into Wales to raise what strength he can against Col. Laugharne and the Pembrokeshire forces, and in his retreat we hear that he useth great strictness in forcing the country along with him, and not only sweeps away the men but all the cattle, horses, provisions, and what he can find out, before him. We had a party that fell upon his rear, but he is gone further towards Pembrokeshire, but we hope Col. Laugharne is in good condition to receive him. . . . .

DOCUMENT LXXII. A.D. 1645.

—— ——.

Nantwich, 26th March, 1645.[1]

[1] *Perfect Passages*, No. 24, April 9th. (K. P., large 4to., 16—12.)

LXXIII.

Interception of Ammunition for Chester—Fresh Siege laid to Hawarden Castle. April 4.

DOCUMENT LXXIII. A.D. 1645.

SIR,

I had intelligence that there was some ammunition come from Anglesey towards Chester, and being come on this side of the Dee I marched into Flintshire to meet them, but they hearing of us got into Hawarden Castle, whither the country people drove in many carriages, and the malignants fled thither with their wives and children, thinking that we would only have faced that place; but I have left a strength before it, who are undermining it, which stands upon sand, therefore the more easy to dig. There is good store of powder and ammunition in it. And leaving a party there I marched to Goozanna,[1] and fell upon the enemy there, which garrison I took from them, and therein the Governor (a Captain) and 27 prisoners more, amongst which some officers. And from thence we marched to block up Chester on the Welsh side, which we have done. The enemy at our approach set fire to Handbridge, but by reason of our speedy march we gained Manly House from them, killed divers, took a captain and many other prisoners, and wounded many more besides, and pursued them to the bridge over which they fled into the city. Of which, if the Irish rebels come not, I hope shortly to give a good account.

WILLIAM BRERETON.[2]

April the 4, 1645.

[1] Gwysaney.

[2] *Perfect Occurrences*, the 15th week. (K. P. 16—13.)

LXXIV.

The Archbishop of York complains to the Lord Digby, of Sir John Owen, of Cleneney, being put over his head in the Government of Conway.

My verye good Lord,

I have written sundrye letters of late unto your Lpp. conce^r^ninge the state of his Mtyes affayres in these parts wth mine owne hand, but without any name subscribed. But hea inge noe returne from Oxenford all this while, I conceive they are miscarried, and am sorye for it. By this bearer, your Lpp's most humble servant, I shall neede to write nothinge, his knowledge in all these pa^r^ticulars beinge noe waye short of myne. I shall onlye saye that he is a valiant and faythfull servant of his Mtye, hath soe showed himself dureinge his abode in these parts, hath acted all that is don for the defence of Beuemorice Castle, and more would have done if his uncle hadd not been wrought about to disable him; or if his Mtye hadd entrusted him with more power, as I (and I beleeve your Lpp.) desired. But all things must be as God by his immediate vicege^r^ent shall determin to effect and bringe about, amongst all true and faythfull subiectes.

DOCUMENT LXXIV. A.D. 1645.

Sr John Owen is likewise governor of this place, and intimateth a desire to have the Government of this castle, wch his Mtye (before any Commission granted to any of the three Princes) hadd upon high and deare considerations passed over unto me and my assignes, and wch from bare walles I have repayred, victuayled, and ammunicioned at myne owne charges; and for wch I am more likelye to give his Mtye a good accompt then this gentleman is, who, w^th^out my costes and charges, was never able to have repayred the towne (as now it is), nor hath any armes but what I len'd him to defend it. Coronel Jones can tell you howe I sett him out from this countye, to drive the rebels out of Denbigshyre. But, I know not by what meanes,

16a

DOCUMENT LXXIV. A.D. 1645.

he is much abated of what he was in the esteeme of these countyes. And I praye God he may give noe worse accompt unto his Mtye then the Bpp. of Yorke hath don for these 3 yeares. Valour will not doe the business: he must have prudence and experience wth all that will governe a countrye, environed with enemies, and destitute of all money. And this man professeth openlye he will consult noe man, nor ioyne with any his felowes and betters, the Commissioners of Arraye in this coutye, as his p'decessors, the two Princes, have hitherto done.

If his Mtye shall deliver unto your Lpp. any papers received by this bearer, w[ch] are copies of peticions w[ch] these 3 countyes have addressed unto the Kinge and Prince Rupert, upon some rumoures w[ch] S[r] John Mennes and Wyat[1] hadd some months agoe scattered about. I beseech you to rep'sent unto the K. and the Prince the effect of them, and I shall praye to God to putt into his Mtye's heart a discerninge spiritt to distinguish betweene such as have don and suffered soe much for his Mtye and his iust cause, and these sharkes and children of fortune who knowe not howe to subsist, but by this fowle waye of license and imposture. For myself, as I have ever lived, soe am I resolved to die (w[ch] now I expect dailye), his Mtye's most faythfull servante, and my lord,

Your Lpp's most affectionate poore freynd,

Jo. Eborac.

Conwaye, 13th of April, 1645.

To the right honourable his Noble Lord, the Lord
Digbye, principall secretarye to his Mtye.,
p'sent these.[2]

[1] I have seen it somewhere stated, but have missed my reference, that Dudley Wyatt was deputy-governor of North Wales under Rupert.

[2] State Papers Dom., Charles I. Bundle 319, fol. 270.

LXXV.

The Defenceless Condition of Chester after the Departure of Princes Rupert and Maurice, from the Relief of Beeston Castle—Lord Byron to Lord Digby. April 26.

My Lord,

I receaved, togeather wth y^r^ Lopps. lettre, a double comfort, both the assurance of y^r^ Lopps. recovery from a dangerous sicknesse, and that I still continew that place in y good opinion wheare with I have ever thought myselfe soe much honored. I may add another wch is the [hope I have shortley to enioy your Lop^s^ much longed for conversation, when you may ease my oppressed thoughts of a burthen which is almost grown to unweldy for them any longer to beare][1] for the present I shall only inform y^r^ Lopp. and humbly desyre you to acquaint his M^aty^ wth the condition of this place, and the strong necessity there is of a speedy and powerful reliefe. I know it is usual for men to recommend the safty of those places wheare theire owne commandes ly as of highest concernment to his Maties service, but truly I have wholy drawne my thoughts from any such self-partiality, and only consider this place now as really it stands in relation to his Maties affairs, both in this Kingdome and Ireland, wherein it is inferior to none other that I knowe as drawinge wth it all Wales, Lancashire, wth the north of England, and what suplyes his Matye can expect either out of Ireland or Scotland. The two Princes, havinge united their forces and releaved Beeston Castle, were earnestly intreated by mee to cleare this country (before they departed) of those petty garrisons that infested Chester, but other considerations at that tyme hindred the effectinge of it, and therefore wth a promise that the army should continew in a distance till Chester were furnished both wth victuall and ammunition, I was contented to returne and

DOCUMENT LXXV. A.D. 1645.

[1] What is in brackets thus [ ] is in cypher in the original.

DOCUMENT LXXV.
A.D. 1645.

undertake the Government of that garryson, but the buysynesse of Hereford[1] interveninge, Prince Rupert was suddenly called away before either ammunition or victuall could be brought into Chester, and togeather wth his Highnesse marched away the remainder of the old Irish regiments, wth some other horse and foot, to the number of at least 1,200, soe that I was left in the towne only with a garryson of citizens, and my owne and Colonell Mostin's[2] regiment, wch both togeather made not up above 600 men, whereof the one halfe beinge Mostin's men, I was forced soone after to send out of towne, findinge them by reason of their officers, who weare ignorant Welch gentlemen, and unwillinge to undergoe any strickt duty, far more preiudiciall to us than usefull. The rebels findinge the Prince retreated wth his army, and the country emptied of all souldiers (but such as were necessary for keepinge the garrysons), returned wth all their forces to blocke up Chester on all sides, wch ever since they have continewed, and wth all layed siedge to Hawarden Castle. The Welch, though they have men for number, and armies sufficient to beat the rebels out Wales, yet either will not or dare not stir, notwithstanding the many orders I have sent them. The truth is that soe long as that cursed Commission of Array (or at least such Commissioners as are in it) have any power there, the Kinge must expect noe good out of North Wales, and I am confident were it not for the castles wch are well provided both wth men, victuall, and ammunition, that country had long since taken part with Brereton and Midleton. Thus your lord^sp^ sees I am left in a condition neither to offend others or defend myselfe yf pressed by a considerable army of the enemy, wch I am advertised now is advancinge towards mee: the Scots being invited by the Ordinance of Parliament, (wch gives them Chester if they can win it) to joyne w the Lancashire forces and the Cheshire; [besides this, if speedy releafe come not the want of powder will be sufficient to blow mee up, there being not full 18 barrells in the store, nor any publicke magazine of victuall, nor any money for publicke pre-

[1] This refers to the rising of the club-men or country-people to defend their property from plunder.

[2] Roger Mostyn, I presume, who was afterwards knighted; a very staunch Royalist.

servation]. I have the more fully related my condition to your Lop. to the end, that if any misfortune should befall mee before reliefe come it may appeare how litle accessary I have beene to it, and for those poore meanes, I have left to maintaine this place. Y[r] Lord[spp] may bee assured I shall improve them to the uttermost for his Ma[tye's] service, and how unfortunate soever he may be, shall leave an accompt of my charge befitting an honest man, and one whom I hope y Lord[sp] shall not blush to owne for DOCUMENT LXXV. A.D. 1645.

Y[r] L[pp's] most humble and faithful servant,

JOHN BYRON.

Chester, Ap. 26, 1645.

For the Right Hon[ble] the L[d.] Digby, Principall Secretary of State.[1]

[1] State Papers Dom., Chas. I., 1645. Vol. 319, fol. 289.

LXXVI.

The Parliamentarians under Laugharne defeated at Newcastle Emlyn by General Gerard, and driven back to Pembroke and Tenby—Haverfordwest and Picton Castle taken by the Royalists. April 1645.

A.

DOCUMENT LXXVI. A.

A.D. 1645.

To the Honourable Committee of the two United Kingdoms of England and Scotland.

A True Narration of the present condition of the County of Pembroke and Army there, together with the Harbour of Milford, exhibited by such of the County as have been eye-witnesses and have solemnly covenanted with God to advance to their utmost His glorious cause, now managed by the two Houses of Parliament,

Who sadly remonstrate to your Honours that when it pleased God to give a great blessing to the said county, not only plentifully to cast off, but also for a good while to be nourished and miraculously to be preserved by His great power and providence, raising them so beyond all probabilities from a handful of naked men to become a pretty considerable body of armed men. The resolved Commanders and Worthies there, for discharge of their faithfulness in so great a trust, having a tender eye also to the exonerating and easing of a county almost worn out by the pillaging and oppression of the enemy and necessary quarter of friends, put on a resolution and marched out of their own county to Cardigan, where, after they had possessed themselves of the said town and castle, and indeed wonderfully relieving the said castle afterwards when it was strongly besieged by General Gerard, they besieged the Castle of Emlyn about six miles distant from Cardigan, being the enemy's next and only garrison in that quarter. Where (after they had

DOCUMENT LXXVI.A. A.D. 1645.

been there near a fortnight) upon the 27th day of April last, being the Lord's day, about six o'clock in the morning, there came a very strong party of the enemy's horse from England, besides other foot very numerous, who suddenly and secretly fell upon our men, slew and took most of our foot companies,[1] besides many horse, drove the rest into their garrisons, being about 30 miles remote from the place of their defeat, and forthwith advanced into the County of Pembroke, faced Haverfordwest, and summoned it. The soldiers no sooner quitted the said town, by reason of its openness, and that they might the better preserve the other garrisons of Pembroke and Tenby, being far more strong and considerable, but the inhabitants were constrained to surrender it upon very slender quarter. There they seized upon much of our ammunition and arms, imprison, plunder, and abuse the well-affected townsmen, range everywhere about the country, pillage and destroy that which should be the present and future livelihood of our army, and have given us a sure testimony that they will leave nothing undone that mischief and violence can invent against a distressed county. This done they drew all their forces towards the garrisons of Pembroke and Tenby, and are very confident either to overmaster them, or in fine to distress them till they yield. Notwithstanding, the Major-General [Laugharne], Mayor of Pembroke [Poyer], and the resolute Commanders there, have firmly by God's blessing determined to stand by their trust, and resolve rather honourably to lose their lives, together with their said towns and garrisons, than basely by yielding betray them, with their religion and liberties.

They further make known to your honours the most dangerous condition of the Harbour of Milford, which the enemy doubts not to block up by planting great ordnances to keep out such shipping as might relieve the Town and Castle of Pembroke; and this very probably they will very speedily do, if a timely expedient be not found out to prevent them.

It were but rashness and indiscretion in them to intimate the dangerous consequence of a delay as of other things so well known to your Honours. The public importance of the said Haven, being the only Harbour to friend, between Plymouth and Liverpool,

[1] "400 of our men were killed and taken in the field."—*Exchange Intelligence*, No. 2, for May 22.

DOCUMENT LXXVI. A. A.D. 1645. bloody Ireland's greatest curb and terror, the mariner's security if preserved; nay, they are verily persuaded, and so are all that know it, that there is not one place in England, *consideratis considerandis*, than that; though some ignorantly (we hope not maliciously) to the great prejudice of the State do slight it. They presume no farther, but humbly submit themselves to your Lordships, and from a bleeding and most tender heart they do commend the condition of the public and that place, together with their own sad estate and condition, to the grace and mercy of a good God and the known wisdom of this honourable Committee for their more speedy relief.[1]

B.

The Royalists' Account of it. Wednesday, May 7.

DOCUMENT LXXVI. B. A.D. 1645. To stop these barbarous rebels in their career, his sacred Majesty, with his army, went this day into the field; and, for a prosperous omen, this morning an express was brought to his Highness Prince Rupert from General Charles Gerard, who, since that full victory obtained over Major-General Laugharne before Newcastle-Emlyn, hath taken Haverfordwest and Picton Castle.

The manner of that action at Emlyn (for though the certain news of it was brought to court nine days since, yet the particulars came not till this morning) was briefly thus: General Gerard, knowing that all the rebels of Pembrokeshire (with their assistants), under Major-General Laugharne, had besieged a garrison of his Majesty (called Newcastle) at Emlyn, in Carmarthenshire, on the borders of Cardiganshire and Pembrokeshire, resolved upon their speedy relief, and marched above 100 miles in that one week through a country from whence he had no kind of assistance, either of men, money, or provisions; yet came upon the rebels so unexpectedly (by marching in small bodies, several ways) that,

[1] From a pamphlet, entitled "An Exact and Humble Remonstrance touching the late conflict of Armies in and near the County of Pembroke, &c. London: Printed by J. M., 1645." (K. P. 209—16.)

till they took some prisoners of his forlorn hope, they did not believe he was in the field. However, the rebels had little time to consult, for General Gerard fell upon them with so well-ordered speed and courage that he presently put them to a total rout, killed 150 in the place (besides those slain in the pursuit—which was continued full seven miles), took 486 prisoners, with 20 commanders, besides inferior officers, 120 good horse, one piece of ordnance of 9lb. bullet, almost 700 arms, and (which we cannot omit) among the prisoners were all the English-Irish, whom the Earl of Essex, in his letter to his Highness Prince Rupert, said were to expect no quarter. The bloody consequence of which is now manifest, if his Highness urge their own ordinance against them.

This happy victory was no sooner obtained, but General Gerard marched next morning to Haverfordwest (24 miles from Emlyn) where the rebels had a strong garrison, which the General resolved to storm; but this blow had made such impression on these rebels that they no sooner descried his Majesty's forces at the one end of the town but the rebels ran out at the other, in such strange confusion that very many of them were taken prisoners. These affrighted rebels not staying to take anything along with them, but left behind all their cannon (which are four pieces of ordnance), whereof two very fair brass guns, all their arms (betwixt five and six hundred), all their ammunition and victual, with two colours of horse, and four of foot. This town being of such consequence to his Majesty that it gives possession of one side of Milford Haven and six parts of seven of Pembrokeshire, which is the only county of South Wales wherein are any rebels.

For that other garrison which the rebels held at Cardigan Castle is now to be reckoned ours, for the very day the rebels there had intelligence of this great defeat at Emlyn and the gaining of Haverfordwest, they conceived themselves but lost men to stay there to be taken; and, therefore, in as much haste as their brethren, they all ran from Cardigan, both town and castle, after they had fired the castle, where they durst not stay to see it quite burned, but fled in haste to sea—their last refuge,—leaving behind them at Cardigan four pieces of ordnance which they did not so much as dismount.

From Haverfordwest General Gerard marched that very night

DOCUMENT LXXVI. B. A.D. 1645. over the water to Picton Castle (belonging to Baronet Phillipps), which the rebels have made a very strong hold; where he presently sent in his summons, but the rebels being obstinate, about 12 o'clock that night he fell on and stormed it, and mastered it in less than an hour, with the loss of nine common soldiers hurt and taken, but not one officer, only Col. Butler (a valiant gentleman) received a shot whereof he is now past danger. In the castle were found three barrels of powder, 150 arms, Baronet Phillipps's son and two of his daughters, a good round sum of ready money, and 12 trunks of plate, besides £500 more in money going to sea. The castle itself is very strong and in good repair, where General Gerard placed a sufficient garrison, and marched the next day to Carew Castle, near Pembroke, which (we hear since) is also taken: the remnant of the rebels being now driven to their last stake at Pembroke and Tenby at the very water-side, which are all the garrisons these rebels have now left.[1]

C.

Additional Excerpts.

DOCUMENT LXXVI. C. A.D. 1645. Col. Gerard hath left Montgomeryshire, and is said to be marched into Pembrokeshire. His forces have driven away what cattle they could light upon—some make mention of no less than 1,800 sheep, besides other cattle, but some of them were rescued by Sir William Brereton.[2]

From Wales there came this day intelligence that Gerard hath plundered much about Tregaron and Lampeter, and swept away the provisions of the county, and noised it abroad for a victory

[1] *Merc. Aulicus*, 4-11 May, 1645, p. 1578. (K. P. 210—17.)

[2] *Merc. Veridicus*, No. 4, 10th May. (K. P. 206—14.)

Yet we had a small party of our Pembroke forces about Ledy [Cledey] and Kilrhedyn, which some of Gerard's horse fell upon, and did some small hurt to, but had as much done to them. The Committee of Pembroke had nearly reconciled all the differences of that county.[1]

DOCUMENT LXXVI. C. A.D. 1645.

And now we desire the reader to call to mind that the 23rd of this month [April] last year, the barbarous rebels of Pembrokeshire drowned many gentlemen for refusing their cursed Covenant, and that very day this year it hath pleased God to revenge their blood on that whole body of rebels, who (as the express testifies) are all routed by General Gerard, before Newcastle Emlyn, on the borders of Pembrokeshire. Three hundred were killed in the place and five hundred taken prisoners, with all ordnance, arms, and ammunition, and whatever belongs to a complete victory; whereby they at Westminster will save £2,000, for on Wednesday (last week) they made an ordinance for sending £2,000 to the forces in Pembrokeshire, under Major-General Laugharne.[2]

The enemies' forces under Col. Gerard, after they had taken Haverfordwest, which is about seven miles from Milford Haven, durst not adventure to come nearer the Haven (though the malignants reported it to be taken), but went plundering and pillaging the county towards Pembroke, where Major-General Laugharne is ready to receive them. The enemy are said to be about 5,000. They took in Haverfordwest only four drakes; our men that were in it went out at one end of the town as they came in at the other.[3]

The sad news of all our Welsh party in Pembroke, the Haven of Milford, and other parts thereabouts, so well-affected to the Parlia-

[1] *Perfect Passages*, No. 29, May 8.

[2] *Merc. Aulicus*, 27th April, p. 1565.

[3] *The Kingdom's Weekly Intelligencer*, No. 100, 20th May. (K. P. 208—13.)

DOCUMENT LXXVI. C. A.D. 1645. ment, being driven quite out of the field, if not more, was confirmed. We see how good intelligence our adversaries have, for this they talked ten days since. It would be of evil consequence should they gain the Haven, as why not? Make they but a fort or two on the land, and they will command the ships, and we be so yoked in the Irish Seas that we shall never be able to pass.

Many serious discourses passed this day [May 20] about the relief of Pembroke, Tenby, and the recovery of Milford Haven, and if possible to enable our party to take the field again. But the work is difficult, and the difficulty lies in recovering what is lost more than in keeping what we have. The Castle of Haverford being taken it will be a very hard pull.[1]

[1] *Moderate Intelligencer*, No. 12, 20th May. (K.P. 209—7.)

LXXVII.

A Diary of the King's sojourn in South Wales after the Battle of Naseby.

DOCUMENT LXXVII. A.D. 1645.

Thursday, June 18 [from Wolverhampton], to Bramyard, co. Hereford, and to Hereford that night, twenty-six myle; this march was very bad way, hilly and woddy. Very poor churches and thin in this part of Worcestershire and Herefordshire. King's troops to Brinsop, afterwards to Pembridge.

Col. Barnabas Scudamore, brother to the Lord S., is Governor of Hereford City. Mr. Coningsby was Governor of Hereford first, and when Sir William Waller came against it, and shott a piece of cannon against it, and killed one man, 'twas rendered upon conditions. 2,500 soldiers in it. Waller stayed about a month and left it. Then Col. Mynne was Governor, and was killed at Red Marley, in Glostershire, by Massey's men. Then Prince Rupert put in Col. Scudamore.

Gentlemen of Herefordshire.

K.[1] John Scudamore, Viscount Sligo in Ireland, lives at Hom Lacy, three miles from Hereford, now prisoner in London. £4,000 per annum.

R. —— Coningsby, of Hampton Court (for every manor-house is called a Court here), Governor of Hereford. £4,000 p. a.

R. Sir Robert Harlow [Harley], of Brampton Brian Castle;

[1] K. signifies for the King; R., rebel.

DOCUMENT LXXVII. A.D. 1645.

he kept it pro. Parl., and 1644 the King's forces, under the command of Woodhouse, won it and pulled it downe. £1,500 p. a.

K. Sir Walter Pye, of Myndee, in Dowchurch parish; his father was Master (£25,000 p. a.) of the Court of Wards: owns Kilpek Castle in this shire, near Hereford; the last decayed, a park about it now.

K. Sir William Croft of Croft, killed near Ludlow, at Stoke Castle, a garrison of Parliament; since, his house beat down by us lest the Parliament should [again] garrison in it. £2,000 p. a.

K. Sir Giles Bridges at Wilton, Bart.

N. Sir Richard Hopton; two sons with the King, at Frome near Ledbury, Usurrer.

Sir John Kerle of Marckle.

K. Mr. Wallop Brabazon at Eaton by Lemster, his father an Irish baron. £1,000 p. a.

K. Sir Robert Whitney of Whitney, £1,000 p. a.

K. Sir Humfrey Baskerville of Ersley Castle, travailer. £300 per ann., was £3,000.

K. Mr. Tompkins of Monington; burgess for Webley. £1,200 p. a.

K. Mr. Roger Dansey of Brinsop Court. £800 p. a.

Baskerville of Canon Peawne, small estate; first for the Parliament, then for the King, then theirs, then taken prisoner by us, and [with] much adoe gott his pardon, and now *pro Rege*, God Wott.

Here in Herefordshire a quarter of mutton 14d.; rye 12d. a bushel. Rye is the best grain, grows generally in the county, and oates and pease; little timber in the shire.

The day before we came to Hereford his Majestie had intelligence that Fairfax had appeared before Leicester, and that the Lord Loughborough had yielded it upon conditions: to march away, the soldiers sans armes, officers with swords.

At Hereford, Wednesday, 25th June, the K. knighted Sir Dudley Wyatt and sent him to France.

Munday, 30th June, the King's Horse Guards removed to Gresmond, com. Monmouth. There is the walls of an old castle on the north side of the towne, moted, but in part dry upon the quarry of stone.

Garrisons in Com. Monmouth.

DOCUMENT LXXVII. A.D. 1645.

K. Monmouth. S[r] Thomas Lundsford is Governor; Herb. Lundsf. Governor.

K. Ragland Castle. Ye h'itation of ye Marq. of Worcester. His 4th son Charles, Lord Somerset, is Governour. 300 foot. No contribution, and constantly paid.

K. Abergaveny. Col. Jas. Prodgers is Gov.; Charles Prodgers, Lift.-G.

K. Chepstow. Sir John Winter is Governour. Ye county pays for 500. 100 [or 300] men now in it.

K. Newport. Col. —— Herbert, first son to the Ld. Cherbury. 50 men; contribution for 500.

Chief Inhabitants of Monmouthsh.

K. H. Herbt., Marquesse of Worcester, lives at Ragland Castle, his whole estate *ubiq.* was esteemed 24 thousand £ p. a. Lord Herbert is his eldest son.

N.[1] Sir William Morgan, lives at Tredegar.

K. Mr. Tho. M., son to S Wm. of Marghen [Machen].

K. Sir Philip Jones of Treowen, Kt., 2 sons in armes *pro R.*

K. Sir William Herbert of Colbrook.

K. Sir George Probert at Pantlace.

K. Sir Trevor Williams, Baronet, of Llangubby.

Sir Charles Kemes [crossed out].

Mr. Davie Lewis, of Llantheney, esq.

Mr. Wm. Baker at Abergaveny; Mr. Hen. Baker.

Tuesday, 10th of July, his Matie left Hereford and marched to Abergaveny, Com. Monmouth. He marched onely with these horse; King's troope; Queen's troope; Pr. Rupert's tr. of life-guard; Pr. Rupert's regt. of horse.

The Governor of Hereford with the gent. of the shire attended ye K. to Mr. Pritchard's house, neare Gresmond, where ye K. dyned. There his Majesty knighted Sir Henry Linghan [Lingen] of Herefordsh.

[1] It is difficult to say whether this is K or N. It looks more like N.

DOCUMENT LXXVII. A.D. 1645.

David Mathew, esq., of Landaffe. £600 p. a.

Marmaduke Mathews, of Landaffe, esq., a lease.

Sir Nicholas Kemys, Baronet, of Kaven Mably, a fine seate. £1,800 p. a.

—— Morgan, esq., of Ruperrie, a faire seate. £1,000 p. a.

George, Lewis, esq., of Llystalyboon. £400 p. a.

Walter Thomas, esq., of Swansey, was Governor. £600 p. a. His son high sheriffe.

Jenkin Morgan, esq. £300 p. a. Serjeant-at-Arms to the K. Towards the mountains, westward.

Wm. Basset, esq., of Bromiskin. £600 p. a. £20,000 in p. [? personalty].

All aforesaid, and so generally, against any that are against the King. Men from £40 to £200, above 100 men more in this county.

Garrisons in Glamorgansh.

K. Cardiffe. Sir T. Tyrell made Governor by Genll Gerard. Sir Anthony Mansell was first governor, killed at Newbury. Wm. Mathew, of St. Faggin's [succeeded him?]. Sir Nicholas Kemys was governor when Gerard came, and put out himself, and then Tyrell put in.

K. Swansey. Walter Thomas, first governor, put in by the K. before Gerard came. Then Col. Rich. Donnel was made by [Gerard].

This county never dealt with the militia. Never admitted.

Thursday, July 31, in the Castle of Cardiffe, the King knighted his coronet, Sir John Walpoole.

Monday, 4 Aug. King's guards marched toward Brecknock.

Tuesday, 5. His Majesty left Cardiffe, and went that night over the mountaynes to Brecknock.

Wednesday to Radnor. By the way dyned at Sir [Henry] Williams, Baronet's howse and fine seate in Brecknockshire

Thursday to Ludlowe. In his march he was accompanied with these horse: General Gerard's; his life guards, 300; Sir Marmaduke Langdale's; Sir William Vaughan's. Sir Thomas Glemham's foot that came from Carlisle to Cardiffe, marched as the King's life-guards. His horse in all 300. DOCUMENT LXXVII. A.D. 1645.

Friday to Bridgnorth, a pretty towne. Sir Lewis Kirke is Governor.

[Thence by Lichfield, Tedbury, Chatsworth, to Newark, and afterwards to Oxford, which was reached August the 28th.] [1]

[1] From "The Marches, Movings, and Actions of the Royal Army, his Majesty being personally present, from his coming out of his winter quarters at Oxford, May 7, 1645, to the end of August following." By Richard Symonds. Harl. MSS., 911, folios 77-143.

DOCUMENT LXXVII. A.D. 1645.

Ea. of Lindsey, High Chamb'lain, Ea. of Lichf., Lord Kernwagh, and his reg[t] of guards went from Ruperrie to Cardiffe, there dyned, and in the afternoon went to a rendezvous of the countrymen and inhabitants of Glamorganshire. There he met the gent[n] of the county in a body on horseback, and ye rest drawn up in a battaile, winged with horse and a reserve. His Ma[tie] returned that night to Cardiffe.[1]

At this rendezvous in com. Glamorgan some articles or propostions were tendered to his Ma[tie], w[ch] if he would please to grant they would march and continue in a body for the defence of his Majesty and their countrey.

Propositions were: That the garrison of Cardiffe might be governed by a country gentleman of their owne.

Wednesday, 30 July, this body of the inhabitants of Glamorgansh. had their rendezvous within 4 myle of Cardiffe at Kevenon [this name is crossed out.] They lay in the field this night and provision brought unto them.

Thursday, this body chose their officers of their own countrey. Every hundred chose their owne captain, &c. Their rendezvous was at Kevenon, 4 myles from Cardiffe, ye same place as ye day afore. This day the King and they agreed upon their propositions. Friday the rendezvous was at Llantrissant. They first called themselves the Peaceable Army.[2]

Cheife Inhabitants of Glamorgansh.

David Evans, esq., Com[r.] of Array, of Neath towards Carmarthensh. £1,000 per annum.

Bushie Mansell, esq., of Burton Ferrie. £1,100 p. a.

[1] This rendezvous was at St. Fagans. Speaking of this place, Symonds says:—"Near the church stands a fair house within the old walls of a castle, called St. Faggin's; the heir of Mr. Edw. Lewis, Esq., owes it. In the orchard of this house, under an old ewe [yew] tree, is a spring or well within the rock, called St. Faggin's well. Many resort from all parts to drink it for the falling sickness, and cures them at all seasons. Many come a year after they have drank of it, and relate their health ever since."

[2] They were, in fact, Club-men, whose chief object was the defence of themselves and property.

Sir —— Mansell, Baronet, of Margam. £4,000 p. a. *Infra etat.* Sir Edw. Scabright married his mother.

—— Llougher, esq., of [Loughor ?] £400 p. a.

Sir Edward Stradling, Baronet, of St. Donats' Castle. £4,000 p. a., if out of lease.

—— Turberville, esq., of the Skerr; descended from one of the 12 knights that came in with Fitzhamond at the Conquest. £600 p. a.

Edw. Kerne [Carne], esq., of Wenny. £1,000 p. a. Fine seate; a priory.

——. Winne, of Llansaner, esq. £600 p. a.

Sir Edw. Thomas, Baronet, of Bettws. £1,600 p. a.

Sir Richard Basset, of the Beaupre, Kt. £1,000 p. a.

John Van, esq., of Marcrosse. £500 p. a.

Sir John Awbrey, Baronet, of Llantrithid. £1,000 p. a.

Wm. Powell, Barrister-at-law, of Bonvilstowne. £300 p. a.

David Jenkins, of Hensol, Judge of the three counties, Carmarthen, Cardigan, and Pembroke; £20,000 in p. [? personalty]. £1,200 p. a., raysed *a nihilo.*

Miles Button, esq., of Cottrell. £400 p. a. Ancient in this place. Buttons, of Wiltshire, descended hence.

Robert Button, esq., of Worlton. £400 p. a.

Sir Thomas Lewis, K of Penmarke. £800 p. a.

Nicholas Lewis, esq., his elder brother, of Carn Llwyd. £400 p. a.

Wm. Thomas, esq., of Wenvoe. £2,500 p. a.

Wm. Herbert, of Coggan Peele, esq. His father was slain at Edghill. £1,000 p. a. Near the sea.

Edw. Lewis, esq., de Van and St. Faggins. £5,000 p. a., all improvable.

Humphrey Mathew, esq., Colonel of the County, had his commission from the King, of Castle Menich, or Monk's Castle. £800 p. a.

——. Mathew, esq., of Aberaman. £800 p. a.

Edward Prichard, esq., of Llancayach. £800 p. a.

Sir Wm. Lewis, K[t] of Killachvargod. £400 p. a.

Thomas Lewis, esq., of Llanishen. £500 p. a.

William Herbert, esq., of the Fryars, in Cardiffe. £1,000 p. a.

DOCUMENT LXXVII. A.D. 1645.

King's troope q[uartered] this night at Treargaire, Broingwinc, Bettus, and Clethey [Clytha], Com. Monmouth, near Ragland Castle.

Castles in Com. Monmouth.

Chepstow—now habitable; Lord Marquis of Worcester owes it.

Ragland—idem; Marq. of W. lives in it.

Monmouth—idem owes it; habitable.

Uske—Philip, Earl of Pembroke owes it; h'itable.

Caerlien—idem; ruined.

Newport—idem; ruined.

Abergaveny—Nevill, Baron thereof, owes it; ruined.

Arnold—Lord Abergaveny owes it; ruined.

Casgwyn, or White Castle—Marquis of Worcester owes it; ruined.

Gresmond—idem owes it; ruined.

Skenfrith—idem owes it; ruined. These three last were belonging to the Dutchy of Lancaster.

Langebby—Sir Trevor Williams in it; strong and inhabited and fortified; 60 men in it.

Cast-roggy—Marq. of Worc.; ruined.

Pencoad—Sir Edw. Morgan lives in it. Very faire. Now High Sheriffe.

Pen Howe—Sir Edmund Morgan lives in it; very faire.

Beeston (Beeston near Seaverne)—Bishop of Llandaffe owes it, and habitable.

Callicot, Trewilliam, Greenfeild Castles; no ruins left.

Thursday, July 3rd, his Matie went to Ragland Castle and lay there. There is an old proverb in this shire:—"*Pyn ddel y Brenin i Raglan, yna y bydd duedd y Cymre.*"[1]

His Majesty stayd at Ragland till Wednesday, July 16, 1645. About the 8th of July ye 2 troopes were going to Black Rock, and the King intended to goe over had not Goring's newes stopt.

H. W. and R. S.,[2] Friday, 4 July, to Brecknock, where Colonel-

[1] "When the King comes to Ragland, then will be an end to the Welsh."

[2] Symonds himself.

General Herbert Prise lives and is Governor. Colonel Turbervil Morgan is Governor under him.—5th, to Golden Grove, ye sweet and plentifull seat of Vaughan, Earle of Carbery, in Ireland.

Wednesday, July 16, his Matie attended with the D. of Rich., Earls of Lindsey, Lichfield, Kernwagh [Carnewarth], Lords Digby and Bellasis; his two troopes went to Sir Wm. Morgan's house, com. Monmouth, and dyned, and that night to Cardiff. The castle is the ancient possession and barony of the Earl of Pembrooke. To meet the Comm[issioners] to rayse men and settle the towne.

Thursday night his M^tie lay at S^r Wm. Morgan's. .

Friday to Ragland.

Parliament shipps [at this time] tooke many of Swansey boates, and some from Cardiff. July 17, came a gent. to Cardiffe with newes to the King that Lord Montrose had beate the Scots near Edenbrugh; killed Baillie their Lift.-Gen^ll, routed the rest. Montrose about 8,000 foot, 2 troopes of horse.[1]

Tuesday, July 22, his Matie went to Creeke, Mr. Moore's house, attended with the D. of Richm., Ea. of Lindsey and Lichfield, Lords Digby and Astley, his servants and other gent., and mett Pr. R. from Bristoll. Ye resolution was to send over the horse as soon as may be, and put all the new-raised foot in the Principality into garrisons. His Majestie returned that night to Ragland, his Highness the P. to Bristoll.

Thursday, 24 July, came intelligence to Bristol that S Thomas Fairfax had taken Bridgwater the day before. . . . .
The Scots at this time, about Wednesday, 23 July, stormed a house called Canon Frome, a garrison of the Kings in Herefordsh., Col. Barnard, Governor. All were put to the sword.

Thursday, 24 July, the K. came to Black Rock, intending to gett over towards Bristoll. Ye gent^n of Wales persuaded earnestly his stay, and immediately raised the hoop-hoop. The newes of Bridgwater's unexpected losse rather stayed him.

Sunday, July 27, 1645. His Matie lay at Ruperrie [Ruperra], a farie seate of Mr. Morgan, Com. Monm. This day the castle of Aberg'eny burnt, viz., the habitable part. Ye garrison drawn out and quitted.

Tuesday, July 29. His Matie attended by the Duke of Richm.,

[1] At this time, too, came news of Goring's defeat in the West.

LXXVIII.

Lord Digby to Prince Rupert, as to the King's intention to stay in Wales.

DOCUMENT LXXVIII.

A.D. 1645.

May it please your Highness,

I have received this day the enclosed account from General Goring of his last ill success and present condition; as also a letter from your Highness containing your resolutions as to Bristol. His Majesty hath had a debate here in council upon the whole matter of his affairs, and commands me to state unto your Highness his opinion in all particulars resulting from it, which if it concur with your Highness's judgment, you will be pleased to apply yourself and your order where you shall judge them necessary accordingly; but if not, your Highness is earnestly desired by his Majesty to hasten over hither to him, that his Majesty may take a clearer and fuller review of his business by your Highness's presence and assistance, and that resolution upon the whole may be settled with your approbation. There are three things of principal consideration in our business:—One, what to be done in the West, in order to the resisting Fairfax; another, what to be done in Wales, in order to the preserving of it, and to the forming of a new force here; and how the King should dispose of his own person . . . . To the second, concerning Wales, it is thought absolutely necessary that it be not abandoned, but that the horse, with General Gerard, according to your Highness's directions, be drawn back and disposed of to the best advantage for the defence of it, to which purpose his Majesty hath sent him orders to stop his march round to the West, and to command his attendance on his Majesty to advise of the rest. It is conceived that if Wales be well managed, and let see that we intend the defence of it, far greater levies may yet be made here, especially if it be found fit for the

DOCUMENT LXXVIII. A.D. 1645.

King to stay in these counties, and that the news be true, which was yesterday brought us very positively by a Major from Carnarvon, that my Lord of Glamorgan is landed in Anglesey, with a very great body of Irish;[1] and he that brought the news swears that he met with Sir Marmaduke Llangdale himself going with his horse to join with them. To the third point, which concerns the King's own person, it is conceived that General Goring, being now so far retreated into Devonshire, and the enemy following, it is not possible for any more forces from hence, or for any of those on the other side, not yet joined, to pass to him, and that for the King's person it cannot be conveyed thither without infinite danger; and were that practicable it would be very imprudent to engage both his and his sons person in the same corner upon such uncertainties, before so powerful an enemy, whereas probably his person cannot contribute much more to the strengthening of General Goring out of Devonshire and Cornwall than the Prince of Wales's will do without him, so that it is unanimously understood here to be the safest and most effectual course for his Majesty to cherish these parts with his presence. To endeavour new levies here, and out of them, and what may be hoped from Ireland, to form a new army, where in the interim it is hoped that what with these new levies of the 15th, with Charles Gerard's remaining foot, and with his horse recalled, it will be safe enough for him, yea, though the Scots should come into Wales, for we should be able to starve a great army, and beat a little one; especially if your Highness should think fit to send back hither those men that went over with Sir Bernard Astley, which is only proposed unto your Highness, to do therein as you think fit. . . . .

Your Highness's most humble faithful servant,

GEORGE DIGBY.

Ragland Castle, July 13th, 1645.[2]

[1] The Earl of Glamorgan had been for some time over in Ireland, trying to obtain the assistance of the Catholics there, and was empowered secretly by the King to offer them very liberal terms.

[2] Warburton's "Prince Rupert," iii., 141.

DOCUMENT LXXX. A.D. 1645.

Tuesday, his Ma[tie] marched towards Chester, attended with Montague Ea. of Lindsey, Ea. of Cork, Ea. of Lichfield, Lord Digby, Lord Astley, Lord Gerard. His force with him were his own reg[t] of Life-Guards, consisting of these troops: the King's; the Queene's, commanded by S[ir] Edw. Brett, the Major of the regiment; Earl of Lichfield's, Lt.-Col. Gourdon, Scot., commanded it. They were most Scotch officers; Sir Henry Stradling's troope w[ch] came from Carlisle with S[ir] Thomas Glemham. Toto, about 200. Lord General Charles Gerard was also there with the K., with his gallant troope of life-guard, 150 men. Col. Herb[t] Price his horse; Sir Marmaduke Langdale's brigade; Sir Thomas Blakstone's brigade, and Sir William Vaughan's brigade, and General Gerard's horse marched before all night toward Holt Castle, a garrison of the King's, commanded by Sir Richard Lloyd, where we have a pass of boats over y[e] river. Their business was to fall upon those horse and foot that lay before Chester. The King went into Chester and lay at Sir Francis Gamul's house: his guards watched in the street. The enemy, who were gotten into the outworkes which secured the suburbs, had made a breach the day before; and had entered had it not bin most gallantly defended.

Wednesday, 24 of September. Contrary to expectation Pointz his horse were come betweene Nantwiche and Chester to releve those forces of their party who were afore Chester, and to fight the King, as appears by his letters, intercepted by Sir Rich. Lloyd, to this purpose directed to Jones who sometimes was student in Lincoln's Inn, and commanded the horse that besieged Chester, thanking them for keeping their ground, notwithstanding the King's approach, and tells them a neare relation or accompt of the King's strength, of his tired over-marcht horse, of his number of dragoons, of his resolution to engage them if possible.

This morning, Sir Marma. Langdale, on Chester side of the river Dee, and not far from Beeston Castle, charged Pointz his horse, beat them and took some cornets. But they beat us agen for't.

About 12 of the clocke, those horse w[ch] came with the King and 200 foot were drawne out of Chester. 900 prisoners of ours taken and carried to Nantwiche, whereof about 20 gentlemen of the King's own troope.[1] Beeston Castle was besieged at this time.

[1] For a list of the prisoners then taken, see next Document.

DOCUMENT LXXX. A.D. 1645.

Thursday, 25. This night I saw a rainbowe within a mile of Denbigh, at 5 in the morning, and the moone shined bright; 'twas just against the moone. About 9 and 10 in the morning the King left Chester and went to Harding Castle, governed by Sir Wm. Neale, stayed 3 houres, and that night to Denbigh Castle. Sir M. Langdale's rendezvous was early this morning within 2 myles of Holt Castle.

Denbigh Castle is governed by Mr. Salisbury, repaired by him and his kinred at their owne cost. Had his commission from the King 2 years since. Friday, 26 Sept., rested. Satterday, 27, was a general rendezvous 3 myles from Denbigh. Newes again that Montrose had routed David Leslie about Kelso on the borders; that Prince Maurice was coming with 1,000 horse to us, and was at Chirke. All was reanimated and expected to follow Pointz to the North.

Sunday, 28. After sermon, about noone, came intelligence that the enemy's horse came over the river. A little afore we heard that they were gone toward Scarborough (so ill intelligence hath the King); but they went but into fresh quarters about Nantwich to refresh.

About one of the clocke afternoon, the K. marched through Ruthyn, where there is a large castle and fortified, to Chirke Castle, com. Denbigh. Watts knighted. Here P. Maurice met us with his troope, and those of P. Rupert's horse that came from Bristoll, Lucas's horse, &c., toto 600 or 700.

Munday, 29. Leaving Oswestree (a garrison of the rebells) on the left hand to Llandisilio and Llandreinio, com. Montgomery, where the army lay in the field; some cheifes in some houses.

Tuesday, from thence early at daybreak, marched, leaving Shrewsbury 3 myle on the left hand; that night late and teadiously to Bridgnorth. The rear guard got to Wenlock Magna, com. Salop. In this march three or four alarms by Shrewsbury horse, and five or six of them crost the way and killed and took some.

Wednesday, rested, 1st October. Thursday, 2, the King marched to Lichfield [and so to Newark].[1]

[1] Symonds's "Continuation of the Marchings of the Royal Army, &c." Harl. MSS., 944.

LXXX.

Journal of the King's Second Visit to South Wales after raising the Siege before Hereford; and thence to Chester and Denbigh. September, 1645.

DOCUMENT LXXX
A.D. 1645.

Saturday [Sept. 6th.] The King determined to go to Abergaveny. [He was then at Weobley, Herefordshire], but 'twas altered: the guards to Letton, his Majesty to Hereford.

Sunday to Ragland; guards to Treargaire, &c.

Thursday, Sept. 11. The K., attended with his guards, went to Abergaveny; returned at night to Ragland. His business was to commit the five cheife hinderers from relieving Hereford. His Majesty at Abergaveny committed Sir Trevor Williams, but he was bayled, Mr. Morgan, of T. [Tredegar?], Mr. Herbert, of Colbrooke, Mr. Barker, [and] Mr. ——, chief hinderers of the counties of Monmouth and Glamorgan to releve Hereford.

During the time of the King's being at Ragland, when he first came he sent Sir Marmaduke Langdale with his horse to Cardiffe, with Lord Astley and 100 foot out of Monmouth . . foot out of Raglan, Chepstow, &c., to parley with the Glamorganshire Peace Army, who were agens reson. Both armyes met 8 myle off Cardiffe. The Peace Army seeing Lord Astley's resolution to fight, though not considerable in number, agreed to lay down their arms and provide 1,000 men and arms within a month for the King, money, &c.

The next day or two after, ye enemy sent them ammunition and arms by sea, landed in Pembrokeshire. Then these rogues, hearing of the loss of Bristol, joined with the Pembrokesh. forces. Sir Marmaduke Langdale marched toward Brecknock.

Friday, Sept. 12, in the afternoon, his Matie attended with his guards, left Ragland, and marched some miles towards Heref., but returned; the guards to Abergaveny. Satterday the K. rested at Ragland. Gerard's horse at this time the King was at Ragland were about Ludlow. 2,000 of the enemyes horse about Lemster.

Sunday, 14., about noon, his Matie left Ragland and marched to Monmouth; thence that night to Hereford.

Monday, 15 Sept. His Matie in the morning, attended with his guards, marched some myles towards Bromyat, but by reason Gerard's horse had not orders soon enough to appear at the rendezvous, &c., his Matie returned to Hereford, accompanied with P. Maurice and General Gerard. His Matie read a letter from Montrose of his thorough victory in Scotland. Guards to Madley.

Tuesday, Sir Marmaduke Langdale's horse came to quarter about Biford, &c., Genl Gerard's horse at . . Poyntz his horse, above 2,000, was come to Lemster. This morning we received orders to move, but remanded; so rested.

Wednesday, Sept. 17. The whole army mett at a rendezvous upon Arthurstone Heath, near Durston Castle, com. Hereford; and from thence his Matie marched to Hom Lacy, the seate of Ld Viscount Scudamore. This day the nearest enemy, and whose business it was to attend the King's motion, viz., Pointz and Rossiter's horse, were about Lemster, co. Heref. Guards to Rolston.

Thursday, Sept. 18. The rendezvous was over Wye at Stockdye in Heref. Marched thence over the river Aroe, betwixt Morden and Wellington. Intelligence at the rendezvous this morning that the s^{d} enemy had marched all night, and were about betweene us and Worcester. This night to Presteyne, com. Radnor.

Friday, 19. This day we marched from Presteyne, and, except in the first three myle, we saw never a house or a church over ye mountaynes—they call it 10 myle, but 20—till we came to Newtowne, com. Montgomery. Satterday rested.

Sunday, 21 Sept. Over the mountaynes: less barren than the day before, by . . . Sir Arthur Blaney's house to Llan Vutlyn [Llanfyllin], a borough towne in Montgomeryshire.

Monday, 22. Over such mountaynes to Chirke Castle, com. Salop. There the King lay. . . . Watts is Governor. The guards to Llangothlyn, a market towne, com. Denbigh, three myle from Chirke. Newes this day that Col. Willm Legge, the Govern^{r} of Oxon, was committed. That P. Rupert's commission was declared null.

That part of the outworks at Chester were betrayed to the enemy by a captain and liett.: both apprehended.

The King sent to Watts to send to Lord Byron to Chester to hold out 24 hours.

LXXIX.

The Royalists defeated on Colby Moor—Haverfordwest taken by Major-General Laugharne. July 28th, 1645.

DOCUMENT LXXIX. A.D. 1645.

On Tuesday, the 28th of July, 1645, the enemy's main body being at Haverfordwest, we drew forth out of garrisons of Pembroke and Tenby with five hundred and fifty foot, and two hundred horse and dragoons (being the most that could be spared with security out of the towns), and two small guns, and marched that day to Caneston, within five miles of Haverfordwest, there met seven of the enemy's scouts, killed one and took the other six. That day Captain Batten arrived at Milford, and by Divine ordination above hopes landed 150 seamen to increase our foot. We kept the field till Friday, the 1st of August, no enemy appearing; then Major-General Stradling and Major-General Egerton drew forth out of Haverford with 450 horse, 1,100 foot, and four field guns, into Colby Moor, three miles from Haverford, and there put themselves in array for a fight. A small party of our horse, guarded on both sides with 150 musketiers, charged their whole body, began the encounter about six of the clock in the afternoon, and continued very fierce and doubtful near an hour, but in the conclusion the enemy's horse were totally routed; the residue of our horse fell on some part to do execution upon the foot, the other to pursue the horse speeding for Haverford. We killed of the enemies an hundred and fifty, took about seven hundred prisoners, in them men of note, Lieut.-Col. Price, Major Brande, Major Guddinge, Capt. Jones, Capt. Wade, Capt. Price, Capt. Thomas, Capt. Lloyd, Capt. Dawkins, Capt. Morgans, with 22 lieutenants and inferior officers, four guns, five barrels of powder, near eight hundred arms, all their carriages and provision, and chased them home to their garrison; the night then approaching we might not beset the town to keep in their horse, but drew back to the field, so that in the night the enemy deserted the town and fled, leaving a garrison in the castle. Saturday we entered the town and besieged the castle, began our battery on Monday, but spent much ammunition to little purpose. DOCUMENT LXXIX. A.D. 1645.

Tuesday, giving over, we fired the outer gate and scaled the walls, gained the castle, took prisoners an hundred and twenty common soldiers, and near 20 commanders and officers, whereof were Colonel Manley, the Governor, Lieut.-Colonel Edger, Major Hawton, Capt. Bushell, Capt. Thomas, Capt. Bandley, Capt. Moore, and Capt. Cromwell, one piece of ordnance, an hundred and twenty arms, some pillage to the soldiers besides the provision. Yesterday, being the 8th of August, we had a day of publique humiliation and thanksgiving in Pembroke and Haverford and the Leager. This day we drew our force of horse and foot before Carew Castle, and are drawing up our ordnance to plant them before the castle, relying upon the Lord of Heaven for a blessing; in all these actions, we bless God, we lost but two men and about sixty wounded, none mortally.

ROWLAND LAUGHARNE.[1]

[1] From a pamphlet, entitled "A True Relation of the late Success of the Parliament's Forces in Pembrokeshire, &c." Printed for Edward Husbands, August 25th, 1645. (K. P. 222—6.)

LXXXI.

Great defeat of the Royalists at Rowton Heath, near Chester, by General Pointz, Sept. 24th, 1645—*List of prisoners taken.*

DOCUMENT LXXXI. A.D. 1645.

Sir Philip Musgrave, Major-General.

Colonels:—Sir Thomas Dabridge-court; Sir Thomas Dacres, Sir Michael Constable, Sir Thomas Gore; Sir Henry Stradling, Phelim Heyter, Weston (son to late Lord Treasurer); Gifford, Cromwell, and Fletcher.

Lieut.-Colonels:—Matham, Millington, Hatton, Salkeld, Ruly, Broughton, and Rutherford.

Majors:—Williams, Morris, McDougall, McDoole, and Lacymouth.

Captains:—Martin, Swinlue, Henshaw, White, Gibbon, Starling, Shelley, Conyers, Johnson, Dixon, Press, Lowther, Willey, Morton, Simpson, Bell, Boulton, Vaughan, and St. Michael's. The last was a Captain of the Queen's troop; with him was taken a scarf which the Queen took from about her neck, and gave him to wear as colours for her.

Lieutenants:—Cottrell, Morgan, Bartrom, Astleby, Story, Colborne, Constable, Mansfield, Skipwith, Jefferson, Power, Brook, Whitney, and Elliot.

Cornets:—Elsing, Julian, Rainsford, Morley, Peirson, Fitzwilliams, and Smith.

Quarter-Masters, 4; Trumpets, 5; Corporals, 2; Gentlemen of the King's Life Guard, 17; twenty more gentlemen; Troopers, between 800 and 1,000.

Slain, two Lords (of whom Earl of Lichfield was one); two Knights (Sir Brian Stapleton was one); one Colonel, one Lieutenant-Colonel, and 300 and more officers and common soldiers.[1]

[1] From a pamphlet, entitled "The King's forces totally routed on Rowton Heath, &c. Printed for Ed. Husbands, September 29th, 1645." (K. P. 227—18.) See for an account of this conflict, several pamphlets printed at the time, and Parry's "Royal Progresses" p. 364. Also ante p. 270.

LXXXII.

Carmarthen Surrenders to Major-General Laugharne, October 12, 1645; *and the County declares for the Parliament.*

To the Honourable William Lenthall, Speaker to the Honourable House of Commons.

MR. SPEAKER,

Since the taking of Picton Castle[1] and freeing the whole County of Pembroke from the power of the enemy, the first action, worthy your knowledge, God vouchsafed I should effect, was the taking of Carmarthen Town and Castle. It was performed this day.[2] At nine o'clock in the morning 1,500 club-men of the county marched out at one gate and I entered at the other. The strength of the club-men in all the adjacent counties since their last association, my endeavouring to recruit in the best measure I could, and the unsettledness of the Commissioners of Array and other of the gentry of Carmarthenshire in their treaty for peace with us, lost me some time which might have been more useful in action. Their solicitations received birth before the taking of Carew Castle,[3] but after their loss of Picton I discerned more importunity in their prosecution. It were impertinent to rehearse all particular passages. The copies of the letters and conditions between us, with my declaration sent herewith (observing the order of them), will manifest the effect of what I should signify. Their first letter to me and the Committee, they sent to receive the King's approbation before they conveyed it to us; and all they did passed, though privately, by allowance of Major-General Stradling and Lovelace, the Governor of Carmarthen, which breeds my doubt they have yet rotten cores; and I shall try before I over-much trust them.

DOCUMENT LXXXII. A.D. 1645.

[1] About the 20th September. See *Scottish Dove*, No. 101. (K. P. 227—10.)

[2] October 12th.

[3] About the middle of September

DOCUMENT LXXXII. A.D. 1645.

On Friday the Commissioners drew 1,500 club-men into town, and with the townsmen undertook the defence, dismissing the Governor and his soldiers. Our forces lying then at St. Clears, six miles short of Carmarthen, staying for some carriages that were not yet come up. The next day we appeared in several bodies, 600 horse and 2,000 foot, before the town, and spent the evening in the interchange of parleys. At eleven at night we concluded, and this morning put it in execution; some of the manifestly "criminous" deserted the town and fled with the enemy. Some troopers and captains daily fall in to us, and the club-men in Cardiganshire resist the enemy, detain their contributions, and (in compliance with Col. Lewes, who neglecteth no means to win them) as I hear, declare for the King and Parliament. Our horse shall advance to-morrow to assist them, and in few days I hope to give a very good account of the two counties. The Glamorganshire gentlemen I desired (and I heard were ready) to appear upon the borders to wait my actions against Carmarthen, if the surrender had not prevented them. The town [is] very spacious, requiring no less than a thousand men in garrison. If we could give pay we should not want men, and these we have, with little encouragement, would deem no enterprise too hard. If it would please the State to afford some supply for money and clothing, I doubt not they should speedily reap the fruit of them. I restrain plunder, and use the country with all lenity. I shall not I hope repent it, or forget that I am, Sir,

Your most humble servant,

ROWLAND LAUGHARNE.

Carmarthen, 12th October, 1645.

Negotiations.

Copy Letter from Commissioners and Gentry of Carmarthenshire to the General and Committee in Pembrokeshire.

GENTLEMEN,

We, taking into consideration the unhappy effects that war (being continued) may produce between the County of Pembroke and the neighbouring Counties of Carmarthen and Cardigan, and

DOCUMENT LXXXII. A.D. 1645.

others, the unity whereof is requisite under many relations, to the preservation of which you and we equally pretend, namely, our religion, loyalty, and laws, though we have been hitherto so unhappy as to endeavour the preserving of these by destroying one another.

To prevent, therefore, the continuance of these miseries, we have formerly felt and the fears of worse that may ensue (if possibly it may be), and that we may move towards these ends, we severally profess to be the same, with better assurance of obtaining them, we conceive (that if your concurrence be had therein) that a treaty between a certain number commissioned out of these two counties and yours may produce a better effect to every of us than the hostility between us hath hitherto done, or (if continued) is like to do.

In order to this (if you approve thereof) you may name your number of persons, with the time and place where to give meeting, sending likewise your safe-conduct for the proportionable number commissioned out of these counties, and the like shall be sent to you from this. Thus desiring your speedy answer, we remain

Your servants,

Ed. Vaughan,	John Vaughan,	Rice Rudd,
Jo. Vaughan,	John Vaughan,	Henry Myddelton,
Rowland Gwyn,	George Gwyn,	John Lewis,
Robert Birt,	John Harr,	Thomas Lloyd.
Francis Lloyd,	Carbery,	

Laugharne's Answer.

Gentlemen,

Your letter of the 5th September we received this 25th of the same. If your desires be answerable to your expressions for peace, we shall upon what terms may be warrantable admit a treaty, conditioned you make full declaration of your obedience to the King and Parliament, and testify your resolution therein by present seizing, delivering to us, or detaining in your own power

DOCUMENT LXXXII. A.D. 1645.

those scattered horse of the enemy yet in your country. With these limitations we hereby engage for the safety of any four gentlemen among you (so they consist not of any member that deserted the Parliament) to repair to this town within the next three days, and to return with their necessary attendants; and we shall be ready upon your compliance to protect the common people and such of the gentry as we shall find capable of protection, and refer the exempted to Superior Judicatures. In the interim, in suspense of our expectations, we are,

Your servants,

ROWLAND LAUGHARNE, LEWIS BARLOW, SAMPSON LORT,
THO. BOWEN, JOHN LORT, THO. JONES.

Haverfordwest, 25th September, 1645.

From the Commissioners of Carmarthenshire to Laugharne and the Committee.

GENTLEMEN,

Expecting this day to have understood the full sense of the inhabitants of this county, that thereby we might have been armed with power to have treated as was in your letter mentioned, you may understand the country met not (as we expected), therefore we consider ourselves not in condition to send unto you according to our undertakings. This we thought fit to intimate you,

Your humble servants,

RICE RUDD, ED. VAUGHAN, HENRY MYDDELTON,
JOHN VAUGHAN, JOHN VAUGHAN, GEORGE GWYNNE.

Oct. 2nd, 1645.

SIR,

We hear you are advanced into this county, which makes us send this bearer to receive your command, which shall be performed by us, who profess and declare ourselves to be for the King

DOCUMENT LXXXII. A.D. 1645.

and Parliament, and will, with the best assistance we can, aid you with our lives and fortunes in anything that may conduce to the Parliament's service.

Your humble servants,
EDWARD VAUGHAN, HENRY MYDDELTON,
JOHN VAUGHAN, JOHN VAUGHAN.

Llangendysccn (?), October 10th, 1645.

For our honoured friend Major-General Laugharne, these.

[Laugharne writing from St. Clears on the same date asked two of them to give him a meeting at that place]; their answer was:—

SIR,

We received your letter, and rest your servants for the affection you express. Our late coming into the town prevents our waiting on you this night. We are 1,500 men in town, who are resolved for King and Parliament. To-morrow four of us will not fail to wait on you. We desire you not to march till then. The castle we have not as yet, but it has been promised us to-morrow; which with the hazard of our lives we will keep for the King and Parliament. Your declaration shall be published to the people, and if they declare not as we do their forced obedience shall make them rue their obstinacy.

Your servants,
EDWARD VAUGHAN, JOHN VAUGHAN, JOHN VAUGHAN,
CHARLES GWYNNE, HENRY MYDDELTON.

Carmarthen, 10th October, 1645.

[Certain conditions were requested by the town and county before declaring for the Parliament, to which Laugharne could not agree; and ultimately the following declaration was signed, and the town surrendered]:—

We, whose names are subscribed, in the name of ourselves and all the inhabitants of this town and county, do absolutely declare for King and Parliament, and will with our lives and fortunes

DOCUMENT LXXXII.

A.D. 1645.

assist the forces raised by the Parliament against any other whatsoever as shall seek to invade these countries, and so desire to be received into the King and Parliament's protection, according to the declaration of Major-General Laugharne; and for contribution we willingly submit proportionably to our neighbouring countries. 11th October, 1645.

Tho. Griffith, Mayor	John Hughes	Henry Vaughan
David Bevan	Walter Chapman	Samuel Hughes
Robert Lewis	Edward Vaughan	Thomas Powell
Tho. Woodford	John Vaughan	John Awbrey
Robert Ioy } Vice-Com.	Henry Vaughan	Anthony Morgan
John David } Vice-Com.	Henry Middleton	John Gwynne
John David	George Gwynne	John Lloyd
Robert Brand	John Vaughan	Edward Vaughan
Robert Griffith	John Harris	William Lloyd
Rich. Thomas	Thomas Williams	John Newskay[1]
Edward Jones	Francis Howell	

[1] From a pamphlet, entitled "Major-General Laugharne's Letter, &c. London: Printed for Edw. Husbands, &c., October 28th, 1645." (K. P. 231—15.)

LXXXIII.

Monmouth taken for the Parliament by Col. Morgan, Governor of Gloucester, assisted by Sir Trevor Williams, October 24; *and an attempt to regain it.*

A.

Col. Morgan's Letter to the House of Commons.

GENTLEMEN,

My desire is to acquaint you with our proceedings in this county since the reducing of Chepstow,[1] and how we have caused Major-General Washington, who had 1,500 horse and foot, besides a great faction in the county, to quit it and refuse to fight with us. My forces consisted of 1,500 horse and foot, and the Monmouthshire club-men, under Sir Trevor Williams,[2] being 1,500 foot and 200 horse. Both these being joined, we concluded to attempt Monmouth, in which design it pleased God to prosper us. Upon the first attempt we got the town, the enemy betaking themselves to (their last refuge) the castle, which being three days besieged, discovered our mines which were almost ready to spring, and then they beat a parley, which we entertained, DOCUMENT LXXXIII. A. A.D. 1645.

[1] Chepstow (Town and Castle) was surrendered by Col. Fitzmaurice, the Governor, upon quarter of life only, to Col. Morgan, on the 10th October, having undergone several days' seige. Scudamore, the Governor of Hereford, attempted a diversion of the seige, but failed. At Chepstow were taken the Governor, Major Bridgman, 3 lieut.-colonels, 6 captains, 50 inferior officers and common soldiers, 30 horse and saddle, with 17 pieces of ordnance, 10 barrels of powder, 300 arms, &c.—*A Diary or an Exact Journal*, No. 75, October 23. (K. P. 230—2.)

[2] Of Llangibby. We have seen him before for the King; but he had changed before the King came to Raglan, for he was of those whom the King seized at Abergavenny as a "hinderer" to the relief of Hereford. Ante Document lxxx.

DOCUMENT LXXXIII. A. A.D. 1645.

concluding the delivery of the castle, with all the arms, artillery, ammunition, and provisions therein (save only the officers [who were allowed] to march away with their horses and arms), immediately unto us, for the Parliaments' use, which was instantly acted; and they were sent with a convoy to Hereford.

We took in the castle seven pieces of ordnance, four sling pieces, 300 muskets, 600 pikes, ten barrels of powder, with bullet and match proportionable, 24 barrels of 'Peter' and brimstone, and a reasonable quantity of all sorts of provisions. By these successes all South Wales is brought into a good condition, and declare themselves for the Parliament. So I rest, gentlemen,

Your servant,

THOMAS MORGAN.[1]

Monmouth, October 24, 1645.[2]

B.

The failure of a Design to betray Monmouth.

DOCUMENT LXXXIII. B. A.D. 1645.

SIR,

On Saturday morning [the day after the surrender of the castle] the Governor marched to Gloucester with all his foot, leaving only 100 in the castle, under the command of Capt. Foster, and the town to Sir Trevor Williams's charge, the country assisting

[1] Of the Tredegar family. Further particulars relating to the capture of Monmouth are given in two letters annexed to the above, from which it appears that Sir H. Lunsford was the Governor at this time. On perceiving Sir Trevor Williams joining with Col. Morgan, the townspeople of Monmouth are said to have laid down their arms. "Sir Trevor Williams is left Governor, and deserves to have it establised by the Parliament, having engaged all the country for the Parliament." Col. Kyrle also did very good service.

[2] From a pamphlet, entitled "Two Letters from Col. Morgan, Governor of Gloucester, to several Members of the House of Commons, &c., relating the manner of taking the Town and Castle of Monmouth, &c. Printed for Thos. Bates, at the Sign of the Maiden-head on Snow-hill, Holborn Conduit, 1645." [Oct. 28.] (K. P. 231—14.)

DOCUMENT LXXXIII. B.

A.D. 1645.

him in that service. The Governor had no sooner gone for Gloucester, but the country (being instigated by some malignants in the town) began to draw homewards, and told Sir Trevor Williams plainly that they did not come to keep garrisons, and they departed the same night every man to his own home, leaving the town destitute of strength. Whereupon Sir Trevor Williams desired Capt. Foster he might have the assistance of his men to keep the town; but he having the charge of the castle thought it not his duty to forsake that, but resolved to keep it to the utmost hazard of his life and fortune. Thereupon, Sir Trevor Williams, seeing the danger he was in (Raglan Castle being within seven miles of it), and the malignants gathering together and giving out words that the town would be their own by the morning, sent a post to the Governor of Gloucester to acquaint him, and also to the Forest of Dean for present supply, upon which Lieut.-Col. Kyrle and Capt. Gainsford came at 12 o'clock that night with 200 men, and before 12 o'clock next day with 500 more, who guarded the town till the Governor had sent 200 commanded men of Gloucester for the keeping thereof. The garrison of Monmouth being put in a posture of defence, and the malignants' design prevented, proclamation was made by Sir Trevor Williams and Lieut.-Col. Kyrle that upon Monday following those people that were suspected to be against the Parliament should depart the town upon pain of death, whereupon divers families of malignants were put out. . .

Yours assured,

C. W.

Monmouth, Nov. 4, 1645.[1]

[1] Extract from a pamphlet, entitled "A Full Relation of the Desperate Design of the Malignants for the betraying of Monmouth. &c." Printed for Thomas Bates, &c. (K. P. 232—19.)

LXXXIV.

Sir William Vaughan defeated by Col. Mytton near Denbigh. November 1, 1645.

To the Honourable William Lenthal, Esq., Speaker of the Honourable House of Commons.

DOCUMENT LXXXIV. A.D. 1645.

HONOURABLE SIR,

It pleased the Most High, who commands all the armies in Heaven and earth, to magnify his power this day by a memorable victory over the enemy near Denbigh, of which (being appointed thereunto by the Commanders whose many other employments transmit it to this pen), I shall render as full an account as may be expected from a work yet indigested.

Sir William Brereton, upon his return to Cheshire, found the work for reducing Chester and Beeston Castle in a good posture; but the enemy, esteeming Chester the masterpiece of the Kingdom, extended their utmost endeavours for the relief thereof, gathered into a body about Denbigh, waiting an opportunity for the effecting of that high design, without which they gave up those parts as utterly lost. Sir William, reserving a competent strength to make good both leaguers, sent away Col. Jones and Adjutant Louthiano, dexterous and trusty men, with the Cheshire forces and auxiliaries of the Counties of Lancaster, Derby, Warwick, Montgomery, and Salop, the whole about 1,400 horse and 1,000 foot, being the cream of all these parts of the Kingdom. The enemy, under the command of Sir William Vaughan (as our best intelligence by the prisoners gives us) were about 1,700 horse and 400 foot. On Thursday night we marched to Mold, on Friday to Ruthin, where, having intelligence the enemy was at Denbigh (reported to be a far greater number), we hastened thither upon Saturday, November 1, accompanied by that active gentleman, Gen. Mytton, and part of his auxiliaries, the rest being left at Chester. The Forlorn Hope, forty out of every regiment, was commanded by Capt. Otter, Captain of the Reformadoes, a gallant soldier, and Capt. William Edwards, a Cheshire Captain and well-deserving

DOCUMENT LXXXIV. A.D. 1645.

gentleman, who, coming to Whitchurch, a mile from Denbigh, were in a lane flanked by the enemy's horse and dragoons, so that they were forced to make good that pass with the Forlorn Hope and Cheshire dragoons, under the command of Capt. Finch and Capt. Holt, stout and resolute men. These, with the Forlorn Hope, behaved themselves gallantly, and maintained the pass till the foot came up, the most part of which, with the Warwick and Derbyshire horse, commanded by Major Sanders and Major Hokesworth, seconding the Forlorn Hope, bare the burden of the day, whilst the Reformadoes, Cheshire horse, and 400 Lancashire foot, were intended for a greater service; for the Commanders finding that straight lane too difficult a pass to fall through upon the enemy, were marshalled in open field. These last mentioned (by the advice of some who knew the country) were drawn thence by Denbigh Green, a way near four miles in compass, to fall upon the enemy upon even ground, which, whilst drawn off, the foot (exceeding forward to engage themselves on the whole), beat the enemy out of the lane, and routed both horse and foot, driving them under the command of the castle, where they rallied themselves; but the Forlorn Hope, Derby and Warwick horse, with the foot, encountered them again, and utterly routed them, whom the horse chased eight miles in the way to Conway, making great execution on the way, taking many prisoners, and 500 or 600 horse, and so long pursued that not above seven score were left together.

To give everyone his due in this service would savour too much of vain-glory. But this I may modestly report: that everyone endeavoured to exceed each other in gallantry, whose spirits God had raised to so high a pitch as might suit to a work of so high a nature. It is conjectured by those who are best able to give account herein, that above 100 of the enemy were slain, about 400 taken prisoners, with divers men of quality. It is not known that any of ours are slain, and few wounded.

. . . . . .

Your Honour's most humble servant,

NATHANIEL LANCASTER.

Denbigh Town, Nov. 1, 1645.[1]

[1] From a pamphlet, entitled "A True Relation of a Great Victory obtained by the Parliament Forces, &c., against the King's Forces, &c., near Denbigh." (K. P. 232—14.)

LXXXV.

Brecknockshire Declares for the Parliament—The Declaration of the Gentlemen and Inhabitants of the County. Nov. 23, 1645.

DOCUMENT LXXXV. A.D. 1645.

We, the gentry and inhabitants of the County of Brecknock, whose names are subscribed, do declare and profess that we are fully satisfied in conscience that the two Houses of Parliament, now sitting at Westminster, are the true and undoubted lawful Parliament of England, and the Supreme Court of Judicature of the Kingdom, to whose judgment and determination we do and will in conscience of our loyalty, and not by terror or restraint, submit ourselves, our lives, and fortunes.

We are also persuaded and confess that the arms taken up and continued by authority of Parliament in this Defensive War, are raised and continued in their own just defence, and for the just defence of the Protestant religion, the person and honour of the King's Majesty, the privileges of Parliament, and the liberty of the subject. And that the forces raised or to be raised within the Kingdom of England, or dominion of Wales, without their consent, are raised and employed for destruction of Parliaments, fomenting and establishing of Popery, prelacy, and an illegal and arbitrary Government.

In apprehension whereof we do unanimously resolve, and firmly engage and undertake, that we, with all persons under our power and command, will from henceforward, to the extremest hazard of our lives and fortunes, adhere to and assist the forces raised or to be raised by authority of Parliament, against all other forces raised or to be raised against them, or without their consent. And we shall willingly and cheerfully join with Major-General Laugharne, and those three associated counties of which he is Major-General, and with the County of Glamorgan, with whom we are already associated, and contribute our utmost assistance

DOCUMENT LXXXV. A.D. 1645.

and endeavours, proportionably to the said respective counties, in such way as Major-General Laugharne shall think fit and meetest for the service of the Parliament.

And from this resolution and engagement we shall not swerve or recede, by adhering to the contrary party, or embracing a detestable neutrality, either by persuasion, dread, or any other motive whatsoever.

Howell Gwyn, Vic.-Com. Brec.[1]	Will. Walbeoff[10]	Daniel Winter
	Will. Vaughan	William Haynes
Edward Rumsey[2]	Tho. Walbeoff[10]	Thomas Bowen
John Williams[3]	Meredith Lewis[11]	Walter Lloyd
Lewis Lloyd[4]	Lewis Jenkins	Henry Jones
Edward Williams[5]	William Herbert	John Thomas
Roger Vaughan[6]	Edward Games[12]	John Win
William Morgan[7]	Tho. Williams	Hugh Meredith
John Gwyn	Will. Watkins[13]	Jeffrey Lewis
Thomas Gunter[8]	Tho. Lloyd	John Lewis
Edward Gwyn	William Jones	Edward Aubery[14]
Richard Games[9]	Thomas Roberts	

[1] Of Glanbran, H. S. 1645. [2] Of Crickhowell. [3] Of Cwmdu.
[4] Of Wernos [5] Of Gwernfigin, H. S. 1659. [6] Trephilip, H. S. 1646.
[7] Of Dderw, H. S. 1655. [8] Of Tregunter, H. S. 1658.
[9] Of Penderyn, H. S. 1625. [10] Of Llanhamlach. [11] Of Pennant, H. S. 1638.
[12] Of Buckland, H.S. 1647. [13] Of Sheephouse, H. S. 1649.

[14] From a pamphlet, entitled "A Declaration of the Gentlemen and Inhabitants of the County of Brecknock, &c. Printed for Edw. Husbands, &c., Dec. 6, 1645," (K. P. 235—9.)

LXXXVI.

Prisoners taken at the Surprisal of Hereford by Col. Morgan and Col. Birch. 18*th December*, 1645.

DOCUMENT LXXXVI. A.D. 1645.

The Lord Brudenell[1]
Sir Thomas Lunsford[2]
Sir Walter Blunt[3]
Sir Henry Spiller[4]
Sir Henry Bedington
Sir Marmaduke Lloyd[5]
Sir George Vaughan
Sir Giles Mompesson
Sir John Stepney[6]
Sir Francis Howard
Sir Francis Lloyd[7]
Sir Richard Bassett[8]
Sir Philip Jones[9]
Sir Edward Morgan[10]
Sir N. Throgmorton[11]
Lieut.-Col. Price[12]
Lieut.-Col. Lewes
Lieut.-Col. Jeffreys[13]
Lieut.-Col. Jones
Major Price
Judge Jenkins[14]
Capt. Wm. Hill
Capt. Thomas Codwallis
Capt. Richard Ballard
Lieut. Gibs
Cornet Denley

[1] After the restoration he became the first Earl of Cardigan. Suffered long imprisonment in the Tower.

[2] Late Governor of Monmouth. [3] Of Sodington, Worcester, Bart.

[4] M.P. for Arundel, 1 Car.

[5] Chief Justice for Counties of Glamorgan, Radnor, and Brecon, of Maesyvelin, Card.

[6] Of Prendergast, Pemb., ousted member for Haverfordwest.

[7] Son of Sir Marmaduke, and Comptroller of the King's Household.

[8] Of Beaupre, Glam., Knt., once Governor of Cardiff.

[9] Of Treowen, Mon., Knt.

[10] Of Pencoed Castle, Mon.; M.P. for Monmouth, 18 Jac. i.

[11] Lieut.-Governor of Hereford. [12] Most probably Herbert Price of Brecon.

[13] John Jeffreys of Abercynrig, Brecon.

[14] David Jenkins of Hensol, Glam. Judge of Great Sessions for Carmarthen, Cardigan, and Pemb. Imprisoned afterwards in the Tower, where he wrote violently against the Parliament, for which and other things he was convicted of, he was condemned to die, but was not executed. When he was taken prisoner there was found on him £6,000 which he had carried with him from garrison to garrison, and would not part with any of it to further the King's cause.—*Old Newspaper.*

DOCUMENT LXXXVI.

A.D. 1645.

Cornet Blood
Cornet Taunton
Quarter-Master Stephenson
Commissary Lingen
Secretary Barne
Mr. George Blunt
Mr. Thomas Blunt
Mr. Edward Blunt
Mr. Windsor
Mr. James Anderson
Mr. Turberville
Mr. Henry Morgan
Mr. J. Phillips } Priests
Mr. J. Taylor }

Mr. Wm. Chambers
Mr. Venner
Peter Merlet, a Frenchman
Mr. Roger Bodnam
Mr. Terringham
Mr. Seaborn
Mr. Mathers More
Mr. John Bemond
Mr. David Powell
Mr. Harrington
Mr. Powell } Chirurgions
Mr. Watson }
Mr. John Ridsen
Mr. Tooley, and twelve troopers

DOCUMENTS

ILLUSTRATING TRANSACTIONS

IN THE YEAR 1646.

LXXXVII.

Efforts made to relieve Chester—The Archbishop of York to the Marquis of Ormond. January 1646.

DOCUMENT LXXXVII.

A.D. 1646.

MAY IT PLEASE YOUR EXCELLENCY,

Yours of the 12th of December I received not until yesterday, which was the 1st of this instant [January] . . . Chester, with the help of some relief put in, on the Welsh side, may hold out three weeks, and much more, were not the poor unruly, who since the pulling down of so many suburbs, do pester that city. The Mayor's wife, always suspected, is gone to the enemy. Our forces from Wales, of some 100 horse (for foot we have none), under the conduct of Major Evet, put in this last supply of meal and powder, whilst the enemy were withdrawn in part to meet Sir William Vaughan, lingering at High Ercall, with 1,500 horse and foot (near which place he cut off 300 rebels in one quarter), in expectation of the main supply from Oxford and Worcester, under the Lord Astley and Sir Charles Lucas, who should add unto his number in horse and foot 2,200 more. We of the Welsh being quite frightened (and three of our five counties being for a great part of them under contribution to the enemy), are not able to make above 300 horse, and scarce so many foot, being, by a piece of ill-conduct in Prince Rupert when he was last in these parts, quite disarmed and discouraged. All these, joined with the foot mentioned in your Excellency's letter, will be more than able, with God's leave, to relieve Chester, and less will not do it. For they set their rest upon this business, and being defeated in this attempt are broken in these parts of the Kingdom.

DOCUMENT LXXXVII. A.D. 1646.

And although, most excellent Lord, the place be in extraordinary danger, and that the loss of it will draw along with it all those hideous consequences mentioned by your Excellency, as the sudden loss of these parts and all communication with that Kingdom, yet dare not I to advise your Excellency to ship your men until I do hear more certainly of the approach of such succours as are destined by his Majesty. Sir William Vaughan himself being drawn to Wenlock to meet them, but expected by a French Lord, who serves the King, Mons. de Saint Pol [Paul], now in my house, to come down the end of this week. I do therefore send a copy of the effect of your Excellency's letter to Chirk and so to Wenlock, to understand punctually and precisely the time of the succour's falling down, that I may send your Excellency the very daily motions of that army, and hereof I look for an answer within three days.

But the exigency of Chester so requiring, I humbly submit it to your Excellency's better judgment whether your Excellency will not with all speed transport those men, who need not advance further than Anglesey, Carnarvon, and the skirts of Denbighshire, but remain so unengaged until the King's horse shall meet and receive them, and they in the meantime will secure these tottering counties. And the vessels that transport them may for eight or ten days lie or ride very securely in that sleeve between Anglesey and Carnarvonshire, until the foot shall punctually understand what to trust unto.

If your Excellency's men do arrive here, they shall be, by God's blessing, provided of good and safe quarters, all along to

DOCUMENT LXXXVII. A.D. 1646.

their joining with the relief, and have necessary refreshment; but I fear me the business will not suffer them to use that plentifully until the action be performed. But who shall assure you of this, my Lord Byron being in Chester, I do not know, but do write to him likewise of that point, and do promise faithfully my own diligence to the utmost of my power to effect it. But I must be clear with your E. that his Majesty hath given me no real commission or authority in this place (although I could have given him, whilst my body was able to bear it, a better account than he hath had of these town and countries). But what I do, is by private interest and for particular ends thwarted and opposed by such as should further the service;[1] yet I hope, in God, I shall be able to do what your Lordship desires in this just and reasonable demand.

. . . . . .

Your Excellency's most humble and faithful servant,

Jo. Eborac.[2]

Conway, 2nd January, 164$\frac{5}{6}$.

[Writing to Lord Astley on the 25th of January, the Archbishop says]:—From the Lord-Lieutenant [Ormond] I have received no answer in writing as yet, though my letters to his Excellency were many since the 1st of January; nor from the Lord Digby any more to the purpose than this enclosed. There is, noble Lord, no relying upon these Irish forces for this service; though if they come they shall be carefully transposed to such a rendezvous as I hear is most fitting for the passage of your Lordship's army. And for that end your Lordship shall be punctually informed of their landing and condition. In the meantime, it is fit your Lordship should understand that under Col. Gilbert Byron, the Lord of St. Paul is in these parts, at the head of 600 (as he saith), but I believe of 500 horse and foot,

[1] Referring probably to Sir John Owen being put over him in the command at Conway.

[2] Carte's Papers, Bodl. Lib., vol. xvi., fol. 242.

good men and well-armed, to be directed and employed by your Lordship. Next, that Lieut.-Col. Roger Mostyn is landed with a piece of a regiment (some 160 men, as Col. Butler tells me) of the Lord Digby's raised in Ireland, of English and some Lorainses (*sic*), and he will be able to make it up 200 upon his own credit (a Commissioner of Array and Peace in this county), and will be after a day or two's refreshment at your Lordship's dispose. . . . . I have it from good and knowing hands, that the armed and fighting men at Chester are above 4,000, whereof many may issue forth.[1]

DOCUMENT LXXXVII. A.D. 1646.

[1] Tanner MSS., vol. lx., f. 386.

LXXXVIII.

The Surrender of Chester to the Parliament, February the 1st, 1646 —Letter from Sir Wm. Brereton to the Speaker of the House of Commons.

DOCUMENT LXXXVIII.

A.D. 1646.

HONOURABLE SIR,

The care of preserving this city from ruin (being the most considerable in this part of the Kingdom), invited [me] to entertain a treaty, wherein at the least ten days were spent in several transactions,[1] the enemy still using protractions and delays in hope of their expected relief;[2] for which end strong preparations were made, whereof we received frequent advertisements from several persons that Astley[3] and Vaughan[4] had united their forces, and lay hovering about Bridgnorth. Their intention was to have joined with the Welsh forces under the Lord St. Paul, with those Irish that came over in December last, and those other now lately landed at Beaumaris, which were part of the Lord Digby's regiment, some whereof are English, and some Lorrainers, as these enclosed intercepted letters mention. To prevent the conjunction of which forces I sent three regiments of horse, the Warwickshire, the Reformadoes regiment, and part of the Staffordshire horse, and some of the Cheshire dragoons, together with Col. Mytton's horse and foot. This party was commanded by Col. Mytton, who marched to Ruthin upon Saturday night, January 24th, intending to fall upon the enemy in their quarters, but they escaped and marched to Denbigh, and so towards Conway. Nevertheless, our forces came most seasonably, for Ruthin Castle was so unprovided, as that we have now great hopes of reducing that strong castle. However, the conjunction of the forces is hereby prevented,

[1] For these see King's Pamphlets, No. 249—30.

[2] See the preceding letter from the Archbishop of York.

[3] Sir Jacob Astley, now Lord Astley.

[4] Sir William Vaughan.

DOCUMENT LXXXVIII. A.D. 1646.

which probably occasioned the enemy's retreat after they had quartered three or four days about Bridgnorth and Shiffnal, and had drawn out some small pieces and two cases of Jacks (?). So as the besieged, being now hopeless of relief, sent out their Commissioners on the 30th of January to treat with ours, whose names are herein enclosed.

The number was proposed by them, and assented to by us, to the end that better satisfaction might be given to the common soldiers when some of their own officers were entrusted and employed in treating and making compositions for them, that they might also be thereby obliged to restrain their soldiers from plunder and violation of what is concluded and agreed upon.

The first day nothing was concluded upon.

This day, January 31st, they were mighty importunate that the treaty might be continued and respited until Monday morning at nine o'clock, which being refused, they delayed not to enter into a treaty. Whereupon it was concluded, to be delivered upon the enclosed conditions, whereunto it was the rather assented to prevent the plunder of the city, which could not have been preserved if it had not ben taken by composition. That which further remains is the satisfying of the soldiers and the settling of the city, which will prove a work of great difficulty, wherein my endeavours shall not be wanting to the utmost of my abilities, or to serve the public in any other employment commanded, and shall ever profess myself to be, Sir,

Your most faithful friend and humble servant,

William Brereton.

Chester Suburbs, February 2nd, 1646.

Though this letter was dated February 2nd, yet I thought fit to stay the messenger until we were able to send you the certainty that we were possessed of the city. What ordnance, arms, or ammunition, or what Irish are found therein, you may expect to receive an account in my next. I do not hear any further reports of the Irish, neither do I believe they will be now less forward to adventure into these parts.

William Brereton.

Chester, February 3rd, 11 of the clock.

Articles concluded upon February 1st, 1646, between the Commissioners appointed on behalf of John Lord Byron, Field-Marshal-General of North Wales, and the Governor of Chester, of the one part, and the Commissioners on behalf of Sir W. Brereton, Baronet, Commander-in-Chief of all the forces of Cheshire and at the Leager before Chester, of the other part, for the Surrender of the City of Chester, with the Castle and Fort thereof.

DOCUMENT LXXXVIII.

A.D. 1646.

1. That the Lord Byron and all Noblemen, Commanders, Officers, Gentlemen, and Soldiers, and all other persons whatsoever now residing in the City of Chester, and the Castle and Fort thereof, shall have liberty to march out of the said City, Castle, and Fort in all their apparel whatsoever, and no other or more goods, horse, or arms than are hereafter mentioned, viz.:—The Lord Byron with his horse and arms, and ten men with their horses and arms to attend him; also his lady and servants, two coaches, and four horses in either of them, for the accommodating of them and of such other ladies and gentlewomen as the said Lord Byron shall think meet, and with 80 of the said Lord's books, and all his deeds, evidences, manuscripts, and writings in his possession—the said Lord, his lady, nor any their attendants, carrying amongst them all above forty pounds in money and twenty pounds in plate. The rest of the noblemen, with their ladies and servants, to march with their horses, each of the said lords attended with four men, their horses, and arms, every such nobleman carrying with him not above thirty pounds in money. Every knight and colonel to march with two men, their horses, and arms: no such knight or colonel to carry with him above ten pounds in money. Every lieut.-col., major, and captain of horse, with one man, their horses and arms, not carrying with them above five pounds in money. Every captain of foot, esquire, graduate, preaching minister, gentleman of quality, the Advocate and Secretary to the Army, every of them with his own horse and swords, the ministers without swords, none of them carrying with them above fifty shillings, and the ministers to have all their own MSS. of notes and evidences. Lieutenants, cornets, ensigns, and other inferior officers in commission, on foot, with every man his sword, and not above twenty shillings in money.

DOCUMENT LXXXVIII.

A.D. 1646.

All troopers, foot soldiers, gunpowder-makers, cannoneers, and all others not before-mentioned, to march without horse and arms; and that none of the persons before-mentioned shall in their march, after they are out of the city and liberty thereof, be plundered, searched, or molested.

2. [Women to have their apparel; the wives of officers to be allowed to carry with them such sums of money as their respective husbands are entitled to do.]

3. [None to carry out of the city but what is their own and hereinbefore allowed.]

4. [Citizens to be secured in their persons and goods, and the city and liberties to be preserved from plunder. Freedom of trade to be permitted in like manner as other towns, under the protection of Parliament. Tradesmen of Chester to be allowed to go to North Wales on business, but with a pass, and not to be allowed to take more money with them than may be necessary for the journey.]

5. [Such officers and soldiers as are sick or wounded to remain until their recovery, and then to have passes to Conway Castle, or any other garrison of the King not blocked up.]

6. That the said Lord Byron, Noblemen, Commanders, Gentlemen, Officers, and Soldiers, and all others that shall march out of the town, shall have liberty to march to Conway, and five days are allowed them to march thither with a convoy of 200 horse. The Welsh Officers and Soldiers to have liberty to go to their own homes; and all of them to have free quarter in their march and twelve carriages, if they shall have occasion to use so many, which carriages are to be returned on the sixth day, and passes be given them for their safe return to Chester, and that they be secured until their return thither.

7. [No soldiers to be inveigled from his colours with any promise.]

8. [Citizens who have families in Chester, and are now in remote places, to have like privileges as those now resident therein.]

9. [The friends of the Earls of Derby and Lichfield, or any whose dead bodies are not yet interred in Chester, to have two months to take them thence, but not to be attended with above twenty horse.]

DOCUMENT LXXXVIII. A.D. 1646.

10. That no church within the city, evidences or writings belonging to the same, shall be defaced.

11. That such Irish that were born of Irish parents, and have taken part with the rebels in Ireland, and now in the city, shall be prisoners.

12. [Horses and arms, not allowed to be taken out, to be brought to the Castle Court and the Shire Hall respectively.]

13. That in consideration hereof, the same city and castle, without any slighting or defacing thereof, with all the ordnance, arms, ammunition, and all other furniture and provisions of war therein whatsoever, except what is allowed to be carried away and herein-mentioned, with the County Palatine Seal, Sword, and all records in the castle, without diminution, embezzling, or defacing, be delivered unto the said Sir William Brereton, or such as he shall appoint, for the use of the King and Parliament, upon Tuesday next, being the third of this instant February, 1646, by ten of the clock in the forenoon.

14. [The fort, with all arms, &c., to be delivered to Sir W. Brereton.]

15. [All prisoners in the city, who have been in arms for the Parliament, to be set at liberty upon the signing of these Articles.]

16. [The Convoy to suffer no injury.]

17. [Anyone violating these Articles to lose the benefit thereof.]

18. [Hostages to be given for the performance of all the said Articles.]

Signed by us, the Commissioners appointed on behalf
of the Right-Honourable the Lord Byron.

Edmund Verney[1]	John Johnson[5]
John Robinson[2]	Christo. Blease[5]
Thomas Cholmondeley	William Ince[5]
Peter Griffith[3]	John Werden
Henry Leigh[3]	Edward Moreton[6]
Thomas Throp[4]	Thomas Bridge[6]

What is done by the Commissioners is confirmed by

JOHN BYRON.

[1] Knight, Colonel. [2] Lieut.-Col., formerly Governor of Holt Castle.
[3] Lieut.-Colonels. [4] Sergt-.Major. [5] Aldermen. [6] Divines.

Commissioners for Sir Wm. Brereton.

DOCUMENT LXXXVIII.

A.D. 1646.

Col. John Boothe	Roger Wilbraham, Esquire
Col. John Bowyer	Adjut. General Louthian
Col. Robert Duckenfield	Jona. Bruen, Esq.
Col. Michael Jones	Lieut.-Col. Hunt
Col. Chidley Coote	Lieut.-Col. Venables
Col. John Carter	Master Bradshaw[1]

[1] From a pamphlet, entitled "Sir W. Brereton's Letter concerning the Surrender of the City of Chester, &c. Printed for Edw. Husbands, Feb. 6, 1646." (K. P. 244—20.)

LXXXIX.

A Revolt in Glamorganshire—Cardiff Castle besieged by Royalists, under Mr. Carne, the High Sheriff—Relieved by Major-General Laugharne, assisted by Sir Trevor Williams. February 1646.

DOCUMENT LXXXIX. A.D. 1646.

Colonel Morgan, the Governor of Gloucester, hearing that the enemy about Raglan had done so many mischiefs and increased so fast; and having consideration of the hard service of Monmouth garrison, so environed with the enemy on all sides, ordered a party of about 200 foot and 100 horse to set up a garrison at Llanarth, Sir Philip Jones's house, which is about three miles from Raglan. Notice whereof being brought to Raglan, Sir Charles Kemeys sent out Capt. Westman with a party of horse and foot to obstruct them from garrisoning there, and the meanwhile others were sent to alarm Monmouth. But we having notice of their design, deferred the business to a more fit opportunity. In the meantime, the enemy plundered the country; and the Governor of Monmouth, having lately escaped the danger of treachery by discovering the design in due time,[1] took the like care to prevent the like now, in case any should be on foot. He caused the port-cullis to be let down, and the draw-bridge to be pulled up; and the country people on the borders of Brecknockshire, many of them were forced to ship away their goods, and make what speed they could for Bristol to preserve themselves and what they had, for the enemy carried away many well-affected people prisoners to Raglan. And the meanwhile Carne,[2] the High Sheriff of Glamorganshire, revolting, was as barbarous in those parts, plundering the country and forcing the inhabitants to serve him; and having possessed himself of Cardiff Town, which was not strong enough to oppose an enemy, now prepared for a siege. Yet the castle was kept against them, for we had very honest, godly, and faithful officers there then, viz., the Governor, Col. Prichard, Col. Leighton, sometime of the Plymouth regiment, and others, who, apprehending the danger they were in in time,

[1] See ante lxxxiii. b.

[2] Edward Carne of Ewenny.

stored the castle with what provisions and ammunition they had, and many honest men had the best of their goods carried in thither. Some went in person, and thither the Governor and our forces belonging to that garrison retreated, with a resolution to hold out to the last man rather than to yield to that renegado crew, to whom many club-men were joined. He having not arms enough for them at first, sent to England for both arms and ammunition, and other officers, from whence was speeded supply for him, and Sir Charles Kemeys with a party from thence marched to join with them. Major-General Skippon speeded them what relief could be by sea, both of salt, coals, and other provisions, and he and Col. Morgan raised what forces they could, and sent all the sailors they could get, the Vice-Admiral, with other ships, assisting herein. The meanwhile Major-General Laugharne prepared all the forces he could about the south-west of Wales, and drew off his men from Aberystwith, all being laborious to relieve those parts before the enemy had rested there and were grown too strong for us. Sir Trevor Williams also drew up all the forces he could make to assist in so considerable a design, which required the more haste because we had certain intelligence that Sir Charles Kemeys was joined with them, and that they were of horse and foot nigh 3,000, and did daily increase, and so were still likely to do, except we did speedily dissipate them.

On Monday, the 16th of February, 1646, the Vice-Admiral approached near for giving notice to Col. Prichard of relief coming, and within sight of the castle hanged out their colours to let them know for whom they were, and for what purpose they came, and shot off one piece of ordnance, and then another, and so six pieces were shot off, to let them know at the castle that relief was then at hand. At the sight of which ship, and hearing of which pieces, our men [in the castle] gave a great shout, and were very glad. Col. Prichard, the Governor, Col. Leighton, and the rest, sat in council, and ordered strict quarter, and encouraged the soldiers to prepare for a storm, which they might fear, upon the enemy understanding that relief was coming, and withal put them in mind how far God had already preserved them, encouraging them still to trust in God who had so kept them till He had perfected His work, which they hoped would now suddenly be. The soldiers expressed much resolution, crying out they would never yield

DOCUMENT LXXXIX. A.D. 1646.

whilst they were able to withstand the enemy, not doubting but to see them dissipated. Their resolutions were the stronger against them, because there were many amongst the enemy that were notorious Papists, some Jesuits, Popish priests and friars, and divers of their officers supposed to be such. One Father Morgan, a Jesuit, they had taken before, who was sent over to Bristol, where he is now a prisoner, a notorious rogue, who vapoured much at the hearing of the enemy's gathering and strengthing themselves about Cardiff for the King. Now, it so pleased God, that the waters rose very high for the transporting of our men, and they rose very much at Awst passage, which was as ill for the enemy to hinder their flight from us. . . . . .

But all this while the design went on for the relief of our friends in Cardiff Castle, and the dissipating of the forces in those parts, which took good effect. So soon as the enemy had intelligence of the approaching of Major-General Laugharne, who marched with about 250 of his own horse and foot, and some others of the country that rose and joined with him, the enemy having first summoned the castle, to which they had a denial, drew off from before Cardiff Castle into a great field to fight us. We marched up to them, and fell upon them with such gallantry that we routed them and made them fly several ways. Carne himself stayed not to keep them together, but like a vagabond ran up and down, bemoaning himself, and glad he was he had a nimble horse, not to charge, but fly with. Major-General Laugharne hath given so great a blow to Sir Charles Kemeys, and of his Raglan forces hath killed and taken so many, that of above 3,000 there are not above seven score of them left upon rally, nor those likely to get to Raglan, for Col. Morgan and Sir Trevor Williams came in both very seasonably, and are all pursuing. Col. Morgan is got between Sir Charles Kemeys and Raglan. It is a very bloody fight—2,000 killed and taken. A great number of arms we have taken, and have rescued many cattle which they had plundered from the country people, and much of their ammunition and plunder, it being a very great victory.[1]

From a phamphlet, entitled "A Great Overthrow given to the King's Forces in Wales, &c. London: Printed for Mathew Walbancke, 26th Feb., 1646." (K. P. 249—8.)

XC.

Surrender of Ruthin Castle to the Parliament—Major-General Mytton to the Speaker of the House of Commons. 8th April, **1646.**

Honourable Sir,

The reducing of this Castle of Ruthin hath cost me more time and ammunition than I expected when I first laid siege to it. At last, having a mine almost in readiness to spring, and batteries prepared for a demi-cannon and culverin to play upon it, it was this day agreed to be surrendered upon the conditions in the inclosed Articles, which I am willing to accept, having perfect information by some that escaped out of the castle, that there was in it provision sufficient for two months longer, which now I find to be true. And if I should have forced it, I must have hazarded many men, and made the place unserviceable, which is of very great use to the reducement of this country, it being the most convenient place for a garrison in all North Wales, as things now stand with us. Yesterday, before the break of day, a part of the enemy, out of Denbigh Castle, being about six score, and thirty mounted fire-locks, fell upon Captain Rich. Price's quarters, about two miles from this town; but he was vigilant, and his scouts performed their duty so well that they were drawn into the field before they came upon them, which gave him opportunity to avoid them, and convey the alarm to this town. And thereupon, Colonel Carter, with a standing horse guard, which we are fain to keep in the field constantly to secure our out-quarters, and Captain Simkies, with my own

DOCUMENT XC. A.D. 1646.

DOCUMENT XC. A.D. 1646.

troop, which was then upon the guard in this town, drew out, and fell between them and Denbigh, and within half-a-mile of their garrison met with them, and charged them so gallantly that they broke in upon them, killed seven of them (as is said) upon the place, and in the pursuit took four captains, one lieutenant, and two cornets, divers troopers, &c., above forty horse, with the loss of one man of our side. The siege of Hoult hath of late been of great difficulty and hazard to those few men I have there, for the drawing off of the Cheshire fire-locks from that service without my privity gave the enemy an advantage to burn the guard the fire-locks kept (which cost the country much to fortify), and about forty dwelling-houses more in the town, and exposed my men (who lay in open quarters, and fewer in number than the enemy within were), to their power, which necessitated my men to be upon continual duty. Upon the first of April the enemy sallied out and fell upon Major Sadler's quarters, resolving to put all my men in that house to the sword, which they had been like to effect had not a guard which was placed in a mount erected by us three days before relieved them. In this storm I lost five men, and fifteen wounded; of the enemy, there were killed their Commander, Captain Cottingham, a Papist, a lieutenant, and two more, and many wounded. There hath been never a day since but they sallied out constantly twice or thrice a day, and as constantly "beaten in." This service, and the furnishing of such garrisons which are reduced, occasions the expense of much powder and match; and therefore I humbly desire that the honourable House will be pleased to grant that I may have a hundred barrels of powder and four or five hundred fire-locks sent me, and that some course may be prescribed to convey it down speedily; the carriage and convoy of the last powder I had, cost above half as much as the powder was worth. And further, that they will be pleased to appoint a governor for this castle [Ruthin]. Lieutenant-Colonel Thomas Mason is a very faithful, active, and godly gentleman, and the most knowing man in his profession that we have in these parts, having been a soldier above twenty years, and lost his command in Ireland because he refused to bear arms against the Parliament. And if this place were worthy of him, I should make bold to recommend him to their consideration.

This, nevertheless, I leave to their wisdom to determine, and rest your very humble servant, DOCUMENT XC. A.D. 1646.

THOMAS MYTTON.[1]

Ruthin, 8th April, 1646.

Articles agreed and concluded between Mr. Robert Fogge, Chaplain to Colonel Thomas Mytton (Major-General of North Wales), and Captain Edward Thelwall, Commissioners on the behalf of the said Major-General, of the one part, and Master John Reynolds, Deputy-Governor of the Castle of Ruthin, of the other part.

1. It is agreed and concluded by the parties above-mentioned, that the Castle of Ruthin shall be surrendered unto Major-General Mytton aforesaid, or to his assignees, on Monday next, April 12th, 1646, by ten of the clock in the forenoon, without any dismantling, demolishing, or defacing the same, or any works now made in or about the same.

2. That all the ordnance, arms, ammunition, provision, and goods now in the castle be left safe and no way harmed, saving the particulars hereinafter mentioned.

3. That the said Deputy-Governor shall march away quietly and without molestation, with his sword and one case of pistols, and six gentlemen with him, and each of them his sword.

4. That the rest of the soldiers and officers, the Irish only excepted (who are barred by the Ordinance of Parliament), to pass to their respective habitations, or to convoy with a safe-conduct, they behaving themselves civilly.

5. That the said Deputy take only with him two trunks, containing only therein his wearing apparel, and some few clothes and lining of his sisters, and that a cart be provided for the carriage thereof.

6. That in the meantime there be a cessation of arms on both

[1] From a pamphlet, entitled "A Letter to the Speaker of the House of Commons, concerning the Surrender of Ruthin Castle to Thomas Mytton, Major-General of North Wales, &c. Printed for Edward Husbands, &c., April 14, 1646." (K. P. 257—9.)

DOCUMENT XC. A.D. 1646.

sides, and no advantage taken by admitting any strength of men or ammunition into the said castle, other than the hostages agreed upon by both parties.

And for the firm confirmation of the premises, the parties to these presents have interchangeably set thereto their hands this 8th day of April, anno dom. 1646.

ROBERT FOGGE.

EDWARD THELWALL.

I also agree to the Articles above-written,

JOHN RAIGNOLDS.

I do consent to what my Commissioners have agreed herein,

THOMAS MYTTON.

All the arms and ammunition, bag and baggage, were also to be surrendered to the Major-General, and the Irish were to be left to be tried according to the Ordinance of Parliament.

XCI.

Aberystwith Castle, after a long siege, is Surrendered to the Parliament, April 14, 1646.

Copy of a letter from Major-General Laugharne's quarters.

SIR,

Though we have lain long before Aberystwith Castle, which is a place of great strength, yet it hath pleased God at last to give it into our hands. I have sent you here enclosed the copy of the Articles of Agreement between Col. Rice Powell and Col. Ro. Whitney for the surrender thereof. When you read them you will find we have gained good terms from them, so that now we are ready to be put into a capacity for further service, either for Carnarvon, or to assist against Raglan, or what other service shall be thought meet, if the soldiers have but money.

DOCUMENT XCI. A.D. 1646.

Your servant,

E. L.

April 14, 1646.

[The Articles were signed on the 12th day of April by Robert Whitley (*sic*), Joseph Whitley, John Bellay, Miles Somner, Charles Haughtley, William Vives, James Plot, and John Wynne, and were eleven in number, containing among others, conditions that the officers should march with their swords by their sides, the soldiers without arms; that the prisoners belonging to the garrison, and then at Haverfordwest, or elsewhere, should be set at liberty, and with passes to go to their Colonel to Carnarthan (Carnarvon), and that the Colonel, and five more in his company, with their horses and swords, may have safe-conduct to the King.] [1]

[1] From a pamphlet entitled "Four strong Castles taken by the Parliament's Forces, &c. London: Printed for Mathew Walbancke at Gray's Inn Gate, April 27, 1646." (K. P. 258—8.)

XCII.

General Mytton's proceedings in North Wales—Carnarvon, Denbigh, Flint, and Holt Castles besieged, and Negotiations for the Surrender of Anglesey. April—June.

DOCUMENT XCII.

A.D. 1646.

SIR,

We received yours bearing date the 26th of this instant [May]. . . . We are glad of your hopes of money, wherein if you and we are disappointed, it will endanger not only our own brigade, but also the whole work of North Wales, that now, through God's blessing upon the active and vigilant endeavours of our General, and the forces under his command, is reduced into a very hopeful condition. We have closely besieged Holt Castle, Denbigh, Carnarvon, and Flint, all places of exceeding great strength. Our forces are so many that all the countries under our command can hardly afford us provision. We are put to use our utmost skill to get maintenance this way; then you may judge how hard it is with us for want of pay, without which our soldiers will not continue patiently to go on in their hard and difficult duty that hitherto they have undergone; harder than which, we dare boldly say, hath not been in any place since the Wars; and, besides, many of our soldiers with us are auxiliaries from Lancashire, who are most unreasonable men if they are disappointed in their pay. . . . .

For news we acquaint you with the above several sieges we are engaged upon. Each of them hath enforced much care and resolution, being all places of very great strength, well-manned and victualled. They have made many sallies, but all of them repulsed with loss, especially Carnarvon, which siege was laid and is managed by our General himself, the Commander-in-Chief. Each siege has made works suitable to the condition of the place. Our hopes must be of starving, not storming any of them.

Denbigh we laid siege to so soon as we took Ruthin, which

now is six weeks since. Its Governor [William Salesbury] is a very wilful man, and hath very nigh 500 able-fighting men in it. It hath in its situation all the advantages for strength that any castle can have. There are many gentry in it and some riches. And it would do well that as they are notoriously refractory so they may be made notoriously exemplary, by the justice of the Parliament upon them and their estates according to their demerits. The countries have improved their interests, and many other ways have been used, but all ineffectual. Their hearts are as hard as the very foundation of the castle itself, being an unpierceable rock. There are mounts raised round about it, and approaches for battering of a tower called the Goblin's Tower: hoping thereby to deprive them of the benefit of a well in that tower; which, can we attain, we may then soon expect the castle through want of water—they having but one well more, which is usually (as it is reported) dry in June or July every summer.

Carnarvon siege the General himself lay, although with exceeding difficulty. The enemy had as many men as the General (if not full as many, yet very nigh, and as good men as England hath.[1]) Yet, notwithstanding, he at his first approach to the town beat in the enemy from their ambushes that they had laid, as also out of the suburbs and from a rock of very great concernment, without any considerable loss. The enemy have made since the siege, which hath been now very nigh one month, two desperate sallies. At the first they lost, slain and taken prisoners, seven or eight, and we but one. At the second [were] taken 17, a lieutenant, and four more [officers]. Our Lieut.-General was in danger at the sally. Had not the country appeared cordially the siege could never [have] continued thus long. Mr. Glynne, Mr. Recorder's brother, Bart. Williams, and some others, are most assisting. They have formerly got relief by sea, but we have now so many boats and ships that we hope they now despair of any more relief that way; they are in great want of water. This day the General gives them a second summons. God grant it may take effect.

Yesterday went Commissioners, Col. Roger Pope, Col. John

[1] Lord Byron and most of those who issued out of Chester had come to Carnarvon.

DOCUMENT XCII. A.D. 1646.

Jones, and Edwards, Esquire, to Anglesey, with propositions from our General for the surrender of that island to him for the Parliament. He formerly had summoned it, and after two or three weeks' consideration they desired to treat either by Commissioners or propositions. The General, therefore, sent both. We hear since that they have turned out all strangers and refuse to afford any relief to Carnarvon. We expect an answer within a few days.[1]

Flint Castle.—Two days after the siege was laid, 46 of the enemy's horse broke away, but all came in or are gone to their homes. Sixteen came into us to Hawarden, about ten went into Chester, and the rest, being Welshmen, are gone to their homes. There is no hold in all North Wales free from a siege, but Conway, Harlech, and Rhuddlan Castle, of which also you will hear something very shortly.

Holt hath being besieged ever since the taking of Chester. It is a very strong place.[2] Starving is the only wayth at we can use against that place. Sir, you may perceive that we neither have been nor are idle. We hope the Lord will continue to bless our endeavours, for which we beg your prayers.

Your assured friends and servants,

RICH. PRICE, GEORGE TWISTLETON.[3]
THO. MASON,

[1] See post Document xciv.

[2] Sir Richard Lloyd was Governor.

[3] From a pamphlet, entitled "An Exact Relation of the whole proceedings of gallant Col. Mytton in North Wales, assured under the hands of several Commanders of note, &c. London: Printed for Robert Chapman." [June 5th.] (K. P. 264–1.)

XCIII.

Carnarvon Town and Castle Surrendered to Major-General Mytton, June 4, 1646.

SIR,

In my last I advertised you of an agreement to capitulate with the Lord Byron for the surrender of Carnarvon. Six Commissioners were chosen—three for Major-General Mytton, and three for the Lord Byron. His Lordship sent out Col. Edward Vere, Col. John Vane, and Lieut.-Col. Disney; and on our side were chosen Col. Thomas Glynne, Col. John Carter, and Sergt.-Major Hierome Zanchy, who have effected the work; so that Carnarvon is agreed to be surrendered to us: agreed by both parties upon this treaty, and by each signed. I have here enclosed sent you the copy of the Articles whereupon it is to be surrendered, which I hope will give very good satisfaction and content to the State.

DOCUMENT XCIII. A.D. 1646.

I am sure it is a very considerable service, it being a place of great strength and of great use. And we are now to fall upon other designs for the reducing of these parts to the obedience of the Parliament; but I must tell you they are here, for the matter of religion, most ignorant and brutish people, who know very little of God; and it is heartily to be wished that some honest and godly-painful ministers would come to preach the Gospel to them. Indeed, there are some prelates and prelatical clergy in Carnarvon very malignant, and such as the people are like to profit little by, except they will study to preach Jesus Christ more than, for ought I can hear, they have done. The country-towns hereabouts have been quite without all manner of preaching almost. But blessed be God, we are in a fair way to reduce these parts to the obedience of the Parliament, who, I doubt not, will take care to send a powerful ministry so soon as North Wales is totally reduced.

I hope that very shortly you will hear good news from Anglesey, which is the place of greatest consequence in all these parts (this

DOCUMENT XCIII. A.D. 1646.

that we have taken in, being very considerable also), Beaumaris being a place that hath been of very great use to the King. I hope it will now be suddenly in our hands, which is of great consequence, because of the conveniency of bringing in of divers foreign forces thither, as hath been often done to serve the King against the Parliament and Kingdom. I trust in the Lord that now God will be pleased to put an end to all the troubles of these parts, that we may meet in peace. The King hath now no more garrisons maintained by his party against us in all North Wales, save only five, and all of them either are or will be besieged (if not a part of them surrendered) within six days. Indeed, some of them, it may be, will prove hard to be reduced, and may hold out long. Our Major-General Mytton is very active, even to be admired, in hastening to make an end of the work. Col. Glynne doth us service since he joined with us, and, truly, Col. Carter is a very pretty gentleman, and full of action. The country are no little glad of the hopes they have to enjoy what they have in peace, which is in a good way for them. There are in Carnarvon with the Lord Byron many gentlemen of quality, most of the chief officers that came from Chester, some bishops, and divers malignant clergy. The works are exceedingly good and regular, high works and thick, and deep moats. I cannot give you the exact number of the ordnance, arms, ammunition, and provisions, till we be possessed of the castle, but after we have taken a note of them, I will send you a list by the first opportunity. But this much I can assure you, that they were so strongly fortified, that they little thought that Carnarvon would so soon have been in our hands when Byron went thither. But blessed be God, this work is now put out of question, and by the next, I believe you will hear something both of Anglesey and Flint Castle, but this is all at present, from

Your humble servant,

S. R.

Carnarvon, the 5th of June, 1646.

[The Articles were signed on the 4th of June by the Commissioners above named; and provided (1) that the Lord Byron, Governor of the Town and Castle, all officers in the commission, and gentlemen of quality, with their servants, should have freedom to march out unmolested to their homes or friends, and to be allowed

DOCUMENT XCIII. A.D. 1646.

three months to make their peace with the Parliament, or to obtain leave to go beyond the seas, they doing nothing in the meantime to the prejudice of the Parliament; (2) that the inferior officers and common soldiers should have liberty to march to Worcester; and if that town was besieged when they got there, they were to have free passes to go to their respective homes; (3) that sick and wounded should remain until their recovery; (4) that none be searched on going out, their word alone being taken that they took nothing contrary to the Articles; (5) for sufficient carriage; (6) that Sir William Byron, Lieut.-Col. John Robinson, Col. Shakerley, Capt. Hassal, Capt. Alcock, Capt. Bennet, Archdeacon Price, and the clergymen in the town, have the benefit of the Articles; (7) the town to be saved from plunder; (8) the Irish to await the order of Parliament, and for the surrender of the Town and Castle, with all the ordnance, arms, ammunition, and provisions therin.][1]

[1] From a pamphlet, entitled "The Taking of Carnarvon, &c. London: Printed by Jane Coe, June the 11, 1646." (K. P. 264—17.)

XCIV.

Anglesey and Beaumaris submit to the Parliament.
June 14th, 1646.

DOCUMENT XCIV. A.D. 1646.

Articles of Agreement concluded and agreed upon the 14th day of June, 1646, by Col. Roger Popé, Col. John Jones, and Thomas Edwards, Esq., Commissioners appointed by Major-General Mytton, of the one part; and Lieut.-Col. John Robinson, Dr. Robert Price, and Major David Lloyd, for and on behalf of Col. Richard Bulkeley, and the rest of the gentlemen in Beaumaris Castle, of the other part.

1. That all men in the castle shall have full benefit of Major-General Mytton's propositions, and his best assistance to dispense with their past delinquency.

2. That they in the castle shall appoint a gentleman, who shall have a pass to go to the Parliament, to intercede according to their desires.

3. That they shall have four months' time to make their peace with the Parliament, and no ordinance of sequestration be put in execution until the pleasure of the Parliament be declared, provided that they procure the Parliament's pleasure signified within those four months.

4. It is agreed (and concluded by the general intendment of Major Mytton's propositions), that all the gentlemen in the castle shall take away whatever is their own (provisions of victuals, ammunition, artillery, and muskets of the veteran trained-bands excepted.)

5. That as many of the inhabitants of this Island of Anglesey that have in any way opposed the submission to Major-General Mytton's proposition, may be equally taxed and charged with other inhabitants of this county; and that their former oppositions may not be made use of to their prejudice.

DOCUMENT XCIV. A.D. 1646.

6. That the arrears due to the officers and soldiers in the castle shall be duly paid by the county, viz.: £50 in hand, and the rest within one month.

7. That in consideration thereof, and the desire of peace—the Castle of Beaumaris, with all things therein contained (according to the intendment of Major-General Mytton's propositions, and the Agreement made between him and Lord Bulkeley), shall be delivered up to Major-General Mytton's Commissioners upon Tuesday morning next, by 8 o'clock at the farthest. And the soldiers now therein to march out at the same hour. Signed by

Roger Pope,	John Robinson,
John Jones,	Robert Price,
Thomas Edwards,	David Lloyd.
For Col. Mytton.	*For Col. Bulkeley.*[1]

[1] *Perfect Occurrences*, 26th week, 26th June. (K. P. 24—14).

XCV.

The Siege and Surrender of Raglan Castle. June—August, 1646.

A.

Col. Morgan, the Governor of Gloucester's Letter to the Speaker of the House of Commons.

DOCUMENT XCV. A.

A.D. 1646.

HONOURABLE SIR,

I shall give you herein a short account of our passages before Raglan Castle. You shall receive enclosed my last[1] summons to the Earl of Worcester, and his answer, by which it will appear unto your Honour how wilful and obstinate they still continue there. Our duties here are very hard, by reason of the enemy's often and strong sallies, who are strong in number and power. I have a heavy burden upon my shoulders, but I hope with the additional forces that comes from his Excellency [Sir Thomas Fairfax], and who are now upon their march, I shall the easier undergo it. This day the enemy made a strong sally-out with horse and foot; but, I thank God for it, they were beaten in again. We pursued them to the very works, and did very good execution upon their horse and foot, with no loss at all on our side. His Excellency, Sir Thomas Fairfax, hath been pleased to furnish me with mortar-pieces, guns, and other materials, for the effecting of this work, which I hope will be with me very

[1] The first summons was sent on the 3rd of June. To that the Marquis sent a refusal, unless he had the King's consent. Being blamed by Col. Morgan for keeping a garrison against the Parliament, the Marquis replied, "The true reason of my keeping forces here, is not in defiance of the Parliament, but to preserve myself, according to the law of nature, from the insolencies of the common soldiers on both sides. Seeing you think it not fit to grant a civil and reasonable request, we must here, to the last man, sell our lives as dear as we can—this not out of obstinacy or any ill-affection, but merely to preserve that honour that I desire should attend me at my death. God assist them that are in the right!"—*Coxe's Monmouthshire*, p. 146.

suddenly. I have no more at present, but that I subscribe myself to be, Sir, DOCUMENT . XCV. A. A.D. 1646.

Your most humble servant,

THO. MORGAN.

From the Leaguer before Raglan Castle,
June 29, 1646.

[ENCLOSURES.]

For Henry, Earl of Worcester, Governor of Raglan Castle.

MY LORD,

By his Excellency's command, this is my second summons, whereby you are required forthwith to deliver to me to the use of both Houses of Parliament the Castle of Raglan, with all the ordnance, arms, ammunition, and provisions, and all other necessaries that belongs to War, that are now in it, which, if you will be pleased to do, you may haply find mercy as other garrisons have had; and if you do refuse, expect nothing but the ruin of yourself, your family, and this poor distressed country. For I must acquaint your Lordship that his Excellency, Sir Thomas Fairfax, having now finished his work over the Kingdom, except this castle, hath been pleased to spare his forces for this work, who are now upon their march this way with all materials fit for it; though I made no doubt but I had of mine own strength sufficient to effect it, if your Lordship will deny to submit to this summons; and [if] more blood must be spilt your Lordship may be confident that you shall receive no favour from both Houses of Parliament. So, expecting your answer this night by 9 o'clock, I rest,

Your Lordship's servant,

THO. MORGAN.

From the Leaguer, before Raglan,
June 28, 1646.

Upon the faith and honour of a soldier this is a true copy of his Majesty's letter to the Governors of Oxford, Lichfield, Wallingford, and Worcester, and of all other garrisons in the Kingdom of England and Dominion of Wales, which I thought fit to present to your Lordship, whereby you may clearly see what

DOCUMENT XCV. A. A.D. 1646.

probability of relief you are like to have.[1] And to give you further satisfaction, upon Tuesday last I was in Oxford, where I bought this paper to present this news unto you. Upon Wednesday last Oxford and Farringdon met together, and everyone marched to their own homes. The Princes [Rupert and Maurice] are to march beyond the seas. These things being as clear as the sun I leave to your consideration.

For Col. Morgan, Commander-in-Chief of the Forces before Raglan.

Sir,

I have received this day two advertisements from you; the first I did read containing, as you would have me believe, a true copy of his Majesty's Warrant to several garrisons, upon honourable terms to quit, &c. But truly, Sir, it is not in the power of man to make me think so unworthily of his Majesty, that to one [who], in the opinion of the world, hath given himself and family so great a remonstrance and testimony of his and their faith and fidelity towards him, that he would not please so much as to name the name of Raglan. I entreat you to give me leave to suspend my belief. And for your second summons, it makes it too evident that it is desired I should die under a hedge like a beggar, having no house to put my head into, nor means left to find me bread; wherefore, to give you answer, I make choice (if it so please God) rather to die nobly than to live with infamy. Which answer, if it be not

[1] The following was the King's Warrant referred to:—"Charles Rex,—Having resolved to comply with the designs of our Parliament in everything which may be for the good of our subjects, and leave no means unessayed for removing of differences between us, therefore we have thought fit, the more to evidence the reality of our intentions of settling a happy and firm peace to require you upon honourable conditions to quit those towns and castles entrusted to you by us, and to disband all the forces under your several commands.—Given at Newcastle the 10th of June, 1646.—To our trusty and well-beloved (by name) Governors of our Cities and Towns of Oxford, Worcester, Lichfield, and Wallingford, and all other Commanders of any other towns, castles, or forts within the Kingdom of England or Dominion of Wales."

pleasing unto you, I shall not think you worthy to be styled by me, DOCUMENT XCV. A A.D. 1646.

Your loving friend and servant,

H. WORCESTER.

From my house at Raglan,
June 28th, 1646.

For Henry, Earl of Worcester, Governor of Raglan Castle.

MY LORD,

Since it is not in my power to make you, nor your son believe anything concerning the surrender of these garrisons, by his Majesty's order, that comes from me or any of our party, once more, and the last before I send your answer to his Excellency, Sir Thomas Fairfax, I shall give your Lordship way to send an officer with another of mine to those Lords in Oxford to whom his Majesty's letters were directed for your better satisfaction. This I do, my Lord, with a respect to prevent your utter and the ruin of this poor country, so much occasioned by your Lordship's obstinacy. I expect your present answer, and rest

Your servant,

June 28th, 1646. THO. MORGAN.

For Col. Morgan, Commander-in-Chief of the Parliament's Forces before Raglan.

SIR,

In respect of your mentioning of any respect or kindness towards me, lest to be divulged to the world might do you any prejudice, I have thought fit in your own letter to return you thanks for the same. And for Sir Thomas Fairfax, were he here with all his army, he should receive no other answer from me than you have had. I hope I serve (though not so well as I should) a Master that is of more might than all the armies in the world, and to His Holy will

DOCUMENT XCV. A. A.D. 1646. and pleasure I submit myself, and yourself, to do what you think fitting; and so rest

Your friend and servant,
H. WORCESTER.

From my dwelling at Raglan,
June 28th, 1646.[1]

B.

The Siege conducted by Lord-General Fairfax.

DOCUMENT XCV. B. A.D. 1646.

SIR,

In my last I acquainted you with the General's leaving of Bath, and coming in person to the siege before Ragland, where he was entertained with great acclamations by the soldiers. After which he sent a summons to the castle, to which a dilatory answer, though not an absolute denial, was sent.[2] A civil reply was made to it, and after a day's consideration the Marquis took occasion to write a calm letter to the General, expressing how much he did respect the General's family, and what long acquaintance he had with his grandfather; in conclusion, invited to have some propositions sent him, which were accordingly sent.[2] The conditions were honourable for the soldiery, but as to the Marquis himself [he was] to submit to the mercy of Parliament. The Marquis having considered of these, remained doubtful whether the Parliament would confirm what the General should grant, in case they should agree, to which the General returned answer, assuring him that what he concluded of, would be performed. Whereupon, Thursday, August 13, the Marquis sent out a drum, desiring leave to send out his Commissioners on Friday, at 10 o'clock, whereupon, he said his Excellency should see he would not be an obstruction to peace, which we conjectured was as much as to say, he would send

[1] From a pamphlet, entitled "A Letter to the Hon. Wm. Lenthal, &c., from Col. Morgan, &c. Printed for Edw. Husbands, &c." July 3, 1646. (K. P. 266—16.)

[2] The first summons from Fairfax was dated the 7th August.

a positive answer to our propositions. And thereupon the drum was returned, with a safe-conduct for the Commissioners' coming forth, and a cessation of arms from ten o'clock till three. The Commissioners appointed on our part to meet theirs were Col. Birch, Mr. Herbert, one of the Commissioners of Parliament residing with the army, and Major Juliday [or Tuliday] whose commission was to receive what they should deliver, and present it to the General.

I shall now give you an account how near our approaches are made unto the castle. That which is our main work is about sixty yards from theirs, and that is the most. We have planted four mortar-pieces, each of them carrying grenade shells, twelve inches diameter, and two mortar-pieces, planted at another place, carrying shells about the like compass; so that in case the treaty do break off we are then ready to show by what extremity they must expect to be reduced. This we are very confident, that the grenadoes will make them quit their works and out-houses, and solely betake themselves into the castle, which will be a work of time before we are able to undermine it, in regard we must mine down the hill under a moat, and then their works, before we can come to the castle. Yet we conceive it feasible to be done with some loss. Our engineer, Capt. Hooper, a painful and honest man, with exact running trenches, which are made so secure as if they were works against a storm, will (with God's blessing) come within ten yards in a few days, and then I believe we shall make galleries, mines, and many batteries. The General is every day in the trenches, and yesterday appointed a new approach, which the engineer of this army, returned from Worcester, is to carry on with all expedition.

During the parley yesterday, which held from nine till two, they permitted us to come to their works, stand close to their stockades and trenches, and discourse with them; so little do they regard our knowledge of their works. The propositions sent out by the Marquis yesterday were as high as ever any garrison yet propounded, to which the General sent a short and positive answer, letting his Lordship know his propositions deserved no answer, and as for himself he must expect no other conditions but to submit to the mercy of the Parliament, and gave him time till this day at

DOCUMENT XCV. B.

A.D. 1646.

10 o'clock to receive his final answer. We are all persuaded if he could but have leave to go beyond the seas, the soldiers having honourable conditions, he would submit; and were it not better to grant a man of 84 years these terms, that probably will be in his grave before the affairs of Parliament will give leave to call him to trial, and thereby save the lives of many an officer and soldier who have adventured their lives in the Parliament's cause, than to gain this old man's carcase at so dear a rate? Col. Rainsborough is already come to the Leaguer, and Col. Hammond is this day expected. The Marquis hath this morning sent word that he will treat upon the General's propositions. Whereupon, the treaty is appointed at Mr. Oates's house, about a mile and a half from Raglan, where it is to begin this afternoon at two o'clock. The General's Commissioners are Col. Morgan, Col. Birch, Mr. Herbert, Quarter-Master-General Grosvenor, Lieut.-Col. Ashfield, and Major Juliday. By the next you shall hear further from

Your assured friend and servant,

Usk, August 15th, 1646.[1] W. C.

The Surrender.

Sir,

On Wednesday last, Aug. 19 [Raglan] Castle was surrendered to his Excellency, Sir Thomas Fairfax. The enemy were no sooner marched forth but his Excellency entered the castle, took a view of it, and had some conference with the Marquis, and afterwards went that night to Chepstow, where he was liberally entertained by the Committee, and came from thence yesterday to Bath.

The Castle of Raglan was as strong a piece (as I have seen) encompassed with a deep moat, besides the river. There were

[1] From a pamphlet, entitled "An Exact and True Relation of the many Messages that have passed between Sir F. Fairfax and the Marquis of Worcester, &c. London: Printed for Fra. Coles, in the Old Bailey, August 19, 1646." (K. P. 274—18.)

in it near 500 officers, gentlemen, and soldiers (a list of the chief of whom I have enclosed). Divers of the officers and soldiers refused passes, saying that they could go anywhere without passes, so that many of them are not comprised in the list; twenty pieces of ordnance, not above three barrels of powder; but they had a Mill with which they could make a barrel a day, which would supply them sufficiently. There was in it also great store of corn and malt in several rooms, the true quantity whereof I cannot give you. There was also a store of wine of all sorts, and beer. The horses they had left were inconsiderable, and those almost starved for want of hay, of which they had none, and not many oats, so that the horses ate their own halters for want of meat, and were tied with chains. Those who marched forth had not the least incivility offered them by the soldiers, who (as formerly during this War) were very punctual in observing the Articles. DOCUMENT XCV. B. A.D. 1646.

. . . .

Your real friend and servant,

W. C.

Bath, August 21, 1646.[1]

C.

Articles for the Surrender of the Castle.

1. That the castle and garrison in Raglan, with all ordnance, arms, &c., shall be delivered without wilful spoil unto his Excellency, Sir Thomas Fairfax, or such as he shall appoint to receive the same, on Wednesday next, the 19th day of this instant August, by 10 o'clock in the forenoon, in such form as shall be expressed in the ensuing Articles. DOCUMENT XCV. C. A.D. 1646.

2. That upon the said 19th day of August, the officers, gentlemen, and soldiers of the garrison, with all other persons therein, shall march out of the said garrison with their horses and arms, with colours flying, drums beating, trumpet sounding, matches

[1] From a pamphlet, entitled "A Letter from his Excellency's Quarters, &c. London: Printed by Bernard Alsop, Aug. 27, 1646." (K. P. 275—13.)

DOCUMENT XCV. C. A.D. 1646.

lighted at both ends, bullets in their mouths, and every soldier with twelve charges of powder, match and bullet proportionable, and bag and baggage, to any place within ten miles of the garrison where the Governor shall nominate; where, in respect his Majesty hath no garrison in England, nor army anywhere in the Dominion of Wales, their arms shall be delivered up to such as his Excellency shall appoint to receive them, where the soldiers shall be disbanded, and that all, both gentlemen and soldiers, shall have the benefit of these Articles, except persons excepted from pardon and composition[1]—they engaging themselves not to bear arms against the Parliament, nor do anything during their abode in the Parliament's quarters prejudicial to their affairs.

3. That all such as desire to go to their homes or private friends shall have the General's pass and protection for their peaceable repair to, and abode at the several places they shall desire to go unto; the officers and gentlemen to pass with their horses and arms, and all with bag and baggage.

4. [Officers and gentlemen to have three months to make peace and compound with the Parliament—passes to be given to such as should desire to go beyond the seas, provided they go within three months of the surrender.]

5. [Sick and wounded to remain in the castle till recovery.]

6. [All officers, gentlemen, and soldiers, to be protected from being questioned, affronted, plundered, or injured, during the said three months; such as break any of the Articles above to be punished]; and that all these Articles may be faithfully observed, according to the true intent thereof, without any cavil or mental reservation to infringe them, or any of them.[2]

[1] The Marquis himself was one of the persons excepted from pardon.

[2] *A Perfect Diurnal.* No. 160. 24th August, p. 1285. (K. P., large 4to., 26—4.)

D.

A List of Officers and Gentlemen who Surrendered at Raglan.

DOCUMENT XCV. D.

A.D. 1646.

Marquis of Worcester
Lord Charles Somerset
Sir Philip Jones, Knight
Col. Ratcliffe Gerard
Col. Price
Col. John Morgan
Col. Ralph Neale
Lieut.-Col. Hen. Somerset
Lieut.-Col. Charles Somerset
Sergt.-Major Price
Sergt.-Major Ch. Prichard
Sergt.-Major Lewis Thomas
Capt. Wm. Pugh
Capt. Wm. Brett
Capt. Wm. Inglesby
Capt. Jo. Morgan, senr.
Capt. Jo. Middlemore
Capt. Valentine Progers
Capt. Robert Tipper
Capt. Jo. Morgan, junr.
Capt. W. Pulton
Capt. Anthony Garnons
Capt. Dennis Corwen
Capt. Wm. Andrew
Capt. John Pointz
Capt. John Fant
Capt. Jas. Scudamore
Capt. Hugh Connor
Capt. Joseph Luker
Capt. Silvester Halsall
Capt. Thomas Cowley
Capt. John Jones
Capt. John Fitz-james
Capt. Richard Yeomans
Lieut. Progers
Lieut. Wm. Prichard
Lieut. John Pierson
Lieut. Rowland Jones
Lieut. Jo. Swinglehurst
Lieut. Thomas Cole
Lieut. Christo. Blunt
Lieut. Wright
Lieut. Bryan
Lieut. John Collins
Lieut. Williams
Lieut. Corry
Lieut. Thomas Powell
Lieut. Arthur Lewis
Lieut. John Rudston
Lieut. Thos. Ambrose
Cornet Hen. Waddock
Cornet Edw. Stanley
Cornet John Ailsworth
Cornet Wm. Water
Cornet John Cowell
Cornet John Gwillim
Ensign George Elliot
Ensign Richd. Halsall
Ensign Price
Ensign John Reade
Commissary W. Willin
Quarter-Master Jo. Prichard
Quarter-Master Thomas Hore
Quarter-Master Thomas Hughes
Quarter-Master Hangston
Quarter-Master Arthur

Esquires and other Gentlemen of Quality.

William Moore
William Porskin
John Powell

DOCUMENT XCV. D.

A.D. 1646.

Robert White
John Glascock
John Parshall
Lewis Scabard } Surgeons
John Powell }
Hen. Wall
John Smith
Wm. Danby
Christo. Metcalfe
Math. Aylworth
Tho. Phillips
Ben. Seaborne
Geo. Seaborne
John Seaborne
Rich. Seaborne
Thomas Price, senr.
Henry Fenwick
John Fenwick
William Jones
Thomas Chanock
James Powell
John Alenson
Valentine Smith
Rob. Thomas
Tho. Owen
Charles Gwynn
Humph. Evans
Rich. Watkins
Edw. Watkins
Thos. Powell
Rich. Crump
Thomas Davies
Rich. Davies
John Andrews
Wm. Morgan
Charles Clark
John Heeley
Thomas Watkins
Henry Williams
Rich. Blunt
Anth. Abbot
Tho. Baldwyn
Mr. Halland
George Hardwing
Humph. Price
Wm. Gwynn
Fra. Crathorne
David Mathews
Luke Hill
Henry Harries
Richard Williams
Robert Frampton
William Jane
George Watkins
John Jones
Wm. Watkins
John Wharton
William Hill
Thomas Lee
Thomas Arick
James Jones, surgeon
Rich. Williams
Wm. Moore
John Robinson
Corp. Peter Bryan
Corp. James Lewis
Corp. Jas. Progers
Doctor Bailey

There were also the Earl of Glamorgan's Lady, the Lady Jones, Mrs. Frances Yeomans, Mrs. Jane Jones, two of the Lord Gerard's sisters, and divers others of quality.[1]

[1] *Perfect Occurrences*, 35th week, 28th August. (K. P. 26 – 7.)

XCVI.

Conway taken by storm by Col. Mytton, assisted by the Archbishop of York. August 18th. The Castle summoned.

DOCUMENT XCVI. A.D. 1646.

On Saturday, the 8th of this instant [August], General Mytton returning to his military employment at Conway Castle [and called] a Council of War, to which was joined the grand advice of Doctor Williams, sometimes Archbishop of York, where he [the General] represents unto them his intentions, concerning the surprisal of the town of Conway, together with the former order for the managing of that service. It was concluded by all to be feasible, though full of doubt and hazard, and not to be effected without much loss, yet they resolved to use their best skill; and endeavour to commend the success and blessing to God. Resolute and approved men of his own horse and foot were employed, preparations of grenadoes and ladders made ready, and provisions. The service [was] thus prosecuted and effected.

Capt. Simkis was appointed to give and continue an alarm to the town on the North side; that while the enemy that were upon guard advanced themselves to defend and secure that part of the town, Major Elliot on the South side, and Capt. Camburs [? Chambres] and Capt. Gethin in two other places, with three select companies of resolute men, might as they were ordered make their advantage of that opportunity . . . Such was the resolution and gallantry of the soldiers, that though some were knocked down and crushed with horses, others cast off the ladders (which were ten yards high, and yet proved a yard and a half too short), that they renewed the action, drawing up over the author [*sic*, ?] by the army, till a considerable company were got over; which being done they fell into the town, surprised the main-guard, killed a corporal and a gentleman there, wounded many, took a major, one Capt. Wynne, an old cow-driver,

DOCUMENT XCVI. A.D. 1646.

four lieutenants, four ensigns, twenty-two soldiers of fortune, and fifty townsmen in arms. Many [Irish] were commanded to be tied back to back, and to be cast over-board, and sent by water to their own country! There was one great gun taken, 200 arms, ammunition answerable, wine, corn, and victuals good store, and considerable booty for the soldiers. The guards being sent for, the town secured, and all things quiet, the General sent this summons for the surrender of the castle [to Sir John Owen] namely:—

Sir,

I cannot but be sensible of the misery you have brought upon your country by holding this town and castle from the obedience of the King and Parliament.

Now it hath pleased God to give this town into our hands. I can do no less than put you in mind, that your holding of the castle can produce no other probable effect than the effusion of Christian blood, and the ruin of your country. And by what anthority you do it I am ignorant: the King being come into our quarters,[1] and [it being] made known unto you that he is not able to relieve you. I cannot omit to tell you what a desperate condition you will bring yourself and estate into, if you will persist in your way but few days. I do, therefore, summon you to deliver the castle into my hands for the service of the Parliament, and expect your answer within two hours.

Your servant,

Tho. Mytton.

Conway, August 9th, 1646.

[*Sir John Owen's Reply*].

Sir,

I received yours yesterday, and this day I send you mine. I wonder you should tax me with bringing misery upon this country, which my conscience tells me I am free of, especially in doing my endeavour to hold it in obedience to his Majesty.

Now you have gotten the town, I expect no other title from

[1] The King by this time, despairing of his affairs, had surrendered himself to the Scotch Army.

DOCUMENT XCVI. A.D. 1646.

you than of the castle, which title I will maintain with my life. For the effusion of Christian blood, far be it from my heart, only I must seek to defend myself and those that are with me. As for the ruin of the country, let the blood of those that lost it fall upon them that were the contrivers of it. I free you and yours. And if you would know by what authority I hold this place, I have formerly given you an answer. You writ that the King was in the Parliament's quarter. I believe he was never further from them; and withal you believe he hath made it known unto me he is not able to relieve me: this point I doubt very much. You tell me [into what] a desperate condition I will bring myself and estate, in persisting in not yielding to your desires. I can be nothing bettered unless you have an absolute power from the Parliament. As for your summons, I shall hold this castle as long as it pleaseth God, for his Majesty. Yet, if you shall accept of such conditions as I shall propound, which shall be honourable for us both, I will be content to treat with you only,

And rest, Sir, your servant,

J. OWEN.

[General Mytton replied he would receive any propositions Sir John Owen had ready. Sir John desired three days to prepare them, and they were expected on Wednesday, the 12th of August.][1]

The castle held out, however, until the 18th of November.[2]

[1] From a pamphlet, entitled "Conway taken by storm by Major-General Mytton, with the assistance of the Archbishop of York, &c. London: Printed by J. C. (August 19), 1646." (K. P. 274—17).

[2] Whitelocke.

XCVII.

Col. Salesbury surrenders Denbigh Castle to General Mytton.
October 26, 1646.

DOCUMENT XCVII.
A.D. 1646.

HONOURED SIR,

I can now assure you of the surrender of Denbigh Castle for the service of the Parliament. Sir William Myddelton commanded here in-chief under General Mytton; but the General was here himself in person, and during all the siege deported himself with much gallantry and wisdom. He agreed with Mr. Salesbury, the Governor, who (according to the Articles) marched out to the place agreed on this night, and there they laid down their arms and scattered several ways. I have sent you (here inclosed) a list of the particulars that we are possessed of, and the names of the most notorious amongst them. The place is exceeding strong, and, though the terms be high, yet the benefit is great of reducing it. The General hath called a Council of War for the reducing of the other three. Col. Carter is in capitulation at Holt,[1] where, had they not by sallies had some relief on the Cheshire side, they could not have been so high. But I doubt not but Conway and Harlech will also suddenly submit.[2] Doctor Williams is no little vexed that Owen hath put such a trick upon him. His brother[3] looks to the actions of Conway, and will oppose or surrender as he sees him do. Thus in brief, &c.,

Yours humbly to be commanded,

—— ——.

Denbigh, the 26th of October, 1646.

[1] Sir Richard Lloyd was Governor of the castle at this time.

[2] Conway surrendered on the 18th November; but Harlech held out till the March following.

[3] Sir John Owen's brother, Col. William Owen, was Governor of Harlech Castle.

There was taken at the surrender on Tuesday, one piece of ordnance, 200 arms, muskets, pikes, &c., which they marched out with, and afterwards surrendered to Major-General Mytton; many barrels of meal, a great quantity of wheat, with other corn and victuals very plentiful. Some hundredweights of lead and bullets [but] no great quantity of powder and match, which they most wanted.

The names of the most eminent men of the castle that marched out were:—Mr. William Salesbury, the Governor of the Castle; Sir William Gerard, a Papist of Lancashire, in the exceptions from mercy. Doctor Nicoll, sometime Dean of Chester, that acted much against the Parliament; Mr. Richard Charles, of Charley, a notorious Papist and an incendiary. 200 men in all—officers, gentlemen, and soldiers—marched out.[1]

Certain passages during the Siege.

[The first summons to surrender the castle was dated the 17th of April from "Denbigh Town," to which the Governor returned answer that he did "resolve to make good this place till I receive our King's command and warrant of my discharge." Carnarvon and Beaumaris Castles having been surrendered to General Mytton, he again summoned Salesbury to deliver up Denbigh Castle, this second summons being dated "Lleweny, 24th June, 1646," to which the following answer was returned]:—

Sir,

In answer to your letter of the 24th of June last, it cannot be (being so closely besieged) that I should be altogether ignorant of the affairs of this Kingdom in general, much more in the particulars, contrary to what you suppose. What the Castle and Town of Carnarvon, the Castle of Beaumaris, with the whole Island of Anglesey, have done doth nothing concern me. That must lie upon their account who were therein entrusted by our King. Now for the holding of this castle, I do hold it in its proper and due

[1] *Perfect Diurnal*, No. 171. (K. P. 26—23, large quarto).

DOCUMENT XCVII. A.D. 1646.

obedience to our King; and when I have 'need' of relief (as I formerly wrote) I am confident my good God will assuredly send it me, who hitherto hath mercifully protected me. As for the ruin of this innocent country, I am heartily sorry that so noble a gentleman, so generally beloved as yourself, of so ancient and so worthy a stock, should be made the prime actor therein, contrary to the laws of God and the fundamental laws of this Kingdom. But for further prevention of the loss of innocent Christian blood (of which I am very sensible), 'if you' withdraw your forces from before this castle and country I shall give you good assurance that this garrison shall neither be hurtful nor burdensome to the country, desiring your consent that I may send two gentlemen to our King (who entrusted me) to be assured of this pleasure. Till when, with God's leave, I shall cheerfully run the extremest hazard of war as shall please God. Lastly, for your summons. When I see the authority you have from our King and his Parliament commanding me to deliver this place to your hands, I shall, with God's help, return you a speedy, honest, and plain answer. Till then

Your well-wishing servant,

WILLIAM SALESBURY.

[Other messages having passed, General Mytton on the 31st of August wrote to say that it was not in his power to allow him to send any one to the King; that it had been denied also to the besieged at Oxford, Worcester, Raglan, and elsewhere. But somehow or other, whether by Mytton's connivance or with his knowledge does not appear, the loyal old Governor managed to send the following message to the King]:—

MAY IT PLEASE YOUR MAJESTY,

I have presumed to make my humble address to you by this gentleman, Mr. Eubule Thelwall, to let your Majesty understand that this castle hath now for several months been closely besieged. What matter of action hath in that time happened I humbly refer your Majesty to his relation, wherein I do beseech your Majesty to give him credit. Praying for your Majesty's health and happiness,

I remain, your Majesty's loyal subject,

WILLIAM SALESBURY.

The King's Answer.

CORONELL SALESBURY,

I heartily thank you for your loyall constancie, and assure you that whensoever it shall please God to enable me to show my thankfullness to my friends I will particularly remember you. As for your answer, I refer you to thease messengers to whom I have clearly declared my mind. Commend me to all my friends. So I rest your most assured friend,

DOCUMENT XCVII. A.D. 1646.

CHARLES R.[1]

Newcastle, the 13th September, 1646.

[1] Another letter accompanied this, being a copy of the Warrant sent to Oxford, Worcester, &c. (see ante p. 316), whereupon the castle was surrendered.—*Parry's Royal Progresses*, pp. 373—379.

DOCUMENTS

ILLUSTRATING TRANSACTIONS

IN THE YEAR 1647.

XCVIII.

The Surrender of Harlech Castle: the last Stronghold which held out for the King in England and Wales. March 15, 1647.

DOCUMENT XCVIII. A.D. 1647.

Articles of Agreement concluded and agreed upon by and between Thomas Edwards, Adjutant-General, and Major Edward Moore, Commissioners appointed and authorised by Major-General Mytton, of the one part; and Sir Arthur Blayney and Capt. William Edwards, Commissioners appointed and authorised by Col. William Owen, Governor of Harlech Castle, of the other part; for and concerning the rendering of the garrison of Harlech Castle to the use of the Parliament.

[These Articles were twelve in number, all of them of an honourable character.]

1. [Provided for the marching out of the Governor, officers, and soldiers, with all military honours, to a place within four miles

DOCUMENT XCVIII. A.D. 1647.

of the garrison, where the common soldiers were to lay down their arms; and that the gentry and clergy therein should have the benefit of the Articles. The common soldiers were to march the first night to Festiniog.]

2. [That the Governor and all others should have freedom to pass to their homes or friends, or to go beyond the seas—that no friends should be prejudiced for entertaining them.]

3. [The Governor and others to have the use of horse to remove their property.]

4. [None to be molested or searched for the space of six months, they doing nothing to the prejudice of the Parliament. Sick and wounded to have fit accommodation until their recovery.]

5. [The violation of the Articles to be visited upon the violator only, and satisfaction to be given at the judgment of any two or more of the Commissioners, they being equal on each part.]

6. [All persons to have, if they wish, certificates to show that they were in the castle, so as to have the benefit of the Articles.]

7. [Officers and gentlemen to have horses to travel to their homes without payment.]

8. [The Town and Corporation to enjoy all their former rights and privileges.]

9, 10, and 11. [Further stipulations regarding property.]

12. That in consideration whereof, the Castle of Harlech, with all the ordnance, arms, ammunition, and provision of war, with all magazines and stores thereto belonging, &c., shall be delivered to General Mytton, or whom he shall appoint, in the state they now are, without waste, &c., for the service of the Parliament, upon Monday next, by ten of the clock, or thereabouts, being the fifteenth day of this instant March.

THOMAS EDWARDES.
ED. MOORE.

I do confirm what my Commissioners have herein agreed.

THO. MYTTON.[1]

[1] The original of this is at Brogyntyn, in the collection of J. R. Ormsby-Gore, Esq., M.P., who now represents the old royalist house of Cleneney. —*Arch. Camb.*, vol. i, p. 261.

Further Particulars.

DOCUMENT XCVIII. A.D. 1647.

March 13, 1647. The Articles for the delivery of Harlech Castle were signed. The next day Mr. Robert Foulkes, being in the castle, died, and was buried at Llanfair. The 16th day, being Tuesday, the Governor, Mr. William Owen, delivered the keys of the castle to General Mytton.

There were in the castle, of gentlemen, the Governor [Mr. William Owen]; Sir Hugh[1] Blayney, Knight; Mr. Foulkes; Mr. John Edwards of Chirk, who being somewhat aged, died in February; Capt. William Edwards, his son; Lieut. Roger Arthur; Lieut. Roberts; John Hanmer, son of Richard Hanmer of Pentre-Pant; William Edwards of Cefn-y-Wern; Ancient [? Ensign] William Williams, was shot in the hand about All-hallowtide, and died the 19th of January; Meredith Lloyd of Llanfair in Careinion; Roger Burton; Francis Mason; Peter Simon; William Thomas; and Thomas Arthur, the Governor's man.

Besides these were twenty-eight common soldiers; their duty was performed as follows:—

1st Squadron.—1. The Governor and Lieut. Arthur.
2. Capt. Wm. Edwards and John Hanmer.
3. Meredith Lloyd and William Edwards. These went the round by turns, and Burton went to the guard on the new wall.

2nd Squadron.—1. Ancient Wm. Williams, by himself.
2. Lieut. John Roberts and Thomas Arthur.
3. Francis Mason and Peter Simon. William Thomas on the new wall. These went the rounds every other night; they were on the guard appointed. Seven sentries stood every night, wherein were fourteen soldiers; their relief was hourly, and their duty every other night.[2]

[1] Should be Arthur.

[2] Mostyn MSS.; *Parry's Royal Progresses*, p. 385;

XCIX.

Fresh Revolt of the Royalists in Glamorganshire—Ostensibly against the Committee of Usk, but really to declare for the King.

A.

Major-General Laugharne's Account.

To the Speaker of the Honourable House of Commons.

MR. SPEAKER,

The first rumour of his Majesty's departure with the army hath put the delinquents in Glamorganshire to their old frenzy: the enclosed papers will express their present posture, and shorten my relation. The leaders of them are of the principal delinquents engaged in the former revolt of that county, and whom the Parliament's clemency for offences past hath occasioned to this ungrateful relapse. Divers of the well-affected gentry of that county disfavour their courses, and cast about for their own security. Some of them are come hither to me, and I am drawing up my forces thitherward to suppress the Insolency; and find my soldiers, I thank God, very cheerful and inoffensive (*sic*) when they came, not capitulating for any conditions. I shall (God willing) never desert my first principles for the Parliament of England. The issue of this insurrection, probably, will occasion speedy and frequent records of this address by him, who is, Sir,

DOCUMENT XCIX. A. A.D. 1647.

The State's and your loyal servant,

ROWLAND LAUGHARNE.

Carmarthen, 17th June, 1647.

[ENCLOSURES.]

To the Honourable Major-General Laugharne.

SIR,

It hath pleased God to make Sir Thomas Fairfax's army a miraculous means of the King's restitution (in appearances). These

DOCUMENT XCIX. A. A.D. 1647.

counties, very apprehensive of their long-desired liberty and present sufferings, have already declared for the King and Sir Thomas Fairfax. Now that there might be nothing untimely done to your prejudice, we thought it fit to communicate so much of our business as can be no way prejudicial to yours. We should be very glad to hear how you look upon our proceedings, and unfeignedly rest

Your humble servants,

THO. NOT, RICH. BASSET,
EDWARD THOMAS, JO. STRADLING.
THO. THOMAS,

To the High Constables of the Hundred of Miskin, and to every of them.

SIR,

We require you forthwith to direct your Warrants to the petty constables of the several parishes within your hundred, that they summon all able men from sixteen to sixty to appear before us at Cowbridge to-morrow by nine o'clock in the morning with all horses fit for service, or dragoons, and all such arms as are defensive or offensive, as they have, or can come by, for the use of the King's Majesty and Sir Thomas Fairfax, General, for the preservation of the peace and safety of this county. Hereof fail not, as you owe your allegiance to his Majesty.—Dated 13th Junii, 1647.

EDW. THOMAS, THO. NOT,
RICHARD BASSET, GRENVILE WEEKS.

To the Honourable Major-General Laugharne.

SIR,

There hath happened a business in Cowbridge which may (except you be pleased to interpret it in a fair sense) be liable to a

DOCUMENT XCIX. A. A.D. 1647.

misconstruction. The truth is, the Committee, as is known, had an intent to seize on the persons of divers gentlemen, some whereof, for their security, betook themselves to Cowbridge, and there made bold with the magazine, without any the least meaning of opposition or disrespect to you; to whom, by many civilities, they are much obliged. And being certain of his Majesty's conjunction with Sir Thomas Fairfax's forces, they conceived they had been wanting to themselves, in not providing so well for their safety as they could. And they more than hope you will be so far from being any way displeased with it, as to receive assistance from you in their first and necessary defence; whereby you shall eternally oblige the whole country, and more particularly

Your most humble servants,

Jo. Stradling,	Will. Basset,
Tho. Stradling,	Robert Thomas,
Jo. Vanne,	Thomas Basset,
Will. Basset,	David Buckley,
Rich. Gwyn,	Jo. Walter,
William Merrick,	Miles Watkins,
Edward Seis,	Jo. Powel,
George Gibbon,	Rich. Wilcocke,
William Fleming,	John Stradling,
Theodore Basset,	John Jones,
Richard Basset,	Rice Merrick,
Henry Stradling,	Robert Coroche.

Cowbridge, 14th June, 1647.

To his Excellency Sir Thomas Fairfax, General of the Parliament's Forces.

May it Please your Excellency,

These last days there appeared a sudden and violent distraction in Glamorganshire. I shall use all power and diligence to allay it, and expect your Excellency's order for my proceedings, and

DOCUMENT XCIX. A. A.D. 1647.

the rather, in that the turbulent party, as I am informed, pretend your Excellency's authority for what they do. The enclosed copies of some expresses I received out of these parts, and of one of the delinquent's Warrants, will supply what I here omit. The chief actors are ancient malignants of a deep stain, and can pretend no grievance, but the just and conscientious proceedings of the Committee according to the Ordinances of Parliament. Other gentlemen well-affected and of good quality in the county are not engaged with them, but stand upon their guard. This is all I can at present in that affair, present to your Excellency, with my humble service and readiness to obey what commands you will please to impose on

Your Excellency's most humble servant,

ROWLAND LAUGHARNE.

Carmarthen, 17th June, 1647.

To Major-General Laugharne.

NOBLE SIR,

We have in a former letter made bold to intimate unto you the necessity of our present posture, which we, in the name of the whole county, must still affirm to be no ways tending to the diminution of your respect with us, but meant only for the vindication of our estates and liberties from the unjust and arbitrary disposition of Committees here, on the mediation of whose friends we have, notwithstanding, thus far complied with their desires. Yet upon assurance given that the inhabitants of this county may enjoy their liberties and estates, and all taxations (other than such as are for the army) be forborn until, by God's blessing, the present unsettledness of supreme affairs be composed, we shall not further proceed with these terms whereon we now insist.[1] This, for

[1] These terms were set forth in certain propositions sent in (by a gentlewoman) from Llandaff, to Col. Prichard, Governor of Cardiff, on the 15th June; and ran as follows:—"To avoid the shedding of Christian blood, the country are content, that upon good assurance of what follows, presently to disband, and every man to repair to his home (namely)—That the inhabitants of the

aught we can yet discover to the contrary, may in a very few days determine our differences. However, we shall not fail to advertise you of what further course the prosecution may engage us to; and ever remain

DOCUMENT XCIX. A. A.D. 1647.

Your humble servants,

RICHARD BASSET, JOHN STRADLING,
HENRY STRADLING, THOMAS NOT,
THO. STRADLING, HENRY BASSET.
CHARLES KEMEYS,

St. Lythan's Down,
15th Junii, 1647.

Sir Thomas Fairfax to Major-General Laugharne.

SIR,

I am very glad that by your watchfulness and diligence you have so timely prevented the inconvenience of the rising of these men in Wales (according as your letters mention). I believe too many are apt to take advantages of the present discomposure of affairs to work their own ends, though it be to the disturbance of the whole Kingdom. It is very true I have made some representations to the Parliament, and I hope their wisdom and justice will so answer our expectations as that we shall speedily see a happy composure of all differences, and a settlement of all rights, both to the King, the Parliament, and the People, to the comfort and satisfaction of all men that wish well to peace and righteousness. I desire you still to continue your care in those parts to prevent any evil of this kind, and to let all men know that I cannot in the least allow of such proceedings, but shall

county, lay and clergy, living according, and conforming themselves to the known laws of the Kingdom, be permitted to repossess their liberties and estates, in such manner as was before the setting up of the Committee here. All taxations, other than such to General Laugharne, to be respited; and this to be inviolably observed until it be clearly manifested what the issue will be between the King, his Parliament, Sir Thomas Fairfax, and the Army, which God grant may be to His glory and the peace of the Kingdom."

DOCUMENT XCIX. A. A.D. 1647.

send to your assistance to suppress them, if need so require, and that you do give me seasonable notice thereof. I rest

Your very loving friend,

THO. FAIRFAX.

Berkhamstead, June 25, 1647.

Laugharne to Fairfax.

MAY IT PLEASE YOUR EXCELLENCY,

My letter of the 17th inst. informed your Excellency of a violent distraction in Glamorganshire, which I have been diligent to allay without the effusion of innocent blood. The country hearing of my approach deserted the chief actors, who, to the number of fifty, all well mounted, are fled the country. The names of them are subscribed to the letters I sent your Excellency, only some few added. They had convened 1,500 to 2,000, pretending authority for so doing; but the country are made sensible how they were seduced; and I shall neglect no diligence to settle quietness, and remove the disturbers of it. This account in duty I conceived myself bound to give your Excellency, and remain

Your humble servant,

ROWLAND LAUGHARNE.

Cardiff, 21st Junii, 1647.

[Writing from Uxbridge, 29th June, Sir T. Fairfax acknowledges Laugharne's diligence as "an acceptable service to the Kingdom," and orders him to withdraw his horse and foot from Glamorganshire "into those counties where they were formerly quartered."][1]

[1] From a pamphlet, entitled "A Full Relation of the whole Proceedings of the late Rising, &c., in Wales, &c. London: Printed for Francis Leech. July 2, 1647." (K. P. 320—9.)

B.

Another Account—A Letter from the Committee at Usk.

Sir,

I thought fit to acquaint the House with a late commotion in our neighbour-county of Glamorgan. The Warrant for summoning the county is for King and Sir Thomas Fairfax. The design intended doth appear to be contrived by [Judge] Jenkins and other delinquents in the Tower. All persons affected to the King's service were to raise and seize on all the faithful-religious people in the several counties, and particularly such of the Committee as acted most eminently for the Parliament; declaring as if the King and Sir T. Fairfax were joined together and marching to London against the Parliament.

DOCUMENT XCIX. B.

A.D. 1647.

The chief actors in the county are Sir Richard Basset, Sir Edward Thomas (men I take it who have compounded at Goldsmith's Hall), Sir Thos. Not, Major Weeks, and others who have been in arms on the King's side. Their first rendezvous was small, not yet above 1,000 men, unarmed; the common people seeming very adverse to new divisions, having had a sweet taste of peace already. They are marched within 2 miles of Cardiff, where the Governor, Col. Prichard, and some gentlemen of the Committee, act faithfully and valiantly: who sent to this County of Monmouth for aid in their distress; thereupon the High Sheriff of this county sent a summons for the Committee to meet at Usk, at which meeting we resolved [to assist]; and the High Sheriff is resolved to raise the *posse comitatus*, and with his horse, and such as can be got elsewhere, endeavour the relief of our friends. We are resolved and declare that whoever acts or stirs in this commotion will be left to the mercy of the soldiery; that seeing that the lenity and goodness of the Parliament and Committees here (to their enemies) will not prevail, severity I hope will keep them in awe, and (by God's blessing) quiet.

The foundation of this insurrection was mischievously plotted as pretending to oppose illegal Committees; and to join with the King and Sir Thomas Fairfax. The reputation of that army is great in the Kingdom, and especially in these parts, who had such

DOCUMENT XCIX. B. A.D. 1647.

large and ample experience of the civility and valour of that army as not to be forgotten [at Raglan]. And many, I may say thousands, that honour the Parliament, and that ever have, and still will, oppose the Cavalierish design, will stick to that army. Some intimation came to the people of a difference between the Parliament and the Army to our Enemy's rejoicing; but I hope hell itself will not be able to divide them whom God hath so joined, honoured, and blessed together in all designs for the good of this poor Kingdom. . . . . Col. Birch's men seem willing to come to our assistance had they power to dispose of themselves. Col. Kyrle is ordered to march for securing of Monmouth; but more forces will be requisite thoroughly to quash this commotion, for there will be found some false brethren now going with the High Sheriff, and our horse, to secure some desperate delinquents, if they be not fled. We narrowly missed some that are gone from Glamorganshire to the King. What their intent is we know not. If the Parliament would send us a little money it would do us a mighty pleasure, for we want it much; our godly ministers are threatened with destruction, &c. I have here enclosed you some passages between the Governor of Cardiff and those up in arms. Major-General Laugharne is sent to and is marching towards that country. The Irish forces have offered their services from Somersetshire.

Yours &c.,

Usk, June 19th, 1647. —— ——.

[ENCLOSURES.]

A Letter to Col. Prichard, Governor of Cardiff.

SIR,

There were (for a good accommodation between us) sent by a gentlewoman some overtures in writing. We desire you will be pleased to return your speedy answer by this drummer unto

Your servants,

JOHN STRADLING, EDWARD THOMAS,
HENRY STRADLING, THOMAS NOT,
THO. STRADLING, CHARLES KEMEYS,
ROBERT THOMAS, RICHARD BASSET.

Landaff, June 16, 1647.

The Reply.

GENTLEMEN,

I received your letter by your drummer, wherein you are pleased to own a paper delivered to me by a gentlewoman, which, being unsubscribed by you and undirected, could not rationally challenge an answer from me. But, gentlemen, before I shall conceive myself to be in a posture to further intercourse with you, I shall desire to propound this question to you:—By what authority have you disturbed the peace of this county and assembled the inhabitants thereof in a martial way? and what commission you have to invade a garrison held for the service of the King and Parliament? And, having received a satisfactory answer to this demand, shall make a further answer to your letter. In the meantime, I subscribe myself, &c., DOCUMENT XCIX. B. A.D. 1647.

EDW. PRICHARD.

Cardiff, June 16.

For Sir Edward Thomas and the rest of the Gentlemen at Landaff.

SIR,

We have hitherto shown ourselves very willing to bring on that conclusion for which we have justly raised these forces, which you then declined. We are, therefore, resolved (God willing) to pursue our ends by the most peaceable and advantageous ways to the disburdening of this afflicted country, and the vindication of our rights and liberties; which, if you resist, you must appear before the world to be guilty of that blood which shall be shed.

Your servants,

JOHN STRADLING, THO. NOT,
HEN. STRADLING, RICH. BASSET.[1]
EDW. THOMAS,

Landaff, June 17.

For the Governor of Cardiff.

[1] From a pamphlet, entitled "A Declaration of the Proceedings of divers Knights and other Gentlemen in Glamorganshire, &c. London: Printed for I. Coe and A. Coe, &c." (K. P. 318—5.)

DOCUMENTS

ILLUSTRATING TRANSACTIONS

IN THE YEAR 1648.

C.

Outbreak of the Second Civil War.

A.

Poyer refuses to disband, and commences Hostilities.

DOCUMENT C. A. A.D. 1648.

SIR,

Colonel Fleming received letters and orders from the Parliament and his Excellency, and upon receipt thereof (after advice with his officers) he sent a drum with the Ordinance of Parliament and the summons, as the last to be sent to him [Poyer] to deliver up Pembroke Castle within twelve hours, or he and all with him to be proclaimed rebels and traitors.

An answer was hourly expected by Colonel Fleming, but came not within the time limited. Yet at last the drummer returned, not with Colonel Poyer's consent to surrender, but with propositions to this effect:—

1. That £1,000 might be paid unto him, which he saith he hath disbursed.
2. That the officers and soldiers be paid part of their arrears according to the proportion of others, and sufficient security for the rest.
3. That the Governor (and also the rest of the officers and soldiers) have liberty to go whither they will with security.

And so far is Colonel Poyer from surrendering of the castle, that he hath discharged several pieces of ordnance upon the town, and battered several houses, to the great prejudice of the inhabitants. DOCUMENT C. A. A.D. 1648.

He also made shot by divers ordnance with small shot at the soldiers, and hath wounded eleven, some of which is feared to be mortal.

After this Colonel Fleming (with the advice and upon the desire of the gentlemen of the county) treated with him, and promised to give him £200 in money; and to have the same terms for himself, and the officers and soldiers with him, as other supernumeraries that are or have been disbanded elsewhere.

Also that his arrears should be audited, and security given to him for payment of what shall be upon account due to him.

And it was also further offered unto him, that he should have the security of the gentlemen of the county, whom he hath much oppressed, that they would relinquish all suits or actions at law against him.

But all these offers from Colonel Fleming and the gentlemen of the county could not prevail upon him, but he put out his flag of defiance, and will not yield.

There is some fear that Tenby Castle will revolt from the Parliament.

Captain Penn (according to the order of the Committee of Safety) hath prepared assistance for Col. Fleming, with ammunition and other necessaries for the resisting of him.

Pembroke, March 15, 1648.[1]

B.

A Declaration in vindication of the Officers and Soldiers under the command of Major-General Laugharne, from divers false reports and slanderous aspersions cast upon them.

For the clearing of ourselves and the rest of the Commanders, Officers, and soldiers under the command of Major-General Laugharne, DOCUMENT C. B. A.D. 1648.

[1] From a pamphlet, entitled "A Bloody Slaughter at Pembroke Castle in Wales, &c. Printed at London, by Robert Ibbitson, in Smithfield, neere the Queen's Head Tavern, 1648." (K. P. 357—5.) Contains also a Declaration from the Chief Officers under Major-General Laugharne.

DOCUMENT C. B. A.D. 1648.

from such false reports and scandals as are raised upon us; and for the satisfying of the public, we have thought fit to declare that our intentions are really to submit and yield obedience to the Ordinance of Parliament, and his Excellency's orders thereupon for disbanding, and are resolved accordingly to disband, at such time and place as the Committees of the several counties shall think fit and appoint (so that the forces be altogether); and on the delivering us our debentures and our payment of the two months' pay complete, in the said Ordinance allowed. And, notwithstanding the scandalous reports bruted through the counties, that we endeavoured to seize upon and imprison the persons of some of the Commissioners and Treasurers appointed for the service of disbanding, and that the forces that are lately sent into the garrison of Tenby are intended to hold the said garrison against the Parliament and his Excellency, and also that others of our forces are intended to join Poyer in the Castle of Pembroke. We, for the manifestation of the truth, do further declare that it was never in our intentions to seize upon any one or more of the Commissioners or Treasurers, nor shall we ever presume to attempt it; neither had we ever the least thought or intention to strengthen the town of Tenby against the State and his Excellency. But we do engage ourselves that when and wheresoever the said Commissioners shall please to appoint a rendezvous for the disbanding the forces together, that the soldiers that are now in Tenby shall likewise appear before them to disband.

And for Colonel Poyer, we declare ourselves innocent of his actions, as may appear by our former desires to his Excellency for power to reduce him to obedience of the Parliament.

PAT. COZEN,	AD. BEALE,
WILL. SHUTTLEWORTH,	HEN. ADDYS,
RICH. POWELL,	PHI. BOWEN,
HUGH LAUGHARNE,	WIL. MARICHURCH.[1]

Carmarthen, the 10th of March, 1648.[2]

[1] This declaration notwithstanding, most of the above soon after did join Poyer.

[2] From a pamphlet, entitled "A Bloody Slaughter at Pembroke Castle in Wales," &c. Printed in 1648. (K. P. 357—5.)

CI.

Col. Poyer defeats Col. Fleming—Takes the Town of Pembroke and victuals the Castle.

Right Honourable,[1]

Since my last unto you of the 14th inst., the work for reducing of Pembroke Castle hath been much retarded, and businesses have happened contrary to our expectation. For the insolent deportment of the Governor having awakened again a discontented party in this Kingdom, which began to fall asleep and to acquiesce to the orders of Parliament, have now taken a resolution upon them to aid and assist the said Poyer: two thousand [hundred it means] of Major-General Laugharne's men, who came out of South Wales, being joined with him.

DOCUMENT CI. A.D. 1648.

Col. Poyer, having notice of their advance, forthwith dispatched a private messenger from the castle to acquaint them, that upon their approach near, he was resolved to make a sally and to fall upon our forces in their quarters, and desired that they would be in readiness to fall on upon the other side, which accordingly they did, insomuch that our party was surrounded. But immediately upon receiving the alarm they prepared to receive them and drew up into several bodies, and charged the party commanded by Poyer himself; and had totally routed them, had not the new revolters charged them on the rear. However, Col. Fleming and his party defended themselves gallantly for the space of half an hour, and engaged themselves very much for the preservation of their ordnance and artillery, but being over-powered and unprovided for their coming, were forced to retreat.

They have slain divers, and a great many are wounded. Col. Fleming himself is missing, but it is hoped is not slain. Our men are all dispersed, and about twenty or thirty are carried prisoners

[1] Who he was is not stated.

DOCUMENT CI. A.D. 1648. into the castle. The number of those killed is not yet certainly known, but we hope not many, and that which supports our confidence therein is their good appearance about Gloucester (?) and the towns adjacent. The Commissioners that went thither are most of them taken. They have also taken two great culverins, which Col. Fleming landed to maintain a battery, and carried them into the castle together, with all the arms and ammunition.

Col. Poyer hath taken Pembroke town, and from thence victuals the castle. He sends out parties daily for the fetching-in of provisions out of the country. And he hath a design to fortify the town of Pembroke, and to garrison those that are come in for his assistance therein.

We have likewise received further advertisements from South Wales, that another party of Major-General Laugharne's men are revolted from the obedience and command of the General, and hath taken possession of Tenby Castle, and do pretend to keep it for the King and Parliament according to their former engagement and covenant. Here is great talk in these parts of the raising of a new army for the King: the royal party giving out very high speeches; but we hope care will be taken for the sending of such a strength to South Wales, as, it is hoped, will soon reduce those parts and bring the new revolters to condign punishment.

The insolent Colonel hath declared his resolution to the inhabitants of Pembroke, and hath sent a declaration and propositions to the late Commander-in-Chief of the Parliament forces, a copy whereof I send you herein,[1] and remain, &c.,

JOHN WILSON.[2]

Gloucester, 28th of March, 1647.

[1] See ante, p. 344.

[2] From a pamphlet, entitled "The Declaration and Resolution of Col Poyer, &c. London: Printed for R. W. (March 31), 1648." (K. P. 358—11.)

CII.

More Troops Revolt—Poyer Summons the County—Landing of Forces from Bristol—Poyer gives them Fight—Attacks Henllan.

WORTHY SIR,

The miseries of the destroyed County of Pembroke do very much increase. This evening a vessel arrived here that came yesterday morning out of Milford, and brings news that Poyer is near 500 strong in foot, and that Capt. Addis's troop, one other troop of Major-General Laugharne's horse are fallen in to him, which amounts to about 100. He is daily raising more forces, both of horse and foot, and to that end doth frequently muster the country into Pembroke Town, who do out of pure fear obey him, and make very full appearances before him with bills, halberts, and such other weapons as they can get; and out of them, upon Saturday last, he pressed 100 men, besides what he hath since pressed in the country. He hath assessed all the country parishes about him to a tax near treble as much on any parish as the three-months' assessment for the army is, which he forceth the inhabitants to bring into him in money or provision, or both. Such as do refuse he threateneth to plunder. He hath imprisoned Mr. Lort, Mr. Bowen, and Mr. Poyer (?), with several others, and made them all pay their ransoms.

DOCUMENT CII. A.D. 1648.

On Tuesday last,[1] a little before night, the two companies of soldiers that went down by water from Bristol landed near Henllan, in Milford, and on Wednesday were set upon by two troops of horse, and about 100 foot of Poyer's, in Pulchran [Pwllcrochan] Church and churchyard, but they maintained the place, and are not taken, as the report was, but had conditions upon treaty to march away with their arms, and are gone to Cardiff upon engagement not to land again in Milford.

The same day Poyer beset Henllan House, where was Mr.

[1] No means of finding out what date this is.

DOCUMENT CII. A.D. 1648.

White, Mr. Roger Lort, Adjutant-General Fleming, Mr. John Lort, and several other gentlemen and Commissioners who were met together about the accommodating and quartering of the new-landed soldiers. All of them were in great danger of being taken, but they also by a stratagem escaped and are got on ship-board. One Butler, a Colonel of the King's army, a grand malignant, commanded the foot that were about the house, and had provided bars of iron, sledges, and other instruments, for the breaking open of the doors of the house.

By this, and what hath formerly been certified, you may see the settled resolution and activeness of Poyer and his adherents to raise a New War, which I am confident will grow to such a head on a sudden, if not timely prevented, in those malignant and discontented parts, as will not easily be overcome.[1]

[1] Anonymous Letter, without date or address, printed in *The Perfect Weekly Account* for 5-12 April. (K. P. 359—20 & 26.)

CIII.

As to the Disbanding of Laugharne's Forces—Extract from a Letter from Brecon. April 8.

The disbanding of Major-General Laugharne's forces goes on very successfully and peaceably. The several companies and troops disbanded being as followeth:— DOCUMENT CIII. A.D. 1648.

Col. Lewis's foot company	Col. Lewis's troop
Capt. Jones's troop	Capt. Griffiths's troop of dragoons
Capt. Lloyd's troop	Capt. Thomas Vaughan's troop

All these showed a willingness to obey the Parliament's orders, notwithstanding they received orders from Col. Powell, on pains of death, to be that day at Carmarthen and to bring three days' provisions with them. Col. Horton, it is thought, by this time, hath entered Pembrokeshire, and confined Poyer to a narrower compass than he had. Some troops of Major-General Laugharne's men are gone with him to testify their fidelity to the Parliament against those who have revolted, which, with some others joined, makes him between 1,200 and 1,300 strong. Likewise, Lieut.-Col. Read, with eight companies of Col. Overton's regiment, are marched after him very well appointed; and at the coming away of the last messenger were as far as Cardiff.

Poyer as yet hath but very few horse, and is not able to keep the field, but will be again sufficiently penned up in the castle upon the appearance of the additional forces sent down.

Brecon, April 8, 1648.[1]

[1] *The Perfect Weekly Account*, 12th April. (K. P. 359—20.)

CIV.

The Advance of Col. Horton into Glamorganshire.

DOCUMENT CIV.

A.D. 1648.

Sir,

Colonel Horton, with the forces ordered to reduce Poyer, are all advanced as far as Neath, and Col. Okey is joined with them. The enemy is encouraged [? encamped] on this side the river Towy, which runneth through the middle of Carmarthenshire, whither the forces are marching to give them battle, if they have but the stomach to fight. Some skirmishes they have had already. Col. Fleming gave them an alarm at Havethry (?) where, with a party of horse and dragoons, he beat up their quarters, and after a light skirmish took 12 horse and men prisoners. It is supposed that most of the officers and soldiers that were under the command of Laugharne will come in to the Parliament's forces when they see they must fight. Two captains are come in already, and Powell's declaring absolutely for the King will bring in others. Malignants come in daily unto them, and show themselves in great numbers at the rendezvous; but when they shall come to fight they will quickly leave them, and, as it were, slip their necks out of the collar again. Horse-meat is a great trouble to the Parliament's forces upon the barren mountains, and want of money as great, without which it is hard to purchase other provisions.

Swansea, April 17th, 1648.[1]

[1] From a pamphlet, entitled "The King's Majesty's last Speech in the Isle of Wight." (K. P. 361—3)

CV.

The State of South Wales—The Earl of Carbery and Sir Richard Pryse discountenance the Insurrection—The Smiths cut down their bellows, and many leave their houses on the approach of the Parliaments's Forces—A Letter from South Wales.

SIR,

The malignants from many places do yet come in unto Poyer,[1] and use their endeavours to strengthen him, and what they can they persuade the Welsh to assist them; and to that end many lies and fictions are spread abroad, the better to animate and encourage the simple misled Welsh to join with them, as that the City of London hath declared against the Parliament, &c. But it is hoped that their assistance will not be anything so great as they expect, for the Earl of Carbery, who hath once been engaged against the Parliament, and formerly a Commander in the King's army, as also Sir Richard Pryse,[2] and others, have withdrawn themselves out of their society, and also out of that country, who may happily by their example move others to do the like. DOCUMENT CV. A.D. 1648.

The Earl of Carbery and others have likewise declared their dislike of their undertakings, and would not have that there should be so much as any suspicion that they will either join with them or associate with them; for they do declare and engage their honour that they will neither join with them nor assist them, neither shall any of their friends so far as they can persuade or hinder them; but, on the contrary, they will engage with and assist the Army against them. His Lordship hath also voluntarily

[1] Among others, Sir Henry Stradling, Major-General John Stradling, Lieut.-Col. Thomas Stradling, Lieut.-Col. John Butler, Col. Morgan Governor of Gloucester, Col. Rich. Donnell (late Governor of Swansea for the King).—*Merc. Elenticus*, No. 22. (K. P. 361—10.)

[2] Of Gogerddan. Elsewhere it is said that Sir Richard Pryse was active in helping Poyer—probably he joined with him at the first, but afterwards left him.

DOCUMENT CV. A.D. 1648.

explained many other tokens of love and affection to the Parliament and Army.

Yet, the more is the pity, some of those parts are miserably bent to oppose the Parliament and the Army, as appears by this: for as the Parliament forces march forward they make away and carry with them their wives, their children, and drive away their cattle, with what goods they have or can get together, and flee into the woods and into the mountains, leaving their houses empty. Many of their smiths are also gone, they themselves having cut down their bellows before they went; for they being a spiteful mischievous people, have in many places spoiled and carried away what they conceive may be of use to our forces; and in some places there is neither a horse-shoe to be had, nor a place to make it, if one would give 40s. to have a horse shod. Therefore, some extraordinary and unusual course must be taken to end this trouble, and bring down the stomachs of these little-less-than-barbarous people.

It is reported that Major-General Laugharne is come in unto Poyer; but whether it were he or not we cannot tell; but the Welsh lately shot off all their guns to welcome some person of quality. The Welsh care not for fighting, but upon passage, and scarce then either, except they have a good opportunity. For the Welsh have always been observed to be cowards [shades of Picton do ye hear!] and seldom act but upon advantage. Col. Horton hath taken fifty of the Welsh soldiers prisoners, ten of whom are gentlemen, who were taken fortifying a house at Broshock (*sic*),[1] for whose exchange a drummer hath been sent unto Poyer.

This present Monday, being the 8th of this instant May, [rumours of another fight in Wales.][2]

[1] Probably alluding to the capture at Builth. Post. p. 360.

[2] From a pamphlet, entitled "The Desires and Propositions of Lord Inchiquin, &c." (K. P. 365—2).

CVI.

Brecknock taken by Col. Horton—A Fight between him and Col. Powell in Carmarthenshire—Death of Col. Fleming. April 29.

RIGHT HONOURABLE,

I am sorry I have occasion to write such red letters. We looked for peace, but behold fresh alarms. DOCUMENT CVI. A.D. 1648.

Col. Horton, since his first coming hither, hath deported himself well (according to his strength, for he is very ill).

There were divers gentlemen of the county, Mr. Games and others, had drawn in some to garrison this town [Brecon] for the King, who do daily increase their strength. It is reported they are about 5,000, and mostly armed. The malignant gentlemen wear blue ribbons in their hats, with this motto—

I long to see C. { [a crown] } R.
His Majestic { [a rose] }

Col. Horton sent a party hither, who took this place, and ten gentlemen of the county (who should have been chief officers here) prisoners, with divers others.

From hence he marched towards Carmarthen, where Col. Powell was then drawing up his army, consisting of English, Scotch, Irish, but mostly Welsh, and many are come from London. They declare for God and King Charles.

Col. Powell, upon the advance of Col. Horton, took an alarm and placed several parties to keep some passes, whilst he retreated with his whole army. And divers bridges were broken down in several places to stop the English from coming upon them.

Col. Horton beat up some quarters, and took some stragglers, and faced the whole army divers days. But the Welsh were got upon the top of a large hill, to which they came. The English would have drawn them down; but they would not, and stood to their ground though they were faced in several places. Col. Horton advised with his officers whether he should march up the

DOCUMENT CVI. A.D. 1648.

hill to force them to engage, but it was not thought fit to do so, as it would give [the enemy] too much advantage. Then the English wheeled off, supposing that that might allure them to fall upon the rear, and so get them to engage; but still the Welsh kept the hill and would not come down. Then Col. Horton sent Col. Fleming with a party of horse and dragoons to gain a pass on the other side of the army, some seven miles from his own quarter. The party that marched with him on his design were two companies of dragoons and one troop of horse. As soon as ever the English approached, the Welsh quitted the pass and retreated to their army, and gave them an alarm on that side. Then Col. Powell sent out a Forlorn Hope, commanded by Major Roach, to oppose Col. Fleming. Both parties met and engaged. The fight was short but very sharp, and divers of the Welsh were wounded, some slain, and the whole Forlorn Hope totally routed, which was pursued very far into the Welsh quarters; and no reserve or relief near Col. Fleming, who had then taken many prisoners. Col. Butler was then sent up from Col. Powell with a reserve to the Welsh, who ambuscaded the way, and whilst the English were in pursuit, rose upon them, and so overpowered them that they were all forced to fly and shift for themselves, leaving most of their horses behind. Yet divers of the Welsh were slain, and many wounded. And of the English there were four killed, and Captain Molyneux shot through the thigh. Col. Fleming with 119 more got into a church, which they kept against them a-while; but after a parley, agreed to surrender upon quarter of their lives. But gallant, valiant Col. Fleming is slain by an unhappy accident, with a pistol in his own hand.

Col. Horton hath sent a drummer to Col. Powell for exchange of prisoners, for he hath about 50 prisoners (and some very considerable ones), besides those that were taken before he came into these parts; and he endeavours daily to give them battle.

They give out in the Welsh quarters that the King is come to London, that bishops are established, and the Book of Common Prayer set up again in all parts about London. And that the City of London have cut off thousands of the Army, and other such like fictions they spread abroad to animate the people to comply with them.

Here is a great desire that some eminent Commander would come with additional strength, because Col. Horton hath his health very ill.[1] DOCUMENT CVI. A.D. 1648.

Brecknock, April 29th, 1648.[2]

[1] The eminent commander here desired was soon forthcoming in the person of Oliver Cromwell.

[2] Anonymous Letter, entitled "A Great Fight in Wales, &c. Printed at London by Robert Ibbitson, &c., 1648." (K. P. 362—2.)

CVII.

Fight in Carmarthenshire—Emlyn Castle is fortified—Poyer defies Cromwell—State of the Country.

DOCUMENT CVII.

A.D. 1648.

SIR,

Col. Poyer, Col. Powell, and the rest of the malignants, begin to be very fearful; and it is thought repent of their undertakings. Col. Powell being lately at Carmarthen, Col. Horton marched towards him, but the Welsh having notice thereof, pulled and broke down all the bridges, and endeavoured to stop the passages, so that when Col. Horton came to Portragorthy [? Pont ar-Gothi], he found the bridge down and Poyer's men at the passage. Col. Horton made towards another passage, and the rebels in a fear retreated to several holds. The Parliament forces being joined, followed them. Some slight skirmishes have happened, but nothing of great consequence is done as yet.

The Welsh people being more afraid than hurt conceived that they should receive strange cruelties from the soldiers of the Parliament, whereupon they quite left their dwellings, and drove all their cattle into the mountains. Col. Horton is very diligent in his service, and with all possibility endeavours to straiten them, because malignants flock unto [the enemy] daily, to hinder his getting provisions. [They] muster the country as they had [already] done in several places; where, at one time, appeared about 4,000, in another place 3,000, and in another 2,000, many of them being armed. And Powell, the better to engage the people, declared himself for the King. Here are divers porters, butchers, and such like rascally fellows, come hither from London. The Welsh endeavoured to make good their ground against the Parliament forces, and encamped near the river Towy, about twenty (*sic*) miles from Pembroke [shire it must be]; but when Col. Horton came they all retreated. Emlyn Castle is fortifying; and two companies of Col. Laugharne's men, under the command of Capt. Cozens and Capt. Aires [? Addis] are to keep it. They had an intent to have put a garrison in the Castle of Aberystwith, in Cardiganshire, but I hear they have deserted it. Monmouthshire is quiet. In Herefordshire, Major Saunders hath quelled the malignants there, and taken Col. Sherington Talbot prisoner. Poyer makes away from the presence of Col. Horton. DOCUMENT CVII. A.D. 1648.

Col. Horton hath had another great fight with Poyer, and divers men slain on both sides; but the number thereof I cannot justly give an account of. It is said that Capt. Powell (of the enemy's party) hath received a mortal wound, and divers other commanders of note. And, indeed, divers fell on our side; but that which terrifies us the most is the fall of a great soldier—a man endowed with valour and resolution.[1] Both parties draw nearer and nearer; and it is said Poyer is resolved to fight; so is Col. Horton. But Poyer is more in number than the party now against him; therefore, high time it is that the rest of the forces designed for this service be forthwith dispatched thither, which we hope will soon be effected. For Poyer gives out high speeches, and says that he fears neither Fairfax, Cromwell, nor Ireton, but is resolved to fight it out to the last man. We hear that Lieut.-General Cromwell is designed for this service, and that he is upon his march hither with several regiments of horse and foot. The [enemy] hath also received the same tidings, and Poyer gives out that they will give him a field and show him fair-play, and that he will be the first man that shall charge against *Ironsides*: saying, that if he had a back of steel and a breast of iron he durst and would encounter with him. Most of the inhabitants in these parts are fled to the mountains, being troubled with too much malignancy; and Mr. Vulcan hath shown himself a great enemy to our proceedings, for divers smiths in several towns have cut up their bellows, broken down their smithies, and made all their materials unserviceable. So that we cannot get a horse shod not in twenty or thirty miles riding.

Your obliged friend,

T. Sands.[2]

Carmarthen, the 3rd of May, 1648.

[1] Col. Fleming is probably here alluded to.

[2] "The Declaration and Resolution of Col. John Poyer, concerning Lieut.-General Cromwell, &c." London: Printed for J. G., 1648 [May 8.] (K. P. 365—6.)

CVIII.

Suppression of Insurrectionists in Brecknockshire and Radnorshire—Col. Horton encamps at St. Fagans—Major-General Laugharne joins Poyer.

A.

Col. Horton's Letter to General Fairfax.

DOCUMENT CVIII. A.
A.D. 1648.

MAY IT PLEASE YOUR EXCELLENCY,

In my last I made mention of sundry gentlemen of the Counties of Brecknock and Radnor, met at Builth to consult about the raising of those counties to join with Col. Powell, and my sending a party to apprehend them, the success whereof was the taking of one Mr. Hugh Lloyd (one of the excepted persons), Lewis Lloyd, late Sheriff of Brecon, and one of his sons, Marmaduke Lloyd, and some others.

After the ammunition was come up to us at Brecknock: we being upon a serious debate of our next motion, which was proposed for Pembrokeshire, we were [informed] by some special friends in Glamorganshire, that the body of the enemy was fallen down into that county, having a design upon Cardiff, both by face and feigned friendship, tempting the cordial and constant-minded Governor, and Mr. Bushey Mansell, to come in unto them; so that we were necessitated for the preservation of that place and prevention of the enemies' design of entirely raising the Counties of Glamorgan and Monmouth (which in the judgment of wise and faithful men was thought to be no less probable than dangerous), to march with all possible speed towards Cardiff, which was done with much difficulty, by the reason of all [the] ways [being] over the mountains, very unseasonable weather, and want of accomodations both for horse and man. At last we passed the river Taff, at Landaff, about a mile above Cardiff, and came to St. Fagans, upon the river Ely, whither the enemy intended to have advanced the same night, which occasioned their stop at St. Nicholas, two miles from us on the other side of the river Ely, being a place much for their advantage, where we could make no use of our horse, and because, for want of food, we could not rationally attempt anything upon them. This morning the enemy is drawn off from St. Nicholas towards Penmark and Fonmon[1] Castle. Major-General Laugharne came to them on the 4th of May, and on the first sent two letters, one to the Commissioners of this county, and another to myself, the copies of both which, with our answers, I have herewith sent to your Excellency.

It hath been formerly represented to your Excellency by our most knowing and faithful friends in these parts, how improbable it was that one party, though more considerable than ours is, should of itself be able to subdue the enemy in the field, reduce Pembroke, and keep all South Wales from rising, being generally inclined to it by reason of the malignancy of most of the gentry, who lead the common people which way they please, as we find by every day's experience. And, without doubt, tumults will grow greater and their numbers increase, if such a strength be not assigned to these parts as may attend both the motion of the enemy and to awe those places which are most apt to rise. Capt. Creed, with three troops of Col. Thornhaugh's regiment, doth very good service in this kind, being now quartered about Glasbury bridge,[2] which is a great pass near the conjunction of the Counties of Hereford, Radnor, and Brecon. Col. Philip Jones, with his company from Swansea, hath (for an assistance) been with us in all our march, and himself many ways helpful to us. I had frequently acquainted your Excellency with our condition, the temper of these parts, and the state of the enemy, had I not been hindered, both from intelligence from my friends and likewise from sending to your Excellency—the country people searching all passengers and abusing them. I am much afflicted I can give your Excellency no better account of South Wales; but in one word I must say again,

[1] "Fulmon" he calls it.
[2] On the Wye.

DOCUMENT CVIII. A. A.D. 1648.

that it is generally against the Parliament, so that what our condition hath been, and is like to be, before any supply can probably be sent hither, your Excellency may easily perceive. Yet, by God's assistance, I shall use my best endeavour (with my life) to prove myself still faithful to the Kingdom's interest, and

Your Excellency's most humble servant,

THO. HORTON.

St. Fagans, May 6, 1648.

B

Laugharne disputes Col. Horton's right to Command in Wales—Correspondence between them.

Major-General Laugharne to Col. Horton.

DOCUMENT CVIII. B. A.D. 1648.

SIR,

I desire you would let me know by what power you first came and still remain in these counties of my association, I being commissioned Commander-in-Chief of these parts by an Ordinance of Parliament? and upon what grounds the injury of seizing on some of my troops was offered, and the taking of the whole attempted, without satisfaction rendered them in point of pay, according to the instructions of the Parliament to the Commissioners for disbanding such supernumeraries? I should gladly be satisfied in these particulars, otherwise your perseverance in these affronts to myself and the soldiery, and the country, will not be without some difficulty. Sir, if you please to withdraw your forces out of this county, it may be a special means to prevent several inconveniences, besides the necessary resolutions which otherwise must be forced upon, Sir,

Your servant,

ROW. LAUGHARNE.

St. Nicholas, 4th May, 1648.

For Major-General Laugharne.

Sir,

I thought that it had not been unknown to you that his Excellency the Lord Fairfax is General (by Ordinance of Parliament) of all forces both in England and Wales, and is empowered to dispose of them into such places and in such manner as he shall see cause for the preservation of the peace of this Kingdom. In order to which, he commanded me into these counties with the forces now under my command, occasioned by Col. Poyer's refusing to disband according to the Ordinance of Parliament and his Excellency's orders to that end, and Col. Powell's adhering unto him, notwithstanding whoever should do so were adjudged and declared traitors by the Parliament; as also Col. Poyer's and Col. Powell's (with others, and their confederates) issuing out warrants (without the least colour of authority) for the tumultuous raising of the Counties of South Wales; their entertaining Capt. Arram's (? Addis) company of foot after they had received their month's pay, and had been by the Commissioners of this county declared disbanded; their inviting and gathering together most of the officers and soldiers which were disbanded in this county, and the joining of all these with the most active Cavaliers both in these and other parts into a body, to the great disturbance of the peace and much impoverishing of these counties; as also the apparent laying the foundation of a New War; besides the affronts put upon two companies of foot (sent by his Excellency to assist the reducing of Pembroke Castle) by some of your forces, which was owned by Col. Powell, before anything was attempted upon Capt. Agborow's troop, called yours, who, notwithstanding the mutual engagement betwixt the Commissioners of this county, myself, and the Captain, that his troop should not depart this county, where they should lie secure until disbanded; yet Capt. Agborow having received £400 in order to disband, gave private orders (as I can clearly prove) to his Lieutenant to march (upon my advance) to join with Col. Powell; which orders the Lieutenant did observe, refusing to return to this county to receive the rest of his disbanding money, though thereunto desired by the Commissioners. Whereas I now understand that you are come down into the country, considering

DOCUMENT CVIII. B. A.D. 1648.

DOCUMENT CVIII. B. A.D. 1648.

the former trust the Parliament reposed in you and your late obligations to them, I would have rather believed that you came with an intention to join with us for the suppressing of that tumultuous assembly with you, than to appear amongst and own those who have so manifestly violated the authority of Parliament, which you seem to maintain and insist upon in your letter to me, Sir,

Your obedient servant,

May 5th, 1648. THO. HORTON.

Major-General Laugharne to the Parliament's Commissioners.

GENTLEMEN,

I cannot be ignorant how the sole command of these associated counties was conferred upon me by Ordinance of Parliament; nor of the injuries and affronts put upon my men, instead of receiving their pay allowed them by the Parliament, and agreed upon by some of yourselves. Truly, I was very confident my past services for your country hath merited much better of you than that such miscarriages should happen in my absence, and to your knowledge unrighted. However, if you please to appear with your country, and to continue your endeavours in prevention of the slavery threatened it, you shall not fail of the most effectual assistance that lie in the power of

Your humble servant,

ROWLAND LAUGHARNE.

St. Nicholas, 4th May, 1648.

[The Commissioners reply much in the same tone as Col. Horton, adding that they wondered "that not only your forces lying in other counties, but likewise those who had received their money and debentures, and had been departed and disbanded; yea, and a great part of the inhabitants of Carmarthen, Pembroke, and Cardigan, should be drawn into this county, we know not any colour of the authority of Parliament for such proceedings."][1]

[1] From a pamphlet, entitled "A Declaration by Major-General Laugharne, &c. London: Printed for Lawrence Chapman, May 15, 1648." (K. P. 366—8.)

CIX.

The Battle of St. Fagans, May 8th—Utter Defeat of Laugharne's Forces—Stragglers Retreat to Pembroke—Col. Horton's Letter to Lenthall, Speaker of the House of Commons.

Sir,

I shall give you a narration (according to my own observation, and the help of some of the officers with me), both of the manner and success of our late engagement with the enemy, near St. Fagans The enemy having drawn off from Saint Nicholas to Llancarvan, Penmark, and Fonmon Castle, Friday, the fifth of May. On the Lord's Day, at night, they advanced towards us again to St. Nicholas; by which we did presently apprehend that they intended to fight with us, and were induced to such a belief, the rather, because they knew two days before that Lieut.-General Cromwell was coming towards us. This made us draw in all our horse close that night, as we had done divers nights before, and prepare for the work in the morning; and about seven in the morning our scouts discovered their body about a mile and a half from our quarters, upon which we drew out, and took the best ground we could. Major Bethel commanded the horse on the right wing, Major Barton on the left, and Colonel Okey and his Major with the Dragoons on both wings with the horse. The enemy advanced fast with a strong forlorn of foot and about six Pickering horse; Lieutenant Godfrey with a forlorn of 30 horse and 20 dragoons charged and routed them, doing good execution, which gave us the advantage of a new ground; so we advanced with horse and foot upon them, Capt. Garland with two hundred fire-locks on foot, and Captain Nicholets (this bearer), with Colonel Okey's own troop of dragoons, mounted with some horse on the right wing, disputed the first encounter very hotly, where he showed much resolution, and beat the enemy out of two closes and over a little brook, and there maintained their ground under command of the enemy's shot, until the forlorn of foot com-

DOCUMENT CIX. A.D. 1648.

DOCUMENT CIX. A.D. 1648.

manded by Captain Lieutenant Fann, and some horse from the left wing, came to their relief; and then they beat the enemy from hedge to hedge before them, until they came to a bridge where the enemy's greatest body were placed. The horse all this while and dragoons following this first success with much vigour, were constrained to stand the enemy's shot for some time before the foot (though they made great haste) could come up to them; and presently the first division of foot, commanded by Lieutenant Colonel Read, fell close up to the enemy's front; Major Wade with the second division got over the little brook on the left flank of the enemy; Major Barton likewise, with the left wing of horse, with much celerity passed over a boggy place and the little brook to second those foot; and some of the enemy's horse coming on to charge the foot, were gallantly resisted and beaten back by Captain Hughes. By this time the horse and dragoons on the right wing were gotten over also, the enemy's foot standing very stoutly to it, until our horse began to surround them, and then they presently all ran, and we cleared the field, our horse and dragoons pursuing them for eight or ten miles. The enemy's horse, which they say were five hundred, were employed in their rear to keep up their foot, and we never saw after we were engaged, above sixty horse in a body all the fight. Their whole number of horse and foot is confirmed to be about 8,000—they had about 2,500 musketeers by their own confession, besides bills, pikes, and clubs. We took up the day we fought above 2,000 fire-arms, with pikes, Welsh bills, and other weapons great store, ten barrels of powder, and all the rest of their ammunition in the field, and most if not all their colours. The number of prisoners that are taken are about 3,000. (I have here enclosed a list of the officers as they gave in themselves to the Marshal.) Some hundreds of them were disarmed four or eight miles from the place we fought, which we let go. Captain Wogan, a Member of the House of Commons,[1] sent down by them into these parts, carried himself from the first to the last with great resolution, encouraging the soldiers and engaging himself in the head of the service. Captain Jones, who came off from the enemy to me long since, with a troop of sixty horse, behaved himself

[1] Thomas Wogan, Member for the Cardigan Boroughs—the Regicide.

DOCUMENT CIX. A.D. 1648.

likewise very well, as also all other officers and soldiers, who I can truly say kept their order in the performance of their service to the admiration of the enemy, as some of them confessed.

And that God's mercy may be the more magnified in this late happy success over our enemies, I think it now seasonable to make known unto you the straits we were in, and difficulties which compassed us about; we having a potent enemy lying within two miles upon much advantage of ground, before us the high mountains, close to us on the right hand the sea, near unto us on the left Chepstow taken and Monmouthshire beginning to rise in our rear, besides our great want of provisions and long and hard duty, all which seemed to threaten our sudden ruin. That God should please in this condition so to own us, as to make a way for us through the midst of our enemies, and to scatter them every way is a mercy not to be forgotten, especially by those who have more immediately tasted of it. Witnessing the truth of these things as they are herein expressed by

Your faithful and most humble servant,

THO. HORTON.

Bridge-end, May 13, 1648.

A List of the Names of the Officers taken by Col. Horton, May 8, 1648.

Field Officers.	*Captains.*	
		William Matthews
Major-General John	William Purve	Jo. Floyd
Stradling	Tho. Bowen	William Williams
Colonel Harris	Jo. Thomas	Hugh Floyd
Lieut.-Col. Matthews	Jo. Rice	Charles Aubray
Major Hopkins	James Lewis	Richard Hopkins
Major Philips	Richard Esmond	Richard Hopkins
Major Stedman	Griffin Bowin	Robert Mathews
Major Gwyn	Captain Lieut. Bartlet	John Owen
Major Adis	Captain Lieut. Hewit	Rowland Matthews
Major Hopkin Dawkins	Rowland Lewis	Richard Jones
Quarter-Master-Gen.	Edmond Price	James Matthews.—
Harris.—10.	William Cradock	24

DOCUMENT CIX.

A.D. 1648.

Lieutenants.	*Ensigns.*	*Reforma. Gent.*
Button	Jo. Harris	Samuel Howel
Valentine Swale	Tho. Hopkins	Herbert Jeffreys
Jeremy Wise	David Walter	Parson Owen
William Richard	Rowland Prothero	Humph. Matthews
Owen Prichard	Jo. Williams	David Parry
Prothoe	Morris ap Richard	Rich. Lloyd
John Thomas	Jo. Keys	Robert David
Tho. Talbot	Nat. Gee	Rob. Nicoll
Pew	Tho. Richard	William Button
Jo. Jenkins	Gabriel Herbert	Geo. Davis
Jo. Morgan	William Llewelyn Griffith	Rol. Phillips
David Lloyd	Ariam Morfew	Mr. Ryley
Jo. Griffith	Walter Williams	Morgan Prist
Williams	John Barrison	Bar. Davey
Tho. Powell	Griffith Thomas	Jos. Hance
William Griffith	Barthol. Rutter	Ed. Thomas
Lewcas	Rice John	Hugh Conyer
Will. Suttleworth	Owen Bowen	Jo. Thomas
Walter Floyd	Morgan Roberts	Mr. Thomas
Griffith Thomas	Rice Howel	Hugh Sayer—20
Jo. Graver	James Annis	*Chyrurgions.*
Jo. Griffith	Tho. Williams	Robert Williams
Walter Jones	James Harman	Richard Maren
Hugh Taylor	Lewis Christopher	
Thos. Malson	Matt. Stacey	Peter Nicoles, Drum-Major
Lewis Jones	Hewin Richard	With 2,900 common soldiers and non-commissioned officers.[1]
Tho. Morgan	John Backster	
William Peregrine	Ed. Thomas.—28	
Tho. Jenkins		
Tho. Jones.—30		

[1] From a pamphlet, entitled "Confirmation of a Great Victory in Wales, sent in a letter from Col. Horton, &c." (K. P. 367—15.)

DOCUMENT CIX.

A.D. 1648.

Slain of the Welsh.

Lieut.-Col. Thomas Laugharne
Lieut.-Col. Howell
Major Bushey
Major Evan Thomas
Major Smith
Capt. Turberville, a Papist
Capt. Powell of Lantrade
40 Officers more
150 Common Soldiers
Gen. Laugharne wounded and fled
Col. Powell fled with 100 horse
Col. Poyer keeps Pembroke Castle, with 100 men.[1]

Another List sets forth the following additional Names as having been taken Prisoners.

Col. Philip Gammage of Newcastle
Col. Rich Grime
Col. Howel Games
Lieut.-Col. Wogan of Pembroke
Lieut.-Col. Lewis of Redla
Major Phillips
Major Christo. Mathews of St. Anal
Capt. Wm. Button
Sir Marmaduke Lloyd and his son
Mr. Hugh Lloyd
Doctor Lloyd
Mr. James Walcot
Mr. Walter Lloyd
Mr. George Anderson
Mr. Roger Games
Mr. Walter Powell
Mr. Edward Games
Mr. Roger Williams
Mr. Devereux Grafton
4,000 Clubmen dispersed
350 arms broken and whole
50 colours
360 horse; and all the ammunition, bag, and baggage.[2]

[1] From a pamphlet, entitled "A List of the Prisoners taken and those that were slain by Col. Horton in South Wales, &c. Printed at London, by Robert Ibbitson, &c., 1648." (K. P. 365—33.)

[2] *Ibid.*

CX.

Flintshire and Denbighshire declare their fidelity to the Parliament.

DOCUMENT CX. A.D. 1648.

A Declaration and Resolution of the Sheriffs, Justices of the Peace, and other of his Majesty's well-affected Subjects in the Counties of Flint and Denbigh, at a general meeting held at Wrexham, the 9th of May, 1648.

First.—It is resolved that the present distemper of the times, and danger imminent upon this country, doth necessitate the putting of the same into a posture of defence against any that shall be in arms against the Parliament.

Secondly.—It is resolved that we shall, in pursuance of the solemn League and Covenant, in all just ways, resist and suppress all forces whatsoever, either native within these counties of North Wales, or those that shall from foreign countries invade these parts, contrary to the authority of both Houses of Parliament, to the contempt thereof, and the disturbance of the public peace, in order whereunto it is further resolved,

Thirdly.—That the declaration of this resolution be published throughout the Six Counties of North Wales, with intimation of our desires—That all well-affected persons therein will join and subscribe with us, with whom we oblige ourselves, to a mutual defence of each other in this engagement; and the taking of subscriptions is referred to the Commissioners of the Assessment of £6,000 *per mensem*, of the said respective counties, and to such as they or any of them shall appoint.

Fourthly.—That those persons that shall subscribe these resolutions shall improve their interests in their several limits, to engage all persons well-affected, both horse and foot, to be ready with their arms for the defence and preservation of the peace of the country in the obedience of the Parliament; and to yield their assistance in the suppression of any insurrection or unlawful tumultuary meeting of such as have been in arms against the Parliament. DOCUMENT CX. A.D. 1648.

Fifthly.—That the names of such persons as shall be engaged to be in readiness in the county of Denbigh, be returned to the Governor of Denbigh,[1] who, with the advice and assistance of the High Sheriff of that county, Sir Thomas Myddelton, Simon Thelwall, Esquire, the elder of Plas-y-Ward, the Commissioners for the £6,000 per month, the Committees of North Wales, or any four of them, shall have power to appoint fit men to draw together and conduct such persons for the service aforesaid as occasion shall require, and as they shall receive orders from the said Governor, and any four of the persons aforesaid.

Sixthly.—That the names of such persons as shall be engaged to be in readiness for the same service in the County of Flint, be returned to the Governor of Denbigh, who, with the advice and assistance of the High Sheriff of that county, Col. Thomas Ravenscroft, Col. John Addersley, John Salisbury, of Bathgrage, Esq., Capt. Luke Lloyd, the Commissioners for the £6,000 per month, the Committee of North Wales, or any four of them, [shall have power to appoint fit men to draw together and conduct such persons for the service aforesaid] as occasion shall require, and they shall receive orders from the said Governor, and any four of the persons aforesaid.

Seventhly.—That the arms of such of the inhabitants of the Counties of Denbigh and Flint as have been in hostility against the Parliament, be by Warrant called in and brought to Denbigh Castle, for the use of the said counties respectively; and that there be intimation in the said Warrants, that such persons as shall quietly and readily surrender up their arms shall be taken notice of as persons not inclinable to disturb the public peace; and that such persons as refuse to deliver up their arms, or conceal the same, shall be esteemed prone and ready to entertain new commotions, and not persons well-affected to the peace of their country; giving further to understand, it is not our intention by the seizure of arms to add fear or molestation to any that conform; but, on the contrary, we shall cherish such and all others who shall not contrive,

[1] Lieut.-Col. Twistleton.

DOCUMENT CX.

A.D. 1648.

practise, or act something to the disturbance of the country's peace.

Eighthly.—That the Castles of Ruthin and Ruthland be, in pursuance of the order of the Honourable House of Commons,[1] forthwith made more untenable, and that Warrants be immediately sent forth, under the hands of the Justices of the Peace, and Commissioners of the respective counties, or any three or more of them, for that purpose; and the care of the demolishment of Ruthin Castle is referred to Simon Thelwall, of Plas-yn-Ward, Esquire, and the present Governor of Denbigh; and for Ruthland, to Roger Hanmer, Esquire, High Sheriff of the County of Flint.[2]

[1] These castles, along with others, were on the 3rd of March, 1647, ordered by the Parliament to be dismantled.

[2] From a pamphlet, entitled "A Resolution of the Sheriffs and Justices of the Peace, &c., in the Counties of Flint and Denbigh, &c." (K. P. 367—16.)

CXI.

The County of Montgomery resolves to assist the Parliament to suppress the Insurrection. 20*th May*, 1648.

DOCUMENT CXI. A.D. 1648.

The Resolutions and Engagements of us, the Gentlemen, Ministers, and well-affected of the County of Montgomery, whose names are subscribed.

First.—That we do and will adhere (according to our Covenant) to the Parliament of England, now sitting at Westminster, and their adherents. And that we will, to the utmost of our endeavours, according to our several places, assist them against all such as shall oppose them or endeavour the disturbance of the peace of the Kingdom, or the obstructing of the execution of their ordinances or orders.

Secondly.—That for the defence of this county we will forthwith, every man according to his power and ability (according to an express from the Speaker of the House of Commons, and according to the example of several other counties, both in England and Wales), put ourselves in a posture of defence; and for that end, till a further course be thought upon and concluded by the Parliament, we do voluntarily and freely engage, according to our list of subscription, for men, horse, and arms.

Thirdly.—We do unanimously accord, concur, and resolve upon, that we will be in a readiness to assist and help each other for the discovering, securing, and disarming of all ill-affected persons within our county, according to order of Parliament; and also for the suppressing of all tumults, insurrections, and disorders that may arise within our said county, by natives of our county, or any other whatsoever, that shall on any pretences (either by imposing

DOCUMENT CXI. A.D. 1648.

of oaths or otherwise, without order of Parliament), disturb the peace or endanger the persons or liberties of the said county, contrary to the laws of the land.

Mathew Morgan Vic.-Com.	Lloyd Piers[3]	Hercules Hannay
	Gabriel Wynne	Ed. Owens
Ed. Vaughan	Evan Lloyd[4]	Ed. Allen
Hugh Price[1]	William Kyffin	William Feiges
George Devereux[2]	Charles Lloyd	Ambrose Maston
Sam. Moore	Lodowich Myddelton	Vavasor Powell[5] *

[1] High Sheriff for 1654.

[2] Of Nantcriba, Member for the Montgomery Boroughs 1646.

[3] Of Maesmawr, H. S. for 1637 and 1649.

[4] H. S. for 1650.

[5] The famous instrument of the Act for Propagation of the Gospel in Wales—a Presbyterian Minister.

* From the *Perfect Diurnall*, No. 252. (K. P., large 4to., 33—32.)

CXII.

Chepstow after a Siege is taken—Sir Nicholas Kemeys slain—Col. Ewer's Letter. May 25.

SIR,

Lieutenant-General Cromwell being to march towards Pembroke Castle, left me with my regiment to take-in the Castle of Chepstow, which was possessed by Sir Nicholas Kemeys, and with him officers and soldiers to the number of 120. We drew close about it, and kept strong guards upon them to prevent them from stealing out and so to make an escape. DOCUMENT CXII. A.D. 1648.

We sent for two guns from Gloucester, and two off a shipboard, and planted them against the castle. We raised the battlements of their towers with our great guns, and made their guns unuseful to them. We also played with our mortar-pieces into the castle. One shot fell into the Governor's chamber, which caused him to remove his lodging to the other end of the castle. We then prepared our batteries, and this morning finished them, and played all the forenoon with our great guns very hot. About twelve o'clock we made a hole through the wall, so low that a man might walk into it.

The soldiers in the castle perceiving that we were like to make a breach, cried out to our soldiers that they would yield the castle, and many of them did attempt to come away. I caused my soldiers to fire at them to keep them in. Esquire Lewis comes upon the wall, and speaks to some gentlemen of the country that he knew, and tells them that he was willing to yield to mercy. They came and acquainted me with his desire, to which I answered that it was not my work to treat with particular men; but it was Sir Nicholas Kemeys with his officers I aimed at. But the Governor refused to deliver up the castle upon these terms that Esquire Lewis desired, and desired to speak with me at the Draw-bridge. I altogether refused to have any such speech with him, because he

DOCUMENT CXII. A.D. 1648.

refused Lieut.-General Cromwell's summons; but being over-persuaded by some gentlemen of the country who were there, presently I dismounted from my horse and went to the Draw-bridge, where he, through a port-hole, spoke with me. That which he desired was, that he with all his officers and his soldiers might march out of the castle without anything being taken from them; to which I answered that I would give him no other terms than that he and all that were with him should submit unto mercy, which he swore he would not do. I presently drew off my soldiers from the castle and caused them to stand to their arms. But he refusing to come out upon these terms, the soldiers deserted him, and came running out at the breach we had made. My soldiers seeing them come out ran in at the same place, possessed themselves of the castle, and killed Sir Nicholas Kemeys, and likewise him that betrayed the castle, and wounded divers; and took prisoners as follows:—Esquire Lewis, Major Lewis, Major Thomas, Capt. Morgan, Capt. Buckeswell, Capt. John Harris, Capt. Christopher Harris, Capt. Mansell, Capt. Pinner, Capt Dowle, Capt. Rositer, Lieut. Kemeys, Lieut. Leech, Lieut. Codd, Ensign Lewis, Ensign Watkins, Ensign Morgan, with other officers and soldiers to the number of 120.

These prisoners we have put into the church, and shall keep them till I receive further order from Lieut.-General Cromwell. This is all at present, but that I am

Your humble servant,

ISAAC EWER.[1]

Chepstow, May 25th, 1648.

[1] "A Full Relation of the Taking of Chepstow Castle in Wales, &c., expressed in a Letter from Col. Ewer to the Honourable Wm. Lenthal, Speaker to the House of Commons, &c. London: Printed by Mathew Simmons, &c., 1648." (K. P. 369—6.)

CXIII.

The Surrender of Tenby Castle to Cromwell. 31st May, 1648.

SIR,

After a long and tedious siege of this Town and Castle of Tenby, finding a most resolved and stubborn enemy, upon the 14th of May we stormed the town in one place, and were repulsed. Then our men fell on a certain work, where there were some slain, and thirty of the enemies taken prisoners. Presently, after this, they did very humbly seek from time to time that they may march out upon conditions; but our honourable Col. Horton would give no ear to them, knowing the serpentine malevolency of their natures, especially of that proud and insolent Col. Powell, that shameful apostate, who indeed deserves no mercy at all, but that he should be cast into that current of the flood-gate of Justice, and be made exemplary to Posterity and to all perfidious villains.

DOCUMENT CXIII. A.D. 1648.

On Wednesday last we had an humble suit from this proud Powell, to desire that noble Col. Horton to take them into protection and mercy, upon which they did freely and willingly surrender all, both arms and ammunition. There are most part of the gentlemen in South Wales that were in this rebellion against the Parliament and their Army, who were the chief ring-leaders and accomplices of these base apostates, Laugharne and Powell, as I wrote to you before. There are a great many gentlemen of quality. In all there are taken of soldiers and gentlemen between 500 and 600, who are now prisoners at Tenby under Col. Horton.

I praise God the Lieut.-General [Cromwell] is gallant and well. He hath subdued all the rebellious party in South Wales except Pembroke Castle, of which you shall hear more presently. All the gentlemen of South Wales come in to him—I mean all those who were not engaged; and they hold a very fair, and I believe, a real correspondence with him. For the common people, who

DOCUMENT CXIII. A.D. 1648.

are natives of Wales, he did consider that they were but a seduced ignorant people, and they have promised never to take up arms more; but for your arch-cavaliering rogues that were privately invited from London, Worcester, Chester, and other parts of the Kingdom, merely to heighten the mischief in Wales, they are kept prisoners, and it is intended they shall be sent to the West Indies for prevention of further mischief here. . . . . .

One thing I had almost forgotten. They in Pembroke are fain to feed their horse and cows with the thatch of their houses. Poyer pretends his old principles, and doth protest he was not confederate with Laugharne or Powell in that rebellion. Now he is under the lash, he makes show of these colours. . .

W. S.

From before Pembroke, June
the 5th, 1648.[1]

Further Particulars.

[The conditions agreed upon were]:—1. To deliver up all the ordnance, arms, and ammunition of the castle to Lieut.-General Cromwell for the use of the Parliament. 2. That the common soldiers be permitted, those who will, to be transported by Prince Philip or others into Italy. 3. Those soldiers who desire to go home may be permitted, taking an oath never to engage against the Parliament hereafter. 4. That all the officers surrender themselves prisoners, their lives and estates to be at the mercy of the Parliament.

A List of what was taken—Prisoners at Mercy.

Col. Rice Powell	Capt. Beale
Col. Edward Kemeys	Capt. Addis
Col. Donnell	Capt. Powell, and
Sergt.-Major Vaughan	30 Officers.[2]

[1] From a pamphlet, entitled "Exceeding good news from South Wales, &c." (K. P. 370—27.)

[2] Of the other officers and gentlemen then taken were Lieut. Smith, Mr. Culpeper, Mr. Henry Penry, Louis Brucius, Thomas Basset, Rich. Leyson, John Thomas, John Stump, John Bratier, George Lourday, Robert Standen, Thomas Reynolds, and Simon Sway.—*Perfect Occurrences*, No. 75.

One hundred soldiers, to be disposed of according to the Articles; 20 pieces of ordnance; 300 arms; four broken barrels of powder; forty horse; five colours, and the standard of the castle; all their ammunition and provision, bag and baggage.[1]

DOCUMENT CXIII. A.D. 1648.

[1] From a pamphlet, entitled "Two Great Victories, &c. Printed at London, by Robert Ibbitson, at Smithfield, 1648." (K. P. 370—23.)

CXIV.

Fresh Outbreak of War in North Wales—Defeat of Sir John Owen.

DOCUMENT CXIV. A.D. 1648.

Sir John Owen, Commander-in-Chief of the enemy's forces, and whom they called formerly Major-General, against the Parliament, with 140 horse and 120 foot, or thereabouts, was grown so strong by some addition from the country that Major-General Mytton, together with William Lloyd, Esquire, High Sheriff of Carnarvon, were forced for their security to repair to Carnarvon garrison on Saturday, the 3rd inst. Major-General Mytton, with the Sheriff, and what horse, were in the garrison, being about 20, and some foot to the number of 60, or thereabouts, marched forth to the enemy, met them within three miles of the garrison. The Sheriff, who led the horse, so far engaged himself that, being overpowered, he could not come off, but after long struggling, having received seven or eight wounds, became their prisoner, whose barbarous usage towards him cannot be related. They carried him, whilst he was able to sit, from place to place on horseback, his wounds never searched nor dressed; which, had they been, it is conceived would not prove mortal, as by a surgeon's attestation appears, given by him under his hand as followeth:—

[I,] William Griffith, surgeon, being sent for to dress some men belonging to Sir John Owen, found the High Sheriff of Carnarvonshire wounded in seven several places, besides burnings and scars, but no considerable help [had been] afforded for the healing of them, being unsearched, untended, unrolled, from Saturday in the forenoon until Sunday night, only some shallow pledgets of lint on the superficies of the orifices; which wounds, I believe, were all curable if he might have rested on a settled place; but being marched in wind and rain, and cold getting into the wounds, must needs cause death. And this I testify under my hand,

William Griffith.

But when his strength began to fail, they carried him upon a bier; and all this not sufficing to take away his life, they threw him off the said bier with such violence that he presently died, having continued in the languishing condition aforesaid from Saturday till Monday following. After his wounding, fresh clothes being brought to him, Sir John would not suffer him to be shifted, and Major-General Mytton sending to desire that he might come to Carnarvon to have his wounds dressed, with engagement that after his recovery he should render himself again prisoner, it was wholly refused, and no answer returned thereunto. Col. Carter, Governor of Conway, Lieut.-Col. Twistleton, Governor of Denbigh, used their best endeavours to suppress the forces raised by Sir John Owen; and having mounted 30 foot foom Denbigh Castle, with Col. Jones's troop, and about 30 volunteers mounted, being some late disbanded officers, and others well-affected in Denbighshire, as also 70 foot and 30 horse forwarded from Col. Duckenfield, Governor of Chester, together with 30 of Col. Carter's soldiers, marched towards Carnarvon, intending before engagement with the enemy to add some of the forces in Carnarvon; but the enemy prevented this, and met them upon Monday, the 5th of this instant month, upon a plain near the sea-side, between Bangor and Aber. The Forlorns of both parties being drawn forth charged each other with great resolution, but ours at last were forced to a disorderly retreat. The enemy pursued with much courage, and were entertained by our reserve, after some long encounter, to their total routing; and on their retreat Capt. Taylor singled out Sir John Owen, and after some short encounter wounded him, and unhorsing him took him prisoner. There were of the enemy slain about 30; whereof three captains—Capt. Madryn, Capt. Morgan, and another, and 58 taken prisoners, most of them of the horse, whereof many of quality, as by the list appeareth. They threw away their arms, most of which were possessed by us. Few of them had escaped, but that our words were somewhat alike in sound, and the signal on both sides the same: their word was

DOCUMENT CXIV. A.D. 1648.

"Resolution," ours "Religion"; the signal was "without bands," (?) so in the disorderly pursuit we knew not each other. About 50 of their horse got away in a body, and carried three of our men with them, whom we hear since they have put to death; it being according to their resolution, as some of the prisoners confessed, not to give quarter to any they took. Sir John Owen, after he was disarmed, upon discourse uttered these words, "though you have defeated me, yet three-score-thousand men now in arms in Essex and Kent will not be baffled therewith;" and seemed therewith much to comfort himself.

By the barbarous and unchristianlike usage aforementioned by the said Sir John Owen and his rebellious crew towards the gallant gentleman, the late High Sheriff of Carnarvon (who with his life gave testimony of his good affection to the Parliament, maugre the late aspersions endeavoured to be fastened upon him by some persons really disaffected both to him and to the Parliament), as also towards others taken by them prisoners, all unbiassed men and of any ingenuity and conscience, may discover their bloody resolution, and others of their stamp, towards the Parliament and their adherents. . . . .

General Mytton's Letter to the Speaker of the House of Commons.

HONOURABLE SIR,

I have sent you enclosed a relation [the foregoing] of the good success God hath been pleased to give unto the force which were coming to join with me (against Sir John Owen), under the command of Col. Carter and Col. Twistleton, as you will find it expressed under their own hands; and surely it was in a mighty seasonable time—the few foot that I had in Carnarvon, which Capt. Simkies turned out of Anglesey, and a very few horse, being tired with continual duty in marching out to endeavour the obstruction of the enemy's raising of men, which, by the help of the late High Sheriff and Thomas Madryn, Esquire, we did very much prevent until Saturday last, when we marched out with a party, where, meeting with the enemy, the Sheriff was taken prisoner and two more private soldiers, and we took a lieutenant and an ensign, and killed one of them.

The next day after the Sheriff was taken, a great part of the county came in to Sir John Owen, and so fast, that if it had not pleased God to give us this victory and deliverance, this county only had not been lost, but also almost all North Wales; the Island of Anglesey being in so distracted (or rather lost) condition; and which I humbly desire may be speedily taken into consideration. I cannot omit to give your Honour a relation of the unchristian-like usage of that gallant gentleman [the Sheriff] by Sir John Owen and some others during the time he was their prisoner. The note here enclosed, under the Surgeon's hand, will demonstrate one part of it. As soon as he was taken I sent a drummer to see whether he was wounded, who brought me word that he was, very sorely. The next morning I sent a letter to Sir John Owen, to desire that he may come to Carnarvon to recover his health, which, if it pleased God that he did, I did engage myself that he should become a prisoner again, unto which, and two letters more, he sent me no answer at all. He also denied to let him receive a suit of clothes that I sent him for shift; those that he was wounded in being exceeding bloody. And he did carry this gentleman along with him every day, all the way he marched, until it pleased God to take him from such bloody tyrants, and put an end unto his time here in the field, as near as possibly could be discerned [to the time] when Sir John was routed and taken prisoner himself.

There be divers other barbarous things spoken of concerning his usage, which I forbear at this time to write unto your Honour of (till I am better informed of the certainty of them), though I am induced to believe many of them.

I am emboldened to give your Honour this relation, though tedious, not doubting but the Honourable House will be pleased to take some speedy course herein, the lives of your servants being so much concerned (if such men shall go unpunished), and amongst the rest, of him, that is,

Your Honour's faithful and most humble servant,

THO. MYTTON.

Carnarvon, the 6th of June, 1648.

A List of the Prisoners, both Officers and Soldiers.

DOCUMENT CXIV.
A.D. 1648.

Sir John Owen, Major-General
Mr. Richard Lloyd, Colonel
Mr. William Owen
Mr. Hugh Bodwrda
Mr. Joshua Cole
Mr. Robert Wynne
Mr. James Kynaston, Captain
Mr. Mathias Lloyd
Mr. John Wantom
Mr. Thomas Lloyd, Lieutenant
Mr. Robert Wynne, Lieutenant
Mr. John Mathews
Mr. Samuel Conway
Mr. William Saunders, Captain
Mr. Gilbert Fox, Captain
Mr. Arthur Stapleton, Cornet
Maurice Griffith, servant to Sir John Owen

William Hide, of *Cheshire*; John Harrison, of *London*; Richard Thomas, John Thomas, William Pym, Robert Jones, William Jones, Hugh Roberts, Robert Davies, Wm. Richard, Rich. George, Owen ap William, of *Carnarvonshire*; Evan Roberts, Thomas Jones, John Davies, Robert Jones, John Hughes, William Davies, of *Denbighshire*; Ralph Davenport, of *Lancashire*, and William Calladу, of *Hertfordshire*; Walter Morgan, of *Gloucestershire*; Christo. Elmore, of *Lincolnshire*; Robert and Wm. Cresswell, Walter Roe, and Tho. Scotchwell, of *Shropshire*; David Williams and Henry Pugh, of *Merionethshire*; Robert Williams, of *Flintshire*; David Ellis, of *Montgomeryshire*; Benjamin Parr, of *Carmarthenshire*; John Morris, of *Cardiganshire*; John and Thos. Cross, Jeffrey Birch, and John Clark, of *Worcestershire*; Richard Baxter, of *Staffordshire*; Isaac Edwards, of *Anglesey*; and John Cadwalader, of *Carmarthenshire*.[1]

[1] From a pamphlet, entitled "A Narrative, with Letters presented by Capt. Taylor to the House of Commons, concerning the late Success, &c., in Carnarvonshire, against Sir John Owen, &c." (K. P. 371—8).

CXV.

An attempt to seize Denbigh Castle, and to rescue Sir John Owen, kept a prisoner there; Detailed in a letter from Chester, July 8, 1648.

We find the King's party still very active in these parts, these in Anglesey who have revolted[1] will not accept of the indemnity but resolve to keep the Island for the King.[2] Sir John Owen is acting in Denbigh Castle, where, with his confederates, the castle was very near being surprised. DOCUMENT CXV. A.D. 1648.

On Monday night last, the Captain of the Guard for Denbigh Castle being gone to bed, they began to act their design. And there was engaged in this business to surprise Denbigh Castle (where Sir John Owen is prisoner), a corporal and a sentinel belonging to the castle, of the Parliament's soldiers, who had, it seems, been wrought upon by those who carried on the design, to whom large promises were made. These men whom we have discovered (besides others whom we cannot yet find out), to have been corrupted by Sergeant-Major Dolben,[3] Capt. Cutler, Capt. Parry, Capt. Charles Chambres,[4] and some others, who were the chief actors in this plot.

There was a party of the Cavaliers that came that night with scaling-ladders, who came privately to the walls, without giving any alarm at all, the corporal and the two sentinels of the guard being privy to their design and confederacy. And about sixty of the Cavaliers had scaled the walls, and were got over without any opposition at all, and were within the walls half an hour at least before any alarm was given; and it was a hundred to one that we had not been all surprised and ruined; but we were

[1] Capt. Thomas Simkies or Symkys, who had been placed by Mytton Governor of Beaumaris Castle, for instance.

[2] See post p. 400.

[3] Dolton in the old pamphlet.

[4] Of the Llysmeirchion family.

DOCUMENT CXV. A.D. 1648.

miraculously delivered. The aforesaid three-score Cavaliers that were got over, were so near entrance into the inner wards of the castle, that they had but only one horse-lock to break, which the corporal was ready to have assisted them in, to open one of the salley ports.

It so pleased God that the Captain of the Guard could not sleep in his bed, but was much troubled, though he knew not for what, and at last he resolved to rise and walk the rounds with his soldiers, for which purpose he did get up accordingly. When he had drawn out some soldiers to walk with him about the rounds, he went with them, until at last he espied a party get over the wall, and scaling-ladders upon the walls; whereupon an alarm was given to the castle, and the town also by this means took an alarm. But they all yielded themselves prisoners at mercy, only some few that had got back again over the wall. And upon search of the business the corporal was discovered to be going with them to help them to open the gate.

I hope this will be a sufficient warning to them all, to look well about them, both in that castle and also in other parts about us.[1]

[1] From a pamphlet, entitled "Denbigh Castle surprised for the King, &c. London: Printed for the general satisfaction of moderate men, 1648." (K. P. 376—4.)

CXVI.

Oliver Cromwell besieges the Town and Castle of Pembroke, and after a long Siege reduces them. May—July, 1648.

A.

Cromwell to the Committee of Carmarthen.

For my Noble Friends the Committee of Carmarthen.

The Leaguer before Pembroke,
9th June, 1648.

GENTLEMEN,

I have sent this bearer to you to desire we may have your furtherance and assistance in procuring some necessaries to be cast in the iron-furnaces in your County of Carmarthen, which will the better enable us to reduce the Town and Castle of Pembroke.

DOCUMENT CXVI. A. A.D. 1648.

The principal things are: Shells for our mortar-piece, the depth of them we desire may be of fourteen inches, and three quarters of an inch. That which I desire at your hands is, to cause the service to be performed, and that with all possible expedition; that so, if it be the will of God, the service being done, these poor wasted counties may be freed from the burden of the Army.

In the next place, we desire some D cannon-shot, and some culverin-shot, may with all possible speed be cast for us, and hasted to us also.

We give you thanks for your care in helping us and [*word lost*]. You do herein a very special service to the State; and I do most earnestly desire you to continue herein, according to our desire in the late letters. I desire that copies of this paper may

DOCUMENT CXVI. A. A.D. 1648.

be published throughout your county, and the effects thereof observed; for the ease of the county, and to avoid the wronging of the countrymen.

Not doubting the continuance of your care to give assistance to the public in the services we have in hand,

I rest your affectionate servant,

OLIVER CROMWELL.[1]

B.

Oliver Cromwell to the Speaker of the House of Commons.

Leaguer before Pembroke, 14th June, 1648.

DOCUMENT CXVI. B. A.D. 1648.

SIR,

All that you can expect from hence is a relation of the state of this garrison of Pembroke, which is briefly thus:—

They begin to be in extreme want of provisions, so as in all probability they cannot live a fortnight without being starved. But we hear that they mutinied about three days since;—cried out "Shall we be ruined for two or three men's pleasure? Better it were we should throw them over the walls." It's certainly reported to us that within four or six days they'll cut Poyer's throat, and come all away to us. Poyer told them Saturday last, that if relief did not come by Monday night, they should no more believe him, nay, they should hang him.

We have not got our guns and ammunition from Wallingford as yet; but, however, we have scraped up a few which stand us in very good stead. Last night we got two little guns planted, which in twenty-four hours will take away their Mills; and then, as Poyer himself confesses, they are all undone. We made an attempt to storm him about ten days since; but our ladders were too short, and the breach so as men could not get over. We lost a few men, but I am confident the enemy lost more. Captain Flower, of Colonel Dean's regiment, was wounded; and Major Grigg's

[1] Carlyle iii., Appendix No. 11.

lieutenant and ensign slain. Captain Burges lies wounded and very sick. I question not but within a fortnight we shall have the town; and Poyer hath engaged himself to the officers of the town not to keep the castle longer than the town can hold out; neither indeed can he, for we can take away his water in two days by beating down a staircase, which goes into a cellar where he hath a well. They allow the men half-a-pound of beef, and as much bread a day, but it is almost spent. DOCUMENT CXVI. B. A.D. 1648.

We much rejoice at what the Lord hath done for you in Kent. Upon our thanksgiving for that victory, which was both from sea and leaguer, Poyer told his men it was the Prince,—Prince Charles and his revelted ships coming with relief. The other night they mutinied in the town. Last night we fired divers houses, which "fire" runs up the town still; it much frights them. Confident I am we shall have it in fourteen days, by starving.

I am, Sir, your servant,

OLIVER CROMWELL.[1]

C.

Troubles in Monmouthshire—Cromwell orders Col. Thomas Saunders (then at Brecon) to arrest Sir Trevor Williams and Mr. Morgan, the Sheriff of Monmouthshire.

'Before Pembroke,' 17th June, 1648. DOCUMENT CXVI. C. A.D. 1648.

SIR,

I send you this enclosed by itself, because it's of greater moment. The other you may communicate to Mr. Rumsey[2] as far as you think fit. And I have written I would not have him or other honest men discouraged, that I think it not fit at present to enter into contests; it will be good to yield a little for public advantage, and truly that is my end, wherein I desire you to satisfy them.

I have sent, as my letter mentions, to have you remove out of

[1] Rushworth, pt. 4, vol. ii., p. 1159. Carlyle, Letter lix.

[2] Of Crickhowell.

DOCUMENT CXVI. C. A.D. 1648.

Brecknockshire; indeed, into that part of Glamorganshire which lieth next Monmouthshire. For this end: We have plain discoveries that Sir Trevor Williams of Llangibby, about two miles from Usk, in the County of Monmouth, was very deep in the plot of betraying Chepstow Castle; so that we are out of doubt of his guiltiness thereof. I do hereby authorize you to seize him, as also the High Sheriff of Monmouth, Mr. Morgan, who was in the same plot.

But because Sir Trevor Williams is the more dangerous man by far, I would have you seize him first, and the other will be easily had. To the end that you may not be frustrated, and that you be not deceived, I think fit to give you some character of the man and some intimations how things stand. He is a man, as I am informed, full of craft and subtlety, very bold and resolute, hath a house at Llangibby well stored with arms and very strong; his neighbours about him very malignant and much for him, who are apt to rescue him if apprehended; much more to discover anything which may prevent it. He is full of jealousy, partly out of guilt, but much more because he doubts some that were in the business have discovered him, which indeed they have; and also because he knows that his servant is brought hither, and a Minister, to be examined here, who are able to discover the whole plot

If you should march directly into that country and near him, it's odds he either fortify his house or give you the slip; so also if you should go to his house and not find him there; or if you attempt to take him and miss to effect it; or if you make any known enquiry after him, it will be discovered.

Wherefore, as to the first, you have a fair pretence of going out of Brecknockshire to quarter about Newport and Caerleon, which is not above four or five miles from his house. You may send to Colonel Herbert, whose house lies in Monmouthshire, who will entirely acquaint you where he is. You are also to send to Captain Nicholas, who is at Chepstow, to require him to assist you if he, Williams, should get into his house, and stand upon his guard. Samuel Jones, who is Quarter-Master to Colonel Herbert's troop, will be very assisting to you, if you send to him to meet you at your quarters, both by letting you know where he is, and also in all matters of intelligence. If there shall be need, Captain Burges's troops, now quartered in Glamorganshire, shall be directed to receive orders from you. You perceive by all this that we are, it may be, a little too solicitous in this business; it's our fault; and, indeed, such a temper causeth us often to overact business. Wherefore, without much ado, we leave it to you, and you to the guidance of God herein; and rest yours, DOCUMENT CXVI. C. A.D. 1648.

OLIVER CROMWELL.

'P.S.'—If you seize him, bring and let him be brought with a strong guard to me. If Captain Nicholas should light on him at Chepstow, do you strengthen him with a strong guard to bring him. If you seize his person, disarm his house, but let not his arms be embezzled. If you need Captain Burges's troop, it quarters between Newport and Chepstow.[1]

D.

Cromwell threatens Richard Herbert (successor of the Lord Herbert, of Cherbury), residing at St. Julian's, Monmouthshire.

Leaguer before Pembroke, 18th June, 1648. DOCUMENT CXVI. D. A.D. 1648.

SIR,

I would have you to be informed that I have good report of your secret practices against the public advantage; by means whereof that arch-traitor, Sir Nicholas Kemeys, with his horse, did surprise the Castle of Chepstow; but we have notable discovery from the papers taken by Colonel Ewer on recovering the castle—that Sir Trevor Williams of Llangibby was the malignant who set on foot the plot.

Now I give you this plain warning by Captain Nicholas and Captain Burges, that if you do harbour or conceal either of the parties, or abet their misdoings, I will cause your treasonable nest to be burnt about your ears.

OLIVER CROMWELL.[2]

[1] Forster iv., 239; Harris, p. 495; Carlyle, Letter lx.

[2] *Monmouthshire Merlin*, Sept. 1845. Carlyle iii., app. 11.

E.

State of Pembroke in the middle of June.

DOCUMENT CXVI. E. A.D. 1648.

Sir,

This town is almost at the last gasp, being much discontented and divided, occasioned by want of victuals; but Col. Poyer studies how to delude the soldiers, declaring to them that before Monday next he will warrant them relief from Major-General Langdale. Our great guns have played against the walls, and a breach was made by battery, and the assault attempted, but fruitless, being repulsed with the loss of 23, and four on their part. Since which time we have had another fight with them upon a sally-forth with their horse. The business was not long in dispute but very hot, and gallantly maintained by both parties; but at the last we put them to flight, killed nine of them, took twenty prisoners, with the loss of few men, it is said. Major-General Laugharne made one amongst them. We also took about thirty horse and some arms. Major-General Laugharne is recovered of his late wounds, and it is supposed there are 2,000 fighting men in the town. We doubt not but to be masters both of Town and Castle very suddenly.

Pembroke, June 19, 1648.[1]

F.

Oliver Cromwell accounts to Lord Fairfax for the length of the Siege.

Before Pembroke, 28th June, 1648.

DOCUMENT CXVI. F. A.D. 1648.

Sir,

I have some few days since despatched horse and dragoons for the North. I sent them by the way of West Chester—thinking

[1] Anonymous. From a pamphlet, entitled "A Dangerous Fight at Pembroke Castle, &c. London: Printed for R. G., 1648." (K. P. 273—21.)

it fit to do so in regard of this enclosed letter, which I received from Colonel Duckenfield, requiring them to give him assistance in the way. And if it should prove that a present help would not serve the turn, then I ordered Capt. Pennyfeather's troop to remain with the Governor [Duckenfield], and the rest immediately to march towards Leeds: and to send to the Committee of York, or to ask him that commands the forces in those parts, for directions whither they should come, and how they shall be disposed of.

The number I sent are six troops: four of horse and two of dragoons; whereof three are Col. Scroop's, and Capt. Pennyfeather's troop, and the other two dragoons. I could not, by the judgment of the Colonels here, spare more, nor send them sooner, without manifest hazard to these parts. Here is, as I have formerly acquainted your Excellency, a very desperate Enemy; who, being put out of all hope of mercy, are resolved to endure to the uttermost extremity; being very many [of them] gentlemen of quality, and men thoroughly resolved. They have made some notable sallies upon Lieut.-Col. Reade's quarter, to his loss. We are forced to keep divers posts, or else they would have relief, or their horse break away. Our foot about them are four-and-twenty hundred: we always necessitated to have some in garrisons.

The country since we sat down before this place have made two or three insurrections, and are ready to do it every day: so that, what with looking to them and disposing of our horse to that end, and to get us in provisions, without which we should starve, this country being so miserably exhausted and so poor, and we [having] no money to buy victuals; indeed, whatever may be thought, it is a mercy we have been able to keep our men together in the midst of such necessity, the sustenance of the foot for the most part being but bread and water. Our guns through the unhappy accident at Berkley[1] not yet come to us, and indeed it was a very unhappy thing they were brought thither; the wind having been always so cross that since [if] they were recovered from sinking they could not [come to us]; and this place not being to be had without fit instruments for battering, except by

[1] Referring, Carlyle conjectures, to the stranding of the vessel that carried the guns at that place.

DOCUMENT CXVI. F. A.D. 1648.

starving. And truly, I believe the enemy's straits do increase upon them very fast, and that within a few days an end will be put to this business; which really might have been done before if we had received things wherewith to have done it. But it will be done in the best time.

I rejoice much to hear of the blessing of God upon your Excellency's endeavours. I pray God that this Nation, and those that are over us, and your Excellency, and all we that are under you, [may discern] what the mind of God may be in all this, and what our duty is. Surely, it is not that the poor Godly people of this Kingdom should still be made the object of wrath and anger; nor that our God would have our necks under a yoke of bondage. For these things that have lately come to pass have been the wonderful works of God; breaking the rod of the oppressor as in the day of Midian—not with garments much rolled in blood, but by the terror of the Lord, who will yet save his people and confound his enemies, as on that day. The Lord multiply his grace upon you, and bless you and keep your heart upright; and then, though you be not comformable to the men of this world, nor to their wisdom, yet you shall be precious in the eyes of God, and He will be to you a horn and a shield.

My Lord, I do not know that I have had a letter from any of your Army of the glorious successes God has vouchsafed you. I pray pardon the complaint made. I long to [be] with you. I take leave; and rest my Lord, your most humble and faithful servant,

OLIVER CROMWELL.

[P.S.] Sir, I desire you that Col. Lehunt[1] may have a commission to command a troop of horse, the greatest part whereof came from the enemy to us; and that you would be pleased to send blank commissions for his inferior officers, with what speed may be.[2]

[1] Col. Lehunt was one of the officers of the revolted Army who did not desert the Parliament.

[2] Sloane MSS., 1519, f. 90. Carlyle's Cromwell, i., Letter 61.

G.

Some Account of the Siege—Of Skirmishes and Storms.

Honoured Sir,

We cannot yet send you that either Pembroke Town or Castle is taken yet; we hope within few days to be masters thereof. We have made several attempts against the town, and stormed the walls in two or three places, fought with the enemy in the town, worsted them, and beat them up to the castle walls, doing great execution throughout the town, and killing near upon 100 of the enemy in the pursuit. But a major of General Cromwell's not following with the reserve of pikes and musketeers according to order, Major-General Laugharne came in the rear of them with a party of horse, and forced them to quit the town, out of which they were driven, and about 30 of our men killed, some few wounded—the rest made good their retreat. Of the enemy, it is supposed their loss was many more, as appears by the confession of divers who have since deserted that service and come in to the Lieut.-General.

DOCUMENT CXVI. G.

A.D. 1648.

In this conflict Colonel Horton behaved himself with much gallantry, and Colonel Okey's dragoons did exceeding good service, who pursued the enemy almost to the very walls, and made good their retreat with very little loss.

Our batteries are now finished, and an ordnance planted against the town and castle, and have made several breaches; and the Council of War have resolved to storm it again. The reason why the siege continues so long is the want of some great guns and mortar-pieces, which came not until within these few days down the Severn—the wind having been long opposed to them.

Captain Flower, of Colonel Deane's regiment, was lately wounded upon a storm, and Major Grey's lieutenant and ensign slain. Capt. Burges is wounded and very sick. . . . . .

The Lieut.-General is alive and in health, and willing to fight for the liberties of England as he ever did formerly.

Tuesday last we gave the town another strong alarm. One hundred and twenty of Poyer's men laid down their arms, vowing never to take them up again; but by the importunity of Poyer and Laugharne telling them, if relief came not within four days they

DOCUMENT CXVI. G. A.D. 1648.

would yield, and they should hang them, they have engaged again. We are informed that they have not provisions for 14 days. We expect every day that most of them will come to us through want—they only have a little rain-water and biscuit left. But it is still feared that Poyer and Laugharne, when they can hold out the town no longer, will betake themselves to the castle, and leave the rest to mercy. If we get the town, we doubt not to carry the castle suddenly.

Our mortar-pieces have played hard against the town, and done great execution; have battered down many houses, and killed at the least 30 of the enemy, as appears by the confession of two of Poyer's men who came over the walls to us.

From the Leaguer before Pembroke, July 4, 1648.[1]

H.

Cromwell's last Letter to Col. Poyer.

DOCUMENT CXVI. H. A.D. 1648.

SIR,

I have (together with my Council of War) renewed my propositions, [and] I thought fit to send them to you with these alterations, which if submitted unto I shall make good. I have considered your condition, and my own duty; and (without threatening) must tell you that if (for the sake of some) this offer be refused, and thereby misery and ruin befall the poor soldiers and people with you, I know where to charge the blood you spill. I expect your answer within these two hours. In case this offer be refused, send no more to me about this subject.

I rest your servant,

OL. CROMWELL.[2]

July 10, at 4 a 'clock
this afternoon, 1648.

[1] From a pamphlet, entitled "A Great and Bloody Fight at Pembroke Castle, &c. Printed at London to prevent mis-information (July 9th), 1648." (K. P. 375—35.)

[2] *Perfect Occurrences*, No. 81. (K. P. 34—7.) This letter is not given in Carlyle's.

I.

Pembroke (Town and Castle) surrendered to Parliament—Oliver Cromwell to the Speaker of the House of Commons.

Pembroke, 11th July, 1648. DOCUMENT CXVI. I. A.D. 1648.

SIR,

The Town and Castle of Pembroke were surrendered to me this day, being the eleventh of July, upon the propositions which I send you here enclosed. What arms, ammunition, victuals, ordnance, or other necessaries of war are in [the] town I have not to certify you—the Commissioners I sent in to receive the same not being yet returned, nor like suddenly to be; and I was unwilling to defer the giving you an account of this mercy for a day.

The persons excepted are such as have formerly served you in a very good Cause; but being now apostatised I did rather make election of them than of those who had always been for the King; judging their iniquity double, because they have sinned against so much light and against so many evidences of Divine Providence going along with and prospering a just Cause, in the management of which they themselves had a share.

I rest your humble servant,

OLIVER CROMWELL.[1]

K.

Articles for the Surrender of Pembroke.

1. That Major-General Laugharne, Col. Poyer, Col. Humphrey Mathews, Capt. William Bowen, and David Poyer, do surrender themselves to the mercy of the Parliament. DOCUMENT CXVI. K. A.D. 1648.

2. That Sir Charles Kemeys, Sir Henry Stradling, Mr. Miles Button, Major Prichard, Lieut.-Col. Stradling, Lieut.-Col. Laugharne, Lieut-Col. Brabazon, Mr. Gamage, Major Butler,

[1] Copy in Tanner MSS. lxii., 159. Carlyle i., Letter 62.

DOCUMENT CXVI. K. A.D. 1648. Major Francis Lewis, Major Mathews, Major Harnish, Capt. Roach, Capt. Jones, Capt. Hugh Bowen, Capt. Thomas Watts, and Lieut. Young, do within six weeks next following depart the Kingdom, and not to return within two years from the time of their departure.

3. That all officers and gentlemen not before-named, shall have free liberty to go to their several habitations, and then live quietly, submitting to the authority of Parliament.

4. That all private soldiers shall have passes to go to the several houses without being stripped, or having any violence done to them —all the sick and wounded men to be carefully provided for, till able to go home, &c.

5. That the townsmen shall be free from plunder and violence, and enjoy their liberties as heretofore they have done, having freedom to remove themselves and families whither they shall think fit, &c.

6. That the Town and Castle of Pembroke, with all the arms, ammunition, and ordnance, together with the victuals and provisions for the garrison, be forthwith delivered unto Lieut.-General Cromwell, or such as he shall appoint, for the use of the Parliament.

(Signed by)

OLIVER CROMWELL.
DAVID POYER.[1]

[1] *Perfect Occurrences*, No. 81. (K. P. 34—7). Collated with the copy given in Rushworth's Hist. Collection, pt. 4, vol. ii., p. 1190.

CXVII.

Revolt in Anglesey, and the suppression thereof. July—Oct. 1648.

Declaration of the Chief Inhabitants of the Island.

We, the inhabitants of the Isle of Anglesey, whose names are hereunto subscribed, after mature consideration and hearty invocation of the name of God for directions and assistance, do remonstrate and declare to our fellow-subjects and neighbours whom it it may concern, that we, having, according to our bounden duty and allegiance, preserved the said Island in due obedience to our most dread Sovereign Lord, King Charles, during the time of this intestine War and Rebellion, and, by God's blessing upon our careful endeavours, defended the same until the enemy had overmastered the whole Kingdom (a few strongholds only excepted); this being the only county of England or Wales, for two months together, kept entire under his Majesty's authority and command; and being then, through the vast number of men and horse threatened to be poured in upon us (finding no possible expectance of relief), enforced to submit to the then prevailing power; do now out of conscience towards God, and loyalty towards His Anointed, with all humbleness prostrate ourselves, our lives, and fortunes, at his Majesty's feet, resolving with the utmost exposal of all that we are, or have, to preserve the said Island, together with the castles and holds therein, in due obedience to his Sacred Majesty, his heirs, and lawful successors, against all rebellious opposers and invaders whatsoever; and do also with sincerity of heart profess that we will, according to our several degrees, places, and calling, maintain the true Protestant religion, by law established, his Majesty's royal prerogatives, the known Laws of the land, the just

DOCUMENT CXVII.
A.D. 1648.

DOCUMENT CXVII. A.D. 1648.

privileges of Parliament, together with our own and fellow-subjects' legal properties and liberties. And we also do further declare and protest, that we shall and will account all those who do, or shall stand, in opposition hereunto, to be enemies and traitors to their King and country, and accordingly to be proceeded against; being most ready to contribute our best abilities for their reducement and the reinstating [of] our gracious Sovereign (who hath long endured the tyranny and oppression of his barbarous and bloody enemies) to his rights, dominions, and dignity, according to the splendour of his most illustrious progenitors.—Given under our hands the 14th day of July, 1648.[1]

(Subscribed) BULKELEY.[2]

Richard Bulkeley[3]	Owen Arthur	Thomas Symkys[13]
William Gryffyth[4]	John Young	Henry Wynne
John Bodvel	John Price	Wm. Wynne
Henry Owen[5]	William Lewis	Rowland Jones
Owen Holland[6]	Rowland White	William Lloyd
Richard Meyrick[7]	Owen Lewis	William Owen
Henry Lloyd[8]	Godfrey Prytherch	Richard Bodychen
Richard Roberts	John Robinson[10]	John Wynne
Hugh Owen[9]	William Bulkeley[11]	Henry Jones
William Owen	Richard Williams	Henry Owen
J. Turbridge	John Lloyd	Henry Lloyd
Owen Gryffyth	Rowland Bulkeley[12]	Richard Wynne

[1] This declaration was penned by Michael Evans, Lord Bulkeley's Chaplain, and Robert Morgan, rector of Llanddyfnan, "who had skill enough to draw it in high swelling words and bitter language, and sublety enough to impose it upon a well-meaning gentry and soldiers, yet wanted discretion to pen it in that wary way and prudent style which the state off affairs at that time did require"—evidently to the regret of Mr. Williams, schoolmaster at Beaumaris in 1669, in whose MSS. it has been preserved.

[2] Thomas, created Viscount Bulkeley by Charles, 1643.

[3] Eldest son of first Lord Bulkeley, who held the commission of Colonel in the Royalist Army, was killed in a duel with Thomas Cheadle on Lavan Sands in 1650. Cheadle was afterwards hanged for it.

[4] D.D. of Garreglwyd, Chancellor of Bangor.

[5] Of Mosoglan, H. S. 1652.

[6] Of Berw.

[7] Of Bodorgan.

[8] Of Bodwiney, H. S. 1659.

[9] Of Bodeon, H. S. 1654.

[10] Probably Col. Robinson, once Governor of Holt Castle.

[11] Of Coyden, H .S. 1637.

[12] Of Porthamel, H. S. 1653.

[13] Once active as a Captain under Mytton.

Articles entered into, concluded, and agreed upon, the 2nd day of October, 1648, between Sir Thomas Myydelton, Knt., Major-General Mytton, Thomas Myddelton, Esq., Simon Thelwall, Esq., and Col. John Jones, of the one part; and Thomas Viscount Bulkeley, Hugh Owen, Owen Wood, Dr. Robert Whyte, Richard Prytherch, Dr. William Gryffydd, Rowland Bulkeley, Owen Holland, William Bold, Richard Owen, Owen Wynne, Henry Owen, Richard Meyrick, Piers Lloyd, John Bodville, William Bulkeley, Esq., Henry Wynne, Jno. Williams, Randolph Wally, Jno. Owen, F. Howell Lewis, gentlemen, on behalf of themselves and the rest of the inhabitants of the Isle of Anglesey, of the other part.

DOCUMENT CXVII.
A.D. 1648.

IMPRIMIS:—It is agreed by and between the said parties that the Viscount Bulkeley, &c., do, on behalf of themselves and the Island of Anglesey, engage and promise to pay to Col. George Twistleton, treasurer, appointed for the present service, the sum of £7,000, of current English money, within 14 days next ensuing, towards satisfaction of two months' pay to the officers and soldiers employed in this present expedition, and other charges incidental. In consideration whereof, they, the said Thomas Myddelton, &c., do engage themselves effectually to mediate with the Parliament that the personal estates of all the inhabitants within the said Island be freed and acquitted from sequestration, from any tax for the 25th part, &c. As touching the real estates of such of the said inhabitants as come within the ordinance of sequestration, they, the said Sir Thomas Myddelton, &c., do likewise engage themselves effectually to mediate with the Parliament, that they be admitted to compound for the same after the rate of two years' value for all estates of inheritance, and proportionably for all other lesser estates.—In witness whereof, we have hereunto put our hands, this 9th day of October, 1648.

INDEX.

ABER, vol. ii., 381
Abbey Cwmhir, vol. i., 275; vol. ii., 219
Abergavenny, i., 271, 272, 298, 318, 323, 370; ii., 257, 259, 268
Abergwili, i., 17
Abermachnant, i., 343; ii., 94, 100
Aberystwith, i., 27, 277, 337, 339, 355; ii., 299, 305, 358
Abrall, Capt. John, ii., 64
Acton, i., 112, 177, 194; ii., 87, 126, 130
Addersley, John, ii., 371
Adams, ii., 64; George, co. Pemb., ii., 164
Aldersey, John, Chester, i., 202
Anglesey i., 48, 71, 80, 184, 290, 332, 343, 366, 405; ii., 71, 89, 93, 161, 162, 308, 312, 385, 399
Apley, Salop, i., 139; ii., 16
Array, Commission of, i., 99; ii., 4, 8
Ashton, Col., ii., 127
Ashton, Cheshire, ii., 196
Astley, Sir Jacob, i., 307, 313, 316, 318, 322, 344, 351, 354; ii., 268, 288
Aston, Sir Thomas, i., 110, 140, 143, 145; ii., 10, 11, 14, 49, 50, 54, 56
Atcham Bridge, ii., 194
Aubrey, Sir John, of Llantrithyd, i., 303
Awst Passage, i., 153, 257

BAGOT, Col., ii., 86
Bala, i., 342
Bangor, Carnarvonshire, ii., 381
Bangor, Flintshire, i., 221; ii., 171, 183
Barlow, co. Pemb., i., 210; ii., 85, 121, 144, 146, 152, 163, 164 n., 276
Barmouth, i., 355
Barthomley Church, ii., 13 n., 116 n.
Bartlett, Capt., ii., 89, 91, 93, 100, 161, 168, 169
Barton Cross, Cheshire, i., 161, 179
Basset, Sir Richard, co. Glam., i., 307 n., 308, 316, 319, 347, 388; ii., 286, 336, 339, 341, 343
Basset, Thomas, William, and Theodore, i., 387; ii., 337
Baxter, Richard, i., 286
Beacons fired, old method of telegraphy, ii., 82
Beales or Beal, Capt., i., 274; ii., 219, (? 346, 378)
Beaumaris, i., 23, 139, 188, 353, 367, 404; ii., 90, 93, 94, 103, 168, 169, 214, 243, 292, 310, 312, 329
Beachley, i., 257, 270; ii., 210
Beckley, ii., 116
Beeston Castle, i., 190, 197, 284, 288, 329, 345; ii., 52, 225, 245, 270
Benbow, Capt., ii., 236
Berrington, Capt., ii., 64
Bettws, Mon., i., 299; ii., 258
Bible in Welsh, i., 17-19, 60, 163
Birch or Byrch, Col., i., 345; ii., 286, 319, 342
Birdwell, Col. John, ii., 175
Birkenhead, Henry, Chester, i., 111; ii., 15, 17
Birket House, Worall, ii., 209
Birt, Robert, co. Carm., ii., 275
Bishops unpopularity of the English, i., 91
Bishop's Palace at Chester, ii., 14
Black Rock, co. Monmouth, i., 230, 300; ii., 258
Blaxton, Sir William, i., 262; ii., 211
Blayney, Sir Arthur, i., 380; ii., 269
Bledwyn, Lt.-Col. John, ii., 176
Book of Sports, i., 67
Booth, Charles, ii., 65
Booth or Boothe, Sir George, i., 179, 192, 195; ii., 45, 48, 99, 101, 127, 181
Boothe, Capt. John, i., 353; ii., 191, 297
Bosworth, Welsh at, i., 9
Boughton, Cheshire, ii., 10, 14
Bowen, James, co. Pemb., ii. 164
Bowen, George, co. Pemb. ii., 85
Bowen, Hugh, Pentre Evan, co. Pemb., ii., 4, 85, 398
Bowen, Phillip, ii., 346
Bowen, Thomas, Treffloyne, co. Pemb., i., 402; ii., 85, 164, 276, 349
Bowen William, ii., 397
Bowyer, Col., i., 285; ii., 235, 297
Bradford, ii., 65
Bradshaw, Edmund and John, ii., 152
Brase Meole, Salop, 194
Brereton, Lord, ii., 56, 60
Brecknock or Brecon, i., 17, 314, 323, 338, 385, 397; ii., 156, 259, 262, 268, 352, 355, 360, 390

Brecknockshire—Privy Seals, i., 37; ship-money, i., 70; contribute men to resist the Scotch, i., 80; not active for the King, i., 312; inclined to be neutral, i., 318; declares for Parliament, i., 338; ii., 284; list of gentry, ii., 285; suppression of insurrection there, i., 397; ii., 355, 360, 390
Brereton, Sir William, i., 101, 102, 136, 140, 142, 143, 159, 172, 179, 181, 184, 195, 199, 226, 238, 243, 246, 268, 285, 288, 290, 295, 326, 328, 343, 345, 353; ii., 49, 51, 53, 54, 86, 93, 99, 101, 103, 110, 116, 127, 138, 166, 185, 196, 201, 235, 242, 292
Bret, Major, i., 150; ii., 64
Bridgend, letter from, ii., 367
Bridgman, Dr., Bishop of Chester, i., 135; ii., 14, 47
Bridgman, Capt., ii., 51, 57
Bridgman, Orlando (afterwards Lord Chancellor), i., 87, 135, 137, 142, 187, 197 n.; ii., 44, 48, 90, 91, 103
Bridgnorth, Salop, i., 126, 332, 352; ii., 15, 139, 263, 271
Brierwood, Recorder of Chester, i., 110 ii., 11, 14 n., 46
Brigges or Brydges, Sir Morton, ii., 122
Bristol, i., 167, 322, 324; ii., 16, 63, 123, 141
Bromley, Henry, ii., 42
Brongwin, co. Mon., i., 299; ii., 258
Brooke or Brook, ii., 64, 166, 198
Broughton, Major, ii., 88; Colonel, i., 178, 200, 203, 251; ii., 125, 137, 202
Brydges, Sir John, co. Heref., i., 347
Buckingham, Duke of, i., 34, 38, 52
Buckley, David, co. Glam., ii., 337
Builth, ii., 360
Bulkeley, Col. Richard, Beaumaris, i., 367, 405; ii., 212, 400, 401
Bulkeley, Thomas (Baron Bulkeley) i., 103, 139, 182, 184, 365, 367, 405; ii., 89, 93, 313, 400, 401
Bunbury, Cheshire, i., 136; ii., 44, 48
Bushell, Thomas, Master of the Mint, i., 26, 116; ii., 30, 31
Burford, Welsh soldiers at, i., 147
Burghall, of Acton, i., 162, 186
Butler, of Pembrokeshire, ii., 85, 152-154, 293, 353, 397
Butler, Sir Francis, ii., 102, 130, 133
Button, Sir Francis, ii., 127
Button, of Cardiff, i., 303; ii., 397
Byron, Sir John (Lord Byron), i., 188, 191, 195, 201, 245, 250, 289, 328, 342, 350, 361, 365, 406; ii., 105, 123, 125, 128, 196, 201-210, 245, 292-97, 309
Byron, Sir Nicholas, i., 143, 188, 196; ii., 53 n., 124, 137
Byron, Sir Robert, i., 183, 188, 192, 195; ii., 98, 116, 117, 131, 227
Byron, Sir William, i., 366; ii., 311
Byron, Col. Gilbert, i., 351

Caergai, i., 342
Caerleon, ii., 390
Caneston Wood, co. Pemb., i., 309, ii., 266
Capel, Lord, i., 159, 161, 171, 176, 177, 187, 188; ii., 86, 94, 99, 105, 123, 216
Caps and Coats at Powis Castle, i., 241; ii., 195
Carbery, Earl of, i., 103; the King's Lieutenant-General for South Wales, i., 120, 164, 172; at Tenby, i., 174; ii., 82; Haverfordwest, *ibid*; prepares to reduce Town of Pembroke, ii., 119, 140; garrisons H. West, Tenby, Carew, and Roch, i., 205; ii., 140; besieges Pembroke, i., 205; is driven from Pembrokeshire, i., 213; ii., 151; resigns his command, i., 214, 230; ii., 275; refuses to join Poyer in revolt, i., 398; ii., 353
Cardiff occupied by Marq. of Hertford, i., 121, 132; ii., 23-25, 139; taken by Gerard, i., 231; ii., 190; visited by the King, i., 300, 301; ii., 259; difficulties there, i., 304-308, 316; ii., 260, 268; taken for Parliament, i., 319, 354; besieged by Royalists, i., 357, 389; ii., 298; in Second Civil War, i., 404; ii., 360
Cardiganshire refuses to join Pembrokeshire to supply a ship for the King, i., 44; refuses to pay loan, i., 46; summoned to pay ship-money, i., 49, 70, 71; refuses, i., 77; has to contribute men for war with the Scotch, i., 80; parliamentarians there, i., 277; mention of, i., 203, 213, 215, 231; ii., 70, 119, 156, 163, 189, 190
Cardigan taken by Gerard, i., 233; ii., 190, 192; regained by the Parliament, i., 277, 280; ii., 228; defeat of Royalists there, i., 291; ii., 229-234; again falls into hands of Royalists, i., 292; ii., 251
Cardigan Bridge broken down, i., 291; ii., 231
Carew Castle, i., 205, 209, 212, 293, 334; ii., 140, 147, 252, 273
Carmarthenshire maintains right of Parliament to vote taxes, i., 42; want of ships there, 43; contributes to the loan, i., 46; ship-money assessment, i., 49, 70; provides men for war with the Scotch, i., 80; mention of, i., 164, 203, 213, 231, 233, 398; ii., 119, 163, 274-278
Carmarthen—Meeting of Royalists there, i., 204; deserted by them, ii., 147; Col. Laugharne goes thither, i., 214; ii., 148, 156, 161 n.; and takes the town, i., 215;

retaken by Gerard, i., 232; and again won by Laugharne, i., 336; ii., 273-278; letter from, ii., 335; ii., 346, 351, 355, 359; i., 407; ii., 387
Carmarthen Free School, i., 23
Carnarvonshire, i., 71, 80 n., 109, 112, 351; Sir T. Myddelton appointed Major-General, ii., 71
Carnarvon—Imports, ii., 214.
Carnarvon Castle — Prynne a prisoner there, i., 61
Carnarvon besieged by Mytton and taken, i., 365; ii., 307, 309; social condition of, ii., 329; during second Civil War, i., 411; ii., 380
Carne of Ewenny, co. Glam., not favourable to the King, i., 303; revolts from Parliament, i., 356; ii., 298
Carne, cornet, ii, 65
Carrow, Morris, ii., 85; Hugh, i., 232; ii., 191
Carter, Col. John, i., 361, 366; ii, 297, 301, 309, 328
Castlemartin, i., 174, 175, 234
Caus Castle, Salop, i., 139
Cave, Sir Richard, ii., 69
Cefnon, co. Glam., i, 306
Cemmaes, co. Pemb. i., 175
Chambers, Capt., i., 405; ii., 325, 385
Chapman, Capt., ii., 88.
Charles I. See King
Charles, Prince, presented with £100 in Chester, i., 118; ii., 14; visits Raglan, i., 123; ii., 26; the King's solicitude for him, i., 314
Charlton of Apley, ii., 16
Cheadle, John, co. Carnarvon, ii., 214
Chepstow, i. 153, 257, 273, 322, 339, 357, 398; ii., 66, 130, 217, 279, 320, 367, 375, 376, 390
Cheshire, gentlemen of, oppose Privy Seal Loans, i., 37; pay ship-money, i., 73, 80; declares against Array, i., 102
Chester, i., 62, 63, 102, 110, 186, 201, 218, 239, 247, 284, 289, 294, 326, 343, 350, 353; ii., 8, 10, 11, 13, 15, 17, 43, 51, 53, 90, 93, 103, 104, 123, 214, 242, 245, 269, 270, 282, 287, 292, 378, 381
Chester, alluded to, i., 106, 135; ii., 177, 180, 199, 201, 214, 225
Chester, Mayor of, i., 187, 202, 351; ii., 98, 104, 109
Chester, letters from, ii., 14, 17, 111, 116, 130, 133
Chirk, i., 139, 143 n., 162, 180, 221, 276, 327, 332; ii., 171, 173, 174, 269, 271
Cholmondeley, Lady, i., 314; ii., 47, 184
Cholmondeley, Lord, i., 102, 110, 141, 187; ii., 10, 14, 15, 17, 59, 113
Chomley House, Cheshire, i., 190; ii., 184
Chomley, Capt., ii., 51
Christleton, ii., 225
Churches defaced in Denbighshire, i., 181; ii., 114
Churchyard on the condition of Wales, i., 21
Cilgerran, trained bands from, i., 175; ii., 83
Cirencester, Welsh soldiers at capture of, i., 147
Cledey, co. Pembroke, i., 292; ii., 253
Cloth, manufacture of, i. 25
Clytha, co. Mon., ii., 258
Coal Mines, i., 25, 27
Coford, Forest of Dean, i., 149; ii., 63
Colby Moor, i., 308, 321, 399; ii., 157, 266, 292
Common Prayer Book translated into Welsh, i., 18; torn at Hawarden Church, ii., 114
Congleton, Cheshire, i., 140; ii., 49
Coningsby, Governor of Hereford, i., 139, 153; ii., 69, 255
Conway, Archbishop of York fortifies, i., 139; ii., 94; a refuge for the clergy, i., 375; ii., 114; in want of cannon, ii., 168; Sir John Owen appointed the Governor of, i., 217; besieged and taken by Mytton, i., 375, 379; ii., 325, 327, 328; ferry, ii., 94; letters from, ii., 93, 99, 168, 216
Corbett, Sir Vincent, i., 137, 141; ii., 42, 50
Corbet, Pelham, Roger, and Thomas, Royalists, ii., 43
Corbet, Sir John, i., 101, 160, 170; John and Robert, of Stanwardine, Parliamentarians, ii., 122
Cornwall, Sir Richard, ii., 122
Council of the Marches, Court of the, established by Ed. IV., i., 10; abolished, i., 86
Cowbridge, co. Glam., i., 387; ii., 336-7
Cozens, Patrick, ii., 346, 358
Cradock, Walter, and the Book of Sports, i., 67
Creek, co. Mon., i., 300; ii., 259
Crew Hall, Cheshire, i., 190; ii., 12, 13 n., 128
Crofts, Sir William, ii., 69
Cromwell, Oliver, his first speech in Parliament, i., 53; stopped from going to America, 66; an Independent, i., 282, 292; his Welsh ancestry, i., 306, 378; at capture of Bristol, i., 325; sent to Wales to suppress second Civil War, i., 403; ii., 365, 375; takes Carmarthen, besieges Pembroke, and reduces it, i., 407-16; ii., 387, 398
Cromwell, letters of, from before Pembroke, ii., 387-394, 396, 397
Crow Meole, Salop, ii., 194
Cuney, Capt. (co. Pemb.), ii., 147, 152

Dabridgecourt, Sir Thomas, ii., 139, 272
Dallison, Sir Thomas, i., 241; ii., 194, 195
Dalton, Major (Hereford), ii., 70
Darfold Hall, Cheshire, ii., 87, 128
Daugleddau, i., 175
Davenport of Woodford, ii., 62, 88, 175
Davies, Dr. Richard, Bishop of St. David's, i., 17
Davies, Capt. (Flintshire), i., 186; ii., 104
Dawkins, Capt., ii., 266
Delamere Forest, Cheshire, i., 194, 243; ii., 126, 196.
Delves, Sir Thomas, i., 110; ii., 11, 12
Denbighshire — Ship-money, i., 71, 73; men for war with Scotch, i., 80; i., 114; ii., 71, 93, 99, 216; faithful to the Parliament in 1648, i., 409; ii., 370
Denbigh, i., 104, 182, 331, 342, 343, 361, 364, 379; ii., 95, 96, 177, 271, 282, 292, 301, 306, 328, 371, 372, 381; an attempt to rescue Sir John Owen from the castle, ii., 385
Denbigh, Earl of, i., 160, 164, 218, 221, 222, 224-227, 239, 266, 282, 284; ii., 166, 171, 182, &c.
Derby, Lord, death of, i., 141; ii., 15.
Dewsland, co. Pemb., i., 175.
Digby, Lord, i., 242, 298, 301, 325, 332, 353; ii., 243, 245, 259, 264, 270
Doddington House, i., 190
Dolgelly, i., 343
Dolguog, i., 30, 385
Done, Sir Ralph, ii., 127
Donnell, Col. Rich., Governor of Swansea, ii., 353, 378
Drayton. See Market Drayton
Duckenfield, Col., ii., 198, 381, 393
Duddleston, victory obtained by Mytton at, i., 221; ii., 171

Eccleshall Castle, i., 172
Edghill, battle of, i., 126; a satire on conduct of Welsh thereat, ii., 36
Edmunds, Capt. Francis, ii., 152
Edwardes, Captain John, Scalyham, co. Pemb., ii., 4, 85, 143
Edwardes, Thomas, various, i., 366, 380; ii., 43, 308, 312, 333
Edwards, Alderman of Chester, i., 102, 141; ii., 15 n.
Egerton, Peter, ii., 101
Egerton, Richard, of Ridley, Salop, i., 110; ii., 10
Egerton, Major-General, in Pembrokeshire, i., 308; ii., 183, 266; at Carmarthen, i., 334
Ellesmere, Salop—Cavaliers surprised there by Mytton, i., 196; ii., 122, 173, 179
Elliot, John, co. Pemb., i., 176; ii., 4, 85, 121, 164
Elliot, ii., 106, 325
Ellis, Col., i., 143, 164; ii., 55, 56, 202
Emlyn. See Newcastle-Emlyn
Erbury, Wm., Vicar of Cardiff, and the Book of Sports, i., 67
Ernley, Sir Michael, i., 183, 187, 195, 248, 266, 286; ii., 98, 103, 107, 117, 127, 130, 133, 208, 237
Essex, Earl of, at Worcester, i., 100, 107, 112; at Edghill, i., 127, 155, 157; raises siege of Gloucester, i., 169; gives up his commission, i., 284.
Ewer, Col., reduces Chepstow, i., 411; ii., 375
Eyton, Capt., 62
Eyton, Sir Robert and Sir Thomas, ii., 42

Fairfax, Sir Thomas, raises siege of Nantwich, i., 193; ii., 126; intercepted letter of, ii., 138; before Leicester, ii., 256; appointed chief command, i., 284; his success in the West, i., 322; ii., 259; takes Bristol, *ibid*; takes Raglan, i., 374; ii., 318-322
Fairfax, Sir William, at Nantwich, i., 194; ii., 127, 291; killed before Montgomery, i., 251; ii., 202
Falkland—His reply to Flintshire Royalists, ii., 2; his death at Newbury, i., 169
Fashionable gatherings in county towns, i., 31, 102
Fellowship of Bristol, captured at Milford, ii., 76
Fen's Hall, ii., 179
Fleming, Col., sent to take Pembroke Castle from Poyer, who refuses to disband, i., 396; ii., 344, 347, 350, 352, 356
Fleetwood, Sir Richard, ii., 127
Fleming, Wm., co. Glam., ii., 337
Flintshire — Ship-money, i., 71, 72, 77; war with Scotland, i., 80; petition of Royalists, i., 104; ii., 2, 71, 99; faithful to Parliament, i., 409; ii., 370
Flint Castle, i., 180, 184; besieged by Mytton, i., 365; ii., 306, 308
Flint Church defaced by Roundheads, ii., 115 n.
Fonmon Castle, Glam., ii., 361, 365
Forest of Dean, i., 138, 149; ii., 63, 67
Foulkes, Sergt. Richard, ii., 172
Fowler, of Abbey Cwmhir, i., 275; ii., 219
Fox, Sergt.-Major, ii., 64; Col., ii., 176
Frampton Passage, i., 151; ii., 63
Franklin, Lieut. Richard, ii., 176
Frazer, Major, ii., 173
Frodsham, Cheshire, i., 243; ii., 196
Furniture at Raglan Castle, ii., 27
Gainsford, Capt., ii., 64
Games, Edward, co. Brecon, i., 338; ii., 285; joins insurrection in 1648, i., 397; ii., 355

Gamul, Sir Francis, Chester, i., 135, 197 n., 358, 330; ii., 46, 270
Gardiner, Sir Thomas, i., 247
Gay Meadow, Shrewsbury, ii., 18
Gerard, Col. Charles, succeeds Earl Carbery in South Wales, i., 216; lands at Black Rock, Mon., i., 230; ii., 190; drives the enemy into Pembrokeshire, i., 230-236; ii., 190; his character, i., 237; news of his intention to go to N. Wales, ii., 214; called by Rupert to Bristol, i., 240; his cruelties in South Wales, i., 252; goes to Worcester, i., 257, 267, 273; ii., 217; reported to be present at Cardigan, ii., 229-234; assists Rupert to relieve Beeston and returns to South Wales, i., 288, 290; ii., 240; his doings there, and his character, i., 302; denounced at Cardiff and is removed from command, i., 305, 307; accompanies the King from Cardiff to Ludlow, i., 314; ii., 262; present at Rowton Heath, i., 330; stands up for Prince Rupert, and with him goes abroad, i., 334
Gerard, Sir William, ii., 329
Gethin, Capt., ii., 325
Gibbon, George, co. Glam., ii., 337
Gibson, Capt. Edward, ii., 197
Gibson, Col., lands from Ireland in North Wales, i., 183; ii., 98, 102, 107, 117, 127, 129, 132, 227
Giffard of Chillington, i., 172
Gilmore, Major, i., 143; ii., 55
Glamorganshire suffers from pirates, i., 37; summoned to pay ship-money, i., 49, 70, 75; stands alone in its readiness to pay ship-money, i., 78; contributes men to war with Scotch, i., 80; offers resistance to the King, i., 303; ii., 260; list of the chief inhabitants, with value of their estates, ii., 260; list of garrisons, ii., 262; never dealt in the militia, *ibid*; the people there from the Pembrokeshire forces, i., 317, 323; ii., 268; declare for the Parliament, i., 338; revolt i., 356; ii., 298; fresh revolt, i., 387; ii., 335-343; second Civil War, i., 405; ii., 360-369 390
Glamorgan, Earl of, i., 103, 122; his dealings with the Irish Catholics, i., 322, 343, 349; ii., 265
Glasbury, ii., 361
Gloucester—Welsh under Lord Herbert defeated at, i., 148-150; Welsh at second siege of, i., 158
Godwyn, Dr., ii., 70
Golden Grove, i., 46; Dr. Jeremy Taylor there, i., 278; ii., 259
Goodrich Castle, ii., 217
Grandison, Lord, i., 112; ii., 12, 13, 17, 19
Green, Capt., ii., 53
Gresmond, co. Mon., ii., 256
Griffiths, M.P. for Beaumaris, i., 87
Griffith, Sergt-Major, ii., 64
Griffiths, Capt., co. Cardigan, ii., 395
Grosvenor, Lt.-Col., ii., 197
Gunpowder manufactured at Raglan, ii., 321
Gunter, ii., 147, 285
Gwesaney, co. Flint, ii., 242
Gwyn, Howell, High-Sheriff of Brecon-shire, ii., 285
Gwyn, Richard, co. Glam., ii., 337
Gwynne, David, Glanbran, co. Carm., ii., 121, 153, 154
Gwynne, George, co. Carm., ii., 275-278
Gwynne, John, Governor of Tenby, i., 112; ii., 146, 153, 154
Gwynne, Rowland, of Taliaris, ii., 121, 275

Halton Heath, Cheshire, i., 110; ii. 10
Hammond, Col., ii., 320; Major, ii., 127
Hammond, co. Salop, ii., 16
Hamond, Edward, ii., 102
Hampden, John, i., 159
Handbridge burnt, i., 182; ii., 242
Hanmer, Sir Thomas, i., 143 n., 161; Sir John, i., 290; Roger, ii., 372
Hanmer, Flintshire, i., 161
Harlech Castle besieged by Mytton, i., 380; ii., 332; is the last garrison in England and Wales to give in, i., *ibid*; ii., 328, 332
Harley, Sir Robert, ii., 255
Harries, ii., 42, 121
Haslerig, Sir Arthur, ii., 66
Hastings, Col., i., 172; ii., 48, 86
Haverfordwest, i., 41; loans, i., 46; ship-money, i., 72, 77; receives Earl Carbery, i., 175; ii., 83; and is garrisoned, i., 205; ii., 140; quitted by Cavaliers on loss of Pembroke, i., 210; ii., 144; regained by Gerard, i., 234, 246, 292; ii., 192, 249-254; again captured by Laugharne, i., 310; ii., 266; alluded to, i., 336; ii., 305
Hawarden Castle betrayed to the Parliament, i., 180; ii., 99; besieged by Royalists, i., 185, 186, 197; ii., 103, 106, 112, 113; besieged by Brereton, i., 290; ii., 242, 246; visited by the King, i., 331; ii., 271
Hayward, George, ii., 164
Heath, Sir Robert, ii., 30
Henllan, co. Pembroke, i., 174; ii., 340
Herbert, Lord of Raglan. See Glamorgan, Earl of
Herbert, Lord of Cherbury, i., 197 n., 242, 248; ii., 201

Herbert, Sir Pierce, ii., 194
Herbert, William, of Cogan Pool, i, 87; killed at Edghill, i., 129
Herbert, William, of Cardiff, i., 121, 139
Herbert of Colebrooke, co. Mon., i., 324; ii., 257, 268, 319
Herbert, Morgan, ii, 154
Herbert, Richard, St. Julian's ii., 391
Herefordshire in hands of Royalists, i., 134; contributes men for war with Scotland, i., 80; list of gentlemen, ii., 255; price of food there, ii., 256; entered by the Scotch, ii., 259 rising of club-men, i, 289; ii., 359
Hereford, i., 134, 153, 289, 297, 299, 321, 325, 345; ii., 39, 69, 217, 246, 255, 268, 286
Hertford, Marquis of, Commander-in-chief in South Wales, i., 100, 120; takes Cardiff, i., 121; ii., 23-25; raises forces in Wales, i., 131; ii., 38; is defeated at Tewkesbury, i., 32; ii., 39; differences between him and Lord Herbert, i., 145; attacks Hereford, i., 134; at Cirencester, i., 147
Heylin, Peter, i., 60
Heylin, Rowland, i, 60, 63
High Commission Court, i., 64; abolished, i., 86
High Ercal, Salop, i., 118, 266, 351; ii., 288
Highman, co. Gloucester, i., 150; ii., 63
Holcroft, John, ii., 101
Holland, Col., ii., 127
Holm Lacy, Hereford, ii., 269
Holmes, Randle, Chester, i., 189, 201
Holt, Cheshire, garrisoned for the King and taken by Parliament, i., 179; ii., 99, 103; quitted, i., 185, 288, 328; castle besieged by Mytton, i., 363, 380; ii., 302, 306, 308, 328
Holyhead, ii., 94, 100
Holywell Church pillaged, and town full of Papists, i., 180, 181, 184; ii., 111, 115
Hoo Heath, Cheshire, ii., 12
Hooke or Hookes, ii., 65, 175, 176
Hooper, Capt., ii, 319
Horton, Royalist, ii., 62, 185
Horton, Col., sent to repress second Civil War in Wales, i. 396; ii, 351; takes Brecknock, i., *ibid*; ii., 355; advances into Carmarthenshire, i., 400; ii., 352; enters Glamorganshire, ii., 360; defeats Laugharne and Poyer at St. Fagans, i., 404; ii, 365, 369; takes Tenby, ii., 377; assists before Pembroke, ii., 395
Hughes, Capt., ii., 366
Hunckes, Sir Fulke, Governor of Shrewsbury, i, 183, 203, 224, 226, 240, 251; ii., 98, 102, 117, 136, 194
Hunt, Capt. Thomas, ii., 65, 122, 123
Hurleton, Capt., ii, 62
Huson, a spy minister at Shrewsbury, ii., 236

Irish, peace made with, i., 183; forces to be sent over to Chester and Beaumaris, i., 183; ii., 90; their destitute condition, ii., 90; land in Flintshire, i., 183; ii., 98, 109; Brereton attempts to win them over, ii., 101; preparations for their clothing, ii., 104; more transports, i., 188; ii., 125; defeated at Nantwich, i., 126 195,; some revolt to the Parliament, i., 198; ii., 137; cruelty towards them, ii., 161; routed before Montgomery, i., 250; ii., 202; ordnance of Parliament against them, i., 255
Iron furnaces at Carmarthen, i., 412; ii., 387

Jeffreys, Col. John, of Abercynrig, co. Brecon, i., 338, 347; ii., 286
Jeffreys, Herbert, ii., 368
Jenkins, David of Hensol, Glamorganshire. See Jenkins, Judge
Jenkins, Judge, i., 216, 254, 387; ii., 286, 341
Jenkins, co. Cardigan, i., 418
Johnston, co. Pembroke, i., 210; ii., 143
Jones, Sir Philip, Llanarth, Mon, i, 347; ii., 286, 298
Jones, Col. John, the Regicide, i., 243 n.; ii., 308, 312, 381
Jones, Capt. John, of Nanteos, i., 355, 395; ii., 351 (?), 337
Jones, Col. Michael, i., 244, 246, 344; ii., 197, 198, 226, 282, 297
Jones, Col. Philip, of Swansea, i., 243 n., 354, 401, 417; ii., 361
Jones, Owen, ii., 172. Thomas, of Newport, Pemb., ii., 164, 276
Jones, Lieut. Richard, ii., 141, 152
Jones, of Castlemarch, Carnarvon, ii., 214
Jordan, Capt., of the *Expedition*, ii., 76

Keme, Capt., ii., 173-175
Kemes. See Commaes
Kemet, a swordmaker at Hornslow, ii., 68
Kemeys, Sir Charles, i., 358, 388, 415; ii., 299, 339, 342, 397
Kemeys, Col. Edward, ii., 378
Kemeys, Sir Nicholas, i., 406, 408; ii., 375
Kemeys, Capt., ii., 65
Kerry, co. Montgomery, ii., 219
Kidwelly, i., 231
Kilmurry, Lord, i., 135, 137; ii., 45, 47
Kilrhedyn, Pemb., i., 292; ii., 253

Kinderton, Cheshire, ii., 59
King, the, and the Parliament—Disputes between, i., 34-96; quits London, i, 94; Welsh sympathy with, i., 104; sets up standard at Nottingham, i, 107; at Shrewsbury, Chester, Whitchurch, i., 109; ii., 10; his reception at Chester, i., 110-114; commits disaffected persons, ii, 11; at Wrexham, i., 114; ii., 14; back at Shrewsbury, i., 115; ii., 18; departs thence, i., 126; ii., 30; at Edgehill, i., 127; at Oxford, ii., 31; his letter to Bushell, ii., 31; makes peace with the Irish, i., 183; ii., 90; raises siege of Chester, i., 294; his sojourn in South Wales after Naseby, i., 296-316; ii., 255-263; his failure to recruit in South Wales commented upon by the press, i., 319; his second visit to South Wales, i., 321; ii., 268-271; his army defeated on Rowton Heath, i., 330; sojourns in N. Wales, i, 331; intends to stay in Wales, i., 332; ii., 264; flies to the Scotch, i., 371; ii., 315; orders capitulation of garrisons, ii., 316; consents to surrender of Denbigh Castle, ii., 331
Kinnersley, Hercules, ii., 122
Knight, Thomas, ii., 122
Knocking, i., 292
Knowles, Lieut., ii., 65
Knutsford, i., 225; ii., 177, 179, 181, 185
Kynaston, Edward, ii, 42; Roger, ii, 43
Kyrle, Col., i., 259, 341; ii. 210, 281, 342

Lambert, Col., ii., 127
Lampeter, co. Cardigan, i., 275, 292; ii., 219 n., 252
Langdale, Sir Marmaduke, i., 288, 322, 328; ii., 200, 270
Laud, Archbishop, i., 52, 55, 59, 64, 65
Laugharne, John, of St. Brides, i., 140, 210; ii, 4, 143, 164 n.
Laugharne, Major-General Rowland, at Pembroke for the Parliament, i., 140; ii., 141; attacks Carew, i., 207; ii., 141; takes Stackpole and Treffloyne, the Pill, Haverfordwest, and Tenby, i., 208, 209; ii., 141-145; is driven back to Pembroke by Gerard, i., 230-236; takes Laugharne Castle, i., 274; Cardigan Castle, i., 277, 291; ii., 228; and while before Newcastle-Emlyn is defeated by Gerard, i., 292; ii., 230, 240, 249; loses Haverfordwest and retires to Pembroke and Tenby, i., 293; ii., 248-254; victory on Colby Moor, i., 308; ii, 273; takes Carew, Manorbier, Picton, and Carmarthen, i., 335-338; ii, 273-278; in Brecknockshire, i., 338; ii., 285; besieges Aberystwith, i., 355; ii., 299; relieves Cardiff Castle, i, 358; ii, 299; suppresses fresh revolt in Glamorganshire, i., 359; ii., 335-340; is rewarded, i., 359; refuses to disband and revolts from Parliament, i., 393, 397; ii., 354, 360-364; at St. Fagans, i., 404; ii., 365; taken prisoner at Pembroke, i., 415; ii., 397; sentenced to die, 417; goes beyond the sea, i., *ibid*
Laugharne, Major Thomas, ii., 147, 152, 369
Laugharne, William, ii., 85, 164
Laugharne Castle, i., 234, 274; ii, 190, 192, 228
Lee, Sir Richard, ii, 42; Cornet, ii., 65; Launcelot, ii., 122
Lee Bridge, i., 178; ii., 88
Legge, Col William, i., 167, 202, 245, 325, 328; ii., 216, 269
Leigh, ii, 167, 197, 296
Leonard, ii., 176
Lewis, David, of Gernos, ii., 164 n.
Lewis, Capt. George, ii., 146, 153
Lewes, James, co. Pembroke, ii., 85, 121
Lewis or Lewes, Col. James, of Coedmore, i., 337; ii, 164 n., 274, 349
Lewis, Sir John, of Coedmore, objects to ship-money, i., 43, 71
Lewis, John, ii., 275; Lodwick, ii., 121
Lewis, Sir William, of Llangorse, i., 170
Lingen, ii, 64, 65
Llanarth, co. Mon., ii., 298
Llancarvan, ii., 365
Llandaff, i., 91; ii., 343, 361
Llandisilio, co. Montg., i., 333; ii., 271
Llandenis, i., 333; ii., 271
Llandovery, i., 67; ii., 156
Llandreinio, ii., 271
Llanelly, ii., 155
Llanfyllin, ii., 269
Llangibby, co. Mon., i., 318; ii., 217
Llangendeyrn, co. Carm., i., 337; ii., 275
Llangollen, ii., 269
Llanidloes, i., 292
Llantrisant, co. Glam., ii., 260
Llanybyther, ii., 156
Lloyd of Shropshire, i., 160; ii., 62, 122, 176
Lloyd, Sir Francis, i., 197 n., 209, 347; ii., 121, 143, 144, 152, 275, 286, 369
Lloyd, Sir Marmaduke, i., 347, 369; ii., 286
Lloyd, Sir Richard, i., 115, 125, 179, 328; ii., 14, 270
Lloyd, Sir Walter, i., 197 n.; ii., 121
Lloyd, co. Cardigan, ii., 156 164, 275
Lloyd, Griffith, Maesyneuadd, Merionethshire, i, 74
Lloyd, Hugh, co. Radnor, i., 276; ii., 175, 220, 360

Lloyd, Hugh, Foxhall, Denbighshire, i., 73
Lloyd of Kilrhuc, ii., 164
Lloyd, Lewis, of Wernos, co. Breck., i., 338; ii., 360
Lloyd of Llanworda, i., 139
Loans, illegal, raised by the King, i., 44-47
Long Parliament, meeting of, i., 84
Lort, of co. Pemb., i., 164, 208, 350; ii., 4, 85, 142, 163, 164, 276, 349
Lothian, Adjudant, i., 344; ii., 181, 184, 226, 282, 297
Love, Christopher, of Cardiff, i., 283
Lovelace, i., 232, 337; ii., 273
Ludlow, ii., 180, 202
Lyster, Sir Thomas, i., 118; ii., 42

MACCLESFIELD, i., 290
Mackworth, Humphrey, i., 160; ii., 122, 123
Madock, ii., 65
Madrin, ii., 176
Mainwaring, Dr., Bishop of St. David's, i., 52
Mainwaring, i., 111, 137, 161; ii., 15, 17, 45, 181, 227
Malpas, Cheshire, i., 246; ii., 198
Manorbier Castle, Pemb., i., 335
Mansel, Bushey, co. Glam., i., 404; ii., 360
Marbury, i., 137; ii., 45
Marches, Court of the Council of the, i., 86
Market Drayton, i., 172, 201, 295; ii., 87, 173
Marrow, ii., 88
Marrow, Col., 226, 243; ii., 107, 173, 179-188, 196
Marston Moor, i., 227, 238
Marychurch, Capt. Wm., co. Pemb., ii., 152, 346
Mason, ii., 62, 302, 306
Massey of Coddington, ii., 62
Massey, General (Governor of Gloucester), i., 148, 167, 257, 259, 270, 272; ii., 67, 210, 211, 219
Mathavarn, co. Merion., i., 275; ii., 219
Maurice, Prince, in N. Wales, i., 284-289
Maxie, ii., 200
Meldrum, Sir John, i., 249; ii, 178, 204
Mennes, Sir John, i., 240; ii., 136, 137, 168
Merionethshire and ship-money, i., 49, 71, 73; Scotch War, i., 80, 275; Royalists there, i., 342; ii., 71
Merrick, William and Rice, co. Glam., ii., 337
Middlewich, Cheshire, i., 143, 190, 191; ii, 54-61, 116, 128, 131, 198
Middleton, Henry, co. Carm., ii., 121, 275, 279
Milburn of Wonastow, Mon., i., 262
Milford Haven, i., 43, 165, 173, 206, 216, 274, 309; ii., 76, 141, 189, 219, 249
Militia, the question of the, i., 95, 99; Committee of in Pembrokeshire, i., 100; ii., 4
Milton Green, Cheshire, ii., 10
Mint at Shrewsbury, i., 117; ii., 30
Miskin, co. Glam., ii., 336
Mold, i., 180, 344; ii, 99, 282
Monk, Col. (afterwards General), made prisoner at Nantwich, i., 195; ii, 127, 129, 132
Monmouthshire refuses to pay unsanctioned subsidies, i., 42: no ships there, 43; levy of men for war with Scotland, i., 80; forces levied there by M. of Hertford, i., 122; by Lord Herbert, i., 149, 154, 258; lukewarmness, i., 261; ii., 139; list of chief inhabitants, ii., 257; of garrisons, ii., 256, 258; not active for the king, i., 312, 318, 323; rising of clubmen under Sir Trevor Williams, i., 340; ii., 279; revolt there, ii., 298, 299, 359, 360, 367, 390
Monmouth, i., 153, 259, 272, 322, 340, 341; ii., 66, 210, 217, 268, 279, 298, 342
Montford Bridge, ii., 174, 183, 194
Montgomery, i., 242, 248, 252, 264; ii., 201-209, 212, 214
Montgomeryshire—Ship-money, i., 71, 80, 275; ii., 71; keeps aloof from second Civil War, ii., 373
Moore, Edward, ii., 122; Richard, *ibid*; Samuel, *ibid*; i., 286
Morgan, Col. Thomas, Governor of Gloucester, i., 339, 341, 347; ii., 279-281, 286, 314-320, 353 n
Morgan, Sir Wm., Tredegar, i., 300; of Machen, i., 324; ii. (?), 390
Morgan, i., 240, 347; ii., 28, 64, 156, 164, 286
Morton, ii., 173
Morton, Corbet, i., 288; ii., 235
Mostyn, co. Flint, i., 180, 184
Mostyn, various, i., 186, 197 n.
Mostyn, Col. Sir Richard, i., 104, 112, 142, 290, 350; ii., 104, 246, 291
Moulton, Capt., i., 216, 235, 236, 273; ii., 159, 191
Myddelton, Sir Hugh, i., 162
Myddelton, Sir Thomas, i., 60, 101, 139, 162, 170, 172, 176, 179, 182, 184, 190, 219, 221, 239, 247, 248, 264, 275, 292, 342; ii., 71, 86, 93, 95, 99, 101, 103, 138, 166, 175, 178, 179-181, 189, 194, 203, 212, 226, 246, 371
Myddelton, Sir William, i., 342; ii., 177, 226, 328
Mytton, General Thomas, i., 160, 172, 176, 196, 219, 221, 222, 224, 240, 248, 268, 285, 287, 344; ii., 86, 87, 123, 166, 171, 175-177, 179-188, 194, 235, 282, 301, 306, 309, 325, 328, 332, 380-384

NANNEY, Capt. John, i., 343
Nantwich, Cheshire, i., 112, 140, 144, 161, 172, 185, 190, 192, 224; ii., 12, 33, 43, 49, 51-53, 126-133, 166, 175, 177, 179, 194, 196, 198, 225, 270
Narberth, co. Pembroke, i., 175; ii., 83
Neath, co. Glamorgan, ii., 352
Neutrality in Cheshire, i., 136, 137; ii., 44
Newcastle-Emlyn, i., 234, 277, 337, 339; ii., 190, 192, 230, 248-254, 358
Newport, Francis, i., 87; ii., 180, 181
Newport, Lord Richard, i., 118; ii., 30
Newport, Salop, i., 294
Newport, Mon., ii., 390
Newspapers, remarks on, i., 97, 230, 319
Newtown, i., 247, 327; ii., 219, 269
Nichols, ii. 122 n., 329
Northop Church, i., 181, 290; ii., 111
North Wales, outbreak of second Civil War, i., 409, 410; ii., 380-384
Northwich, Cheshire, i., 190, 243; ii., 54
Not, Sir Thomas, co. Glam., i., 388; ii., 336, 338, 341

OFFICERS, list of Royalist, taken prisoners at St. Fagans, ii., 367, 395
Okeley, Richard, ii., 43
Okey, Colonel, at St. Fagans, ii., 365
Organs in churches pulled down, i., 181
Orme's Head, ii., 94, 100
Ormond, i., 145, 183, 187; ii., 89, 91, 93, 98, 99, 103, 109, 116, 125, 128, 161, 208
Oswestry, garrisoned for the King, i., 140, 221; ii., 171; taken by Earl Denbigh, i., 222; ii., 173; attempt to regain it, i., 224-226; ii., 177-188; mention of, i., 285, 333; ii., 203, 212, 271
Ottley, Sir Francis, i., 108, 134, 198, 224; ii., 42, 134, 135-139
Over, Cheshire, ii., 50
Overton, Col., ii., 351
Owen, Alban, Henllys, co. Pembroke, ii., 4, 85
Owen, Arthur, of Orielton, i., 103; ii., 147, 164 n.
Owen, George, of Whitchurch, Pemb., herald, i., 168
Owen, Sir Hugh, of Orielton, co. Pemb., i., 101, 103, 139, 176, 210; ii., 4, 85, 121, 145, 157
Owen, Dr John, Bishop of St. Asaph, i., 91
Owen, Sir John, of Clenency, co. Carn., i., 103, 114, 118, 167, 217; ii., 243, 326, 327, 380-384
Owen, Dr. Morgan, Bishop of Llandaff, i., 91
Owen, Sir William, Condover, Salop, ii., 42, 236
Owen, William, of Pakington, Governor of Harlech, ii., 332

PEMBRIDGE CASTLE, i., 273; ii., 218
Pembrokeshire—Refuse to pay subsidy not sanctioned by Parliament, i., 42; too poor to supply a ship for the King, i., 43; contributes to General Loan, i., 46; ship-money, i., 71, 74; war with the Scotch, i., 80; Committee of Militia, i., 100; ii., 4; Earl of Carbery and Royalists there, i., 164, 175; ii., 76, 82-85; landing of Papists there, ii., 80; "Hue and Cry," *ibid*; protestation of gentry, ii., 119; cleared of Royalists, ii., 146-157; associated with Cardiganshire and Carmarthenshire, ii., 163; success of Royalists, i., 234; ii., 189, 240; again freed of Cavaliers, i., 335
Pembroke—Town and castle garrisoned for Parliament, i., 139; ii., 82-85; Lord Carbery prepares to reduce it, i., 205; ii., 120, 140; Laugharne, assisted by Swanley, drives him away, i., 206-212; ii., 146-157; Gerard appears before it, i., 234; ii., 192; but quits the county without taking it, i., 293; Poyer, refusing to disband, establishes himself there, i., 393; ii., 344-350; besieged and taken by Oliver Cromwell, i., 415; ii., 375, 387-398
Penllyn, North Wales, i., 343
Penmark, co. Glam., ii., 361, 365
Perrott, ii., 85, 163
Petition of Rights, i., 51, 53
Pill, Milford Haven, i., 208; ii., 142-144
Pirates, i., 37
Phillipps, Sir Richard, of Picton Castle, i., 293; ii., 4, 85, 121, 164 n., 230
Phillips, Hector, Cardigan, i., 71.
Phillips, Col. James, Priory, Cardigan, i., 277
Phillips, John, co. Pembroke, ii., 85, 121, 164
Phillips, Thomas, co. Salop, ii., 43; various, ii., 176, 197
Picton Castle, i., 293, 334; ii., 254, 273
Pierpoint, William, i., 157, 282; ii., 122
Plague in London, i., 36
Pontargothi, i., 400; ii., 358
Pope, Col. Roger, ii., 307, 313
Powell, Capt. (Col.) Rice, for the Parliament, i., 279, 291; ii., 147, 152, 229, 305; joins Poyer in his revolt, i., 394; ii., 351, 352, 355, 358, 377
Powell, Thomas, co. Pemb., ii., 163
Powell, Vavasor, ii., 374
Powis, Lord, i., 197, 241; ii., 195, 213, 239
Powis Castle, i., 241, 264; ii., 212
Poyer, David, of Pembroke, ii., 397

Poyer, Col. John (Mayor of Pembroke), fortifies Pembroke for Parliament, i., 139; assists in its defence, i., 206, 210; ii., 141, 147, 152; takes Carew Castle, i., 212; his resolution of fidelity to the Parliament, ii., 249; refuses to disband, takes possession of Pembroke, and heads a revolt, i., 395; ii., 344; denounced by some officers, ii., 345; defeated at St. Fagans, i., 405; ii., 365; retreats to Pembroke, which is besieged by Oliver Cromwell, i., 405-407; ii., 387-398; made prisoner, i., 417; ii., 398; tried for high treason and executed, i., 417
Prees Heath, ii., 86
Press, the, i., 97
Press at Shrewsbury, i., 119; ii., 30
Presteign, i., 327; ii., 269
Price, Sir John, of Newtown, i., 197, 265, 275, 292; ii., 203, 213, 215
Price, Col. Herbert, Brecon, i., 87, 103, 154, 197, 338, 347; ii., 69, 70, 156, 157, 268
Price of Rhiwlas, i., 342
Price, Capt. Richard, N. Wales, ii., 301, 306
Price, various, ii., 70, 85, 201, 311
Prichard, the Vicar of Llandovery, i., 67
Prichard, Col., of Llancayach, Glam., i., 303; ii., 299, 341, 343
Privy Seals, attempt to borrow money on, i., 36
Progers, Col., ii., 217
Protestants, massacre of, in Ireland, i., 90
Prynne, William, i., 60, 140
Pryse, Capt. Richard (? Gogerddan), i., 278; ii., 232; as Sir Richard Pryse he refuses to join Poyer in his revolt, i., 399; ii., 358
Pryse, Sir Richard, Gogerddan, i., 77; ii., 121
Puritanism, i., 60, 63, 65
Puritan gallantry in Monmouthshire, ii., 262
Pwllcrochan, co. Pemb., ii., 349

Radnorshire contributes to Illegal Loans, i., 46; ship-money, i., 71, 77, 80, 275, 335; suppression of insurrection there, ii., 360
Radnor Castle (?), ii., 28, 262
Radnor, old, i., 315
Raglan Castle garrisoned for the King, i., 138; visited by Prince of Wales, i., 123; ii., 26, 27; alluded to, ii., 211, 217; visited by the King after Naseby, i., 299, 300; ii., 258; and a second time from Oxford, i., 322-325; ii., 268, 299; siege and surrender of, i., 369-374; ii., 314-322; list of prisoners there, ii., 323
Rainsborough, Col., ii., 320
Ravenscroft, Col., co. Flint, i., 180; ii., 99, 371
Red Castle. See Powis Castle
Reinking, Col., i., 286, 287; ii., 235
Rhyddlan Castle, i., 375; ii., 94, 100, 372
Rivers, Lord, i., 102, 110, 141; ii., 10, 14
Roach or Roch Castle, co. Pemb., i., 205, 210, 234; ii., 140, 145, 190
Roach or Roch, Major, co. Pemb., ii., 356, 398
Robinson, Col. John (Flint), i., 179; ii., 99, 296, 311, 312
Roch. See Roach
Roman Catholics, i., 69, 146, 183; massacre of Irish Protestants, i., 90, 322, 349
Roos, co. Pemb., i., 210., 234
Rossbridge, i., 153, 273; ii., 66
Rowton Heath, Cheshire, i., 110, 330; ii., 14, 270, 272
Rudd, Sir Rice, co. Carm., ii., 121, 275
Rudd, Archdeacon, i., 164; ii., 153
Rumsey, Edward, co. Brecon, ii., 285, 389
Ruperra, co. Mon., i., 304; ii., 259
Rupert, Prince, comes to the King at Shrewsbury, i., 112; ii., 19, 31; at Edghill, i., 127; at Cirencester, i., 147; appointed to command North Wales, Cheshire, and Shropshire, i., 198; ii., 134; his power increases, ii., 166; powder for him intercepted, i., 221; ii., 171, 173; defeated at Marston Moor, i., 227; retreats to Cheshire, i., 239; thence to Bristol, i., 245; ii., 214; relieves Beeston, i., 288; ii., 245; suppresses clubmen in Herefordshire, i, 289; counsels peace, i., 310; loses Bristol, i, 324; ii., 268; and his commission, ii., 269; quits England, i., 334; alluded to, ii., 168, 169, 175, 186, 195
Ruthin, i., 139, 164, 245, 332, 344; ii., 93 215, 271, 282, 292, 301, 306, 372

St. Asaph, i., 91
St. Clears, i., 337; ii., 274
St. David's, i., 52, 65, 173, 273; ii., 76
St. Fagans, co. Glam., i., 404, 406; ii., 260, 361, 362, 365-369
St. Lythans, Glam., ii., 339
St. Nicholas, co. Glam., ii., 361, 365
St. Pere, co. Mon., ii., 139
Salesbury, Capt. (Royalist), i., 112; ii., 17
Salesbury, Capt. (Parliamentarian), i., 179
Salesbury, John, i., 197 n., of Bathgrage; ii., 371
Salesbury, Col. William, i., 104, 128, 182, 331; ii., 93, 94, 271, 307, 328-331
Sandbach ale, ii., 117; mention of, i., 189, 190
Sandford, Capt., i., 186, 193; ii., 107, 132

Sankey, or Zanchy, i., 162, 243; ii., 196, 198, 226, 309
Scriven, Sir Thomas, i., 178; ii., 42, 88
Scudamore, Lord, i., 139, 154; ii., 70, 255
Scudamore, Col. Barnabas, i., 289, 346; ii., 256
Sea Hall, Salop, i., 288
Seis, Edward, co. Glam., ii., 337
Shakerley, Col., ii., 311
Sheffnal, Salop, ii., 293
Ship-money, i., 43; first warrant for, i., 48; general levy of, i., 69-77; declared illegal, i., 86
Shrewsbury—Ship-money, i., 72, 77; the King there, i., 100, 118; ii., 10-30; full of Papists, i., 115; ii., 16; the King's departure, i., 118; ii., 30: Mint and Press established there, i., 116, 119; ii., 30, 31; Lord Capel in disfavour there, i., 183; ii., 94; Sir Francis Ottley receives Prince Rupert there, i., 198; ii., 134; scarcity of money, ii., 136; influx of Irish, i., 200; ii., 137; Rupert returns thither after Marston, i., 239; ii., 166; faced by Mytton, ii., 194; Prince Maurice there, i., 285; taken by the Parliament, i., 285-287; ii., 235; alluded to, i., 139, 188, 218, 224, 225, 252, 266, 333; ii., 30, 87, 94, 137, 173, 176, 180, 199, 202, 271.
Shropshire, i., 37, 80, 159, 160, 171, 285, 316; ii., 16, 19, 42, 122, 166
Slebech Estate, i., 335
Smiths, loyalty of the Welsh, i., 402; ii., 354
South Wales, outbreak of second Civil War, i., 387; ii., 344
Smith, Capt. William, Vice-Admiral, i., 173, 174, 206-210, 217; ii., 29, 76, 142-153, 164, 228
Solemn League and Covenant, i., 170, 215
Somerset, Lord Charles, i., 272; ii., 65, 217; Lord John, i., 149, 152; ii., 63
Sports, Book of, i., 67
Stackpoole Court, co. Pemb., i., 205, 208; ii., 142
Stamford, Earl of, ii., 38-41
Star Chamber, Court of, i., 58; abolished by Long Parliament, i., 86
Stedman, John, co. Cardigan, ii., 121
Steinton Church, co. Pemb., i., 209; ii., 143
Stepney, Sir John, of Prendergast, i., 103, 164, 197, 210; ii., 4, 85, 121, 144, 153, 286
Stradling, Sir Edward, of St. Donats, i., 128, 167
Stradling, Major-General, i., 308, 334-337; ii., 266, 273-278
Stradling, John Henry, i., 330; and Thomas, i., 415; ii., 336-339, 342, 343, 353, 397
Strafford, the Earl of, i., 35, 83; Welshmen and his trial, i., 87; ii., 34
Sunday in Wales, i, 67
Swanley, Capt. Richard, Admiral, at Milford Haven, i., 173, 207-210; ii., 142-153, at Carmarthen, i, 215,; throws Irish into the sea, i., 233; ii., 161, 164 n., 189; rewarded by Parliament, i., 217
Swansea, i, 319, 418; ii., 351, 353, 361; summoned by the Parliament, i., 215; ii., 158; boats belonging to, ii., 259; gives in to the Parliament, i., 354; Col. Philip Jones made Governor, i., 357; Cromwell's visit, i., 407
Tarvin, Cheshire, i., 243, 268; ii., 196, 198
Taylor, Dr. Jeremy, prisoner at Cardigan, i., 278; ii., 229
Tenby, in hands of Royalists, attacked from sea, i., 194; ii., 82; garrisoned for the King, i., 205, 209; ii., 140; stormed by Laugharne, i., 211; ii., 145, 146, 192, 194; i., 234, 246; outbreak of second Civil War, i., 407; ii., 345; taken by revolters, ii., 348; and reduced by Cromwell, i., 408; ii., 377
Telegraphic substitute—firing of beacons, ii., 82
Tewkesbury, great defeat of Welsh at, i., 132, 133; ii., 39-41
Thomas, Sir Edward, co. Glam., ii., 341
Thomas, Lewis, ii., 64; John, ii., 65; Thomas and Robert, ii, 337
Thelwall, Capt. Edward, ii, 303; Eubule, ii., 330; Simon, i., 213, 140-148, 152, 371
Tilston Hill, Salop. ii., 52
Tipton Green, ii., 175
Tong Castle, Salop, i., 288
Torperley, Cheshire, i., 142; ii., 47, 48, 52
Towy, river, i., 401; ii., 352, 358
Trawscoed, co. Cardigan, letters from, ii., 154-157
Treargaer, co. Mon., i., 299; ii., 258
Tredegar, Mon., ii., 259, 268
Trefloyne, co. Pembroke, i., 205, 209; ii., 142
Tregaron, co. Cardigan, i., 292; ii., 252
Trevor, Arthur, i., 135, 137, 145, 251; ii., 162, 169, 208
Trevor, Col., i., 245; ii., 197, 192, 209, 214, 227
Twistleton, Col., i., 409, 410; ii., 371, 381
Tyler, Col., i., 200, 202; ii., 125, 127, 195, 202
Tyrrell, Sir T., Governor of Cardiff, i., 304, 307

Vane, Col. John, i., 366; ii., 209
Vann, John, co. Glam., ii., 337
Vaughan, Sir Henry, of Golden Grove, i., 103, 197, 207, 210; ii., 142, 144, 153

Vaughan, John, of Trawscoed, co. Card., i., 87, 103, 197 n., 213; ii., 154-157
Vaughan, of co. Carm. and Card., ii., 121, 275-278
Vaughan, Rice, ii., 163; Capt., ii., 229; Cornet, ii., 65
Vaughan, Capt. Thomas, co. Card., ii., 351
Vaughan, Sir William, i., 267, 294, 343, 351; ii., 125, 199, 209, 282, 289
Vavasor, Sir William, i., 168
Verney, Sir Edmund, i., 342; ii., 296

Waller, Sir William, i, 150, 152, 153; ii., 63, 66, 67
Walton, hundred, co. Pemb., i., 232; ii., 190
War first talked of in Parliament, i., 100; declared by the King, i., 107
Waring, of Shrewsbury, ii., 30, 43
Waring Bridge, ii., 58
Warren, of Trewern, co. Pemb., ii., 4, 85, 121, 164
Warren, John, ii., 106, 175
Warren, Col. (from Ireland), i., 118, 195; ii., 117, 127, 129, 132, 202
Watts, Col. John (Chirk Castle), i., 276; ii , 224
Wellington, i., 109
Welsh language, no newspapers in, i., 98
Welshpool, i., 240, 264, 342; ii., 194, 195, 212
Welsh roads, ii., 66
Wem, Salop, garrisoned for the Parliament, i., 172; ii., 86, 123; Lord Capel defeated, i., 176; ii , 87; women of, i., 177; threatened by Rupert, ii., 167; alluded to, i., 223, 225, 285; ii., 172, 173, 177, 178, 194, 215, 235
Wenlock Magna, i., 157; ii., 271
Weobley, Heref., i., 326
Whitchurch, Pemb., i., 168
Whitchurch, Salop, i., 110, 159, 329; ii., 10, 79, 166, 184, 198
White, of Pembrokeshire, i., 164
White, Griffith, of Henllan, co. Pemb., i., 174, 350; ii., 4, 80, 81, 85, 150, 164
Whitley, Col. Robert, ii., 305
Whitmore, Sir Thomas, of Apley, i., 126
Whittington, ii., 180
Wigmore, of co. Heref., ii., 64, 65
Wilbraham, Sir Richard, i., 110, 136; ii., 11, 12, 15, 17, 47
Wilbraham, Roger, ii., 15, 47, 297
Wilbraham, Thomas, ii., 33
Williams, Dr. John. See York, Archbishop of
Williams, Roger, founder of Rhode Island, i., 66
Williams, Col. Sir Trevor, of Llangibby, co. Monmouth, prisoner at Gloucester, i., 263, 272; ii., 64; at Monmouth, a Royalist, ii., 217; turns for the Parliament, i., 318; imprisoned by the King, and let out on bail, i., 344; heads clubmen, and assists in taking Chepstow and Monmouth, i., 340, 341; ii., 279; appointed Governor of Monmouth, ii., 280 n.; suspected by Cromwell and ordered to be arrested, i., 413; ii., 390; Cromwell's idea of his character, ii., 390, 391
Williams, Sir W., of Vaenol, co. Carn., i., 365; ii., 307
Willis, Sir Richard, i., 164, 178, 196, 333; ii., 124, 130
Winter, Sir John, i., 257, 270; ii., 139
Wodehouse, Sir Michael, Governor of Ludlow, i., 139
Wogan, John, Rowland, and Thomas, of Wiston, co. Pemb., i., 43, 74; ii., 4, 147, 152, 164, 369
Wogan, Capt. Thomas, Member for Cardigan, i., 420; ii., 366
Wonastow House, co. Mon., i., 262
Worcester, Marquis of, i., 103, 120, 261, 323, 340; ii., 211, 258, 268, 314-318, 320
Worrall, co. Chester, ii., 93, 214
Wrexham, i., 114, 125, 179, 181, 184, 185, 187; ii., 14, 17, 20, 93, 95, 112, 114, 140
Wroth, of Llanvaches, and the Book of Sports, i., 67
Wynne, Col., of Melai, i., 178; ii., 88
Wynne, George, ii., 102
Wynn or Wynne, ii., 104, 176, 325, 400

York, Archbishop of (Dr. John Williams), as Bishop of Lincoln, persecuted by Laud for opposing High Churchism, i., 59; roughly used by the mob, i., 90; his correspondence with Ormond as to the state of North Wales, i., 179, 182, 184, 187, 217, 351; ii., 89, 93, 94, 99, 161, 168, 214, 288; with Lord Digby, ii., 243; with Lord Astley, ii., 289; he turns round to the Parliament, i., 376-378; ii., 325; and helps to take Conway, *ibid*

Zanchy, Sergt.-Major. See Sankey

www.ingramcontent.com/pod-product-compliance
Lightning Source LLC
Chambersburg PA
CBHW032143010526
44111CB00035B/992
* 9 7 8 3 3 3 7 0 1 5 2 0 6 *